Lecture Notes in Computer S

T0250773

Commenced Publication in 1973
Founding and Former Series Editors:
Gerhard Goos, Juris Hartmanis, and Jan van Leeuwen

Editorial Board

Jana Dittmann   Stefan Katzenbeisser
Andreas Uhl (Eds.)

Communications and Multimedia Security

9th IFIP TC-6 TC-11 International Conference, CMS 2005
Salzburg, Austria, September 19 – 21, 2005
Proceedings

 Springer

Volume Editors

Jana Dittmann
Otto-von-Guericke-Universität Magdeburg
Institut für Technische und Betriebliche Informationssysteme
Universitätsplatz 1, 39106 Magdeburg, Germany
E-mail: Jana.Dittmann@iti.cs.uni-magdeburg.de

Stefan Katzenbeisser
Technische Universität München
Institut für Informatik
Boltzmannstrasse 3, 85748 Garching, Germany
E-mail: katzenbe@in.tum.de

Andreas Uhl
Universität Salzburg
Department of Scientific Computing
Jakob Haringer Strasse 2, A-5020 Salzburg, Austria
E-mail: uhl@cosy.sbg.ac.at

Library of Congress Control Number: 2005931928

CR Subject Classification (1998): C.2, E.3, D.4.6, H.5.1, K.4.1, K.6.5, H.4

ISSN   0302-9743
ISBN-10   3-540-28791-4 Springer Berlin Heidelberg New York
ISBN-13   978-3-540-28791-9 Springer Berlin Heidelberg New York

Springer is a part of Springer Science+Business Media

springeronline.com

©2005 IFIP International Federation for Information Processing, Hofstrasse 3, A-2361 Laxenburg, Austria
Printed in Germany

Typesetting: Camera-ready by author, data conversion by Scientific Publishing Services, Chennai, India
Printed on acid-free paper   SPIN: 11552055   06/3142   5 4 3 2 1 0

Preface

It is our great pleasure to present the proceedings of the 9th IFIP TC-6 TC-11 Conference on Communications and Multimedia Security (CMS 2005), which was held in Salzburg on September 19–21, 2005. Continuing the tradition of previous CMS conferences, we sought a balanced program containing presentations on various aspects of secure communication and multimedia systems. Special emphasis was laid on papers with direct practical relevance for the construction of secure communication systems.

The selection of the program was a challenging task. In total, we received 143 submissions, from which 28 were selected for presentation as full papers. In addition to these regular presentations, the CMS conference featured for the first time a "work in progress track" that enabled authors to report preliminary results and ongoing work. These papers were presented in the form of a poster session during the conference; an extended abstract of the posters appears in this proceedings volume. From all papers submitted to the CMS conference, the program committee chose 13 submissions for inclusion in the work in progress track.

In addition to regular presentations, CMS 2005 featured a special session on XML security, containing both contributed and invited talks. This special session was jointly organized by Rüdiger Grimm (TU Ilmenau, Germany) and Jörg Schwenk (Ruhr-Universität Bochum, Germany). Their assistance in organizing CMS 2005 was greatly appreciated.

Besides the above mentioned presentations, the scientific program of CMS 2005 featured three invited speakers: Christian Cachin (IBM Zürich), with a talk about the cryptographic theory of steganography, Ton Kalker (HP Labs), with a survey talk on recent trends in the field of Digital Rights Management, and Ingemar Cox (University College London), with a talk about robust watermarking schemes.

We want to thank all contributors to CMS 2005. In particular, we are grateful to the authors and invited speakers for contributing their latest work to this conference, as well as to the PC members and external reviewers for their critical reviews of all submissions. Finally, special thanks go to the organizing committee who handled all local organizational issues and provided us with a comfortable location and a terrific social program. For us, it was a distinct pleasure to serve as program chairs of CMS 2005.

We hope that you will enjoy reading these proceedings and that they will be a catalyst for your future research in the area of multimedia security.

July 2005

Jana Dittmann
Stefan Katzenbeisser
Andreas Uhl

9th IFIP TC-6 TC-11 Conference on Communications and Multimedia Security

September 19–21, 2005, Salzburg (Austria)

Program Chairs

Jana Dittmann, Otto-von-Guericke Universität Magdeburg, Germany
Stefan Katzenbeisser, Technische Universität München, Germany
Andreas Uhl, Universität Salzburg, Austria

IFIP TC-6 TC-11 Chairs

Otto Spaniol, RWTH Aachen, Germany
Leon Strous, De Nederlandsche Bank, The Netherlands

Program Committee

André Adelsbach, Ruhr-Universität Bochum, Germany
Elisa Bertino, University of Milan, Italy
Carlo Blundo, UNISA, Italy
Christian Cachin, IBM Zürich, Switzerland
Ingemar J. Cox, University College London, UK
David Chadwick, University of Kent, UK
Bart de Decker, KU Leuven, Belgium
Yves Deswarte, LAAS, France
Elke Franz, TU Dresden, Germany
Miroslav Goljan, SUNY Binghamton, USA
Patrick Horster, Universität Klagenfurt, Austria
Ton Kalker, HP Labs, USA
Stephen Kent, BBN Technologies, USA
Klaus Keus, BSI, Germany
Herbert Leitold, A-SIT, Austria
Nasir Memon, Polytechnic University, USA
Sead Muftic, Stockholm University, Sweden
Fernando Perez-Gonzalez, University of Vigo, Spain
Günter Pernul, Universität Regensburg, Germany
Reinhard Posch, Technische Universität Graz, Austria
Bart Preneel, KU Leuven, Belgium
Claus Vielhauer, Otto-von-Guericke University Magdeburg, Germany
Moti Young, Columbia University, USA

Local Organization

Dominik Engel
Roland Norcen
Helma Schöndorfer
Michael Tautschnig
Andreas Uhl

External Reviewers

Carlos Aguilar-Melchor
Felix Balado
Lejla Batina
Yannick Chevalier
Stelvio Cimato
Pedro Comesana
Peter Danner
Paolo D'Arco
Liesje Demuynck
Claudia Diaz
Kurt Dietrich
Wolfgang Dobmeier
Anas Abou El Kalam
Martin Feldhofer
Jessica Fridrich
Alban Gabillon
Sebastian Gajek
Steven Galbraith
Clemente Galdi
Jörg Gilberg
Ulrich Greveler
Hazem Hamed
Mark Hogan
Yongdae Kim
Franz Kollmann
Klaus Kursawe
Mario Lamberger
Peter Lipp
Mark Manulis

Björn Muschall
Vincent Naessens
Vincent Nicomette
Rodolphe Ortalo
Elisabeth Oswald
Federica Paci
Udo Payer
Luis Perez-Freire
Thomas Popp
Torsten Priebe
Markus Rohe
Thomas Rössler
Heiko Rossnagel
Martin Schaffer
Peter Schartner
Christian Schlaeger
Stefaan Seys
Dieter Sommer
Anna Squicciarini
Hung-Min Sun
Yagiz Sutcu
Ingrid Verbauwhede
Frederik Vercauteren
Tine Verhanneman
Kristof Verslype
Ivan Visconti
Ron Watro
Johannes Wolkerstorfer
Peiter Zatko

Table of Contents

Applied Cryptography

DRM & E-Commerce

Media Encryption

Multimedia Security

Privacy

Biometrics & Access Control

Network Security

Mobile Security

Work in Progress Track

Special Session: XML Security

Fast Contract Signing with Batch Oblivious Transfer

Ľubica Staneková[1],* and Martin Stanek[2],**

[1] Department of Mathematics, Slovak University of Technology,
Radlinského 11, 813 68 Bratislava, Slovakia
ls@math.sk
[2] Department of Computer Science, Comenius University,
Mlynská dolina, 842 48 Bratislava, Slovakia
stanek@dcs.fmph.uniba.sk

Abstract. Oblivious transfer protocol is a basic building block of various cryptographic constructions. We propose a novel protocol – batch oblivious transfer. It allows efficient computation of multiple instances of oblivious transfer protocols. We apply this protocol to improve the fast simultaneous contract signing protocol, recently proposed in [11], which gains its speed from computation of time-consuming operations in advance. Using batch oblivious transfer, a better efficiency can be achieved.

1 Introduction

Oblivious transfer is a cryptographic protocol in which one party (usually called sender) transfers one of two strings to the other party (usually called chooser). The transfer should have the following properties: The chooser should obtain the string of his/her choice but not the other one, and the sender should be unable to identify the chooser's choice. Oblivious transfer is used as a key component in many cryptographic applications, such as electronic auctions [12], contract signing [4,11], and general multiparty secure computations [8]. Many of these and similar applications make intensive use of oblivious transfer. Therefore, efficient implementation of oblivious transfer can improve the overall speed and applicability of various protocols.

Batch variants of various cryptographic constructions are useful for decreasing computational costs. A batch variant of RSA, suitable for fast signature generation or decryption, was proposed by Fiat [5]. Batch verification techniques [1] can be used for efficient proofs of correct decryptions in threshold systems with applications to e-voting and e-auction schemes.

Simultaneous contract signing is a two-party cryptographic protocol, in which two mutually suspicious parties A and B wish to exchange signatures on a contract. Intuitively, a fair exchange of signatures is one that avoids a situation

---

* Supported by APVT 023302.
** Supported by VEGA 1/0131/03.

J. Dittmann, S. Katzenbeisser, and A. Uhl (Eds.): CMS 2005, LNCS 3677, pp. 1–10, 2005.

where A can obtain B's signature while B cannot obtain A's signature and vice-versa. There are two types of contract signing protocols: the ones that use trusted third party either on-line or off-line [6], and protocols without trusted third party [4,7]. Protocols without trusted third party are based on gradual and verifiable release of information. Hence, if one participant stops the protocol prematurely, both participants have roughly the same computational task in order to find the other participant's signature.

Recently, a contract signing protocol that allows pre-computation of significant part of the most time consuming operations in advance was proposed in [11]. The protocol makes an extensive use of oblivious transfers (its security depends on the security of oblivious transfers) in each protocol run.

Motivation. Oblivious transfer is frequently used in cryptographic protocols. There are many protocols in which a large number of oblivious transfers is employed in a single protocol instance. Therefore, an efficient implementation of oblivious transfer is a natural way to improve the efficiency of such protocols.

Our Contribution. We present a batch RSA oblivious transfer protocol where multiple independent instances of oblivious transfers can be computed efficiently. The security of the protocol is based on RSA assumption, and we prove it in the random oracle model.

We compare actual implementation of batch RSA oblivious transfer protocol with standard RSA oblivious transfer [11], and oblivious transfer based on the computational Diffie-Hellman assumption [13].

We show the usefulness and applicability of our proposal and improve the simultaneous contract signing protocol [11]. The use of batch RSA oblivious transfers instead of pre-computed oblivious transfers leads to more efficient protocol. Both settings were implemented and compared to illustrate exact decrease of computational costs.

Related Work. The efficiency of computing oblivious transfer influences the overall efficiency of many protocols. Our batch RSA oblivious transfer is a modification of the RSA oblivious transfer protocol from [11]. Other constructions of oblivious transfer employ some kind of ElGamal encryption or computational Diffie-Hellman assumption [13].

Similar problem of amortizing the cost of multiple oblivious transfers, based on computational Diffie-Hellman assumption, has been considered by Naor and Pinkas [13]. We compare our approach with their constructions in Sect. 4.

Our security proofs for batch RSA oblivious transfers make use of random oracles. The application of random oracles in the security analysis of cryptographic protocols was introduced by Bellare and Rogaway [2]. Security proofs in a random oracle model substitute a hash function with ideal, truly random function. This approach has been applied to many practical systems, where the ideal function must be instantiated (usually as a cryptographically strong hash function). Recently, an interesting discussion about plausibility of security proofs in the random oracle model appeared in [10].

The paper is structured as follows. Section 2 presents our main result, the batch RSA oblivious transfer, and its implementation. The protocol for contract signing is described in Sect. 3. We analyse an actual implementation of batch RSA oblivious transfer and the savings of computational costs resulting from its application in Sect. 4.

2 Batch Oblivious Transfer

Oblivious Transfer (OT) protocol, more specifically OT_1^2 protocol, allows two parties (sender and chooser) to solve the following problem. The sender has two strings m_0 and m_1 and transfers one of them to the chooser in accordance with the following conditions:

- the chooser selects a particular m_b which he wishes to obtain ($b \in \{0, 1\}$);
- the chooser does learn nothing about m_{1-b};
- the sender does not know which m_b was transferred.

We modify and extend construction of RSA-based OT_1^2 protocol from [11]. Most oblivious transfer protocols employ some kind of ElGamal encryption. This results in increased computational overhead as the chooser must perform at least one modular exponentiation. Using RSA-based oblivious transfer allows to reduce the chooser's complexity, since the public exponent can be made small. Moreover, RSA decryption with distinct private exponents can be implemented efficiently, leading to Batch RSA [5]. We use this idea for further improvement of computational complexity of RSA-based oblivious transfer.

We employ the following notation through the rest of the section. Let $n = p \cdot q$ be an RSA public modulus (i.e. a product of two distinct primes p and q) and let e, d denote public and private exponents, respectively. Let $Z_n = \{0, 1, \ldots, n - 1\}$ and let Z_n^* be the set of all numbers from Z_n relatively prime to n. All computations in protocol descriptions are defined over Z_n, the only exception is bitwise xor operation $\oplus$. We will omit stating explicitly that our operations in the paper are mod n whenever it is clear from the context. The hash function H is modelled as a truly random function (random oracle, see [2]) in the security analysis. For simplicity we write $H(a_1, \ldots, a_l)$ for the hash function applied to the concatenation of l-tuple $(a_1, \ldots, a_l)$. Random, uniform selection of x from the set A is denoted by $x \in_R A$.

We assume the sender (S in protocol description) generates the instance of RSA system and the chooser (C) already has a valid public key of the sender (i.e. a pair (n, e)). Moreover, we assume that the length of H output is not shorter than strings m_0 and m_1. Recall, $b \in \{0, 1\}$ denotes the index of string, which the chooser wants to obtain.

2.1 RSA Oblivious Transfer

The RSA oblivious transfer protocol [11] is a modification of the protocol [9]. Since the protocol is executed multiple times a sufficiently long random string R (chosen by sender) is used to distinguish the instances of the protocol.

1. $S \rightarrow C$: $C \in_R Z_n^*$
2. $C \rightarrow S$: $x' = x^e C^b$, where $x \in_R Z_n$.
3. $S \rightarrow C$: R, E_0, E_1,
   where ciphertexts E_0, E_1 of strings m_0, m_1 are computed as follows:

$$E_0 = H(R, x'^d, 0) \oplus m_0; \qquad E_1 = H(R, (x'C^{-1})^d, 1) \oplus m_1.$$

4. The chooser decrypts m_b from E_b: $m_b = E_b \oplus H(R, x, b)$.

Since the value x' is uniformly distributed in Z_n, the chooser's security is protected in an information-theoretic sense – the sender cannot determine b, even with infinite computational power. The sender's security can be proved in the random oracle model under RSA assumption. The protocol allows pre-computation of value $(C^{-1})^d$, thus allowing efficient implementation of protocols, where multiple instances of oblivious transfer are required.

Remark 1. Roughly the same efficiency can be obtained (without any pre-computation) by generating C^d randomly first and computing C by exponentiation to the short public exponent. This possibility was neglected by the authors of this protocol. Batch oblivious transfer is even more efficient, as we will see later.

2.2   Batch RSA Oblivious Transfer

The main observation regarding efficiency of RSA oblivious transfer is the fact that multiple parallel executions can use distinct private exponents. This allows to reduce computational complexity of sender using techniques of Batch RSA.

We assume that L oblivious transfers should be performed. Let $m_{i,0}$, $m_{i,1}$ (for $0 \le i < L$) be input strings for i-th oblivious transfer. Similarly, $b_0, \ldots, b_{L-1}$ are indices of those strings, which the chooser wants to obtain. The sender selects L distinct small public RSA exponents $e_0, \ldots, e_{L-1}$, each one relatively prime to $(p-1)(q-1)$, and computes corresponding private exponents $d_0, \ldots, d_{L-1}$. For efficient implementation the public exponents must be relatively prime to each other and $e_i = O(\log n)$, for $i = 0, \ldots, L-1$.

The protocol executes L separate instances of oblivious transfer:

1. $S \rightarrow C$: $C_0, C_1, \ldots, C_{L-1} \in_R Z_n^*$
2. $C \rightarrow S$: $x'_0, x'_1, \ldots, x'_{L-1}$,
   where $x'_i = x_i^{e_i} C_i^{b_i}$ and $x_i \in_R Z_n$, for $i = 0, \ldots, L-1$.
3. $S \rightarrow C$: $\{R_i, E_{i,0}, E_{i,1}\}_{0 \le i < L}$,
   where ciphertexts $E_{i,0}$, $E_{i,1}$ of strings $m_{i,0}$, $m_{i,1}$ are computed as follows:

$$E_{i,0} = H(R_i, (x'_i)^{d_i}, i, 0) \oplus m_{i,0};$$
$$E_{i,1} = H(R_i, (x'_i C_i^{-1})^{d_i}, i, 1) \oplus m_{i,1}.$$

4. The chooser decrypts $m_{i,b_0}, \ldots, m_{i,b_{L-1}}$ from $E_{i,b_0}, \ldots, E_{i,b_{L-1}}$:

$$m_{i,b_i} = E_{i,b_i} \oplus H(R_i, x_i, i, b_i), \quad \text{for } i = 0, \ldots, L-1.$$

One can easily check the correctness of the decryption:

$$
\begin{aligned}
E_{i,b_i} \oplus H(R_i, x_i, i, b_i) &= H(R_i, (x_i' C_i^{-b_i})^{d_i}, i, b_i) \oplus m_{i,b_i} \oplus H(R_i, x_i, i, b_i) \\
&= H(R_i, (x_i^{e_i} C_i^{b_i} C_i^{-b_i})^{d_i}, i, b_i) \oplus m_{i,b_i} \oplus H(R_i, x_i, i, b_i) \\
&= m_{i,b_i}
\end{aligned}
$$

Security. The chooser's objective is to hide values $b_0, \ldots, b_{L-1}$ from the sender. The values x_i' are uniformly distributed in Z_n. Thus, the sender cannot compute b_i, even with unrestricted computational power – for each transmitted L-tuple $x_0', \ldots, x_{L-1}'$ and every possible selection of values $b_0, \ldots, b_{L-1}$ there exist suitable choices $x_0, \ldots, x_{L-1} \in Z_n$ (easily computed by the sender himself):

$$
x_0 = (x_i' \cdot C_i^{-b_i})^{d_i}, \qquad \ldots, \qquad x_{L-1} = (x_{L-1}' \cdot C_i^{-b_{L-1}})^{d_{L-1}}.
$$

Hence, all combinations of values $b_0, \ldots, b_{L-1}$ are equiprobable and the sender cannot identify the correct one. The chooser's security is protected unconditionally.

The sender's objective is to hide one string from every pair $m_{i,0}, m_{i,1}$ (not knowing which one exactly). We prove this security property of the protocol in random oracle model, where the hash function H is modelled as a random function.

We compare the protocol with the ideal implementation (model). The ideal model uses a trusted third party that receives all $m_{i,0}$ and $m_{i,1}$ from the sender and $b_0, \ldots, b_{L-1}$ from the chooser. After obtaining all inputs, the trusted third party sends the chooser m_{i,b_i}, for $0 \le i < L$. The ideal model hides the values $m_{i,1-b_i}$ perfectly – no adversary substituting the chooser can learn anything about hidden values. The actual protocol should be comparable with the ideal model in the following sense (for extensive study of various definitions of protocol security in the ideal model see [3]):

> For every distribution on the inputs $\{m_{i,0}, m_{i,1}\}_{0 \le i < L}$ and any probabilistic polynomial adversary A substituting the chooser in the actual protocol there exists a probabilistic polynomial simulator S_A in the ideal model such that outputs of A and S_A are computationally indistinguishable.

Since the ideal model is secure and outputs of A and S_A are indistinguishable, one can conclude that A does not learn more than allowed by security requirements.

The simulator S_A simulates both the sender and adversary A. Therefore, the verb "send" refers to writing data to input or reading data from output of simulated adversary.

1. S_A selects random $C_0, C_1, \ldots, C_{L-1} \in_R Z_n^*$ and sends them to A. It starts to simulate A on this input.

2. A sends values $x'_0, x'_1, \ldots, x'_{L-1} \in Z_n$ to S_A. These values can be computed by adversary A in any way (adversary does not need to follow the protocol).
3. S_A selects random strings $\{R_i, E_{i,0}, E_{i,1}\}_{0 \leq i < L}$ as "sender's answer" and sends them in response.
4. S_A continues the simulation of A and monitors all its queries to H. All queries have the form of a quadruple (R, x, i, b). We say that the quadruple (R, x, i, b) is valid if $R_i = R$ and $x'_i C_i^{-b} = x^{e_i}$. All queries not containing a valid quadruple are answered at random. If A asks for $H(R, x, i, b)$, where the argument is a valid quadruple, then S_A asks a trusted third party in the ideal model for $m_{i,b}$. The simulator sets $H(R, x, i, b) = E_{i,b} \oplus m_{i,b}$ to allow A to decrypt $E_{i,b}$ correctly. Whatever A outputs, so does S_A.

The distribution of simulated communication with the adversary A is identical to the distribution of real communication between the sender and A. The only exception is the case when A asks for any valid pair of quadruples $H(R, x, i, 0)$ and $H(R, x^*, i, 1)$, for $i \in \{0, \ldots, L-1\}$. In this case, the validity of the quadruples implies $x'_i = x^{e_i}$ and $x'_i C_i^{-1} = (x^*)^{e_i}$. It easily follows that $x \cdot (x^*)^{-1}$ is the decryption of C_i:

$$(x \cdot (x^*)^{-1})^{e_i} = x^{e_i} \cdot (x^*)^{-e_i} = x'_i \cdot (x'_i)^{-1} C_i = C_i.$$

The values C_i are chosen randomly by the simulator S_A. Hence, the adversary cannot construct a pair of valid quadruples, assuming the RSA assumption holds. Therefore the output of S_A cannot be distinguished from the output of A in the real communication with the sender.

Remark 2. Random strings R_i are used in the protocol to ensure distinct inputs of H in different invocations of the protocol.

Remark 3. Less direct construction would use triples $(R_i, (x'_i C_i^{-b_i})^{d_i}, b_i)$ instead of quadruples $(R_i, (x'_i C_i^{-b_i})^{d_i}, i, b_i)$. The simulator would determine the correct value of index i by testing validity of all potential triples.

Implementation. The most time-consuming part of the protocol is step 3, where the sender computes $2L$ RSA decryptions. The use of distinct pairs of encryption/decryption exponents enables to apply batch RSA decryption [5]. The sender needs to compute following decryptions in step 3:

$$(x'_i)^{d_i}, (x'_i C_i^{-1})^{d_i}, \qquad \text{for } i = 0, \ldots, L-1.$$

Certainly, only one decryption has to be computed for every i, namely $(x'_i)^{d_i}$. This follows from an observation that $(x'_i C_i^{-1})^{d_i} = (x'_i)^{d_i} (C_i^{d_i})^{-1}$, and C_i can be generated from randomly chosen $C_i^{d_i}$ by encrypting it: $(C_i^{d_i})^{e_i}$ (thus having decryption "for free"). Assuming small size of public (encryption) exponents, the computation can be implemented in such a way that L decryptions $(x'_i)^{d_i}$ require time asymptotically proportional to one decryption, see [5]. Notice, that small public exponents yield efficient implementation of the chooser's part of the protocol as well.

3 LS Protocol

The protocol for contract signing from [11] (we call it LS protocol) is based on construction by Even, Goldreich and Lempel [4]. The main difference between these protocols is a criterion when the contract is considered binding (the original protocol uses threshold acceptance).

Protocols for simultaneous contract signing usually consist of two interlaced protocols. Both participants are in symmetric positions – each of them wants to transfer its own signature in exchange for the other participant's signature. Our description includes both exchanges.

Let us denote by $Sig_A(m)$ a digital signature of a message m created by the participant A. The protocol is independent of chosen digital signature algorithm. Let k be a security parameter, e.g. $k = 128$. For the purposes of contract signing a *C-signature* (or $CSig$) of a message m is defined as a triple:

$$CSig_A(m) = (Sig_A(m, R), Sig_A(R, i, 0), Sig_A(R, i, 1)),$$

for arbitrary $i \in \{1, \ldots, k\}$ and a random binary string $R \in \{0, 1\}^k$ long enough to avoid collisions among instances of the protocol. A C-signature is (considered) valid if and only if all its parts are formed correctly and have valid signatures.

3.1 The Protocol

Alice and Bob simultaneously transfer C-signatures of contract M. A symmetric encryption (e.g. one-time pad) of message m with a key K is denoted by $\{m\}_K$. We denote by $A \leftrightarrow B : OT_1^2(m_0, m_1)$ the instance of an oblivious transfer protocol with A playing the role of the sender (possessing two strings m_0, m_1), and B playing the role of the chooser (and selecting the string which he wishes to obtain randomly). Alice chooses random $R_A \in \{0, 1\}^k$ and random symmetric keys $K_{A,i,b}$, for $i \in \{1, \ldots, k\}$ and $b \in \{0, 1\}$. Similarly, Bob chooses random $R_B \in \{0, 1\}^k$ and random symmetric keys $K_{B,i,b}$, for $i \in \{1, \ldots, k\}$ and $b \in \{0, 1\}$. Let k' be the length of symmetric key and i-th bit of key K is denoted by K^i, i.e. $K_{A,i,b} = K_{A,i,b}^1 K_{A,i,b}^2 \cdots K_{A,i,b}^{k'}$, and $K_{B,i,b} = K_{B,i,b}^1 K_{B,i,b}^2 \cdots K_{B,i,b}^{k'}$.

Both participants check the correctness of received data/signatures immediately (as soon as they can be verified). In case of failure, the participant aborts the protocol.

1. (exchange of the first parts of $CSig$)
   $A \rightarrow B$: $R_A, Sig_A(M, R_A)$,
   $B \rightarrow A$: $R_B, Sig_B(M, R_B)$.
2. (exchange of encrypted parts of $CSig$)
   $A \rightarrow B$: $\{Sig_A(R_A, i, b)\}_{K_{A,i,b}}$, for $i = 1, \ldots, k$ and $b = 0, 1$,
   $B \rightarrow A$: $\{Sig_B(R_B, i, b)\}_{K_{B,i,b}}$, for $i = 1, \ldots, k$ and $b = 0, 1$.
3. (opening one half of encryptions)
   $A \leftrightarrow B$: $OT_1^2(K_{A,i,0}, K_{A,i,1})$, for $i = 1, \ldots, k$,
   $B \leftrightarrow A$: $OT_1^2(K_{B,i,0}, K_{B,i,1})$, for $i = 1, \ldots, k$.

4. (gradual exchange of symmetric keys) For $w = 1, \ldots, k'$:
   $A \to B$: $K_{A,1,0}^w, K_{A,1,1}^w, \ldots, K_{A,k,0}^w, K_{A,k,1}^w$,
   $B \to A$: $K_{B,1,0}^w, K_{B,1,1}^w, \ldots, K_{B,k,0}^w, K_{B,k,1}^w$.

   Transfers are interlaced, so both parties send the pieces in the iteration $w+1$ only when they already received (and verified) the pieces from previous iteration (i.e. w). Alice and Bob check after each iteration that the half of received pieces is equal to the corresponding pieces of the keys obtained via oblivious transfers. They continue the protocol only if the check is successful.

The most computationally demanding task of the protocol is the step 3, where $2k$ oblivious transfers have to be performed. This leaves the room for efficient implementation of the protocol – by employing efficient oblivious transfers, such as our batch oblivious transfer presented in Sect. 2.2.

4   Implementation and Comparison

This section presents actual comparison of oblivious transfer protocols and their impact on efficiency of LS contract signing protocol. All test were implemented in Java and were performed on Pentium II 400 MHz processor.

The Chinese remainder theorem (CRT) is routinely applied to decrease computational cost of RSA decryption. Both RSA-based implementations of oblivious transfer protocols employed CRT. Employing CRT in batch RSA oblivious transfer requires two binary trees for computations mod p and mod q. Results (decryptions) are combined using CRT just like in "standard" RSA.

4.1   Comparing Oblivious Transfer Implementations

We compare implementation of RSA oblivious transfer (Sect. 2.1), batch RSA oblivious transfer (Sect. 2.2), and OT_1^2 protocol proposed by Naor and Pinkas in [13] based on the computational Diffie-Hellman assumption (we denote this protocol NaPi). NaPi computes in subgroup of order r of Z_s, where s is prime and $r \mid s - 1$. For the purpose of our test we choose 160 bit long r. The hash function is instantiated as SHA-1 in the protocols.

The first graph on Fig. 1 shows combined time spent by the sender and the chooser when performing 128 oblivious transfers simultaneously while increasing the length of the RSA modulus n (for RSA-based protocols) or the length of prime s (for NaPi protocol). The second graph presents combined computational time while increasing the number of oblivious transfers computed in parallel. The length of RSA modulus, and the length of prime s is fixed to 1024 bits in this case.

We compare only on-line computations, off-line (pre-computed) parts of protocols are not considered. On-line computation of NaPi protocol requires two modular exponentiations in a subgroup of order r. Since the length of exponents is 160 bits, the protocol is faster than standard RSA oblivious transfer. However, when multiple oblivious transfers should be performed, batch RSA

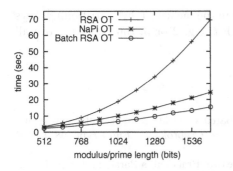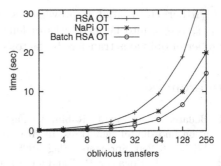

Fig. 1. Comparison of RSA, batch RSA, and NaPi oblivious transfers

oblivious transfer is even more efficient. Moreover, NaPi protocol requires additional off-line computation (three exponentiations), while batch RSA oblivious transfer does not employ off-line computation.

Remark 4. Naor and Pinkas proposed additional constructions of oblivious transfer protocols in [13]. They proposed efficient OT_1^N protocol and used it to implement many OT_1^2 protocols using bandwidth/computation tradeoff. However, such construction relies on a fast communication line between the sender and the chooser. Another OT_1^2 protocol proposed by the authors has the advantage of not requiring random oracles for its security proof (and can be viewed as superior to our construction in this sense). On the other hand, its on-line computational complexity is substantially higher.

4.2   Comparing Implementations of LS Protocol

The most time consuming steps of LS protocol are step 2 and step 3. Computational costs of steps 1 and 4 are negligible. Our implementations use RSA modulus of 1024 bits and 128 oblivious transfers (the length of symmetric keys are 128 bits).

Notice the signatures of the second and third parts of C-signatures, i.e. $Sig_A(R_A, i, b)$ and $Sig_B(R_B, i, b)$, do not depend on actual contract M. Thus, they can be pre-computed off-line. Table 1 compares computational time of LS protocol when step 2 is computed on-line (no pre-computation) or off-line (pre-computed signatures). Using batch RSA oblivious transfer improves computational costs in both cases.

Table 1. Computational time of LS protocol (sec)

	on-line	off-line
RSA OT	57.14	19.61
Batch RSA OT	44.25	6.74

Further substantial improvements can be achieved by partitioning keys $K_{A,i,b}$, $K_{B,i,b}$ into larger blocks of length t, e.g. 2 or 3, thus reducing overall number of oblivious transfers by factor t.

References

1. Bellare, M., Garay, J., Rabin, T.: Fast batch verification for modular exponentiation and digital signatures, In *Advances in Cryptology – EuroCrypt '98*, LNCS 1403, 236–250, Springer-Verlag, 1998.
2. Bellare, M., Rogaway, P.: Random Oracles are Practical: a Paradigm for Designing Efficient Protocols, In *1st ACM Conference on Computer and Communication Security*, 62–73, ACM Press, 1993.
3. Canetti, R.: Security and Composition of Multiparty Cryptographic Protocols, *Journal of Cryptology*, Vol. 13, No. 1, 143–202, 2000.
4. Even, S., Goldreich, O., Lempel, A.: A Randomized Protocol for Signing Contracts, In *Advances in Cryptology: Proceedings of Crypto '82*, 205–210, Plenum Publishing, 1982.
5. Fiat, A.: Batch RSA, In *Advances in Cryptology: Proceedings of Crypto '89*, 175–185, LNCS 435, Springer, 1990.
6. Garay, J., Jakobsson, M., MacKenzie, P.: Abuse-Free Optimistic Contract Signing, In *Advances in Cryptology: Proceedings of Crypto '99*, LNCS 1666, 449–466, Springer-Verlag, 1999.
7. Garay, J., Pomerance, C.: Timed Fair Exchange of Standard Signatures, In *Financial Cryptography '03*, LNCS 2742, 190–207, Springer-Verlag, 2003.
8. Goldreich, O., Micali, S., Wigderson, A.: How to play any mental game – a completeness theorem for protocols with honest majority, In *19th ACM Symposium on the Theory of Computing*, 218-229, ACM Press, 1987.
9. Juels, A., Szydlo, M.: A Two-Server Sealed-Bid Auction Protocol, In *Financial Cryptography '02*, LNCS 2537, Springer-Verlag, 2002.
10. Koblitz, N., Menezes, A.: Another Look at "Provable Security", Cryptology ePrint Archive, Report 2004/152, `http://eprint.iacr.org/`, 2004.
11. Liskova, L., Stanek, M.: Efficient Simultaneous Contract Signing, In *19th International Conference on Information Security (SEC 2004)*, 18th IFIP Word Computer Congress, Kluwer Academic Publishers, pp. 441-455, 2004.
12. Naor, M., Pinkas, B., Sumner, R.: Privacy preserving auctions and mechanism design, In *1st ACM Conference on Electronic Commerce*, 129–139, ACM Press, 1999.
13. Naor, M., Pinkas, B.: Efficient oblivious transfer protocols, In *12th Annual ACM-SIAM Symposium on Discrete Algorithms*, 448–457, 2001.

An Instruction Set Extension for Fast and Memory-Efficient AES Implementation

Stefan Tillich, Johann Großschädl, and Alexander Szekely

Graz University of Technology,
Institute for Applied Information Processing and Communications,
Inffeldgasse 16a, A–8010 Graz, Austria
{Stefan.Tillich, Johann.Groszschaedl, Alexander.Szekely}@iaik.at

Abstract. As more and more security-critical computation is done in embedded systems it is also becoming increasingly important to facilitate cryptography in such systems. The Advanced Encryption Standard (AES) specifies one of the most important cryptographic algorithms today and has received a lot of attention from researchers. Most prior work has focused on efficient implementations with throughput as main criterion. However, AES implementations in small and constrained environments require additional factors to be accounted for, such as limited memory and energy supply. In this paper we present an inexpensive extension to a 32-bit general-purpose processor which allows compact and fast AES implementations. We have integrated this extension into the SPARC V8-compatible LEON-2 processor and measured a speedup by a factor of up to 1.43 for encryption and 1.3 for decryption. At the same time the code size has been reduced by 30–40%.

Keywords: Advanced Encryption Standard, 32-bit implementation, instruction set extensions, S-box, cache-based side-channel analysis.

1 Introduction

The recent years have seen an enormous increase in the number of small and embedded systems in use. Cell phones, PDAs, portable media players, and smart cards are just a few examples of such devices. But also more and more computation is performed totally hidden from the user, e.g. in sensor nodes or RFID tags. Strong cryptographic algorithms should build the basis for achieving all of the security assurances required by the system. However, since embedded systems are generally constrained in resources, the overhead introduced by cryptographic algorithms should be kept as small as possible.

Many symmetric block ciphers require to perform operations which are costly in software, but very cheap when realized in hardware. Typical examples of such operations are bit-level permutations or inversions in the Galois field $GF(2^8)$. Moving the execution of these operations from software to hardware, e.g. through *application-specific (custom) instructions* integrated into a general-purpose processor, can have a significant performance impact [9]. The concept of *instruc-

J. Dittmann, S. Katzenbeisser, and A. Uhl (Eds.): CMS 2005, LNCS 3677, pp. 11–21, 2005.

tion set extensions may be viewed as a hardware/software co-design approach to combine the performance of hardware with the flexibility of software.

The Advanced Encryption Standard (AES) [11] specifies a symmetric block cipher that has found widespread adoption during the last five years. It can be used to encrypt digital communication and data or to guarantee integrity and authenticity. Today, the AES algorithm is prevalent in a plethora of devices, ranging from high-end servers to RFID tags [5]. Most previous work on efficient AES implementation has focused either on "pure" hardware or "pure" software. Our approach is to improve the performance by slight modifications of a 32-bit general-purpose processor in the form of instruction set extensions. In the current paper we propose a single custom instruction which requires little additional hardware and yields advantages for different parts of the AES algorithm.

The rest of this paper is organized as follows. Section 2 summarizes different choices for AES software implementation and also presents some of the benefits of our proposed extension. Section 3 presents our extension and also cites some related work. Section 4 examines the effect of cache size on the performance of different AES implementations, while Section 5 shows the benefits of our proposed extension in terms of performance and code size. Section 6 concludes the paper and gives a short outlook on future work.

2   Implementation Options for AES in Software

AES encrypts or decrypts the 16 bytes of input data in a number of rounds. The number of rounds is 10, 12, or 14, depending on the chosen key size of either 128, 192 or 256 bits. In encryption, each round but the last consists of the four transformations SubBytes, ShiftRows, MixColumns, and AddRoundKey, while a decryption round features the respective inverse operations. The last round is different as it does not include MixColumns in encryption and InvMixColumns in decryption. For each round, a round key has to be derived from the cipher key in an operation called key expansion [4].

All operations except SubBytes can be calculated quite efficiently on general-purpose processors. SubBytes and the key expansion require a non-linear byte substitution involving bit permutations and an inversion in $GF(2^8)$, which is not very well supported by general-purpose processors. Therefore, the inversion is normally implemented as a lookup into a table of 256 bytes. A table of the same size is required for the operation InvSubBytes in AES decryption.

A second implementation option is to perform most of the AES round (Sub-Bytes, ShiftRows, and MixColumns) as 16 lookups into larger tables, commonly referred to as *T tables* [4]. The overall size of these tables can either be 1 kB or 4 kB, whereby the 1 kB table requires additional rotation operations to be performed. The last round can also be realized with lookup by using other tables of either 1 kB or 4 kB size. Decryption requires different tables than encryption. Therefore, an AES implementation able to perform both encryption and decryption may require up to 16 kB of additional memory. Gladman's AES implementation [7] offers the possibility to configure the size of the T tables.

In the remainder of this paper we will use the following notation to refer to the two implementation strategies mentioned before. Any AES implementation which uses large lookup tables to perform most of the round transformations will be denoted as *T lookup AES implementation*. On the other hand, an implementation which calculates the round transformations (except SubBytes and InvSubBytes) will be denoted as *calculated AES implementation*.

T lookup implementations have a number of drawbacks. For compact AES implementations the use of large tables is not desirable. Moreover, the performance of a lookup table-based implementation is highly dependent on memory and cache performance. In Section 4 we demonstrate that, for small cache sizes, the performance of AES with large lookup tables is much worse than that of a calculated AES. Another problem of large lookup tables is an increased factor of cache pollution by an execution of the AES. This means that each execution of AES will throw out a large number of cache lines from other tasks. If these tasks continue they will have to fetch their data from main memory again, thus leading to a degradation in overall performance. Another issue for AES decryption is that it is necessary to use a much more complex key expansion if T lookup is employed. More specifically, the key expansion requires the transformation of nearly all round keys with InvMixColumns, which is a very costly operation.

For calculated AES implementations there are a number of design options on 32-bit processors. The 16 input bytes are represented as a 4×4-matrix, called the *state*, which is subsequently transformed by the AES algorithm. The state can be stored in four 32-bit registers, where each register can either hold a column or a row of the state matrix. Bertoni et al. [2] have shown that a row-oriented AES implementation yields a more efficient implementation of MixColumns and a better overall performance, especially for decryption.

Another option is to either precompute and store all round keys (precomputed key schedule) or to calculate the round keys during AES encryption or decryption (on-the-fly key expansion). The first option occupies more memory and may also require more memory accesses while the second option saves memory at the cost of additional operations in encryption and decryption in order to calculate the round keys.

In the present paper we propose a custom instruction for performing the non-linear byte substitution of SubBytes and InvSubBytes in a small dedicated hardware unit, which we call *SBOX unit*. In this fashion we can completely eliminate the requirement of memory-resident lookup tables. The implementation details of the sbox instruction are described in Section 3. With this instruction it is possible to implement AES with very few memory accesses. If there are enough spare registers to store the state and round key and an on-the-fly key expansion is used, then the only memory accesses required are the loading of the input data and cipher key and the storing of the result. Popular RISC architectures for embedded systems like ARM, MIPS and SPARC offer large enough register files to allow such implementations.

By eliminating the need for lookup tables, all possible threats through cache-based side-channel attacks are also removed [12,18,3]. Cache pollution is kept to a minimum and the performance of AES becomes much more independent of the cache size as shown in Section 4. Another advantage of our proposed extension is the reduction of energy dissipation. Memory accesses are normally the most energy-intensive instructions [15], and hence their minimization will lead to a substantial energy saving.

3   Custom Instruction for S-Box Lookup

For performing the byte substitution operation of AES in hardware we have used the implementation presented in [19] as a functional unit. It can perform the lookup for both encryption and decryption, is relatively small, and can be easily implemented with any standard cell library. We wanted to achieve a high degree of flexibility, and therefore we have designed the new instruction such that it can be used for both column-oriented and row-oriented implementations. The sbox instruction has the following format (in SPARC notation):

sbox rs1, imm, rd

The immediate value imm contains information regarding the operation to perform and the substituted bytes of the source register rs1 and the destination register rd. The sbox instruction performs the following steps:

1. Select one of the four bytes in the source register (rs1), depending on the immediate value (imm).
2. Depending on imm perform forward (for encryption and key expansion) or inverse (for decryption) byte substitution.
3. Replace one of the four bytes in the destination register (rd) with the substituted value, as indicated by imm. The other three bytes in rd remain unchanged.

Figure 1 illustrates the operation of the sbox instruction.

The sbox instruction requires the values from the registers rs1 and rd. Since the second operand of the sbox instruction is always an immediate value, the second read port of the register file is not occupied. It can therefore be used to read in the value of the destination register rd, which is required to form the 32-bit result. The sbox instruction is therefore easy to integrate into most architectures for embedded processors like ARM, MIPS, and SPARC as they all have instruction formats with two source registers.

Our instruction supports both encryption and decryption and can be used to perform all byte substitutions in all AES rounds as well as in the key expansion. It is possible to select the source byte in rs1 and the destination byte in rd in a manner so that the SubBytes and ShiftRows transformation can be done at the same time. The same applies for the InvSubBytes and InvShiftRows operations in decryption.

We have integrated our proposed extension into the freely available SPARC V8-compatible LEON-2 embedded processor from Gaisler Research [6] and prototyped it in a Xilinx Virtex2 XC2V3000 FPGA. In Sections 4 and 5 we will

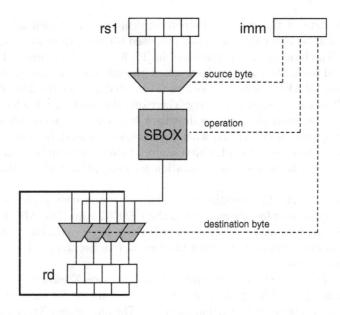

Fig. 1. Functionality of the sbox instruction

state the practical results we have achieved by comparing an AES implementation which uses our sbox instruction with pure-software implementations. Our implementations used a key size of 128 bits, but the results also apply to larger key sizes. We have prototyped the extended LEON-2 on an FPGA board, where the timing results have been obtained with help of the cycle counter which is integrated in the processor.

In order to estimate the area overhead due to our extensions, we have synthesized the functional unit presented in [19] using a 0.35 μm CMOS standard cell library. The required area amounted to approximately 400 NAND gates, which is negligible compared to the size of the processor. When synthesized for the Xilinx Virtex2 XC2V3000 FPGA, the extended LEON-2 (with 1 kB instruction and 1 kB data cache) required 4,274 slices and 5 Block RAMs.

3.1 Comparison with Related Work

Irwin and Page [8] have proposed extensions for PLX, a general-purpose RISC architecture with multimedia instructions, and presented strategies to use multimedia instructions for implementing AES with the goal to minimize the number of memory accesses. The PLX is datapath-scalable, which means that register size and datapath width are parameterizable from 32 to 128 bits (128 bits were used in [8]). Unfortunately, most of the presented ideas do not map very well to 32-bit architectures, and hence we did not use these concepts in our work.

Nadehara et al. [10] have proposed an instruction set extension for AES which calculates the value of a T table entry, i.e. SubBytes and MixColumns, for a single byte of the state. Although implementations which use such an instruction will be faster than with our proposed solution, there are also several drawbacks. The functional unit presented in [10] is larger than ours and it has a longer critical path. Moreover the instruction presented in [10] cannot be used in the last round of AES where MixColumns is omitted and for the key expansion where SubBytes is required separately. Therefore, the need for table lookups for byte substitution remains. Another drawback is a much more complicated key expansion required for decryption when the extension is used, because all round keys must be transformed with InvMixColumns before they can be used in Add-RoundKey [11]. This is a serious limitation for decryption with on-the-fly key expansion.

Schaumont et al. [14] investigated performance and energy characteristics of an AES coprocessor loosely coupled to the LEON-2 core. The AES hardware increased FPGA LUT usage by 70% but still yields lower performance than our extended LEON-2 with just the `sbox` instruction (see Section 5.1 for a detailed performance analysis).

Ravi et al. [13] used the extensible 32-bit processor Xtensa from Tensilica Inc. [16] to design and integrate instruction set extensions for different public- and secret-key cryptosystems (including AES). The augmented Xtensa achieved better performance for AES encryption, but worse performance for decryption when compared to our approach with just the `sbox` instruction. Unfortunately, Ravi et al. do not give details about the functionality and area overhead of the implemented instruction set extensions.

4   Influence of Cache Size on Performance

In order to demonstrate that an AES implementation with large lookup tables does not necessarily deliver the best performance, we have compared implementations with different sizes of lookup tables on an extended LEON-2 with different cache sizes. The influence of cache size on the performance of AES has already been studied by Bertoni et al. [1]. Their work assumes that the cache is large enough to hold all lookup tables. In this section we will examine the situation where the cache may become too small to hold the complete tables.

In our experiments, we have varied the size of the data and instruction cache from 1 kB to 16 kB (both caches always had the same size). The implementations which use T lookup are based on the well-known and referenced AES code from Brian Gladman [7], whereby we have used a size of 1 kB, 4 kB, and 8 kB for the lookup tables, respectively. We have compared the achieved performance to two AES implementations which calculate all round transformations except Sub-Bytes. In one case, a 256-byte lookup table (only S-box lookup) is used, and in the other case our `sbox` instruction is employed. Figure 2 shows the performance for encryption, while Figure 3 depicts the results for decryption.

The performance of the lookup implementations is very bad for small cache sizes. For encryption, the usage of the `sbox` instruction yields a similar performance as the use of big lookup tables on a processor with very large cache.

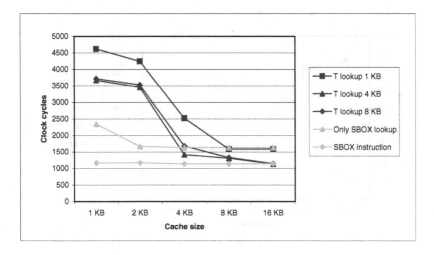

Fig. 2. Performance of AES-128 encryption in relation to cache size

In decryption, T lookup implementations become faster at cache sizes of more than 4 kB. This is due to the fact, that the InvMixColumns transformation is rather complex to calculate and therefore T lookup becomes more efficient than calculation for large caches sizes. The main result of our experiments is that the performance of implementations using the **sbox** instruction is almost independent from the cache size. On the other hand, the performance of T lookup implementation depends heavily on the size of the cache.

5 Comparison of Calculated AES Implementations

The previous section has shown that the performance of AES implementations using T lookup varies greatly with cache size. In this section we aim to highlight the benefits of using the **sbox** instruction in settings where T lookup is not an option, e.g. due to limited memory. To analyze the performance, we have compared a calculated AES implementation (without extensions) to one that uses our proposed **sbox** instruction. We have estimated both the gain in performance as well as the reduction in code size. All comparisons have been done for both precomputed key schedule and on-the-fly key expansion.

The **sbox** instruction performs the inversion in $GF(2^8)$ in a single clock cycle, while a calculated implementation requires a number of instructions for the inversion, which increases both the execution time and the size of the executable. In systems with small cache, the speedup factor for the implementation with **sbox** instruction will be higher than in systems with large cache, mainly because the performance of the calculated software implementation (without extensions) degrades due to cache misses in the instruction cache. Therefore, we have used a LEON-2 system with large caches since we are primarily interested in the speedup due to the **sbox** instruction (and not due to less cache misses).

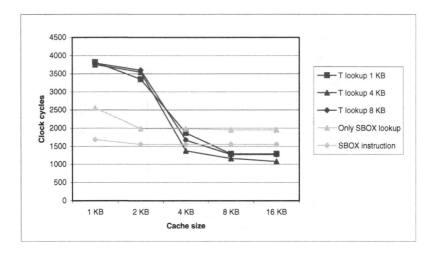

Fig. 3. Performance of AES-128 decryption in relation to cache size

We have also tested a third implementation that uses both the sbox instruction as well as the gf2mul/gf2mac instructions[1], which have been proposed in a previous paper of the first two authors [17]. The third implementation uses the gf2mul/gf2mac instructions to calculate MixColumns in an efficient manner.

All three implementations have been written in C and inline assembly has only been used to execute the custom instructions. For on-the-fly key expansion, we have also tested an assembler-optimized implementation which uses both the sbox and gf2mul/gf2mac instructions. This variant makes optimal use of the large register file offered by the SPARC V8 architecture and performs only a minimal number of memory accesses (8 loads for plaintext and key, 4 stores for ciphertext), which cannot be reduced further.

In the following subsections, we will only comment on the benefits of using the sbox instruction alone. The figures for the additional use of the gf2mul/gf2mac instructions are only stated for the interested reader familiar with [17].

5.1   Performance

Table 1 contains the timings for AES encryption and decryption with a precomputed key schedule. The use of the sbox instruction yields a speedup of 1.43 for encryption and 1.25 for decryption respectively. It can also be seen that the key expansion is accelerated by the use of our proposed extension. For comparison, Table 1 also contains the performance figures for the implementations in [14] and [13] for pure-software and hardware-accelerated AES-128 as far as they are available. Table 2 states the timing results for an on-the-fly key expansion. The figures for decryption assume that the last round key is directly supplied to the

---

[1] The gf2mul (gf2mac) instruction performs a multiplication (multiply-and-add operation) of two binary polynomials of degree 31, yielding a polynomial of degree 62.

Table 1. Execution times of AES-128 encryption, decryption and key expansion

	Key exp.	Encryption		Decryption	
	Cycles	Cycles	Speedup	Cycles	Speedup
[14] (pure SW)	n/a	45,228		n/a	
[14] (HW accelerated)	n/a	1,494		n/a	
[13] (pure SW)	n/a	24,419		24,419	
[13] (HW accelerated)	n/a	1,400		1,400	
Our work (no custom instr.)	738	1,636	1	1,954	1
Our work (sbox instr.)	646	1,139	1.43	1,554	1.25
sbox & gf2mul instruction	345	807	2.02	1,087	1.79

Table 2. Execution times of AES-128 en/decryption with on-the-fly key expansion

	Encryption		Decryption	
	Cycles	Speedup	Cycles	Speedup
No custom instructions	2,254	1	2,433	1
sbox instruction	1,576	1.43	1,866	1.3
sbox & gf2mul instruction	868	2.59	1,126	2.16
sbox & gf2mul instr. (optimized)	612	3.68	881	2.76

AES decryption function. The speedup for encryption and decryption is about 1.43 and 1.3, resprectively.

5.2   Code Size

Savings in code size are mainly due to the fact that the lookup tables for Sub-Bytes and InvSubBytes can be omitted with the sbox instruction and that the code for SubBytes and ShiftRows as well as for their inverses becomes more compact. The figures for the implementation with a precomputed key schedule are stated in Table 3. The code size shrinks by 32% for encryption and by 36% for decryption. Table 4 specifies the code sizes for AES with on-the-fly key expansion. Savings in code size range from nearly 43% for decryption to more than 37% for encryption.

6   Conclusions and Future Work

In this paper we have presented an inexpensive extension to 32-bit processors which improves the performance of AES implementations and leads to a reduction in code size. With the use of our sbox instruction, all data dependent memory lookups can be removed and the overall number of memory accesses can be brought to an absolute minimum. This instruction has been designed with flexibility in mind and delivers compact AES implementations with good performance even if cache is small and memory is slow. In our practical work

Table 3. Code size of AES-128 en/decryption with precomputed key schedule in bytes

	Encryption		Decryption	
	Bytes	Reduction	Bytes	Reduction
No custom instructions	2,168	0%	2,520	0%
sbox instruction	1,464	32.4%	1,592	36.8%
sbox & gf2mul instr.	680	68.6%	792	68.5%

Table 4. Code size of AES-128 en/decryption with on-the-fly key expansion in bytes

	Encryption		Decryption	
	Bytes	Reduction	Bytes	Reduction
No custom instructions	1,656	0%	2,504	0%
sbox instruction	944	42.9%	1,564	37.5%
sbox & gf2mul instruction	628	62.0%	764	69.4%
sbox & gf2mul instr. (optimized)	480	71.0%	596	76.1%

we have observed a speedup of up to 1.43 while code size has been reduced by over 40%. The performance gain is much higher on processors with small cache size. Furthermore, the sbox instruction also improves the resistance of an AES implementation against cache-based side-channel attacks. The extra hardware cost of the sbox instruction amounts to only 400 gates.

As future work we will examine the possibility to provide dedicated and flexible support for the MixColumns operation of AES. Our goal will be to integrate this support with the ECC extensions we have used for AES acceleration in [17].

Acknowledgements. The research described in this paper was supported by the Austrian Science Fund (FWF) under grant number P16952-N04 "Instruction Set Extensions for Public-Key Cryptography" and in part by the European Commission through the IST Programme under contract IST-2002-507932 ECRYPT. The information in this document reflects only the author's views, is provided as is and no guarantee or warranty is given that the information is fit for any particular purpose. The user thereof uses the information at its sole risk and liability.

References

1. G. Bertoni, A. Bircan, L. Breveglieri, P. Fragneto, M. Macchetti, and V. Zaccaria. About the performances of the Advanced Encryption Standard in embedded systems with cache memory. In *Proceedings of the 36th IEEE International Symposium on Circuits and Systems (ISCAS 2003)*, vol. 5, pp. 145–148. IEEE, 2003.
2. G. Bertoni, L. Breveglieri, P. Fragneto, M. Macchetti, and S. Marchesin. Efficient software implementation of AES on 32-bit platforms. In *Cryptographic Hardware and Embedded Systems — CHES 2002*, vol. 2523 of *Lecture Notes in Computer Science*, pp. 159–171. Springer Verlag, 2003.

3. G. Bertoni, V. Zaccaria, L. Breveglieri, M. Monchiero, and G. Palermo. AES power attack based on induced cache miss and countermeasure. In *Proceedings of the 6th International Conference on Information Technology: Coding and Computing (ITCC 2005)*, pp. 586–591. IEEE Computer Society Press, 2005.
4. J. Daemen and V. Rijmen. *The Design of Rijndael*. Springer-Verlag, 2002.
5. M. Feldhofer, S. Dominikus, and J. Wolkerstorfer. Strong authentication for RFID systems using the AES algorithm. In *Cryptographic Hardware and Embedded Systems — CHES 2004*, vol. 3156 of *Lecture Notes in Computer Science*, pp. 357–370. Springer Verlag, 2004.
6. J. Gaisler. The LEON-2 Processor User's Manual (Version 1.0.24). Available for download at http://www.gaisler.com/doc/leon2-1.0.24-xst.pdf, Sept. 2004.
7. B. Gladman. Implementations of AES (Rijndael) in C/C++ and assembler. Available for download at http://fp.gladman.plus.com/cryptography_technology/rijndael/index.htm.
8. J. Irwin and D. Page. Using media processors for low-memory AES implementation. In *14th International Conference on Application-specific Systems, Architectures and Processors (ASAP 2003)*, pp. 144–154. IEEE Computer Society Press, 2003.
9. R. B. Lee, Z. Shi, and X. Yang. Efficient permutation instructions for fast software cryptography. *IEEE Micro*, 21(6):56–69, Nov./Dec. 2001.
10. K. Nadehara, M. Ikekawa, and I. Kuroda. Extended instructions for the AES cryptography and their efficient implementation. In *Proceedings of the 18th IEEE Workshop on Signal Processing Systems (SIPS 2004)*, pp. 152–157. IEEE, 2004.
11. National Institute of Standards and Technology (NIST). Advanced Encryption Standard (AES). Federal Information Processing Standards (FIPS) Publication 197, Nov. 2001.
12. D. Page. Theoretical Use of Cache Memory as a Cryptanalytic Side-Channel. Technical Report CSTR-02-003, University of Bristol, Bristol, UK, 2002.
13. S. Ravi, A. Raghunathan, N. Potlapally, and M. Sankaradass. System design methodologies for a wireless security processing platform. In *Proceedings of the 39th Design Automation Conference (DAC 2002)*, pp. 777–782. ACM Press, 2002.
14. P. Schaumont, K. Sakiyama, A. Hodjat, and I. Verbauwhede. Embedded software integration for coarse-grain reconfigurable systems. In *Proceedings fo the 18th International Parallel and Distributed Processing Symposium (IPDPS 2004)*, pp. 137–142. IEEE Computer Society Press, 2004.
15. A. Sinha and A. Chandrakasan. Jouletrack – A web based tool for software energy profiling. In *Proceedings of the 38th Design Automation Conference (DAC 2001)*, pp. 220–225. ACM Press, 2001.
16. Tensilica Inc. Xtensa Application Specific Microprocessor Solutions. Overview handbook, available for download at http://www.tensilica.com, 2001.
17. S. Tillich and J. Großschädl. Accelerating AES using instruction set extensions for elliptic curve cryptography. In *Computational Science and Its Applications — ICCSA 2005*, vol. 3481 of *Lecture Notes in Computer Science*, pp. 665–675. Springer Verlag, 2005.
18. Y. Tsunoo, E. Tsujihara, K. Minematsu, and H. Miyauchi. Cryptanalysis of block ciphers implemented on computers with cache. In *Proceedings of the 25th International Symposium on Information Theory and Its Applications (ISITA 2002)*. SITA, 2002.
19. J. Wolkerstorfer, E. Oswald, and M. Lamberger. An ASIC implementation of the AES sboxes. In *Topics in Cryptology — CT-RSA 2002*, vol. 2271 of *Lecture Notes in Computer Science*, pp. 67–78. Springer Verlag, 2002.

Self-healing Key Distribution Schemes with Sponsorization*

Germán Sáez

Dept. Matemàtica Aplicada IV, Universitat Politècnica de Catalunya,
C. Jordi Girona, 1-3, Mòdul C3, Campus Nord, 08034-Barcelona, Spain
german@ma4.upc.edu

Abstract. In a self-healing key distribution scheme a group manager enables a large and dynamic group of users to establish a group key over an unreliable network. The group manager broadcasts in every session some packet of information in order to provide a common key to members of the session group. The goal of self-healing key distribution schemes is that, even if the broadcast is lost in a certain session, the group member can recover the key from the broadcast packets received before and after the session. This approach to key distribution is quite suitable for wireless networks, mobile wireless ad-hoc networks and in several Internet-related settings, where high security requirements need to be satisfied.

In this work we provide a generalization of previous definitions in two aspects. The first one is to consider general structures instead of threshold ones to provide more flexible performance to the scheme. The second one is to consider the possibility that a coalition of users sponsor a user outside the group for one session: we give the formal definition of self-healing key distribution schemes with sponsorization, some bounds on the required amount of information. We also give a general construction of a family of self-healing key distribution schemes with sponsorization by means of a linear secret sharing scheme. Our construction differs from previous self-healing key distribution schemes in the fact that the length of the broadcast is almost constant. Finally we analyze the particular case of this general construction when Shamir's secret sharing scheme is used.

Keywords: Group key, self-healing, dynamic groups, linear secret sharing schemes, broadcast.

1 Introduction

Self-healing key distribution schemes enable large and dynamic groups of users of an *unreliable* network to establish group keys for secure communication. In a self healing key distribution scheme, a group manager provides a common key

* This work was done while the author was in the *Dipartimento di Informatica ed Applicazioni* at the *Università di Salerno*, Italy. The author would like to thank people in the Crypto Research Group for their kind hospitality and useful comments. Research supported in part by Spanish *Ministerio de Ciencia y Tecnología* under project CICYT TIC 2003–00866.

J. Dittmann, S. Katzenbeisser, and A. Uhl (Eds.): CMS 2005, LNCS 3677, pp. 22–31, 2005.

to a group of users by using packets that he sends over a broadcast channel at the beginning of each session. Every user on the group computes the group key by means of this packet and some private information supplied by the group manager. Multiple groups can be established by the group manager for different sessions by joining or removing users from the initial group. The main goal of these schemes is the self-healing property: if during a certain session some broadcasted packet gets lost, then users are still capable of recovering the group key for that session simply by using the packets they have received during a previous session and the packets they will receive at the beginning of a subsequent one, without requesting additional transmission from the group manager.

This new approach to key distribution is very useful due to the self-healing property, supporting secure communications in wireless networks, mobile wireless ad-hoc networks, broadcast communications over low-cost channels (live-events transmissions, etc.) and in several Internet-related settings.

Self-healing key distribution schemes were introduced by Staddon et al. in [7] providing formal definitions, lower bounds to the resources required to such schemes as well as some constructions. In [6], Liu et al. generalised the above definition and gave some constructions. Blundo et al. in [1] modified the proposed definitions, gave new lower bounds, proposed some efficient constructions and showed some problems in previous constructions. Finally, Blundo et al. in [2] analysed previous definitions and showed that no protocol could exist for some of them; they proposed a new definition, gave some lower bounds for it and proposed some schemes. All of these papers mainly focused on unconditionally secure schemes.

The contributions of our paper are the following. First of all we formally define self-healing key distribution schemes with sponsorization in Section 2. This definition contains two main differences comparing with the one presented in [1]. The first one is to consider a monotone decreasing family of rejected subsets of users instead of a monotone decreasing threshold structure and the second one is to consider the feature that a coalition of users can sponsor a user outside the group for one session. The first modification allows us to consider more flexible self-healing key distribution schemes that can reach better properties. The motivation for the second modification is to give dynamism to the scheme allowing an authorized subset of users in the group to invite a new user without the help of the group manager. Of course the proposal considers the case in which certain majorities (the coalition of authorized subsets of users to sponsor) can perform this action. This feature has been considered in other distributed protocols as group key distribution schemes [5,4]. In Section 3 some lower bounds on the resources required to such schemes are presented. We give lower bounds on the amount of information given to sponsor a user and on the personal key of a user with this capability. In Section 4 a family of self-healing key distribution schemes with sponsorization is presented. This construction follows in part the ideas of [1] but considering any possible linear secret sharing scheme instead of a threshold one and ideas of [5,4] for sponsorization capability. At the end of the section we comment the security and efficiency of the scheme. Finally we present in Section 5 the scheme obtained when Shamir's secret sharing scheme is used.

2 Self-healing Key Distribution Schemes with Sponsorization

The models presented in [1] and [7] implement self-healing key distribution schemes with good properties. However these models do not consider the possibility that a coalition of users in the group can invite a new user to the group. This feature has been considered in other protocols to distribute keys as group key distribution schemes [5,4]. In this section we propose a model for this feature.

Let $\mathcal{U} = \{1, \ldots, n\}$ be the finite universe of users of a network. A broadcast unreliable channel is available, and time is defined by a global clock. Suppose that there is a group manager who sets up and manages, by means of join and revoke operations, a communication group, which is a dynamic subset of users of $\mathcal{U}$. Let $G_j \subset \mathcal{U}$ be the communication group established by the group manager in session j. Each user $i \in G_j$ holds a personal key S_i, received from the group manager before or when joining G_j. A personal key S_i can be seen as a sequence of elements from a finite set. A user $\ell \in G_j$ can sponsor a user $i \notin G_j$ for session j by giving to him some proof of sponsorization $P_{\ell i}^j$.

We denote the number of sessions supported by the scheme as m, the set of users revoked by the group manager in session j as R_j, and the set of users who join the group in session j as J_j. Hence, $G_j = (G_{j-1} \cup J_j) - R_j$ for $j \geq 2$ and by definition $R_1 = \emptyset$. Moreover, for $j = 1, \ldots, m$, let K_j be the session key chosen by the group manager and communicated to the group members through a broadcast message, B_j. For each $i \in G_j$, the key K_j is determined by B_j and the personal key S_i. This key can also be computed by a user $i \notin G_j$ sponsored by a subset of users $A \in \Gamma$, $A \subset G_j$ by means of B_j and $\{P_{\ell i}^j\}_{\ell \in A}$, for a certain family of subsets $\Gamma \subset 2^{\mathcal{U}}$. Then Γ is the family of authorized subsets to perform a sponsorization, that we suppose monotone increasing (if $A_1 \in \Gamma$ and $A_1 \subset A_2 \subset \mathcal{U}$, then $A_2 \in \Gamma$).

The family of subsets of users that can be revoked by the group manager is the monotone decreasing structure $\mathcal{R} \subset 2^{\mathcal{U}}$ (that is, if $A_2 \in \mathcal{R}$ and $A_1 \subset A_2 \subset \mathcal{U}$, then $A_1 \in \mathcal{R}$). In a natural way we assume that a subset of users which can be rejected cannot be authorized to sponsor a user. Then the monotone increasing access structure Γ satisfies $\Gamma \cap \mathcal{R} = \emptyset$. In order to define the security of the sponsorization capability we also consider the monotone decreasing structure $\mathcal{S} \subset 2^{\mathcal{U}}$ compound by the collection of tolerated coalition of users that can receive sponsorization by a unique sponsor.

Let $S_i, P_{\ell i}^j, B_j, K_j$ be random variables representing the personal key for user i, the proof used by user ℓ to sponsor user i in session j, the broadcast message B_j and the session key K_j for session j, respectively. The probability distributions according to whom the above random variables take values are determined by the key distribution scheme and the random bits used by the group manager. In particular, we assume that session keys K_j are chosen independently and according to the uniform distribution.

We define a $(\mathcal{R}, \Gamma, \mathcal{S})$-*self-healing scheme with sponsorization* using the entropy function (see [3] for more details on Information Theory):

Definition 1. *Let $\mathcal{U}$ be the universe of users of a network, let m be the maximum number of sessions, and let $\mathcal{R} \subset 2^{\mathcal{U}}$ be a monotone decreasing access structure of subsets of users that can be revoked by the group manager. Assume that Γ is the family of authorized subsets of users to perform a sponsorization verifying $\Gamma \cap \mathcal{R} = \emptyset$. We also consider the monotone decreasing structure $\mathcal{S} \subset 2^{\mathcal{U}}$ of the tolerated coalition of users that can be sponsored by a unique sponsor. A $(\mathcal{R}, \Gamma, \mathcal{S})$-self-healing key distribution scheme with sponsorization is a protocol satisfying the following conditions:*

1. *The scheme is a session key distribution scheme, meaning that:*
   (a) *For each member $i \in G_j$, the key K_j is determined by B_j and S_i. Formally, it holds that:* $H(\mathbf{K}_j | \mathbf{B}_j, \mathbf{S}_i) = 0$.
   (b) *Keys $K_1, \ldots, K_n$ cannot be determined from the broadcast or personal keys alone. That is:* $H(\mathbf{K}_1, \ldots, \mathbf{K}_m | \mathbf{B}_1, \ldots, \mathbf{B}_m) =$
      $= H(\mathbf{K}_1, \ldots, \mathbf{K}_m | \mathbf{S}_{G_1 \cup \cdots \cup G_m}) = H(\mathbf{K}_1, \ldots, \mathbf{K}_m)$.

2. *The scheme has $\mathcal{R}$-revocation capability. That is, for each session j, if $R = R_j \cup R_{j-1} \cup \cdots \cup R_2$ is such that $R \in \mathcal{R}$, then the group manager can generate a broadcast message B_j such that all revoked users in R cannot recover K_j (even knowing all the information broadcast in sessions $1, \ldots, j$). In other words:* $H(\mathbf{K}_j | \mathbf{B}_j, \mathbf{B}_{j-1}, \ldots, \mathbf{B}_1, \mathbf{S}_R) = H(\mathbf{K}_j)$.

3. *The scheme is $(\mathcal{R}, \Gamma)$-self-healing. This means that the two following properties are satisfied:*
   (a) *Every user $i \in G_r$ who has not been revoked before session s can recover all keys K_ℓ for $\ell = r, \ldots, s$, from broadcasts B_r and B_s, where $1 \leq r < s \leq m$. Formally, it holds that:* $H(\mathbf{K}_r, \ldots, \mathbf{K}_s | \mathbf{S}_i, \mathbf{B}_r, \mathbf{B}_s) = 0$.
   (b) *Let $B \subset R_r \cup R_{r-1} \cup \cdots \cup R_2$ be a coalition of users removed from the group before session r and let $C \subset J_s \cup J_{s+1} \cup \cdots \cup J_m$ be a coalition of users who join the group from session s with $r < s$. Suppose $B \cup C \in \mathcal{R}$. Then, such a coalition does not get any information about keys K_j, for any $r \leq j < s$. That is:* $H(\mathbf{K}_r, \ldots, \mathbf{K}_{s-1} | \mathbf{B}_1, \ldots, \mathbf{B}_m, \mathbf{S}_B, \mathbf{S}_C) = H(\mathbf{K}_r, \ldots, \mathbf{K}_{s-1})$.

4. *The scheme has $(\Gamma, \mathcal{S})$-sponsorization. This means that the three following properties are satisfied:*
   (a) *Every user $\ell \in G_j$ can generate a proof of sponsorization $P_{\ell i}^j$ to sponsor a user $i \notin G_j$ for session j using his personal key. In other words:* $H(\mathbf{P}_{\ell i}^j | \mathbf{S}_\ell) = 0$.
   (b) *A user $i \notin G_j$ that receives enough sponsorizations from a subset of users $A \subset G_j$ with $A \in \Gamma$ can compute the key K_j in the same conditions that users in G_j. That is:* $H(\mathbf{K}_j | \mathbf{P}_{Ai}^j, \mathbf{B}_r \mathbf{B}_s) = 0$ *for $A \in \Gamma$, $A \subset G_j$, $i \notin G_j$ and $r \leq j \leq s$.*
   (c) *Suppose that a coalition of users $i_1, \ldots, i_u \notin G_j$, not revoked before session j, have received sponsorization from subsets of users $C_1, \ldots, C_u \notin \Gamma$ respectively, with $C_1 \cup \cdots \cup C_u = \{\ell_1, \ldots, \ell_v\} \subset G_j$. This action is performed in such a way that users $\ell_1, \ldots, \ell_v$ sponsor subsets of users $D_1, \ldots, D_v \in \mathcal{S}$ respectively, with $D_1 \cup \cdots \cup D_v = \{i_1, \ldots, i_u\} \subset \mathcal{U} - G_j$; therefore $P_{C_1 i_1}^j \ldots P_{C_u i_u}^j = P_{\ell_1 D_1}^j \ldots P_{\ell_v D_v}^j$. In these conditions, such*

a coalition does not get any information about the value of key K_j. Formally, it holds that: $H(\mathbf{K}_j | \mathbf{P}^j_{C_1 i_1} \ldots \mathbf{P}^j_{C_u i_u} \mathbf{B}_r \mathbf{B}_s) = H(\mathbf{K}_j)$ for $C_1, \ldots, C_u \notin \Gamma, D_1, \ldots, D_v \in \mathcal{S}$ such that $P^j_{C_1 i_1} \ldots P^j_{C_u i_u} = P^j_{\ell_1 D_1} \ldots P^j_{\ell_v D_v}$, $C_1 \cup \ldots \cup C_u = \{\ell_1, \ldots, \ell_v\} \subset G_j, D_1 \cup \ldots \cup D_v = \{i_1, \ldots, i_u\} \subset \mathcal{U} - G_j$ and $r \le j \le s$.

This definition has two differences with respect to the one presented in [1]. First the family of subsets that can be rejected in [1] is $\mathcal{R} = \{R \subset \mathcal{U} : |R| \le t\}$ while in our definition we consider the general case of any possible monotone decreasing structure $\mathcal{R}$, not only threshold ones. This allows us to consider more general self-healing key distribution schemes, where, for instance, some users can be more revocable than others. And the second one is that the possibility of sponsorization is considered. The conditions to define this feature are the following. Condition 4.(a) expresses the mechanism of sponsorization: the information used to sponsor is computed from the personal key. The condition 4.(b) expresses the fact that the information obtained from enough sponsorizations with the correspondent broadcast allows to compute the personal key of the session. The last condition 4.(c) gives us the security condition: a coalition of users outside G_j sponsored by not enough users cannot obtain any information about the value of the key K_j. The key remains secure even if every user receives sponsorization of a coalitions in $\mathcal{S}$.

3   Lower Bounds

In this section we present some bounds for a $(\mathcal{R}, \Gamma, \mathcal{S})$-self-healing key distribution scheme with sponsorization. The first one is a lower bound on the size of proofs of sponsorization and the second one is a lower bound on the size of the personal key.

Proposition 1. *In any $(\mathcal{R}, \Gamma, \mathcal{S})$-self-healing key distribution scheme with sponsorization, for any user $\ell \in G_j$ and $i \notin G_j$, it holds that*

$$H(\mathbf{P}^j_{\ell i}) \ge H(\mathbf{K}_j).$$

Proof. Suppose that there exists a subset of users $C \subset G_j$ such that $C \notin \Gamma$ and $C \cup \{\ell\} \in \Gamma$. From conditions 4.(b) and (c) we have that:

$$H(\mathbf{K}_j | \mathbf{P}^j_{Ci} \mathbf{P}^j_{\ell i} \mathbf{B}_j) = 0 \text{ and } H(\mathbf{K}_j | \mathbf{P}^j_{\ell i} \mathbf{B}_j) = H(\mathbf{K}_j).$$

Then we can apply Lemma 5.1 in [1] finding $H(\mathbf{P}^j_{\ell i}) \ge H(\mathbf{K}_j)$.

$\square$

If the secret keys are uniformly chosen in a finite field $GF(q)$ then $\log |P^j_{\ell i}| \ge \log q$ for any $\ell \in G_j$ and $i \notin G_j$ because $H(\mathbf{P}^j_{\ell i}) \le \log |P^j_{\ell i}|$. That is: every proof of sponsorization must have at least $\log q$ bits. Moreover for a fixed session j and a user $i \notin G_j$, conditions 4.(b) and (c) determine a secret sharing scheme that distributes secrets K_j, with shares $P_{\ell i}^j$ for users $i \in \mathcal{U} - G_j$ realizing structure $\Gamma_j = \{A \subset \mathcal{U} - G_j \; : \; A \in \Gamma\}$. Then: $\max_{i \in \mathcal{U} - G_j} \log |P_{\ell i}^j| \geq \frac{\log q}{\rho^*(\Gamma_j)}$.

With regard to lower bounds for the size of the personal key it can be proved the following result. For any user i belonging to the group since session j and any subset of users $C \in \mathcal{S}$ with $C \cap G_j = C \cap G_{j+1} = \cdots = C \cap G_m = \emptyset$, it holds that $H(\mathbf{S}_i) \geq H(\mathbf{P}_{iC}^j \mathbf{P}_{iC}^{j+1} \ldots \mathbf{P}_{iC}^m)$. Assuming that the proofs of sponsorization are statistically independent and secret keys are uniformly chosen in a finite field $GF(q)$ (using Proposition 1), then $H(\mathbf{S}_i) \geq (m - j + 1) |C| \log q$. So, in this situation every user added in session j must store a personal key of at least $(m - j + 1)|C| \log q$ bits because $\log |S_i| \geq (m - j + 1)|C| \log q$.

With respect to lower bounds on the broadcast information, the one found in [1] is valid for our model with the same proof.

4 A Family of Self-healing Key Distribution Schemes with Sponsorization

To construct this family of self-healing key distribution schemes with sponsorization we follow in part ideas of Scheme 2 in [1] and sponsorization mechanism in [5,4]. Our construction has three main differences with Scheme 2 in [1]. The first one is that we use linear secret sharing schemes instead of Shamir secret sharing scheme as Scheme 2 in [1] does, supporting in this way new properties and features. See [8] for more details on secret sharing schemes. The second one is to increase the information given to users on the personal key. This operation allows a subset of users in a group to sponsor new users in such a way that they obtain the key of the session without the help of the group manager. A secure unicast channel between the sponsors and the sponsored user is necessary. And the third one is that this construction uses a different broadcast than the one in [1]. In fact the broadcast in [1] can also be used in our construction, but ours gives us an almost constant length broadcast. In this section we present this construction, prove the security and analyze the efficiency.

Let q be a prime power and denote by $K_j \in GF(q)$ the session key for group G_j. Let Γ be a monotone increasing access structure. We suppose for simplicity that there exists a public map

$$\psi : \mathcal{U} \cup \{D\} \longrightarrow GF(q)^t$$

which defines Γ as a vector space access structure, with D a special user outside $\mathcal{U}$ (see [8] for definitions). But the construction that we present here can be extended in a natural way to work with any access structure Γ by means of a linear secret sharing scheme realizing it. The use of a specific ψ fixes the properties of the scheme. Let $\mathcal{R} = 2^{\mathcal{U}} - \Gamma$ be a monotone decreasing access structure and $\mathcal{S} = 2^{\mathcal{U}} - \Gamma'$ where Γ' is defined as $\Gamma' = \{A \subset \mathcal{U} \; : \; GF(q)^t = \langle \psi(A) \rangle\}$. Note that $\Gamma' \subset \Gamma$ is a monotone increasing access structure that depends on the function ψ chosen to represent Γ.

We are going to present a self-healing key distribution scheme with sponsorization in which Γ is the family of subsets of users that can perform a sponsorization, $\mathcal{R} = 2^{\mathcal{U}} - \Gamma$ is the family of subsets of users that can be revoked by the group manager and $\mathcal{S} = 2^{\mathcal{U}} - \Gamma'$ is the family of tolerated coalition of users that can be sponsored by a unique sponsor. In order to construct the scheme we need to prove the following lemma:

Lemma 1. *Let $v_1, \ldots, v_n$ be non null vectors in $GF(q)^t$, for q a prime power. If $q \geq n$ then there exists at least one vector $v \in GF(q)^t$ such that $v \cdot v_i \neq 0$ for all $i = 1, \ldots, n$.*

Proof. Let $A_i = \{v \in GF(q)^t : v \cdot v_i \neq 0\}$. First we will prove that for any positive integer $k = 1, \ldots, n$ we have that $|A_1 \cap \cdots \cap A_k| \geq q^t - kq^{t-1} + (k-1)$. The proof is by induction on k.

For $k = 1$ we can take into account that $A_1 = GF(q)^t - \langle v_1 \rangle^{\perp}$ where $\langle v_1 \rangle^{\perp}$ is the $(t-1)$-dimensional orthogonal subspace of $\langle v_1 \rangle$ in $GF(q)^t$. Then $|A_1| = q^t - q^{t-1}$ and, in fact, $|A_i| = q^t - q^{t-1}$ for any i.

If this result is true for k then

$$|A_1 \cap \cdots \cap A_k \cap A_{k+1}| = |A_1 \cap \cdots \cap A_k| + |A_{k+1}| - |(A_1 \cap \cdots \cap A_k) \cup A_{k+1}| \geq$$

$$\geq q^t - kq^{t-1} + (k-1) + q^t - q^{t-1} - (q^t - 1) = q^t - (k+1)q^{t-1} + k$$

because $(A_1 \cap \cdots \cap A_k) \cup A_{k+1}$ is a subset of $GF(q)^t$ that does not contain the null element.

The proof of the lemma ends observing that for $n = 1$ the result is true because $|A_1| = q^t - q^{t-1} > 0$ and for $n \geq 2$ we have $|A_1 \cap \cdots \cap A_n| \geq q^t - nq^{t-1} + (n-1) \geq q^{t-1}(q-n) + 1 \geq 1$ if $q \geq n$. $\square$

Now we describe the different phases of our proposal of self-healing key distribution scheme. In order to design the scheme we need a vector $v \in GF(q)^t$ such that $v \cdot \psi(i) \neq 0$ for all $i \in \mathcal{U}$. Suppose $q \geq n$, then vector v exists applying Lemma 1. For instance, for vectors defining Shamir secret sharing scheme (see [8]) we have that an appropriate vector is $v = (1, 0, \ldots, 0)$.

Set-Up. Let $G_1 \subset \mathcal{U}$. The group manager randomly chooses $t \times t$ matrices $P_1, \ldots, P_m$ and session keys $K_1, \ldots, K_m \in GF(q)$. For each $j = 1, \ldots, m$ the group manager computes the vector $z_j = K_j v + \psi(D)^{\top} P_j \in GF(q)^t$. The group manager sends privately to user $i \in G_1$ the personal key $S_i = (\psi(i)^{\top} P_1, \ldots, \psi(i)^{\top} P_m) \in GF(q)^{tm}$. Note that if we use a linear secret sharing scheme in which a user i is associated with $m_i \geq 1$ vectors, then his secret information S_i consists of m_i vectors of tm components.

Full Addition. In order to add users $J_j \subset \mathcal{U}$ in session j, the group manager sends privately $S_i = (\psi(i)^{\top} P_j, \psi(i)^{\top} P_{j+1}, \ldots, \psi(i)^{\top} P_m) \in GF(q)^{t(m-j+1)}$ to every user $i \in J_j$ as his personal key.

Broadcast. Suppose $R_j \subset G_{j-1}$ with $R_1 \cup R_2 \cup \cdots \cup R_j \in \mathcal{R}$ if $j \geq 2$. By definition we have $R_1 = \emptyset$. The group manager chooses a maximal non-authorized subset of users $W_j \in \mathcal{R}_0 = \overline{\Gamma}_0$ such that $R_1 \cup R_2 \cup \cdots \cup R_j \subset W_j$ and $W_j \cap G_j = \emptyset$

with minimum cardinality. The broadcast B_j in session $j = 1, \ldots, m$ is given by $B_j = B_j^1 \cup B_j^2$. The first part of the broadcast is defined as follows: let us suppose that vectors z_j are divided in two parts $z_j = (x_j, y_j)$ where the x_j is the first part of the binary representation of every component of z_j and y_j is the second part. So x_j and y_j are $\frac{1}{2}t \log q$ bits long. Then $B_j^1 = (X_j, Y_j)$, where:

$$X_j = \begin{cases} x_j & \text{if } j = 1, 2 \\ x_1 + x_2, x_1 + x_3, \ldots, x_1 + x_{j-1}, x_j & \text{if } j = 3, \ldots, m \end{cases},$$

$$Y_j = \begin{cases} y_j, y_m + y_{j+1}, y_m + y_{j+2}, \ldots, y_m + y_{m-1} & \text{if } j = 1, \ldots, m-2 \\ y_j & \text{if } j = m-1, m \end{cases}.$$

The second part of the broadcast is defined as follows: for $j = 1, 2$

$$B_j^2 = \{(k, \psi(k)^\top P_j)\}_{k \in W_j} \text{ and for } j \geq 3, \ B_j^2 = B_{j-1}^2 \cup \{(k, \psi(k)^\top P_j)\}_{k \in W_j}.$$

Sponsored Addition of Users. If a user $\ell \in G_j$ wants to sponsor a user $i \notin G_j$ for session j, then he sends $(\ell, \psi(\ell)^\top P_j \psi(i))$ privately to i (computed from its personal key: $(\ell, \psi(\ell)^\top P_j)$).

For lack of space we do not include the proof of the following result: *the proposed scheme is a $(\mathcal{R}, \Gamma, \mathcal{S})$-self-healing key distribution scheme with sponsorization for $\mathcal{R} = 2^{\mathcal{U}} - \Gamma$ and $\mathcal{S} = 2^{\mathcal{U}} - \Gamma'$.* Observe that the assert $\mathcal{S} = 2^{\mathcal{U}} - \Gamma'$ is strict to ensure condition 4.(c) in the sense that if some $D_i \in \Gamma'$ then sponsored users in D_i by $i \in G_j$ can obtain the key K_j. This happens because $\{(\psi(i)^\top P_j \psi(d))\}_{d \in D_i}$ determines $\psi(i)^\top P_j$: suppose that $e_1, \ldots, e_t$ is the canonical basis of $GF(q)^t$, then they can find scalars λ_{kd} such that $e_k = \sum_{d \in D_i} \lambda_{kd} \psi(d)$, so $\psi(i)^\top P_j e_k = \sum_{d \in D_i} \lambda_{kd} \psi(i)^\top P_j \psi(d)$ and we know that $\psi(i)^\top P_j = (\psi(i)^\top P_j e_1, \ldots, \psi(i)^\top P_j e_t)$; from $\psi(i)^\top P_j$ and the correspondent broadcast, the key K_j can be determined.

We analyze the efficiency of the family of the proposed self-healing key distribution schemes with sponsorization in terms of memory storage and communication complexity. In our construction every user i has to store a personal key of size $|S_i| = t(m - j + 1) \log q$ when the structure Γ is a vector space access structure. The length of the proofs of sponsorization achieve the bound presented in Proposition 1. In our construction, the broadcast length depends on the particular function ψ used. The second part of the broadcast has the same form as the proposed in [1] and its purpose is to perform the rejection capability as well as the computation of the key. Its length depends on the history of rejected subsets $R_2, R_3, etc.$. The first part of the broadcast has almost constant length in every session (in contrast with the length in other proposals, for instance in [1]): B_1^1 and B_m^1 have $\frac{1}{2}tm \log q$ bits and B_j^1 for $j \neq 1, m$ has $\frac{1}{2}t(m-1) \log q$ bits. Then the total number of broadcast bits is $\frac{1}{2}t(m^2 - m + 2) \log q$.

5   A Particular Example Based in Shamir's Secret Sharing Scheme

We will present the particular self-healing key distribution scheme that we obtain using the polynomial Shamir's secret sharing scheme [8] in our general construction. This (t,n)−threshold scheme can be defined with the assignment of vectors $\psi(D) = (1,0,\ldots,0) \in GF(q)^t$ and $\psi(i) = (1,i,\ldots,i^{t-1}) \in GF(q)^t$ for $i \in \mathcal{U}$, and vector $v = (1,0,\ldots,0)$ that verifies conditions of Lemma 1. We should point out that the product of vector $\psi(i)$ by a vector of coefficients can be seen as the image of a polynomial, that is, $\psi(i)w = p(i)$ where $w = (a_0, a_1, \ldots, a_{t-1})$ and $p(x) = a_0 + a_1 x + \cdots + a_{t-1} x^{t-1}$. In a similar way the product of a vector $\psi(i)$ by a matrix can be seen as a polynomial in two variables. With this map ψ we find the following particular self-healing key distribution scheme:

Set-Up. Let $G_1 \subset \mathcal{U}$. The group manager chooses randomly polynomials $P_1(x,y), \ldots, P_m(x,y)$ of degree $t - 1$ in both variables and session keys $K_1, \ldots, K_m \in GF(q)$. For each $j = 1, \ldots, m$ the group manager computes the polynomial $z_j(y) = K_j + P_j(0,y) \in GF(q)[y]$. The group manager sends privately to user $i \in G_1$ the personal key $S_i = (P_1(i,y), \ldots, P_m(i,y)) \in (GF(q)[y])^m$.

Full Addition. In order to add users $J_j \subset \mathcal{U}$ in session j, the group manager sends privately $S_i = (P_j(i,y), P_{j+1}(i,y), \ldots, P_m(i,y)) \in (GF(q)[y])^{m-j+1}$ to every user $i \in J_j$ as his personal key.

Broadcast. Let $R_j \subset G_{j-1}$ with $|R_2 \cup \cdots \cup R_j| < t$ if $j \geq 2$ and by definition $R_1 = \emptyset$. The group manager chooses a subset of users W_j with $|W_j| = t - 1$ such that $R_1 \cup R_2 \cup \cdots \cup R_j \subset W_j$ and $W_j \cap G_j = \emptyset$. The broadcast B_j in session $j = 1, \ldots, m$ is given by $B_j = B_j^1 \cup B_j^2$. The first part of the broadcast is defined as follows: let us suppose that polynomials $z_j(y)$ are divided in two parts $z_j = (x_j, y_j)$ where x_j is the first part of the binary representation of every coefficient of $z_j(y)$ and y_j is the second part. So x_j and y_j are $\frac{1}{2}t \log q$ bits long. The rest of the definition of the broadcast follows the lines presented in Section 4. For instance for $j \geq 3$, $B_j^2 = B_{j-1}^2 \cup \{(k, P_j(k,y))\}_{k \in W_j}$.

Sponsored Addition of Users. If a user $\ell \in G_j$ wants to sponsor a user $i \notin G_j$ for session j, then he sends $(\ell, P_j(\ell, i))$ privately to i (computed from a part of its personal key: $(\ell, P_j(\ell, y))$).

Let us show how the session key computation is performed in this particular case. User $i \in G_j$ has $\{(k, P_j(k,y))\}_{k \in W_j}$ and computes $\{(k, P_j(k,i))\}_{k \in W_j}$. By means of $P_j(i,y)$ of its personal key, he computes $P_j(i,i)$. Then he computes $P_j(0,i)$ using $\{(k, P_j(k,i))\}_{k \in W_j \cup \{i\}}$ where $|W_j \cup \{i\}| = t$. In effect: interpolating these t points he can compute $P_j(0,i) = \sum_{k \in W_j \cup \{i\}} \lambda_k P_j(k,i)$ for some $\lambda_k \in GF(q)$ (again the Lagrange coefficients of interpolation). From the broadcast information the user can compute the key because $z_j(i) = K_j + P_j(0,i)$. For the case of a user i sponsored by a subset of users $A \subset G_j$ with $|A| = t$ he proceeds as follows. User i can compute $P_j(0,i)$ because he has $\{(k, P_j(k,i))\}_{k \in A}$. In effect: since $|A| = t$, then $P_j(0,i) = \sum_{k \in A} \lambda_k P_j(k,i)$ for some $\lambda_k \in GF(q)$ (the Lagrange coefficients of interpolation). Then the key is easy to compute using the broadcast information: $z_j(i) = K_j + P_j(0,i)$.

In this particular construction, a subset of at most $t-1$ users can be revoked, that is $|R| = |R_2 \cup \cdots \cup R_j| \leq t - 1$. Then $\mathcal{R} = \{A \subset \mathcal{U} : |A| \leq t - 1\}$. We also have that $\Gamma = \{A \subset \mathcal{U} : |A| \geq t\}$ and $\mathcal{S} = \{A \subset \mathcal{U} : |A| \leq t - 1\}$ because $\Gamma' = \Gamma$. The bounds presented in Section 3 are achieved.

In this scheme a part of the broadcast is proportional to $t - 1$, the cardinality of subset W_j. The almost constant length for every session of the first part of the broadcast can be observed in the following broadcasts for $m = 9$:

$$B_1^1 = (x_1, y_9 + y_8, y_9 + y_7, y_9 + y_6, y_9 + y_5, y_9 + y_4, y_9 + y_3, y_9 + y_2, y_1)$$
$$B_2^1 = (x_2, y_9 + y_8, y_9 + y_7, y_9 + y_6, y_9 + y_5, y_9 + y_4, y_9 + y_3, y_2)$$
$$B_3^1 = (x_1 + x_2, x_3, y_9 + y_8, y_9 + y_7, y_9 + y_6, y_9 + y_5, y_9 + y_4, y_3)$$
$$B_4^1 = (x_1 + x_2, x_1 + x_3, x_4, y_9 + y_8, y_9 + y_7, y_9 + y_6, y_9 + y_5, y_4)$$
$$B_5^1 = (x_1 + x_2, x_1 + x_3, x_1 + x_4, x_5, y_9 + y_8, y_9 + y_7, y_9 + y_6, y_5)$$
$$B_6^1 = (x_1 + x_2, x_1 + x_3, x_1 + x_4, x_1 + x_5, x_6, y_9 + y_8, y_9 + y_7, y_6)$$
$$B_7^1 = (x_1 + x_2, x_1 + x_3, x_1 + x_4, x_1 + x_5, x_1 + x_6, x_7, y_9 + y_8, y_7)$$
$$B_8^1 = (x_1 + x_2, x_1 + x_3, x_1 + x_4, x_1 + x_5, x_1 + x_6, x_1 + x_7, x_8, y_8)$$
$$B_9^1 = (x_1 + x_2, x_1 + x_3, x_1 + x_4, x_1 + x_5, x_1 + x_6, x_1 + x_7, x_1 + x_8, x_9, y_9)$$

Other schemes can be proposed using our construction with particular linear secret sharing schemes instead of Shamir's secret sharing scheme. For instance, a particular construction in which we have a short broadcast for small revocations of users can be proposed following the same idea presented in [4].

References

1. C. Blundo, P. D'Arco, A. De Santis and M. Listo. Design of Self-Healing Key Distribution Schemes. *Designs, Codes and Cryptography*, Vol. 32, pp. 15–44 (2004).
2. C. Blundo, P. D'Arco, A. De Santis and M. Listo. Definitions and Bounds for Self-Healing Key Distribution. In *ICALP'04*. LNCS, **3142** (2004) 234–245.
3. T.M. Cover and J.A. Thomas. Elements of Inform. Theory. *J. Wiley & Sons*, 1991.
4. V. Daza, J. Herranz and G. Sáez. Constructing General Dynamic Group Key Distribution Schemes with Decentralized User Join. In *8th Australasian Conference on Information Security and Privacy (ACISP '03)*. LNCS, **2727** (2003) 464–475.
5. H. Kurnio, R. Safavi-Naini and H. Wang. A Group Key Distribution Scheme with Decentralised User Join. *Security in Communication Networks, Third International Conference, SCN'02*. LNCS, **2576** (2002) 146–163.
6. D. Liu, P. Ning and K. Sun. Efficient Self-Healing Key Distribution with Revocation Capability. In *10th ACM Conf. on Computer and Com. Security* (2003).
7. J.Staddon, S.Miner, M.Franklin, D.Balfanz, M.Malkin and D.Dean. Self-Healing Key Distribution with Revocation. *IEEE Symp. on Security and Privacy*, (2002).
8. D.R. Stinson. An explication of secret sharing schemes. *Designs, Codes and Cryptography*, Vol. **2**, pp. 357–390 (1992).

Effective Protection Against Phishing and Web Spoofing

Rolf Oppliger[1] and Sebastian Gajek[2]

[1] eSECURITY Technologies, Gümligen, Switzerland
[2] Horst Görtz Institute for IT-Security, Ruhr University Bochum, Germany

Abstract. Phishing and Web spoofing have proliferated and become a major nuisance on the Internet. The attacks are difficult to protect against, mainly because they target non-cryptographic components, such as the user or the user-browser interface. This means that cryptographic security protocols, such as the SSL/TLS protocol, do not provide a complete solution to tackle the attacks and must be complemented by additional protection mechanisms. In this paper, we summarize, discuss, and evaluate the effectiveness of such mechanisms against (large-scale) phishing and Web spoofing attacks.

Keywords: SSL/TLS, phishing, Web spoofing, visual spoofing.

1 Introduction

There are many technologies to protect e-commerce applications. Most importantly, the Secure Sockets Layer (SSL) and Transport Layer Security (TLS) protocols are used to authenticate the Web server and to establish a cryptographically secure channel between the browser acting on behalf of the user and the Web server. The user is typically authenticated with one or several of the following mechanisms: user identification (ID) and password, transaction authentication number (TAN), one-time password, challenge-response mechanism, or public key certificate. The corresponding authentication information is transmitted over the SSL/TLS channel. While the SSL/TLS protocol is—with some minor theoretical vulnerabilities—reasonably secure [1], the way it interacts with the user and the way it is employed in e-commerce applications typically are not [2]. In fact, spoofing attacks—like phishing and Web spoofing—show that currently deployed authentication mechanisms for Web applications are insufficient to protect users against fraudulent Web sites. When spoofing attacks on the Web were first introduced and discussed in [3], they were purely theoretical and only a few incidents really occurred in practice. This has changed dramatically, and contemporary e-commerce applications are severely threatened by phishing and Web spoofing attacks, which have proliferated and recently become a major nuisance on the Internet and WWW. Consequently, there is considerably strong pressure to protect users against these types of attacks.

One could argue that a cryptographically secure end-to-end mutual authentication protocol is all that is needed to protect users against phishing and Web

J. Dittmann, S. Katzenbeisser, and A. Uhl (Eds.): CMS 2005, LNCS 3677, pp. 32–41, 2005.

spoofing attacks. There are several protocols that can be used for this purpose. Even though these protocols are cryptographically sound, the user behavior may induce some security problems. An unsophisticated user may simply recognize a window that pops up and requests to enter his credentials (i.e., authentication information). As long as an adversary is capable of imitating the window, the user can not reliably verify whether the window is legitimate and originated by the browser or whether it is spoofed by malware. Consequently, the user may provide his credentials assuming that they are handled by a secure protocol, whereas in reality they are sent to the adversary. Recently, the term *doppelganger window attack* was coined to refer to this type of attack [4]. The ease of mounting these attacks is worrisome, and the underlying problem is the interface between user and the implementation of the cryptographic system. This problem cannot be solved with another layer of cryptography—the user would have to be interfaced to it again. Against this background, we argue (i) that phishing and Web spoofing is threatening because the corresponding attacks target non-cryptographic components, such as the user or the user-browser interface, (ii) that the implementations of existing cryptographic security protocols, such as the SSL/TLS protocol, do not provide a complete solution, and (iii) that these protocols must be complemented by additional protection mechanisms. This it what this paper is all about. In Section 2, we introduce the relevant attacks and distinguish between five attack levels. In Section 3, we summarize, discuss, and evaluate the effectiveness of corresponding protection mechanisms. In Section 4, we summarize our major findings, and in Section 5, we identify some open research challenges. Finally, we provide some conclusions in Section 6.

2   Relevant Attacks

In *native phishing*, an attacker sends an e-mail to the victim, requesting the victim to reveal and send back (by e-mail) his or her password. Today, more complex and sophisticated phishing and Web spoofing attacks take place. They typically consist of two stages:

1. The attacker directs the victim to a Web site he controls. According to [5], we use the term *mounting attack* for this stage.
2. The attacker uses his Web site to spoof a legitimate Web site of an arbitrary company or organization. We use the term *spoofing attack* for this stage.

There are many mounting attacks. They can be categorized into those operating on the network layer and those operating on the application layer. Examples of network layer mounting attacks are ARP, IP, and DNS spoofing. Examples of application layer mounting attacks are e-mail and URL spoofing or cross-site-scripting. For the purpose of this paper, we assume that there are so many types of current and future mounting attacks, that it is infeasible to protect against all of them. So we only consider spoofing attacks.

Again, there are many possibilities to realize a spoofing attack. For example, in the simplest case, the attacker simulates the look-and-feel of the spoofed site—this is simple, because the attacker can reuse the images and icons from the spoofed site. Although common browsers have a set of indicators that provide information about the connection, two practical concerns remain: on the one hand users are notoriously bad (or untrained) at verifying and validating these indicators and, on the other hand, there are still many possibilities to either manipulate or overwrite them. However, if the browser and server communicate over an SSL/TLS channel, then it is somehow more challenging for the adversary to mount a spoofing attack. This is because there are several *browser's secure connection indicators (BSCIs)* [5]:

- The icon that indicates the use of the SSL/TLS protocol (e.g., the padlock icon in the case of the Microsoft Internet Explorer).
- The certificate dialog that displays information about the server's certificate and the current status of the SSL/TLS connection.
- The location bar that displays the URL (including, for example, the prefix `https` standing for HTTP over SSL/TLS).
- A few menu items that can be used to display information about the status of the SSL/TLS connection.

Following [5], we use the term *visual spoofing* to refer to attacks that tamper with the BSCIs to fool the users about the status of their SSL/TLS connections (e.g., [3,6,7,8,9]). We consider visual spoofing as a powerful and very threatening attack that jeopardizes the security of most of today's Web applications. The details of these attacks are beyond the scope of this paper (a proof-of-concept can be found in [5]). Instead, we focus on mechanisms that can be employed to protect users against phishing and Web spoofing attacks.

To better understand why protection against phishing and Web spoofing is difficult, we look at the entities and components involved in a Web transaction.

- The *user* is the human entity who initiates the transaction.
- The *platform* is the client-side computer system employed by the user to initiate and perform the transaction. It consists of hardware and software (e.g., an operating system).
- The *browser* is the application software that is executed on the platform on behalf of the user to initiate and perform the transaction.
- The *Web server* (or *server* in short) is the server-side computer system that hosts the site and the resources that are requested by the browser.

In this setting, we are ultimately interested in a secure (i.e., authentic and private) channel between the user and the Web server. Such a channel may protect the user against phishing and Web spoofing. Unfortunately, all we have today is a supposedly secure channel between the browser and the Web server— using the SSL/TLS protocol. Note that this is an entirely different situation. Before the user can initiate this channel, he must convince himself (i) that the Web server is authentic, (ii) that the browser is authentic and not compromised in a way that it may leak secret information (e.g., authentication information), and (iii) that the platform is not compromised (otherwise it is not possible to establish a secure channel to the browser in the first place). The last point is the most critical one, and for all practical purposes one must assume that the platform is not compromised, has not been tampered with, and operates soundly.

To evaluate protection mechanisms against phishing and Web spoofing attacks, we need a classification of such attacks. We distinguish between five classes of attacks and corresponding attack levels. In either case, we assume an adversary who is powerful enough to passively and actively attack network communications. We define the following five attack levels:

Level 0: Attacks that implement native phishing as mentioned above.

Level 1: Attacks that implement classical phishing as reported in the media, i.e., the victim is directed to a Web site the adversary controls and the user is asked to reveal his credentials. Note that the adversary does not try to spoof an official Web site. Level 1 attacks are the most popular ones.

Level 2: Similar to attack level 1, except that the adversary tries to spoof an official Web server. The case is an aggravation of the prior one. The adversary imitates the official site's look-and-feel to mislead the user about the real connection.

Level 3: Similar to attack level 2. In this case, however, the adversary additionally employs visual spoofing to hide the attack. This means that the adversary can compromise the browser in some meaningful way. As mentioned above, this includes the capability of tampering an SSL/TLS-connection.

Level 4: Similar to attack level 3. In this case, however, the adversary can compromise the platform on which the browser executes. These attacks are very powerful, because they allow an adversary to install and execute key loggers, Trojan horses, and any other malicious software.

Attacks of levels 0 and 1 are comparably simple to detect even for casual users. Consequently, awareness and education programs may help to have users protect themselves against these attacks. Contrary to that, attacks of levels 2 and 3 are much more difficult to detect (sometimes even for the experienced and well-educated user). This is even more true for attacks of level 4.

3   Protection Mechanisms

In the past, several mechanisms have been developed that can be employed to partially protect users against phishing and Web spoofing attacks. The mechanisms may address the user, the platform, the browser, the Web server, or combinations thereof. For example, the user may be educated not to trust (and click on) anything received over the Internet and to use a different password for every Web site (if possible). Furthermore, the platform may be secured using best practices. This includes, for example, the use of firewalls and intrusion detection systems. For the purpose of this paper, we only address protection mechanisms that can be implemented on the browser or server side, or that can be implemented as a(n additional) interaction between the browser and the server. In the second case, the interaction must be specified and implemented as a protocol—that is either independent from other protocols or enhances an already existing protocol, such as the SSL/TLS protocol.

We mention that several authors have proposed heuristics to detect phishing and Web spoofing attacks (e.g., [10,5,11]). Heuristic protection mechanisms can be as simple as blacklists of known phishing sites (e.g., EarthLink's Toolbar[1] and GeoTrust's TrustWatch[2]) or take into account multiple rules (e.g., Spoof-Guard[3]). Due to space limitations they are not addressed in this paper.

3.1 Browser-Side Protection Mechanisms

There are several mechanisms that can be employed on the browser side to (partially) protect users against phishing and Web spoofing attacks.

- In [12], the author proposes three modifications of the browser: First, the domain names of the Web sites being visited may be hashed, and the resulting hash value (or a prefix thereof) may be displayed by the browser in some appropriate way (e.g., as a two-character symbol). The aim is to make lexically close or homographic domain names look significantly different. Second, the browser may keep track of visited Web sites and notify the user if a new site is being visited (using, for example, some graphical warning sign). To defeat privacy concerns, the domain names of the visited sites may be concatenated with some user-specific random string (before they are hashed). Third, the browser may use heuristics to determine whether a site is suspicious (not addressed in this paper). The first two proposals are simple and effective to protect users against phishing and Web spoofing attacks up to level 2.
- In [3], the authors propose to configure the browser in a way that active Web scripting and programming languages (e.g., Java, JavaScript, and ActiveX) are deactivated. This proposal is effective to protect against phishing and Web spoofing attacks up to level 3; it is, however, neither complete nor practical.
- A user can protect himself against phishing and Web spoofing attacks, if he can properly authenticate the Web server. In theory, he can authenticate the server by verifying its SSL/TLS certificate. More specifically, the user must ensure that the certificate is valid, meaning that it is issued by a trusted certification authority (CA) and has not been revoked. Furthermore, he must compare the certificate's fingerprint with a reference value that is received out-of-band (e.g., published in print media). This is not a trivial task, and we propose that it can be simplified considerably by representing the hash value visually (e.g., [13,14,15]).
- Before the user provides his credentials, he must be sure that the browser is authentic in order to protect himself against visual spoofing attacks (level 3). If the platform supports trusted computing, then user has some certainty

---

[1] http://www.earthlink.net
[2] http://www.trustwatch.com/
[3] http://crypto.stanford.edu/SpoofGuard/

that the browser is indeed authentic. In all other cases, the user has to make sure in one way or another that the browser or components of its GUI (e.g., the BSCIs) have not been tampered with. There are a couple of proposals that protect users against attacks up to level 3.

- In [8], the authors recommend to prevent that the status bar is being deactivated by active Web languages. This proposal is simple and effective at protecting the user against some visual spoofing attacks (as it prevents deactivation of the padlock indicating a trustworthy SSL/TLS connection). It was recently implemented in Windows XP Service Pack 2, for instance.

- In [9], the authors propose to add a secure and tamper-resistant component called TrustBar[4] to the browser to visualize information about the Web site and the CA that issued the corresponding Web site's certificate. According to RFC 3709 [16], it is possible to include logotypes (commonly known as a *logo*, which is the graphical representation of a trademark or brand) in X.509 public key and attribute certificates. Consequently, the TrustBar renders the corresponding logotypes (of the Web site and CA) or display textual representations thereof. A fake site is divulged when a user does not recognize his corresponding visualization on the TrustBar. In addition, for unprotected Web sites, TrustBar displays a highly visible warning. We argue that if future browsers included a TrustBar (or something similar), then users would have a better way to judge and argue about the trustworthiness of Web sites.

- In [17], the authors introduce and propose the notion of synchronized random dynamic (SRD) boundaries. The idea is to distinguish between authentic parts of a browser's graphical user interface (GUI) and rendered content dynamically received from a Web server, and to make this distinction obvious by changing the boundary colour of the real GUI between two colors, blinking in synchrony with a trusted reference window. SRD boundaries are simple and effective, and they do not require any user interaction. However, they do not allow for modular verification of portions of a Web page. Furthermore, the modification of the browser required to implement SRD boundaries are not trivial. This is also true for the modification proposed in [8].

- In [5], the authors adopt an idea of [18] and suggest to authenticate the browser (or the BSCIs, respectively) by applying the concept of personalization with individually chosen background bitmaps.

The first, second, and fourth proposal are useful and worth considering (the third proposal is more complex than the fourth proposal, but achieves more or less the same level of protection).

In summary, our analysis implies that client-side protection mechanisms can effectively protect users against phishing and Web spoofing attacks up to level

---

[4] http://TrustBar.Mozdev.org

3. This is particularly true for protection mechanisms that employ tamper-resistant or personalized browser BSCIs. We recommend that these countermeasures should be adapted in future Web applications, which fail in authentically presenting the connection identifiers. As the visualization of these identifiers is not tamper-proof, the user is unable to distinguish between real and faked components of his user interface and, thus, susceptible to visual spoofing attacks.

3.2   Server-Side Protection Mechanisms

In addition to a proper authentication of the server during the execution of the SSL/TLS protocol, there are a few proposals and corresponding mechanisms that can be used on the server side to (partially) protect the users.

- If the login process is separated into two phases, then the user can enter his user ID in the first phase and his credentials in the second phase. Furthermore, the user can be taught to enter his credentials if and only if the second window is personalized in some meaningful way (e.g., by showing an image selected by the user).[5] We argue that such a mechanism protects the user against phishing and Web spoofing attacks up to level 2 because the adversary's Web site is unable to personalize the second window. However, we judge this mechanism to be ineffective to counteract attacks of higher level. The personalized window can be retrieved by anybody (simply by entering the appropriate user ID) and (mis)used to mount a visual spoofing attack. The only advantage we see is that an adversary must personalize the attack. Since this personalization can be automated, we don't see any real benefit.
- Another idea is implemented in GeoTrust's True Site seal. In short, the seal is a dynamically created "smart icon" that is placed on a Web site to make sure that the site is legitimate and authentic. The browser renders the seal and the user must actively validate it via a trusted party. This mechanism looks promising to protect users against phishing and Web spoofing attacks up to level 2. The major drawback is that the mechanism is passive (meaning that its validation must be initiated by the user), and hence the seal itself may be subject to spoofing attacks.

In summary, we conclude that server-side protection mechanisms are inappropriate for protecting users against this attack generation at all. The reason is lack of content protection or content secrecy, i.e., the adversary is generally able to perceive the same content as the user does. As a result, the adversary is able to imitate the content, i.e., he can copy and paste the Web site's look-and-feel (e.g., brand marks, logos and layout) and camouflage his attack by tampering with all BSCIs. There is no possibility to verify the authenticity and to realize its true origin with means standard Web browsers provide.

---

[5] Such a system has been developed and is being marketed by PassMark Security (cf. http://www.passmarksecurity.com).

3.3   Protection Mechanisms for the Interaction

There are a few proposals that affect the browser, the server, and the way they interact. The proposals are quite complex and are able to protect users against phishing and Web spoofing attacks up to level 2.

- It is useful to restrict the temporal validity of user credentials. This does not completely protect against phishing and Web spoofing attacks, it does, however, make sure that an adversary must operate in real-time.
- In [19], the authors propose a system in which a Web server can enrich its contents with HTML extensions called prooflets. Prooflets in turn can be verified by the browsers using special Web services. In theory, this proposal is appropriate and effective. In practice, however, this proposal has similar drawbacks as GeoTrust's True Site seal.
- In [4], the authors propose a technique called *Delayed Password Disclosure* (DPD) that protects a user executing a password-based mutual authentication protocol against the *doppelganger window attack* mentioned above. The technique is based on augmenting each user password with an easy-to-recognize sequence of images (that are specific to the user, the password, and the Web site). The user enters his password letter by letter, and for every letter he must recognize an image. The technique provides protection against phishing and Web spoofing attacks up to level 3.

In summary, we evaluate these proposals as helpful and effective to counteract level 3 attacks. Taken into account the current situation on the Internet and WWW, it is certainly time to move from user ID and password to more secure (mutual) authentication mechanisms. Particularly, the notion of prooflets and DPD look promising for the future.

4   Summary and Major Findings

As mentioned in Section 2, we are interested in mechanisms that are effective to protect users against phishing and Web spoofing attacks of level 2 and 3 (i.e., without or with visual spoofing attacks). Unless we do not enter the field of trusted computing, we assume that we are not able to protect users against phishing and Web spoofing attacks of level 4.

With regard to level 2, the proposals of [12] are effective and should be implemented on the browser side. Furthermore, we opine that server authentication must be improved. The visual representation of certificate fingerprints is certainly something that should be considered first (since it does not require infrastructural changes). Similarly, systems like TrustBar and True Site are useful to make the notion of a public key certificate and the entire certification process more transparent to the user. However, more research is needed with regard to the usefulness and user acceptance of these mechanisms.

With regard to level 3, the proposal of [3] is by far the most simple and effective protection mechanism. Unfortunately, it is impractical, and hence we must evaluate alternative mechanisms. Making the BSCIs as tamper resistant as possible and personalizing them are certainly good ideas that should be implemented. In particular, the personalization paradigm has been largely ignored by the browser manufacturers. We argue that it is about time to change this and that future versions of browsers should incorporate features that allow users to personalize the BSCIs. Similarly, browser manufacturers should include features that allow users to realize that they have connected to a Web site for the very first time (especially if the connection is secured with the SSL/TLS protocol). The Petname tool[6] for the Firefox browser is a good example. This does not help in the Internet café scenario; it does help, however, in the home PC scenario.

5   Research Challenges

In [20], the author proposes a possibility to improve the security of TAN lists in a way that the user is protected against an adversary reading out the list and misusing the TANs, as well as some simple phishing attacks. The idea is to protect the TAN list in a way that reading a TAN requires a physical act that can be detected easily at some later point in time. One possibility is to use a physical layer that hides the TANs and can easily be rasped away by the user (similar to lots in some lotteries). Furthermore, an authentication code or a prefix thereof can be printed on the physical layer, and the user can be taught to verify the code before he rasps away the physical layer. Alternatively, the code can also be covered by a physical layer that must be rasped away. The corresponding TAN lists are securely delivered, mainly because they are distributed out-of-band (i.e., using an out-of-band distribution channel). This can be simulated, for example, using the short messaging service (SMS) of GSM networks. An interesting research challenge is to find a similar mechanism that does not require an out-of-band distribution mechanism. One possibility is to combine a challenge-response mechanism with a non-trivial redundancy scheme that allows a browser to verify the authenticity of a challenge. Note that this does not protect against adversaries that operate in real-time (i.e., the adversary can simply act as as a relay between the origin server and the user). Consequently, an important research challenge is to find technologies and mechanisms that are able to protect users against adaptive adversaries that operate in real-time. There are many applications (e.g., Internet banking) that could take advantage of such technologies and mechanisms.

6   Conclusions

In this paper, we summarized, discussed, and evaluated the effectiveness of mechanisms to protect users against (large-scale) phishing and Web spoofing attacks. Some mechanisms are simple and effective and should be implemented immediately. This is particularly true for browser-side mechanisms. Server-side mechanisms seem to be advantageous, mainly because they are simpler to deploy but

---

[6] http://www.waterken.com/user/PetnameTool

are also more challenging to design and come up with. In fact, we have found no server-side protection mechanism that can be used to effectively protect users against phishing and Web spoofing attacks. The protection mechanisms for the interaction look promising but still require more analysis. More surprisingly, there is a simple and reasonable secure protection mechanism against many relevant phishing and Web spoofing attacks that employ plain old TAN lists.

References

1. Wagner, D., Schneier, B.: Analysis of the SSL 3.0 Protocol. In: USENIX Security Symposium. (1996) 29–40
2. Clayton, R.: Insecure Real-World Authentication Protocols (or Why Phishing is so Profitable). In: Financial Cryptography. (2005)
3. Felten, W.E., Balfanz, D., Dean, D., Wallach, D.S.: Web Spoofing: An Internet Con Game. Technical Report 540-96, Dept. of Computer Science, Princeton University (1996)
4. Jakobsson, M., Myers, S.: Stealth Attacks and Delayed Password Disclosure. (2005)
5. Adelsbach, A., Gajek, S., Schwenk, J.: Visual Spoofing of SSL Protected Web Sites and Effective Countermeasures. In: Information Security Practice and Experience Conference. (2005)
6. De Paoli, F., DosSantos, A., Kemmerer, R.: Vulnerability of 'Secure' Web Browsers. In: National Information Systems Security Conference. (1997)
7. Lefranc, S., Naccache, D.: Cut-&-Paste Attacks with JAVA. In: ICISC. (2002) 1–15
8. Li, T.Y., Wu, Y.: Trust on Web Browser: Attack vs. Defense. In: ACNS. (2003) 241–253
9. Herzberg, A., Gbara, A.: TrustBar: Protecting (even Naive) Web Users from Spoofing and Phishing Attacks. IACR Cryptology ePrint Archive (2004)
10. Chou, N., Ledesma, R., Teraguchi, Y., Mitchell, J.C.: Client-Side Defense Against Web-Based Identity Theft. In: NDSS. (2004)
11. Jakobbson, M.: Modeling and Preventing Phishing Attacks. In: Financial Cryptography. (2005)
12. Markham, G.: Phishing-Browser-based Defences. (2005) http://www.gerv.net/security/phishing-browser-defences.html#ssl-essential.
13. Perrig, A., Song, D.: Hash visualization: A new technique to improve real-world security. In: Cryptographic Techniques and E-Commerce. (1999)
14. Perrig, A., Dhamija, R.: Déjà Vu: A User Study Using Images for Authentication. In: USENIX Security Symposium. (2000)
15. Dohrmann, S., Ellison, C.: Public key support for collaborative work. In: PKI Research Workshop. (2002)
16. Santesson, S., Housley, R., Freeman, T.: Internet X.509 Public Key Infrastructure: Logotypes in X.509 Certificates. (2004) Request for Comments 3709.
17. Ye, Z.E., Smith, S.: Trusted Paths for Browsers. In: USENIX Security Symposium. (2002) 263–279
18. Tygar, J., Whitten, A.: WWW Electronic Commerce and Trojan Horses. In: USENIX Workshop on Electronic Commerce. (1996)
19. Shin, M., Straub, C., Tamassia, R., Polivy, D.: Authenticating Web content with Prooflets. Technical report, Brown University, Center for Geometric Computing (2002)
20. Oppliger, R.: Sichere Streichlisten. digma **5** (2005) 34–35

Identity Based DRM: Personal Entertainment Domain

Paul Koster, Frank Kamperman, Peter Lenoir, and Koen Vrielink

Information and System Security Department, Philips Research,
Professor Holstlaan 4 (WY71), 5656AA Eindhoven, The Netherlands
{R.P.Koster, Frank.Kamperman, Peter.Lenoir,
Koen.Vrielink}@Philips.com

Abstract. Digital Rights Management (DRM) enforces the rights of copyright holders and enforces their business models. This imposes restrictions on the way users handle content. These restrictions apply specifically in networked environments. Authorized Domain (AD) DRM concepts remove, or at least reduce, several of these restrictions to a large extent, while at the same time taking into account the content providers' need to limit the proliferation of content. In this paper we describe the design and operation of an Authorized Domain system, which we call the Personal Entertainment Domain (PED).

Keywords: Digital Rights Management, DRM, Authorized Domain.

1 Introduction

The concept of Authorized Domain (AD) Digital Rights Management (DRM) [1-3] aims to fulfill the requirements of both the content owners and the users (see section 0), which often appear to be conflicting. For an AD the general idea is that content can flow freely between the devices that belong to the domain, while content transactions between ADs are restricted.

Companies [4-9] and standardization bodies such as DVB (Digital Video Broadcasting) [1] and OMA (Open Mobile Alliance) are investigating and developing the concept of Authorized Domains. Up until now people have taken a device-oriented approach [2], where an AD groups a set of devices that belong to a certain household.

We conducted a study on alternative approaches to device-based AD concepts; these provide better solutions to enable the user to access content anywhere, at any time and on any device. The outcome of that study was that the Personal Entertainment Domain (PED) AD concept was the most promising candidate and this paper therefore presents a realization for such a PED-DRM system. PED-DRM does not have many of the disadvantages of device-based AD and it also represents a feasible solution for the near future.

PED-DRM is characterized by its structure, i.e. the relationship between various entities such as content, devices and persons, and by its policy, i.e. the rules that govern content access and proliferation. The PED-DRM structure is characterized by the fact that one single person is the member/owner of the domain, that content is bound to that person and that a number of devices are bound to the user (see fig. 1).

J. Dittmann, S. Katzenbeisser, and A. Uhl (Eds.): CMS 2005, LNCS 3677, pp. 42–54, 2005.

The PED-DRM policy is characterized by the fact that domain content can be accessed on a set of permanent domain devices without user authentication, allowing convenient content usage at home, including the sharing of content among family members. The only thing people must do is to register their device once to their domain. On all other compliant devices content can be accessed temporarily after user authentication, enabling people to access their content anywhere and at any time. Devices may be a member of multiple domains, both permanent and temporary. This paper presents the architecture and design of a PED-DRM realization together with a trade-off of alternatives and an overview of the requirements and threats for DRM domain concepts in general.

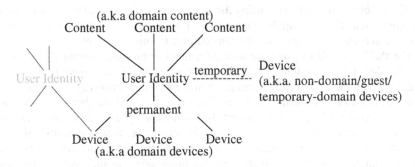

Fig. 1. PED-DRM concept

The outline of this paper is as follows. Section 2 introduces some typical scenarios and requirements for PED-DRM. Section 3 discusses the threat model and attacks. In section 4 we describe the functional design of the PED-DRM system. Section 5 elaborates on the main PED-DRM operations. The paper ends with an overview of related work and conclusions.

2 Scenarios and Requirements

The following scenarios demonstrate some of the typical PED-DRM functionality and the expected user experience and interaction with the system. The upcoming sections elaborate on the technical realization of these scenarios. In the scenarios that follow we assume that a user has a user identity device, such as a smartcard or mobile phone, with which he can authenticate – preferably wirelessly – to other devices. *Access family content at home:* A user operates his media center (a.k.a. Personal Video Recorder) connected to his TV in the living room. He selects a movie his wife bought using the remote control and presses play. The content starts to render (see fig.1: relation between permanent device, user identity and content). *Content access at remote location (guest access):* A user arrives at his hotel and decides he wants to render some content stored on his media center at home. He authenticates to the hotel TV and the TV lists the available content. He selects some content he bought some time ago and renders the content, which is streamed from his home (see fig.1: relation between user identity, temporary device and content). *Device registration to domain:*

A user buys a new TV for his bedroom. He holds his user identity device close to the TV and a menu pops up, asking him if he wants to register the TV to his domain. He confirms the registration using the TV remote (see fig.1: relation between user identity and permanent device). *UI (User Interaction) limited device registration to domain:* A user buys a cheap new music player with flash memory, a USB and preferably a wireless near field communication interface, but no screen. He holds the music player and personal authentication device close to his TV, which then displays the option to register the music player to his domain. He confirms the operation using the TV remote. *Device deregistration from domain:* A user decides to replace his media center with a better one he has just bought and gives his old media center away to his friend. Before giving it away he holds his user identity device close to his old media center and deregisters it using the media center remote and the menu shown on the connected TV. The application on the TV suggests he moves his content and licenses to another device so that he can continue to enjoy his content.

For the PED-DRM design we assume a number of requirements for the various stakeholders of the system. From the point of view of the content provider, the realization of the PED-DRM concept should meet the following requirements: (1) limit proliferation of content that has not been paid for; (2) limit damage in the case of hacked devices; (3) provide support for renewability/revocation of hacked/non-compliant devices; (4) support tracing of devices to facilitate revocation if devices malfunction. The rationale behind these requirements is that the content provider's business model must be sustainable and not break down in the event of an incident with the DRM system that governs the content. From the point of view of the user, the following requirements should be met: (1) in his role as domain and device owner, the user must have control over his domain and devices, i.e. no undesired (de)registrations of his devices to his domain; (2) DRM and domain functionality should work for devices that have limited user interface capabilities; (3) the conceptual complexity for the user must be low, e.g. the user needs to have an overview of his domain and related actions; (4) the solution should be robust, e.g. automatically maintain a consistent state as far as possible; (5) it must be possible to remove broken/offline/stolen devices from the domain. The rationale behind these user requirements is that the user must have maximum control over his devices and content while still not being bothered too much by procedures and technicalities in daily use.

3 PED Threat Model and Attacks

Since PED is a DRM system with a domain concept centered around a user, the typical threat model for DRM systems applies to PED. The DRM threat model assumes that users may be malicious and will attempt to gain unauthorized access to content. To accomplish this goal, the attacker has full control of his local environment, including network and devices, although it is assumed that compliant devices have some form of tamper resistance. Malicious users may use compromised and circumvention devices and software. However, we assume the average attacker has limited computational resources to break cryptography, has only limited capability to disrupt external network communication outside his local environment and does not have access to professional tools. That said, it is possible that there could be a small number of attackers with the skills, technology and resources to perform such attacks. We continue with a number of attacks with a focus on domain- and person-based aspects, because general DRM aspects are assumed to be known [10].

Active attacks on the realization of the domain concept, i.e. grouping of devices according to a certain policy, include (1) malicious user interference with the domain management protocols in the local environment, (2) malicious user interference with license management and distribution in the local environment, and (3) malicious user interference in the distribution of device compliance status information through the heterogeneous and ad-hoc network of domain devices. Furthermore, there are some attacks that relate more to user behavior and the content owner's business models: (4) 'Content club': a large group of people share an account/identity/domain and obtain lots of content in such a way that it is accessible to all individual members, (5) 'Content cannibalization': realizations of the domain concept that include flexible limits, i.e. limits that can temporarily allow more devices to access content than intended, may be faced with domain extensions just before some premium content is released, (6) 'Content filling station': a rendering/storage device is loaded with domain content and then the device ownership is transferred, leaving the content available to the new and old owner for ever, (7) 'Automated domain or license management': intentional limitation or friction, such as mandatory user confirmation, could be frustrated if such operations are automated, making it seem as if a domain has no limitations.

Attacks that involve binding content to persons through licenses and allowing content access based on user presence include: (1) malicious users exploiting procedural processes for person management, e.g. users maliciously requesting replacement user authentication tokens, (2) malicious users exchanging, sharing, trading or cloning their identification and authentication credentials/tokens (3) simultaneous non-expired user authentication sessions that harm premium content releases. Since user behavior is non-technical, it is hard to detect and counter some of these attacks purely by technical means. The challenge is, therefore, to find the correct balance between attacks, threats, risks, countermeasures and user-friendliness.

4   Functional PED-DRM Architecture and Design

Figure 2 shows a functional and data view of the PED-DRM system. The shaded rectangles are data objects. The ovals above the data objects represent the typical PED-DRM functionality. The typical AD aspect of PED-DRM builds upon the user, device and domain management functions (fig.2, right). We have omitted most of the specific details of the DRM functions, e.g. content protection or license creation, because descriptions of these already exist [11;12] and because we have chosen to solve domain functionality independently so as to limit the effect on the traditional DRM functions (fig.2, left). The relation between rights management and domain management, i.e. the management of the set of permanent devices in the domain, is typically realized by means of a user identifier embedded in the license.

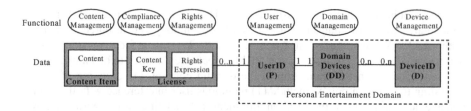

Fig. 2. PED-DRM DRM, identity and domain overview

User/Device Management

The main aspect of user management in PED-DRM is that a user is provided with a UserID certificate and corresponding public/private key pair. The user is not granted access to the private key in order to prevent him from misusing or giving away his private key and enabling someone else to impersonate him. To enforce this, the user's private key must be stored securely on a tamper-resistant user identity device, which also serves as a token that proves the user's presence. The user identity device (hardware and software) must be easy to handle, provide secure computing means and must be hard to clone. Typical solutions for this are smartcards and mobile phones equipped with a SIM card.

Devices in PED-DRM are given a DeviceID certificate. In addition to their identity, devices are also given explicit authorization to fulfill certain functions. This would limit the effects of a security breach by preventing the certificate and keys of a hacked device from being misused for other functions, e.g. keys from a rendering device cannot be used to register other devices to the domain.

The approach outlined for user management contains the most essential elements that provide a working solution. However, this rather straightforward approach also triggers a number of privacy issues. Solutions to this could be found in privacy-enhancing technologies [13], such as pseudonymity services, and use of solutions that for example rely on roles or assertions without revealing the identity involved.

Domain Management

According to the model in figure 2, domain management in PED-DRM concerns the relation between a UserID and a number of DeviceIDs, which is characterized by a DomainDevices (DD) data object. We propose an approach in which DD is a certificate containing a reference to the user of the domain, references to a number of devices, a version number and the signature of the domain manager (ADMCore in fig.3).

DD = { DomainID, Version, UserID, DeviceID1, ..., DeviceIDn, SignDM }   (1)

The first advantage of making DD a certificate is that it shows who issued it. The second advantage of putting all domain members in one certificate is that this allows a simple but secure signaling mechanism to show which devices are in the domain. This can be used effectively to inform deregistered devices and can be used efficiently to obtain and distribute revocation/authorization information. This synchronization mechanism is part of the secure authenticated channel setup, as explained later, which makes it possible for the system to function even when not all devices are online and reachable. The third advantage of the DD certificate is the ability to report domain information to the user on any domain device at any time.

Domain-based DRM systems often base their security on domain key(s) [4;6;7]. In these systems the content key is typically encrypted with the domain key. This has security advantages if devices are hacked because the accessible content to these devices is limited to the domain content. PED-DRM addresses this threat by limiting license distribution to permanent and temporary domain devices, realizing a similar level of security. PED-DRM could also be extended with a domain key.

System Components and Their Interaction
Figure 3 presents the main components – ADMCore, ADClient, UserIdentity and ADMTerminal – that group PED-DRM functionality and the interaction between them. We defer the descriptions of these interactions to section 5 of this paper. The typical connectivity means that enable interaction between the components are also indicated: combined on the same device (local), connected through a network (IP) or via wired/wireless connection with a strict limitation on the distance (e.g. Near Field Communication (NFC) [14]).

The ADMCore, ADClient and UserIdentity must run on a compliant device which has a DeviceID certificate because they manage domain or content-related data. These components must have a compliant implementation, which means that their implementation is subject to robustness requirements. It is beyond the scope of this paper to go into detail about the robustness and implementation rules for each type. The ADMTerminal component is only responsible for UI and control aspects and ADMTerminal is therefore not subject to DRM compliance requirements.

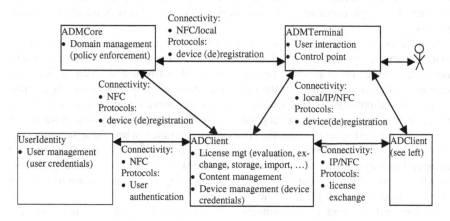

Fig. 3. PED-DRM components and their interaction

With respect to deployment of components over devices and taking into account the characteristics of the PED-DRM system, we foresee that UserIdentity and ADMCore components are combined on one device, e.g. on a smartcard or mobile phone, conveniently referred to as a user identity device in the scenario section. Alternatively, ADMCore runs as a service on the Internet, an approach similar to OMA DRMv2 and Apple's Fairplay. However, in the remainder of this work we assume that ADMCore runs on a device and not in the network. Some characteristics of local domain management are exploited, such as proximity verification, in the knowledge that some other aspects of central domain management are given up, notably central control and easy and direct audit facilities. Ideally, the ADClient and ADMTerminal would also be combined on one device, allowing straightforward AD management operations using the user interface of the device for interaction with the user. Typical devices are hardware- and software-based media centers, connected renders (TVs), etc. Provision has been made for alternative forms of component distribution, e.g. portable devices that combine the ADMCore, ADMTerminal and UserIdentity.

PED-DRM Domain Policy
The domain policy specifies under which conditions entities are entitled to be part of the domain and thereby largely defines the scale of content proliferation in a domain-based DRM system. It is evident that end users prefer a policy with a relaxed regime, while copyright holders, content providers, etc., prefer more tight regimes. As in most other domain-enabled DRM systems, PED-DRM has a domain policy that is fixed for the system. An exception to this is OMA DRMv2, where the domain policy is left to the individual Rights Issuers. Components that can enforce (part of) the domain policy include the ADMCore and ADClient.

We propose a simple and straightforward basic domain policy enforced by ADMCore. The policy is based on a maximum number of devices per domain. So far, the policy is very similar to Apple's Fairplay limit of 5 authorized PCs. Furthermore, ADMCore only registers ADClients that are in direct proximity. This limits the domain size and content proliferation to places where the user goes. Devices may be a member of multiple domains to support sharing of content between people who share devices.

In addition to the basic domain policy, further measures may be required by the content owners, e.g. to further reduce some of the risks associated with the attacks mentioned earlier or to allow a higher number of permanent domain devices. To accomplish this, a balanced set of the following measures may be added to the domain policy. They should be selected with care so that in normal circumstances a user does not encounter them, keeping conceptual complexity low for end users. Note that it may be hard to estimate the resulting content proliferation when these measures are combined. Some examples are: 'membership liveness' meaning that domain membership stays valid for some time, but must be confirmed regularly by the ADMCore; 'rate-limited domain management' meaning that (de)registrations may not exceed a maximum level per time unit.

Options with respect to the domain policy enforced by the ADClient are: the number of domains of which a device may be a member, which is unrestricted in pure PED-DRM; the validity time of the membership; the rate at which the device may register to different domains. Domain policy enforcement by the ADClient may also interact with other non-domain management actions, such as license management, e.g. limiting the exchange of licenses to distance-limited channels, or user authentication, e.g. a maximum number of authentications over time.

5 PED-DRM Operations

We will now describe the protocols and processes of the PED-DRM that realize the main PED-DRM functionality in a secure and user-convenient way.

Device Registration
The protocol for registering a device starts when, under the user's control, the ADMTerminal instructs the ADClient to register itself at the ADMCore. The ADClient requests registration to the domain at the ADMCore with its DeviceID reference. The ADMCore responds to the ADClient with a new DD certificate, including the ADClient's DeviceID, if the device is registered successfully. The ADMCore processes the registration request using the following steps: it verifies the authenticity of ADClient's request (i.e. verify digital signature or use of secure channel), it verifies that the device with DeviceID is not revoked and is not already a member, it executes the PED policy algorithm to determine whether the device may be added to the domain and creates a new DD certificate with the DeviceID reference included and an increased version number. The ADClient verifies the validity of the DD certificate received, stores it and is subsequently able to render domain content based on possession of the DD certificate.

The device registration protocol supports two deployment configurations explicitly. The first is the trivial case where the ADClient and ADMTerminal are located on the same device with an NFC interface to the ADMCore. The second case concerns a device which has limited UI capabilities and an NFC interface to the ADMCore and which is controlled by an ADMTerminal running on another device in the network. Provision has been made for ADClients without NFC interface to be supported in the future using extensions to the protocol or policy.

The requirement that the device registration protocol should protect the interests of the user in his role as domain and device owner is triggered when domain management can be controlled over a network. Device owner consent can be addressed in two complementary ways. The first solution involves user confirmation at the ADClient for registration, e.g. the ADClient device is put in registration mode by pressing a button. This ensures that a remote ADMTerminal cannot add devices to a domain without confirmation at the physical location of the ADClient. The implementation should ensure that a user confirmation only relates to the intended registration session. The second solution comprises authentication of the device or domain owner when devices are registered remotely to prevent abuse such as registration by third parties on the same network. Domain owner consent is implicitly assumed, because the ADMCore must be in physical proximity of ADClient.

The requirement that the protocol must be robust and must inform the user of the status is supported by including acknowledgements, rollback procedures, and DD distribution in the protocol that prevents the ADClient from considering itself a domain member when the ADMCore does not. The ADMCore has to implement the device registration protocol as a transaction due to the fact that communication could fail, e.g. a smartcard stops functioning when it is removed prematurely from the reader. It must perform a rollback procedure when it is re-activated after removal. To speed up the distribution of the new domain composition and thereby contribute to the robustness and consistency for the user as well, the registered ADClient should broadcast the latest DD certificate to other ADClients. The latter is a best-effort approach in addition to the forced synchronization as part of the secure authenticated channel required for the license exchange described later.

Device Deregistration
The device deregistration protocol starts when the ADMTerminal under the control of the user instructs ADClient to deregister itself at the ADMCore. The ADClient sends a deregister request with its DeviceID to the ADMCore, which responds with a new DD certificate that indicates the domain composition. If the ADClient is not available, e.g. if it has been stolen, broken or is offline, then the ADMTerminal may send the deregister request on its behalf. The ADMCore verifies that the DeviceID indicated in the deregistration request is listed in DD, it removes the device from the DD certificate and increases its version number. The ADClient performs the following steps for the deregistration response: it checks the validity of the DD certificate and if it is no longer listed it deletes the DD certificate. Before ADMCore replaces its stored DD certificate, it expects a deregistration confirmation from ADClient to ensure that ADClient received the request and deregistered itself. Unconfirmed deregistrations, including deregistrations of offline devices, may be administered differently and used in the domain policy for future device registrations, such that the protocol cannot be misused to allow for lots of new registrations while the old ones are effectively still present. The new DD certificate should be broadcasted so that other domain devices learn the new domain composition as quickly as possible.

The interests of the domain owner in the deregistration protocol are protected by the requirement that the ADMCore and ADMTerminal must be in close proximity or in direct contact with each other. The presence of the ADMCore implies authorization for the deregistration action. Alternatively, the requirement can also be met if the ADMCore is present near the ADClient that is removed, in combination with a user confirmation or explicit deregistration mode on ADClient to thwart unwanted deregistrations from the local network. The device should ensure that the confirmation or deregistration mode corresponds with the correct deregistration session. The implementation must ensure that the user may not be subject to a denial of service attack consisting of many confirmation requests.

The device deregistration protocol fulfills the requirement that devices must be removable from the domain. Stolen and offline devices are removed effectively over time when the new domain composition is distributed in the form of the DD certificate as part of the secure communication protocol discussed later.

ADClient Reset / Local Deregistration
A local deregistration is required when an ADClient needs to be de-registered from a domain but has no opportunity to communicate with its ADMCore, e.g. someone gives his device away without having his ADMCore in the neighborhood but still wants to prevent the new owner from accessing his content. In this case he needs to perform an autonomous ADClient reset action whereby the ADClient deletes the DD certificate. This approach should not be advocated because there is no automatic means to ensure that ADMCore will remove it from the DD certificate as well. A device should therefore indicate to the user that he needs to perform (offline) deregistration using ADMCore as well.

ADMCore Disaster
If the ADMCore device is broken or lost, a user is no longer able to change the composition of his domain. If the ADMCore is stolen, somebody else will be able to add his own devices and access the content belonging to the original owner, assuming that no additional access control mechanisms are in place. To mitigate this problem, a user requests a new ADMCore device. As part of this process the old ADMCore is revoked, with the result that the devices will no longer engage in AD management protocols with the old ADMCore and DD certificates issued by the old ADMCore will not validate correctly, since the old ADMCore is blacklisted. In effect, the old ADMCore and the old domain are revoked. The user needs to register all his devices to a new domain managed by his new ADMCore.

Secure Authenticated Channel and Revocation
The AD management and license exchange protocols require confidentiality, integrity, authenticity and protection against replay attacks; these are provided by a Secure Authenticated Channel (SAC). Although many general purpose SACs exist, e.g. TLS [15], PED-DRM has some specific features that are highlighted here.

An important aspect for PED-DRM is the exchange of DD certificates as part of the SAC setup phase. When a device receives a valid DD certificate with a higher version number than its stored DD certificate, it replaces the stored DD with the new DD, provided that it is still contained in the new DD certificate, otherwise it removes its DD completely. Inclusion of the DD certificate forces the DRM system to function correctly by ensuring that devices have an updated view of the domain composition. Based on this view, they must decide how they can exchange licenses with other devices and what kind of access they can allow to the content. The exchange of the DD certificate as part of SAC setup facilitates the update of a deregistered device that was deregistered from the domain while it was offline. The viral nature of the DD certificate distribution ensures that eventually the deregistered devices are no longer able to render any further domain content, except when a deregistered device no longer has any contact with its former domain members. The viral nature of DD certificate distribution is made more effective by requiring SAC usage for common operations, e.g. license exchanges, domain (de)registrations and user authentication.

A second important aspect of SAC setup is the support for device revocation. Devices only participate in domain management or license management interaction when the other party is still compliant. Lack of space limits us to only sketch the solution: we propose to use a scheme based on authorization lists, i.e. assertions proving that devices are still compliant, which also uses the viral nature of DD distribution to ensure that all active domain devices obtain fresh authorization/revocation status information related to a domain and user, even when some devices do not have global (Internet) connectivity.

User Authentication
The user authentication protocol consists of unilateral authentication based on a straightforward PKI protocol extended with proximity/presence assertions if necessary. Revocation must be supported on two levels: user identity and user identity device/token. The user identity should be revoked when the private key is compromised. User identity devices should be revoked when the device is broken,

lost or stolen. The user obtains a new UserId device and can use both his old and new content. An additional measure could be that for new content the old UserId device is specifically blacklisted in order to tackle cases where propagation of revocation status information may take some time. For both levels of revocation nothing needs to be done with either content or licenses. The organizational and infrastructural aspects of user authentication and identity management have been omitted here.

License Management
Distribution of licenses is straightforward in PED-DRM. The ADClients must exchange licenses with each other using the SAC. The properties of the SAC ensure that only compliant and non-revoked devices can obtain the licenses.

To reduce the effect in the case of hacked devices, licenses in a PED-DRM are only transferred to and stored on devices that are either domain devices or devices to which the domain user has been authenticated recently. It is preferable if the source device receives some proof of the user identity device via the target device such that it can be sure that the user identity device is or was in close proximity to the target device. A pure form of this approach implies that domain licenses are removed from devices upon deregistration or upon expiry of an authentication session, which might be impractical in some cases since it could unintentionally destroy the last domain license for a content item while not achieving any significant increase in security because the device already possesses the licenses. There is a minor drawback to this approach because licenses cannot be distributed upfront as they can when domain keys are used.

6 Related Work

To put PED-DRM into perspective we compare it with other network-oriented DRM systems. Due to limited space we have restricted ourselves to highlighting some advantages of PED-DRM over other systems. Of course, PED-DRM is not free of pre-requisites, e.g. its dependence on user identification and the hardware tokens and interfaces required for this, none of which are currently commonly used in consumer markets and products.

Person-based access to content at any time and in any place is one of the main advantages of PED-DRM over a number of systems that are device based and/or limit content exchanges to the local network, e.g. SmartRight [4], DTCP-IP [5] and Microsoft's WindowsMedia DRM (MS DRM) [16].

An advantage of PED-DRM (and also of SmartRight, for example) is that it separates domain management and domain policy from the license-issuing functionality, which enables a uniform user experience. This is the opposite from OMA DRMv2, where each rights issuer manages the domains for its content according to its own domain policy, which may be confusing for users buying content at different shops.

PED-DRM's approach is based on the equality of rendering/storage devices (ADClients), which is easy to understand for end users. Current systems, such as Apple's Fairplay or MS DRM, put devices in different classes such as PCs, portables, extenders [17], etc. The complicating factor is that policies vary for each device class, e.g. number of devices allowed per class, permitted functions such as rendering/storage per class, and whether or not a device may further distribute content and licenses to domain devices.

When the relation between persons change, it is quite easy for them to divide up their music in PED-DRM because each person binds his content to his user identity. Solutions such as SmartRight make it more difficult to do this because they are device based and, furthermore, only allow one domain per environment.

7 Conclusions and Discussion

In this paper we have discussed a design and operation of the PED-DRM concept in which (1) content is linked to persons, (2) a person has a number of permanent domain devices, and (3) where content can be rendered on the permanent domain devices or (4) on arbitrary (compliant) devices after authentication. The main characteristics of the design are the seamless access to content on devices that are a member of the domain. Authentication is taken care of by means of a personal smartcard or a device that can act as a user identity device like a mobile phone with a SIM. These two characteristics allow the person of the domain to enjoy his content at any time, anywhere and on any device. It is also possible to share content with relatives or friends by sharing content access devices that can be a member of multiple domains. However, due to the domain policy, which states that the number of devices in a domain is limited and that content can only be accessed on non-domain devices if the owner of the content is in close proximity, the proliferation of the content is still controlled strictly.

The user requirements have been taken into account in the design of the PED management protocols. For example, users have explicit control over what devices are added and/or removed from their PED. The use of close proximity technologies and devices (smartcards) makes the system as user friendly as is possible with the current technology.

The attacks relating to the domain concept realization and person-based content access are addressed by robust protocol and device design and by an appropriate domain policy. With respect to the attacks that deal with user behavior, it is harder to make an assertion. The proposed domain policy for a maximum number of permanent devices per person, and registration of domain devices with a proximity requirement will reduce most threats significantly. However, for some attacks, such as 'Content filling station', it is hard to put in place effective protection without adopting less user-friendly policies like time-outs for domain membership.

Technical challenges for PED-DRM lie amongst others in privacy issues for user identities and in the infrastructure, e.g. availability of authentication mechanisms.

Acknowledgements

We would like to thank our colleagues for their comments and help in the design of the PED-DRM system. Furthermore, we would like to thank the reviewers for their valuable comments on draft versions of this paper.

References

[1]   R.Vevers and C.Hibbert, *Copy Protection and Content Management in the DVB*, IBC Conference Publication, p458-466, Amsterdam, IBC2002, 15-9-2002.

[2]   S.A.F.A.van den Heuvel, W.Jonker, F.L.A.J.Kamperman, and P.J.Lenoir, *Secure Content Management in Authorised Domains*, IBC Conference Publication, p467-474, Amsterdam, IBC2002, 15-9-2002.

[3]   DVB-CPT, *DVB-CPT Authorized Domain: Definition / Requirements*, cpt-018r5, 2002.

[4]   Thomson Multimedia, *SmartRight*, www.smartright.org, 2003.

[5]   5C, *DTCP Volume 1 Supplement E Mapping DTCP to IP (Informational Version), DRAFT Revision 0.9*, 12-9-2003.

[6]   IBM, *IBM Response to DVB-CPT Call for Proposals for Content Protection & Copy Management: xCP Cluster Protocol*, DVB-CPT-716, 19-10-2001.

[7]   John Gildred, Ashot Andreasyan, Roy Osawa, and Tom Stahl, *Protected Entertainment Rights Management (PERM): Specification Draft v0.54*, Pioneer Research Center USA Inc, Thomson, 9-2-2003.

[8]   Eskicioglu, A. M. and Delp, E. J., *An overview of multimedia content protection in consumer electronic devices*, Signal Processing: Image Communication, Elsevier, 2001.

[9]   Willem Jonker and Jean-Paul Linnartz, *Digital Rights Management in Consumer Electronics Products*, IEEE Signal Processing Magazine, Special Issue on Digital Rights Management, 2004.

[10] R.Gooch, *Requirements for DRM systems*, Digital Rights Management: Technological, Economic, Legal and Political Aspects, LNCS2770, Springer-Verlag, 2003.

[11] S.Guth, *A Sample DRM System*, Springer, 2003. Digital Rights Management: Technological, Economic, Legal and Political Aspects.

[12] Open Mobile Alliance, *DRM Architecture: Draft Version 2.0*, OMA-DRM-ARCH-V2_0-20040820-C, 20-8-2004.

[13] Claudine Conrado, Milan Petkovic, and Willem Jonker, *Privacy-Preserving DRM*, SDM 2004, LNCS 3178, Springer, 2004.

[14] Philips Semiconductors, *Near Field Communication*, http://www.semiconductors.philips.com/markets/identification/products/nfc/, 2004.

[15] T.Dierks and C.Allen, *RFC2246: The TLS Protocol (version 1)*, 1999.

[16] Microsoft, *Windows Media Connect - Connectivity Solution for Networked Media Players*, WinHEC2004, 2004.

[17] Microsoft, *Next Generation Windows Media DRM for Consumer Electronics Devices*, WinHEC2004, 2004.

Rights and Trust in
Multimedia Information Management

Jaime Delgado, Víctor Torres, Silvia Llorente, and Eva Rodríguez

Universitat Pompeu Fabra, Passeig de Circumval·lació, 8, 08003 Barcelona, Spain
{jaime.delgado, victor.torres, silvia.llorente,
eva.rodriguez}@upf.edu

Abstract. Multimedia information management, which implies all steps from creation and production to distribution and consumption, is a complex and challenging research area. To have a secure and trusted system we need to take into account aspects such as digital rights management (DRM), certification, control and security. As current solutions rely on proprietary architectures and tools, we propose an open architecture, as general as possible and not restricted to a specific standard, which provides trust and rights management in multimedia information systems. We analyse how the elements of the architecture provide trust to the whole value chain by managing multimedia content and digital rights represented using current standards, such as MPEG-21 and OMA DRM, and we compare it with an alternative approach. Then, we illustrate the system operation through a content composition use case, and finally, we present the software tools that we have already developed and the future work.

1   Multimedia Information Management Architecture

In [1] we proposed an architecture for a system capable of processing multimedia information structured as defined in the MPEG-21 standard [2]. This architecture was refined in [3] and [4] to be as general as possible, considering the requirements from several standards, initiatives and projects like the Open Mobile Alliance (OMA) [5], MPEG-21 [2], Digital Media Project (DMP) [6], FP6 NAVSHP DRM [7] and AXMEDIS European project [8]. Figure 1 shows the basic modules that constitute the new architecture.

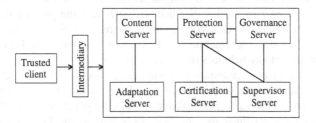

Fig. 1. DMAG-MIPAMS architecture

J. Dittmann, S. Katzenbeisser, and A. Uhl (Eds.): CMS 2005, LNCS 3677, pp. 55–64, 2005.

The architecture, called DMAG Multimedia Information Protection and Management System (DMAG-MIPAMS), whose name is after our group acronym DMAG [9], consists of several modules, where each of them provides a subset of the whole system functionality needed for managing and protecting multimedia content. The following list briefly describes the modules of the architecture:

- **Content server.** It provides the content that final users may request.
- **Protection server.** It is responsible for protecting the content or digital objects, which become protected objects, mainly using encryption techniques and managing the encryption keys.
- **Governance server.** The governance server includes several functionalities: license generation, license storage, authorisation and translation support.
- **Certification server.** It includes registration, authentication, certification and verification of users, tools and devices.
- **Adaptation server.** It performs the adaptation of content and its associated metadata, depending on transmission, storage and consumption constraints.
- **Supervisor server.** It receives reporting messages that include information about different aspects of media usage and stores them for future access.

It is worth noting that currently the architecture does not try to be complete, and some possible modules, such as a payment solution, are deliberately ignored.

2 Provision of Trust

After introducing our architecture, we are going to analyse the elements in the proposed system that provide trust from a business user or a final user point of view.

To provide trust to users it is important to take into account privacy aspects. In the presented system, information regarding content usage must be tracked. Nevertheless, this information will only be accessible to authorised parties. This authorisation will be done by means of party certification, which will provide the authentication in front of the service giving access to the information.

2.1 Use of Licenses

Digital Rights Management (DRM) enables the association of rights and conditions of usage to digital content, written in a digital license that can be embedded together with the content or stored in a separate way.

Digital licenses can be seen as digital documents that establish a contractual relationship between two parties: the license issuer and the granted party. That is, licenses can be used to establish contractual relationships in an e-commerce environment not only for final users (B2C scenario) but also between content creators/providers and distributors (B2B scenario).

Another interesting functionality of digital licenses together with the Governance server is the possibility to keep track of the identity and correctness of the actions performed by any of the value chain players, from the content creator to the final user. The authorisation algorithms use the licenses stored in the Governance server to determine if all the parties (content provider, distributor, final user) use the contents in the right way, according to the rights they are granted by their authorising party.

As we have seen, DRM can be a key element to provide trust in a content management system. In the proposed system, the Governance server provides this functionality through its license creation and authorisation facilities.

2.2 Protection

Protection mechanisms over digital content make it possible to deploy a business model to ensure the accomplishment of the license terms, so that protected objects are safe from unauthorised access, providing trust to the DRM system.

The delivery of protection keys must be performed in a secure and trusted way. On one hand, keys must be delivered through a secure channel. Moreover, they must be inaccessible in the client side. This can be achieved by providing the keys to certified and hence trusted tools in the client side.

2.3 Users and Tools Certification

Any tool in the user side must be trusted and must perform some checks in the server side to resynchronise the local information with the server side in every reconnection. Every time a user tries to do an action over a protected and governed object, the client side module must send the necessary information to the server side so that it can verify not only the user and the device, but also the tool integrity to ensure that the module has neither been modified nor corrupted. By ensuring the tool integrity, we can be sure that it is still trusted from the system point of view. If we want to provide trust from the user perspective, we must trust on the party that is performing the certification, which can be more easily achieved in a B2B scenario than in a B2C scenario. Whereas in a B2B scenario each party usually has a previous knowledge of the rest of the players and even also of the system, which could be formalised in a contract, in the B2C scenario, users usually need to trust on some tools without a real knowledge on how they work or manage their personal information.

The Certification server provides the mentioned functionality to verify the user, device and tool integrity. The tool in the user side must be trusted and must perform some checks in the server side to resynchronise the local information with the server side in every reconnection. Every time a user tries to do an action over a protected and governed object, the client side module must send the necessary information to the server side so that it can verify not only the user and the device, but also the tool integrity to ensure that the module has neither been modified nor corrupted. By ensuring the tool integrity, we can be sure that it is still trusted.

2.4 Supervision and Tracking

Transaction and operation supervision and tracking is another feature that can provide trust in such a system. The Supervisor server is responsible for collecting and interpreting the reporting messages generated by different modules and storing the appropriate information into a specific database. As we have already explained, the information in the reports can be notified to the corresponding party or used to block the access to a user, for accounting purposes or statistical analysis.

3 Existing Standards and the MIPAMS Architecture

As we have already mentioned, our intention is to define the architecture as general as possible so as not to be restricted to a specific standard, but to be able to align it to as many standards as possible. With this aim, we are going to present how it can operate with current standards, such as MPEG-21 [2] and OMA DRM REL [10]. However, in order to have a fully interoperable architecture capable of managing different multimedia formats at the same time, common interfaces for the identified modules should be defined.

MPEG-21 standard defines different mechanisms and elements needed to support multimedia information delivery and management, and the relationships and operations supported by them. In the seventeen parts of the MPEG-21 standard, these elements are elaborated by defining the syntax and semantics of their characteristics.

In the MPEG-21 context, the information is structured in Digital Items, which are the fundamental unit of distribution and transaction. A Digital Item [11] is constituted by the digital content, plus related metadata, such as adaptation information (DIA, Part 7) [12], information related to the protection tools (IPMP, Part 4) [13], rights expressions (REL, Part 5) [14], information to automatically report some actions exercised over the digital content (ER, Part 15) [15] and others.

In the following list, we describe how our architecture has the necessary functionality to cover the different parts of this standard:

- **DID.** Digital objects can have the structure of Digital Items, as defined in the DID part of the MPEG 21 standard.
- **IPMP, REL and RDD.** In MPEG-21 standard the protection and governance of digital content are specified in MPEG-21 IPMP Components, REL and RDD parts. MPEG-21 IPMP Components provides mechanisms to protect a digital item (DI) and to associate licenses to the target of their governance, while MPEG-21 REL specifies the syntax and semantics of the language for issuing rights for users to act on DIs while MPEG-21 RDD [16] comprises a set of terms to support the MPEG-21 REL.
- **ER.** Event Reporting is required within the MPEG-21 Multimedia Framework in order to provide standardised means for sharing information about Events amongst Peers and Users. Such Events are related to Digital Items and/or Peers that interact with them. In the MPEG-21 context, the reporting messages that include information about different aspects of media usage are called Event Reports. In our system, the functionality that involves the management of the event reports is provided by the Supervisor.

OMA Digital Rights Management (DRM) v2 [17] defines mechanisms to enable the consumption of digital content in a controlled manner. The content is consumed on authenticated devices per the usage rights expressed by the content owners. The OMA DRM work addresses the various technical aspects of this system by providing appropriate specifications for content formats, protocols, and the rights expression language based on ODRL [18]. ODRL and MPEG-21 REL are currently the two most important rights expression languages and, although they have a different syntax, their semantics is quite similar.

We have been working for some time in this interoperability issue. After an initial proposal of a simple syntactic mapping [19], [20] we have proposed a specific subset of MPEG-21 REL that is interoperable with the first version of OMA DRM REL [21], [22], [23] and also with version 2 of OMA DRM REL [21], [24], [25], [26]. This work could lead to the specification of an MPEG-21 REL profile, as it is being discussed in the MPEG group after our proposals.

Our architecture enables the use of whatever rights expression language the content creators, providers or distributors want to use, associated to digital objects. Internally, our system can work with a predefined rights expression language and provide some translation mechanisms for converting licenses expressed in other languages to the predefined one. This translation can only be performed under certain conditions, which can be grouped to define rights expressions languages profiles, as stated before.

We have also studied the workflow of OMA DRM in order to provide a generic workflow for DRM systems [27].

4   Relationship of the Architecture with Other Initiatives

Other architectures exist for the management of protected multimedia content. Nevertheless, they correspond to proprietary systems and it is difficult to compare our architecture with them, as they do not follow any standard. Among projects funded by public administrations, the MOSES project [28] developed the OpenSDRM [29] architecture, with which DMAG-MIPAMS has some common points.

The main differences between MIPAMS and OpenSDRM are the following:

- OpenSDRM provides a Wallet, the middleware that requests and manages licenses and performs the authorizations locally. A single wallet can be used on the same device by different applications, whereas in MIPAMS we will have a trusted plug-in for each application or specific trusted application.
- OpenSDRM currently uses ODRL to express the licenses, while MIPAMS proposes different mechanisms, such as translation, to support ODRL and MPEG-21 REL at the same time.
- OpenSDRM provides a Content Preparation Server, which receives raw data and encodes it on a specified format, while adding metadata and protection. On the other hand, MIPAMS leaves this functionality for specific user-side tools, while providing protection, licensing and adaptation functionalities on the server side.
- MIPAMS performs the authorisation of users based on a licenses chain (from content rights holder to party or user), ensuring rights fulfilment in the whole value chain, whereas OpenSDRM uses a single license referred to the party.
- MIPAMS, through supervision and tracking functionalities, enables post-usage billing. OpenSDRM provides an interface for a pre-usage payment solution while, for the moment, MIPAMS leaves this point open for the involved parties.

5   Use Case

In this section we present a scenario to illustrate how the proposed architecture and the processing of protected and governed multimedia content are related.

The scenario we propose is about content composition. Imagine that a publisher has purchased a license that grants him the right to include a still image in one of his electronic publications. The mentioned user has installed in his device a specific editing tool or a plug-in for an already existing tool capable of managing the protected and governed objects of the system. For the sake of simplicity, the license creation for the new composite content has been omitted.

The use case begins when the user (publisher) downloads the protected and governed image and tries to include it in his publication using the editing tool. Figure 2 shows the steps involved in the content composition use case, which are:

1. The user opens in the editing tool the digital object that contains the image.
2. The user tries to include it in his publication ("embed" image).
3. The tool/plug-in connects to the Protection server in order to check if the user is authorised. It sends the following information: requested operation ("embed"), object identifier, user identifier, device identifier and tool/plug-in identifier.

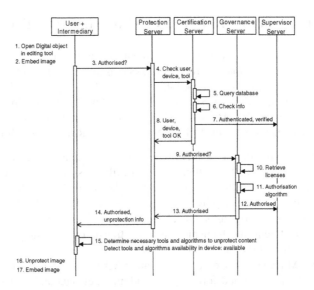

Fig. 2. Content composition use case

4. The Protection server sends the Certification server the received information.
5, 6. The Certification server queries its database and checks that the user and device are registered and the tool/plug-in integrity.
7. An event report is sent to the Supervisor server notifying the successful authentication of the user and verification of device and tool.
8. The Certification server notifies the Protection server that everything is OK.
9. The Protection server contacts the Governance server asking if the user is authorised. This authorisation consists on checking if the user is granted to exercise the right "embed" over the image according to a certain chain of licenses (going from the image creator (or rights holder) to the publisher).

10, 11. The Governance server searches in the database the licenses related to the user and runs an authorisation algorithm over the chain of licenses. The Governance server determines that the user is granted to perform the requested operation and that the distribution chain is correct (all the parties in the license chain were granted by their corresponding license).

12. An event report is sent to the Supervisor notifying the successful authorisation.

13. The Governance server notifies the right authorisation to the Protection server.

14. The Protection server notifies the object viewer that the user is authorised and sends the needed information for unprotecting the content.

15. The tool/plug-in determines the tools or algorithms that must be used to unprotect the object and detects that they are already available in the user device.

16. The tool/plug-in unprotects the image following the unprotection process steps and using the necessary tools and algorithms.

17. The editing tool finally embeds the still image into the electronic publication.In this section we present a scenario to illustrate how the proposed architecture and the processing of protected and governed multimedia content are related.

6 Development of Tools and Demonstrators

At the DMAG [9], we have been working in the MIPAMS trusted architecture and related standards, and have already developed several tools [30], contributed to the standardisation of MPEG-21 and included in the MPEG-21 Reference Software [31]. Some other tools have also been created to deal with ODRL licenses [32]. The tools we present in subsequent subsections are publicly available at [30] and [32].

The implemented tools offer independent and isolated functionality and will be extended and integrated with other modules in the context of the AXMEDIS European project [8] to develop several demonstrators, for several delivery channels. With these demonstrators we will verify the operation of the proposed modular architecture. Moreover, an AXMEDIS framework will be available for presenting the tools implemented in this project.

6.1 Rights Expression Languages and Rights Data Dictionary Tools

REL and RDD developed tools concern the creation and validation of digital licenses.

License Validators. These tools take a license as input and provide a verdict as the output. If the input license is not valid, a report explains the reasons why, according to the validation that has been performed. These tools, which have been implemented as Java APIs that can be run independently or integrated with other modules, include:

- **MPEG-21 REL Schema Checker**. It checks if an MPEG-21 REL license is valid against the corresponding XML Schemas.
- **MPEG-21 ODRL Schema Checker**. It checks if an ODRL license is valid against the corresponding XML Schemas.
- **MPEG-21 REL Validation Rules Checker**. It checks if a schema-valid MPEG-21 REL license is a valid REL License according to the MPEG-21 REL standard specification [14]. A license will be REL syntactically conformant if it complies with all the rules specified in the standard.

License Creators. These tools have been implemented as web applications, formed by a web page containing an HTML form, a servlet for processing the information introduced in this form, a Schema Checker implementation and several auxiliary files, mainly used for formatting the information. The introduction of information is done by means of the HTML form. If all information has been filled, an XML file containing the license is created. Finally, the license syntax is checked with the Schema Checker and returned to the user, who can see the generated license and also store it locally. They include:

- **MPEG-21 REL License Creator**. It allows the introduction of the following information to create a license: Principal, Resource, Right, Conditions and Issuer.
- **ODRL License Creator**. It allows the introduction of the following information to create a license: Asset, Permission, Constraints and Party.

MPEG-21 Authorisation Tools. These tools determine if a user is authorised to perform an action over a resource according to the license terms. In this tools we have used the RDD term genealogy defined in MPEG-21 to determine if a term present in a license (e.g. Adapt) grants a user the permission to perform another action (e.g. Play). We have implemented a specific tool, as a Java API, that consults an RDD ontology placed in an external server, returning all the ancestors of an input RDD term.

- **License Interpreter**. It performs the authorisation according to a unique license and a simple, non-standardised query mechanism.
- **Interpretation Conformance**. It performs a standardised authorisation and query mechanism, which consists on checking not only if the user is authorised according to the source license, but also if the party that issued this license was authorised to do so, and so on, so that the whole licensing chain is checked.

6.2 MPEG-21 IPMP Tools

IPMP developed tools concern the validation and extraction of IPMP information from Digital Items, as explained next:

- **MPEG-21 IPMP Expressions Validator**. This tool parses and validates a set of IPMP Information documents against the XML Schemas specified in them.
- **MPEG-21 IPMP Information Extractor**. This tool obtains the IPMP Information associated to a protected DIDL document or parts thereof. First, the protected element(s) within the DIDL document are identified and presented. Then, the software module obtains and presents the relevant information related to the IPMP tools and the license(s) associated to each one of the IPMP DIDL elements previously identified.
- **MPEG-21 License Extractor**. This tool obtains the license(s) associated to a protected and governed DIDL document or parts thereof. It identifies the protected element within the DIDL document given as input, and obtains the license(s) that govern(s) it, if any.

7 Conclusions

We have presented a general architecture of a system for the distribution and management of protected and governed multimedia content, based on different requirements, not restricted to a specific standard and flexible enough to locate different functionalities in separate machines.

We have analysed the elements in the proposed architecture to describe how they provide trust in different aspects to the global system and the whole value chain.

On the other hand, we have shown how the presented architecture is flexible enough to support current standards such as MPEG-21 and OMA DRM. In the MPEG-21 context, we have described the relationship between MPEG-21 parts and the elements or functionalities of the architecture while, regarding OMA DRM, we have shown how the use of different rights expressions languages can be managed by translation mechanisms and profile definition. Moreover, we have compared MIPAMS with the OpenSDRM architecture.

Then, a use case has been presented showing the successive steps that the system will follow in a content composition scenario, considering authentication, verification and authorisation matters.

Finally, we have presented several tools that have been contributed to the MPEG-21 Reference Sofware part and we have introduced the AXMEDIS project, which will provide a publicly available framework.

Acknowledgements. This work has been partly supported by the Spanish administration (AgentWeb project, TIC 2002-01336) and is being developed within VISNET (IST-2003-506946, http://www.visnet-noe.org), a European Network of Excellence and AXMEDIS, a European Integrated Project, both funded under the European Commission IST FP6 program, and "Projecte Integrat" project, funded by the Catalan Administration (Fundació i2Cat).

References

1. Torres, V., Rodríguez, E., Llorente, S., Delgado, J.: Architecture and Protocols for the protection and management of multimedia information. MIPS 2004, LNCS, Vol. 3311. Springer-Verlag, Berlin Heidelberg New York (2004) 252-263
2. MPEG 21, http://www.chiariglione.org/mpeg/standards/mpeg-21/mpeg-21.htm
3. Torres, V., Rodríguez, E., Llorente, S., Delgado, J.: Trust and Rights in Multimedia Content Management Systems. The IASTED International Conference on Web Technologies, Applications, and Services (WTAS 2005). To be published
4. Torres, V., Rodríguez, E., Llorente, S., Delgado, J.: Use of standards for implementing a Multimedia Information Protection and Management System. AXMEDIS 2005. To be published
5. Open Mobile Alliance (OMA), http://www.openmobilealliance.org
6. Digital Media Project (DMP), http://www.dmpf.org/
7. Digital Rights Management (DRM) Coordination Group of the European FP6 Projects in the area of Networked AudioVisual Systems and Home Platforms (NAVSHP), http://www.rose.es/navshp

8. Automatic Production of Cross Media Content for Multi channel Distribution (AXMEDIS), IST 2004 511299, http://www.axmedis.org
9. Distributed Multimedia Applications Group (DMAG), http://dmag.upf.edu
10. OMA, DRM Rights Expression Language (OMA-Download-DRMREL-V2_0-20041210-C). December 2004. http://www.openmobilealliance.org
11. ISO/IEC, ISO/IEC 2nd Edition FCD 21000-2 – Digital Item Declaration
12. ISO/IEC, ISO/IEC FDIS 21000-7 – Digital Item Adaptation
13. ISO/IEC, ISO/IEC CD 21000-4 – Intellectual Property Management and Protection
14. ISO/IEC, ISO/IEC IS 21000-5 – Rights Expression Language
15. ISO/IEC, ISO/IEC WD 21000-15 – Event Reporting
16. ISO/IEC, ISO/IEC IS 21000-6 – Rights Data Dictionary
17. OMA, DRM Specification (OMA-DRM-DRM-V2_0-20040716-C), July 2004, http://www.openmobilealliance.org
18. Open Digital Rights Language (ODRL), http://odrl.net
19. Polo, J., Prados, J., Delgado, J.: Interworking of Rights Expression Languages for Secure Music Distribution. In: Delgado, J., Nesi, P., Ng, K. (eds.): WEDELMUSIC 2004 Proceedings, IEEE Computer Society (2004) 78-84
20. Polo, J., Prados, J., Delgado, J.: Interoperability between ODRL and MPEG 21 REL. ODRL International Workshop (2004)
21. OMA, DRM Rights Expression Language (OMA-DRM-REL-V1_0-20040615-A). June 2004. http://www.openmobilealliance.org
22. Delgado, J., Prados, J., Rodríguez, E.: Interoperability between MPEG-21 REL and OMA DRM: A Profile? ISO/IEC JTC 1/SC 29/WG 11/M11580. January 2005. http://dmag.upf.edu/DMAGMPEG21Tools/m11580.pdf
23. Delgado, J., Prados, J., Rodríguez, E.: Profiles for interoperability between MPEG-21 REL and OMA DRM. IEEE CEC 2005, IEEE Computer Society, to be published
24. Delgado, J., Prados, J., Rodríguez, E.: A subset of MPEG-21 REL for interoperability with OMA DRM v2.0. ISO/IEC JTC 1/SC 29/WG 11/M11893. April 2005. http://dmag.upf.edu/DMAGMPEG21Tools/m11893.pdf
25. Prados, J., Rodríguez, E., Delgado, J.: Interoperability between different Rights Expression Languages and Protection Mechanisms. AXMEDIS 2005. To be published
26. Prados, J., Rodríguez, E., Delgado, J.: A new Approach for Interoperability between ODRL and MPEG-21 REL. Second International ODRL Workshop. To be published
27. Llorente, S., Rodríguez, E., Delgado, J.: Workflow description of digital rights management systems. OTM 2004 Workshops. LNCS, Vol. 3292. Springer-Verlag, Berlin Heidelberg New York (2004) 581-592
28. MPEG Open Security for Embedded Systems (MOSES) project, http://www.ist-moses.org
29. Serrao, C., Dias, M., Delgado, J.: Using ODRL to express rights for different content usage scenarios. The Second International ODRL Workshop 2005. To be published
30. DMAG MPEG 21 Tools, http://dmag.upf.edu/DMAGMPEG21Tools
31. ISO/IEC, ISO/IEC FCD 21000-8 – Reference Software
32. DMAG ODRL Tools, http://dmag.upf.edu/ODRLTools

Signature Amortization Using Multiple Connected Chains

Qusai Abuein[1] and Susumu Shibusawa[2]

[1] Graduate School of Science and Engineering
[2] Department of Computer and Information Sciences
Ibaraki University, Hitachi, Ibaraki 316-8511, Japan
{abueinq, sibusawa}@cis.ibaraki.ac.jp

Abstract. Amortization schemes for authenticating streamed data have been introduced as a solution to reduce the high overhead that sign-each schemes suffer from. The hash chains structure of amortization schemes and the number of hash values appended to other packets affect the efficiency of the authentication scheme specially against packet loss. Which packets should have hashes appended to the signature packet and how many hashes to append to it have no solutions yet. This paper introduces a new hash chain construction to achieve longer resistance against packet loss and reduces the overhead. The proposed scheme consists of multiple connected chains, each chain links several packets together. Our scheme specifies clearly how to choose the packets that should have hashes appended to a signature packet, in addition to deriving their loss probability. We study the effect of the number of hashes that are appended to a signature packet on the overhead. We introduce a measure so as to know the number of packets receivers need to buffer until they can authenticate the received packets. The number of chains of our model plays a main role in the efficiency of our scheme in terms of loss resistance and overhead.

Keywords: Multicast stream authentication, hash chain, signature amortization, web security.

1   Introduction

Digitally sign each packet using any signing algorithm such as RSA requires high computation and communication overhead and causes delay on both the sender and receivers [1], even if faster signing algorithms are used such as in [2]. Alternatively, Message Authentication Codes (MAC) are introduced such as TESLA in [3], which requires time synchronization between the sender and receivers. Another alternative is amortization schemes, such as Authentication Tree (AT) in [4], Efficient Multi-chained Stream Signature (EMSS) in [3] and Augmented Chain (AC) in [5]. In amortization schemes the stream is divided into blocks, a single packet in each block is digitally signed and the rest of the packets in the block are linked to the signed one using multiple hashes links. The

J. Dittmann, S. Katzenbeisser, and A. Uhl (Eds.): CMS 2005, LNCS 3677, pp. 65–76, 2005.

linked packets form what is known as hash chains. The security of amortization schemes is proven by Gennaro and Rohatgi in [6].

AT requires high amount of overhead, since each packet contains a signature with the authentication information so as to be individually verifiable. EMSS strengthens the resistance against packet loss of the scheme introduced by the authors of [6] by storing the hash value of each packet in multiple locations. EMSS determines the best hash chain construction by experiments and randomly chooses packets that have hashes appended to other packets.

AC uses similar strategy to EMSS so as to achieve longer resistance against packet loss, by choosing packets that have hashes appended to other packets in a deterministic way. AC does not include the means of choosing the number of packets to be inserted between each pair of the original chain.

Both EMSS and AC increases the resistance against packet loss by increasing the number of hashes in each packet, that will in turn increases the overhead [7], [8]. More details about AC analysis is found in [9], where it is applied to two case studies and compared to EMSS.

The authors of [7] and [8] give analysis of hash chains based on graph theory. They show that to increase the authentication probability, which is defined as the conditional probability that a packet is verified, the number of paths from any packet to the signature one should be increased. The main aim of Piggybacking scheme in [8] is to achieve high resistance against multiple bursts.

Signature amortization using Information Dispersal Algorithm (SAIDA) in [10], reduces the overhead of amortization schemes by using erasure codes. According to [11], the computation resources of receivers for the Forward Error Correction (FEC) in SAIDA is high comparing to that of hashes in other amortization schemes. The low computation and communication cost of hashes [12], [13] and [14] makes amortization schemes widely adopted and researchers still have high concern about it [15].

In this paper we will introduce a general construction of our Multiple Connected Chains (MC) model [16] and [17] and analyse the generalization of our model. We will also introduce a measure to determine the maximum number of hashes to be appended to the signature packet. We also show how the loss probability of the packets that have hashes appended to a signature packet is affected by their position, which in turn has a great effect on the authentication scheme. We also study the relation between the number of hashes appended to the signature packet and the overhead. Our solution is efficient in achieving longer resistance against burst packet loss and reducing overhead at the same time.

In Section 2, we introduce MC model. In Section 3, we discuss the efficiency of MC model. In Section 4, we show the required buffer and delay for both the sender and receiver. Section 5 reports a performance evaluation of our model as compared to other models followed by conclusion and future work in Section 6.

2   Multiple Connected Chains Model

Table 1 shows the notation used in MC model. A packet P_i is defined as a message M_i a sender sends to receivers along with additional authentication information. When a stream S consists of N contiguous packets we represent S as:

$$S = \{P_1, P_2, \cdots, P_N\}.$$

We introduce a Multiple Connected Chains (MC) model for multicast stream authentication using signature amortization in which a stream is divided into a number of blocks and each block consists of some packets. A single packet in each block is digitally signed and the rest of the packets are concatenated to the signed packet through hash chains in a way that allows the receiver to authenticate the received packets.

Table 1. Notation

symbol	representation
ν	number of packets containing the hash of P_i
μ	number of hashes appended to the signature
β	number of hashes appended to the packets of the stream
h	hash size (SHA-1 is 20 bytes, MD5 is 16 bytes)
H	total size of all hashes in the stream
γ	number of signatures in the stream
N	number of packets in the stream
k	number of slices in a block
c	number of chains in the stream
δ	communication overhead per packet in bytes
s	signature size (RSA is 128 bytes)
ℓ	loss resistance

A block of MC model consists of c chains, where each chain consists of some packets and the hash value $H(P_i)$ of each packet P_i is appended to packet P_{i+1} in addition to ν other packets P_{i+jc} where $j = 1, 2, \cdots, \nu$. So as for MC model to be constructed and robust against packet loss, we need the value of ν as $\nu \geq 1$. For example, when $\nu = 3$, $H(P_i)$ is appended to P_{i+1}, P_{i+c}, P_{i+2c} and P_{i+3c}. Let $A(c, \nu)$ denote a set of the packets that contain $H(P_i)$, then

$$A(c, \nu) = \{P_{i+1}, P_{i+c}, P_{i+2c}, \cdots, P_{i+\nu c}\}.$$

A signature packet P_{sig} in MC model contains μ hashes of non-contiguous packets chosen from the last c packets preceding P_{sig}. The reason to choose these packets as non-contiguous is that Internet packet loss is burst in nature, and if a packet P_i is lost, packet P_{i+1} is likely to be lost [2], [18], [19]. We mean by non-contiguous packets that the next packet to P_i is P_{i+j} where $j > i + 1$. On the other hand contiguous packets mean that the next packet to P_i is P_{i+1}.

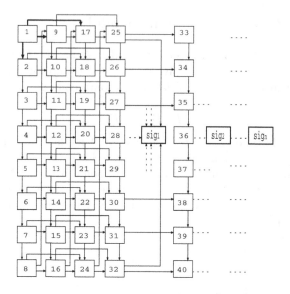

Fig. 1. A construction of MC model when $c = 8$, $k = 4$ and $\nu = 2$

Each signature packet is sent after every kc packets, which determines the block size, where k denotes the number of slices in MC model. The group of the first c packets $\{P_1, P_2, \cdots, P_c\}$ is the first slice in MC model, the group of the second c packets $\{P_{c+1}, P_{c+2}, \cdots, P_{2c}\}$ is the second slice, and so on. Fig. 1 depicts a construction of MC model when $c = 8$, $k = 4$, and $\nu = 2$.

Let E denote a set of the last c packets preceding a signature one, then $E = \{P_{(k-1)c+1}, P_{(k-1)c+2}, \cdots, P_{kc}\}$. Let the first packet of those that have their μ hashes appended to P_{sig} chosen from E denote $P_{(k-1)c+1} = P_{j_1}$, the last one denotes $P_{kc} = P_{j_\mu}$, where μ is the number of hashes appended to a signature packet. So the set of the packets that have their μ hashes appended to P_{sig} is:

$$E(\mu) = \{P_{j_1}, P_{j_2}, \cdots, P_{j_\mu}\},$$

where $j_1 < j_2 \cdots < j_\mu$. In Fig. 1, the sender computes the hash value of the first packet $H(P_1)$, then sends P_1. A hash $H(P_{i-1})$ is appended to every packet P_i, where $2 \leq i \leq c$ before computing each packet's hash value $H(P_i)$ and then sends P_i, where $2 \leq i \leq c$. While $H(P_{i-1})$ and $H(P_{i-c})$ are appended to every packet P_i, where $c+1 \leq i \leq 2c$ before computing each packet's hash value $H(P_i)$ and then sends P_i, where $c+1 \leq i \leq 2c$. Every packet P_i, where $2c+1 \leq i \leq N$ contains $H(P_{i-1})$, $H(P_{i-c})$ and $H(P_{i-2c})$ before computing each packet's hash value $H(P_i)$ and then sends P_i, where $2c+1 \leq i \leq N$.

The sender then appends μ hashes to the signature packet P_{sig_1}, signs it and sends it. The sender experiences a single packet delay since the computations of each packet's hash value and the signature packet depend on previously computed hashes.

So in Fig. 1, the sender performs the following computation processes:

- $H(P_1)$ is computed,
- $(H(P_{i-1})||M_i) \rightarrow H(P_i)$, where $2 \leq i \leq c$,
- $(H(P_{i-1})||H(P_{i-c})||M_i) \rightarrow H(P_i)$, where $c+1 \leq i \leq 2c$,
- $(H(P_{i-1})||H(P_{i-c})||H(P_{i-2c})||M_i) \rightarrow H(P_i)$, where $2c+1 \leq i \leq N$,
- $SA(K, H(P_{j_1})||H(P_{j_2})|| \cdots ||H(P_{j_\mu})) \rightarrow P_{sig_1}$,

where $||$ denotes concatenation, $\rightarrow$ denotes computation, SA represents the signing algorithm, and K represents the private key. The security of these amortization schemes is proven by Gennaro and Rohatgi in [6].

The following steps describes the authentication procedure according to MC model. Since the same operations are performed on every block we only describe it for the first block:

1. Choose value of ν
2. Determine the number of chains c
3. Choose values of μ and k
4. Append necessary hash values to P_i, compute $H(P_i)$ and send P_i, $1 \leq i \leq N$
5. Choose $E(\mu)$
6. Append μ hashes to P_{sig}, sign and send P_{sig}.

3   The Efficiency of MC Model

In this section we introduce factors, such as communication overhead and number of chains, that affect the performance of the authentication scheme, equations to measure these factors and the loss probability of $E(\mu)$.

3.1   Communication Overhead

The communication overhead means the total size of the information added to a packet to authenticate it, such as hashes and digital signature. The number of packets ν, number of hashes μ and number of chains c influence the performance of the authentication scheme.

Since in MC model the packets of $E(\mu)$ are chosen as non-contiguous to each other from the last c packets preceding the signature one, the value of μ is computed as

$$\mu \leq \left\lceil \frac{c}{2} \right\rceil, \tag{1}$$

Since each packet P_i in MC model contains hashes of previous packets, P_1 contains no additional hashes. While each of the rest packets of the first slice $\{P_2, P_3, \cdots, P_c\}$ contains only a single hash, that is, in total there are $c-1$ hashes. Each packet of the second slice $\{P_{c+1}, P_{c+2}, \cdots, P_{2c}\}$ contains 2 hashes of the previous packets, so that in total there are $2c$ hashes. Each packet of the ith slice contains i hashes of previous packets where $i \leq \nu$ except for P_1. In total we have $c - 1 + 2c + 3c + \cdots + \nu c$ hashes in the first ν slices; that is, $(\frac{\nu^2 + \nu}{2})c - 1$. Each packet of the remaining packets $\{P_{\nu c+1}, P_{\nu c+2}, \cdots, P_N\}$ contains $\nu + 1$ hashes of previous packets. In total we have $(\nu + 1)(N - \nu c)$ hashes. Accordingly, the total number of hashes β appended to the packets of stream S is computed as

$$\beta = (\frac{\nu^2 + \nu}{2})c + (\nu + 1)(N - \nu c) - 1. \tag{2}$$

The total size of all hashes H in the stream depends on the hash value the algorithm uses. In general H is computed as

$$H = h\beta. \tag{3}$$

Since there are kc packets in each block, the number of signatures γ in the stream is expressed as

$$\gamma = \left\lceil \frac{N}{kc} \right\rceil. \tag{4}$$

Dividing the overhead by the total number of packets in the stream gives the overhead per packet.

Lemma 1. *The communication overhead δ in bytes per packet is*

$$\delta = \frac{H + \gamma(s + \mu h)}{N}. \tag{5}$$

Proof. Packets of a stream contain hashes and signatures in addition to data. The total of all hashes in the stream is given as H, while every signature packet contains a signature and μ hashes of other packets. Therefore, we have $s + \mu h$ overhead per signature packet. Since we have γ signatures in the stream, the overhead of all signature packets is $\gamma(s + \mu h)$. In total we have, $H + \gamma(s + \mu h)$, dividing this total by N gives the overhead per packet δ.   □

The stream size N is assumed to be known in advance for the above equations. In case N is unknown or infinite, the following equation is obtained:

$$\lim_{N \to \infty} \delta = \lim_{N \to \infty} \frac{H + \gamma(s + \mu h)}{N} = (\nu + 1)h + \frac{s + \mu h}{kc}. \tag{6}$$

Loss resistance ℓ is the maximum number of lost packets the scheme can sustain and still able to authenticate received packets. To resist burst loss of packets, the distance from P_i to the last packet that contains $H(P_i)$ must be longer than the expected burst packet loss length. Accordingly, in our scheme resistance ℓ against burst loss is achieved by

$$\ell = \nu c - 1 . \tag{7}$$

Longer resistance against burst packet loss is achieved by increasing the number of chains c in our model. The number of chains plays an important role in the efficiency of our model, so as to determine the appropriate number c, we introduce a measure regarding burst packet loss length b and the loss resistance

ℓ. The model must resist the expected burst loss b, otherwise, the authentication of the received packets preceding the start of the loss can not take place. Accordingly, $\nu c - 1 \geq b$, that is,

$$c \geq \left\lceil \frac{b+1}{\nu} \right\rceil. \tag{8}$$

Fig. 2 shows how δ for different streams decreases in terms of k when $c = 16$, $\mu = 3$, $\nu = 2$, $s = 128$ bytes, and $h = 16$ bytes. Increasing number of slices k decreases δ. For streams of sizes $N = 320$, 1000, 2000 and 5000, the overhead per packet δ decreases 6.7%, 5.9%, 6.0% and 6.0%, respectively, when increasing k from 3 to 20. Our model construction depends mainly on the number of the

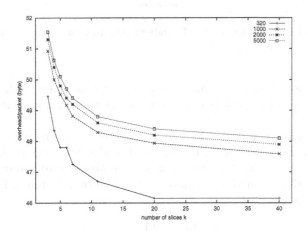

Fig. 2. Overhead per packet in terms of number of slices k for different streams when $c = 16$, $\nu = 2$ and $\mu = 3$

chains c. The increase of c affects δ positively. This effect is shown in Fig. 3 for different chains c and streams, where the number of slices $k = 3$. The overhead per packet δ decreases 27.5%, 16.6%, 14.1% and 12.5% for the streams 320, 1000, 2000 and 5000, respectively, when increasing c from 8 to 64. The effect of μ on the overhead is depicted in Fig.4, when $c = 16$, $k = 3$ and $h = 16$ bytes. The increase of δ is linear with respect to μ. The overhead increment ratio of small streams N is more than that of large ones regarding μ, that is, when N increases the increment ratio of δ becomes less regarding μ. When increasing μ from 2 to 16, the ratio is equal to 3.43%, 2.84%, 2.55% and 2.45% for the streams of sizes 320, 1000, 2000 and 5000 respectively.

3.2   Characterizing Loss Probability with Gilbert Model

In this section we derive the loss probability of $E(\mu)$ in case the packets are contiguous to each other and non-contiguous using Gilbert model. Since in MC

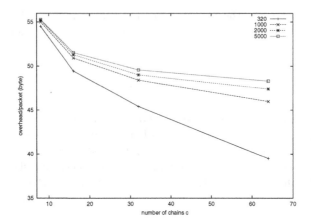

Fig. 3. Overhead per packet in terms of number of chains c for different streams where $k = 3$, $\nu = 2$ and $\mu = 3$

model the packets of $E(\mu)$ are chosen as non-contiguous to each other, the distance between each two packets of $E(\mu)$ as well as the loss probability of these packets depend on c.

Fig. 5 shows the Gilbert model that is used for characterizing burst packet loss. In the figure, r represents the probability that the next packet is lost, provided the previous one has arrived. q is the probability to transit from loss state to received state, and it is opposite to r. The transition matrix P of the Gilbert model is expressed as

$$P = \begin{bmatrix} p_{00} & p_{01} \\ p_{10} & p_{11} \end{bmatrix} = \begin{bmatrix} 1-r & r \\ q & 1-q \end{bmatrix}, \qquad (9)$$

where p_{ij} is the transition probability from state i to state j.

Lemma 2. *Let G be the set of the first signature packet P_{sig_1} and the last c packets preceding it, then $G = \{P_{(k-1)c+1}, \ldots, P_{kc}, P_{sig_1}\}$. Let P_{j_1} and P_{j_μ} be chosen as $P_{(k-1)c+1}$ and P_{kc}, respectively. Let ρ_1 be the loss probability of non-contiguous packets chosen from G whose hashes are appended to the signature one, and ρ_2 be the loss probability of contiguous ones. According to the Gilbert model ρ_1 and ρ_2 are given by*

$$\rho_1 = (1-r)^{c-2\mu+1} \cdot r^\mu \cdot q^\mu, \quad c > 2\mu - 1, \qquad (10)$$

and

$$\rho_2 = (1-r)^{c-\mu} \cdot r \cdot (1-q)^{\mu-1} \cdot q, \quad c > \mu. \qquad (11)$$

Proof. In case of non-contiguity in our model, the first packet is $P_{(k-1)c+1}$, the last one is P_{kc}, and the others are any non-contiguous packets in between the first and the last. When the packets that have hashes appended to P_{sig_1} are lost and the rest packets of G are received, we have μ transitions from non-loss state

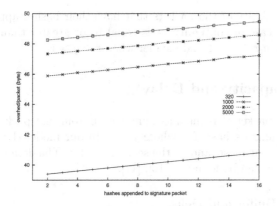

Fig. 4. Overhead per packet for different streams in terms of μ when $c = 16$ and $k = 3$

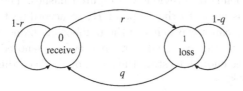

Fig. 5. The Gilbert model for burst packet loss

to loss state and μ inverse transitions. The other transitions are from non-loss state to non-loss state, and the total number is $c - 2\mu + 1$. Accordingly,

$$\rho_1 = (1-r)^{c-2\mu+1} \cdot r^\mu \cdot q^\mu$$

In case of contiguity, packets that have their μ hashes appended to P_{sig_1} are $P_{kc-\mu}$, $\ldots$, P_{kc-1} and P_{kc}. When all of these packets are lost and the other packets of G are received, the loss probability ρ_2 can be derived similarly. □

Lemma 3. *In the Gilbert model, let r be the probability that the next packet is lost, provided that the previous one has arrived, and q be the opposite probability. Then, the relation between loss probabilities ρ_1 and ρ_2 given in Lemma 2 is*

$$\rho_1 \leq \rho_2 \quad when \quad r + q \leq 1,$$

and

$$\rho_1 > \rho_2 \quad when \quad r + q > 1.$$

Proof. Dividing ρ_2 by ρ_1, we get

$$\frac{\rho_2}{\rho_1} = (\frac{1-r}{r} \times \frac{1-q}{q})^{\mu-1}.$$

When $\frac{1-r}{r} \times \frac{1-q}{q} > 1$, we get $r + q < 1$ and $\rho_1 < \rho_2$. On the other hand, when $\frac{1-r}{r} \times \frac{1-q}{q} < 1$, we get $r + q > 1$ and $\rho_1 > \rho_2$. □

The loss probability of the packets that have their hashes appended to the signature one in case of contiguity ρ_2 is equal to or greater than that of non-contiguity ρ_1 when $r + q \leq 1$ and smaller when $r + q > 1$.

4   Buffer Capacity and Delay

The scope of any packet P_i is the maximum length from that packet to the other packet that contains its hash P_j, where $j > i$. In our model the hash of P_i is appended to $P_{i+\nu c}$ at most, and so the scope is $\nu c + 1$. The details of the buffer capacity and delay can be found in [16], [17].

4.1   Sender's Buffer and Delay

The sender experiences a delay of a single packet, since the last packet of a block is signed and it depends on previously computed hashes. The requested buffer size denoted as α, is equal to the scope of P_i, so according to available buffer resources the sender can always choose the number of chains c so as to achieve sufficient resistance to the expected burst packet loss denoted as b. The buffer capacity is then large enough to store the scope of P_i. Accordingly the following relation holds $b \leq \ell \leq \alpha$.

4.2   Receiver's Buffer and Delay

The necessary buffer size for the receiver denoted as α_1 to authenticate the received packets depends on the following factors: the start of the burst loss, its length and the loss of the signature packet. When θ denote the number of consecutive signatures loss and n denotes the number of bursts, the following measures the necessary buffer and delay in number of packets the receiver waits:

$$\alpha_1 = (\theta + 1)kc - \sum_{i=1}^{n} b_i \tag{12}$$

5   Performance Evaluation

In this section we compare our solution with previously proposed schemes, EMSS [2] and AC [3]. The comparison is in terms of hash chain construction and loss resistance.

In terms of hash chain construction, The EMSS does not specify what and how many hashes to be appended to each packet, or to the signature packet. EMSS only determines the best case of the chain construction to achieve high robustness against packet loss by simulation.

AC also does not give a clear method to determine the number of packets to be inserted between every two packets of the original chain. Also, it does not explain clearly the signature packet, which packets to append their hashes to the signature and the number of hashes to be appended to the signature.

Our solution specifies clearly the hashes to be appended to each packet and to the signature one, in addition to introducing a mathematical model and the loss probability.

Loss resistance achieved by EMSS depends on the way that the hash of a packet is appended to other packets. In the case of the scheme "$5 - 11 - 17 - 24 - 36 - 39$", that is, the hash of P_i is appended to P_{i+5}, P_{i+11}, P_{i+17}, P_{i+24}, P_{i+36}, and P_{i+39}, an EMSS achieves loss resistance equal to $i + 39 - i - 1 = 38$ packets. For EMSS to increase loss resistance the hash of P_i should be appended to more packets, which in turn increases the overhead.

The AC achieves loss resistance equal to $p(a - 1)$, where a represents the strength of the chain, and p represents the sender buffer size in the AC scheme. When $C_{a,p} = C_{3,6}$, loss resistance is equal to 12 packets. The way AC can increase the resistance against packet loss is by increasing p or a, which means to append more hashes to other packets that in turn increases the overhead.

Our solution on the other hand, achieves the loss resistance equal to $\ell = \nu c - 1$ as given by equation (7). Note that ℓ does not depend on the number of hashes appended to each packet and requires no extra computation resources, rather it depends on the number of chains c. Longer loss resistance is achieved by increasing c, and this will also reduce the overhead, which is the major advantage of our scheme over those previously proposed.

6 Conclusion

We introduced a generalization of our MC model for signature amortization to authenticate multicast streams. We analyzed the generalization and introduced a measure to determine the maximum number of hashes to be appended to the signature packet. The loss probability of the packets with hashes appended to the signature packet in case they are non-contiguous and contiguous are also discussed. The effect of the number of hashes that are appended to the signature packet on the overhead for different streams is also provided.

Our scheme achieves greater loss resistance against packet loss and lower overhead by increasing the number of chains of our model. The buffer capacity needed by the sender when constructing our model so as to achieve the desired resistance against packet loss is studied. The receivers buffer capacity and delay increases as the loss of signature packets increases.

As future works, derivation of the authentication probability for our model and discuss the optimal values of the number of chains, number of slices, μ and ν of our model. We will also conduct an empirical study to see the performance of our method and compare it to the performance of the existing methods.

References

1. P. Rohatgi: A compact and fast hybrid signature scheme for multicast packet authentication. Proc. of the 6th ACM Conf. on Computer and Communications Security (1999)

2. W. Jiang and H. Schulzrinne: Modeling of packet loss and delay and their effect on real-time multimedia service quality. Proc. of 10th Int. Workshop on Network and Operations System Support for Digital Audio and Video (2000)
3. A. Perrig, R. Canetti, J. D. Tygar, and D. Song: Efficient authentication and signing of multicast streams over lossy channels. IEEE Symposium on Security and Privacy (2000) 56-73
4. C. K. Wong and S. S. Lam: Digital signatures for flows and multicasts. IEEE/ACM Trans. on Networking, 7 (1999) 502-513
5. P. Golle and N. Modadugu: Authenticating streamed data in the presence of random packet loss. Proc. of ISOC Network and Distributed System Security Symposium (2001) 13-22
6. R. Gennaro, and P. Rohatgi: How to sign digital streams. Advances in Cryptology - CRYPTO'97 (1997) 180-197
7. A. Chan: A graph-theoretical analysis of multicast authentication. Proc. of the 23rd Int. Conf. on Distributed Computing Systems (2003)
8. S. Miner and J. Staddon: Graph-based authentication of digital streams. Proc. of the IEEE Symposium on Research in Security and Privacy (2001) 232-246
9. P. Alain and M. Refik: Authenticating real time packet stream and multicast. Proc. of 7th IEEE Symposium on Computers and Communications (2002)
10. J. Park, E. Chong and H. Siegel: Efficient multicast stream authentication using erasure codes. ACM Trans. on Information and System Security, 6 (2003) 258-258
11. T. Cucinotta, G. Cecchetti and G. Ferraro: Adopting redundancy techniques for multicast stream authentication. Proc. of the 9th IEEE Workshop on FTDCS (2003)
12. A. Perrig and J. D. Tygar: Secure Broadcast Communication in Wired and Wireless Networks. Kluwer Academic Publishers (2003)
13. W. Stallings: Cryptography and Network Security Principles and Practices. Prentice Hall (2003)
14. C. Wong and S. Lam: Digital signatures for flows and multicasts. Technical Report TR-98-15. Dept. of Computer Sciences, University of Texas at Austin (1998)
15. A. Lysyanskaya, R. Tamassia, and N. Triandopoulos: Multicast authentication in fully adversarial networks. Proc. of IEEE Symposium on Security and Privacy (2004) 241-255
16. Q. Abuein and S. Shibusawa: Efficient multicast authentication scheme using signature amortization. Proc. of the IASTED Int. Conf. on CIIT (2004)
17. Q. Abuein and S. Shibusawa: New chain construction for multicast stream authentication. Proc. of the ICENCO Int. Conf. on NTIS (2004)
18. H. Sanneck, G. Carle, and R. Koodli: A framework model for packet loss metrics based on loss runlengths. SPIE/ACM SIGMM Multimedia Computing and Networking Conf. (2000)
19. M. Yajnik, J. Kurose, and D. Towsley: Packet loss correlation in the mbone multicast network. Proc. of IEEE Global Internet (1996)

A Key Embedded Video Codec for Secure Video Multicast*

Hao Yin[1], Chuang Lin[1], Feng Qiu[1], Xiaowen Chu[2], and Geyong Min[3]

[1] Department of Computer Science and Technology, Tsinghua University,
Beijing 100084, P.R.China
{hyin, clin, fqiu}@csnet1.cs.tsinghua.edu.cn
[2] Computer Science Department, HongKong Baptist University,
Kowloon Tong, Kowloon, Hong Kong
chxw@comp.hkbu.edu.hk
[3] Department of Computing, University of Bradford,
Bradford, BD7 1DP, U.K.
g.min@brad.ac.uk

Abstract. The problem of controlling access to multimedia multicasts requires the distribution and maintenance of keying information. This paper proposes a new key embedded video codec for the media-dependent approach that involves the use of a data-dependent channel, and can be achieved for multimedia by using data embedding techniques. Using data embedding to convey keying information can provide an additional security and reduce the demand of bandwidth. In this paper, we develop a new statistical data embedding algorithm on compression-domain, then, by combining FEC (Forward Error Correction) algorithm and our proposed key information frame format. After a series of simulation experiments, we find that the new codec can satisfy the special demand of media-dependent approach. At the same time, the codec provides good performance.

1 Introduction

Access control in video multicast is usually achieved by encrypting the content using an encryption key, known as the session key (SK) that is shared by all legitimate group members [1] [2]. Since the group membership will most likely be dynamic with users joining and leaving the services, it is necessary to change the SK in order to prevent the leaving user from accessing future communication and prevent the joining user from accessing prior communication. In order to update the SK, a party responsible for distributing the keys, called the group center (GC), must securely communicate the new key material to the valid users. This task is achieved by transmitting rekeying messages that use key encrypting keys (KEKs) to encrypt and distribute new keys. In addition, any solution to access control should address issues of resource scalability for scenarios of large privileged groups.

---

* This work is supported by the National Natural Science Foundation of China (No. 60372019, 60429202, and 60473086), the Projects of Development Plan of the State Key Fundamental Research (No. 2003CB314804).

J. Dittmann, S. Katzenbeisser, and A. Uhl (Eds.): CMS 2005, LNCS 3677, pp. 77–87, 2005.

The problem of access control for multicasts has been recent attention in the literature, and several efficient schemes have been proposed with desirable communication properties. These schemes can be classified into two distinct classes of mechanisms: media-independent mechanism and media-dependent mechanism [1]. In media-independent mechanism, the rekeying messages are conveyed by a means totally disjoint from the multimedia content; while in media-dependent mechanism, the rekeying messages are embedded in the multimedia content and distributed to those who receive the data.

When media-dependent mechanism uses data embedding techniques to delivery rekeying messages, the issues of reliability of them and transparency for adaptation mechanisms become more pronounced than in the media-independent case. New video codec should face these challenges: 1) transparency for adaptation mechanism;

2) reliability for rekeying message delivery; 3)real-time key embedding;4) Multicast architecture and packetization independence;5) Video Quality; since the rekeying messages are embedded into the video content by modifying the original signal, there will be great impact for video quality. How to make the video quality after key embedding acceptable for users and meanwhile maintain preferable security is another challenge.

In this paper we propose a new key embedded video codec which can solve the challenges mentioned in above. The rest of the paper is organized as follows Section 2 presents our key embedded video codec, including the error resilient embedded video coding and detecting scheme. Section 3 evaluates our codec by a series of simulation experiments. Section 4 contains some concluding remarks. Appendix A proves the validity of our key embedding scheme. Appendix B presents the relationship between luminance in spatial domain and the coefficients in the DCT domain, and infers the luminance alteration method in DCT domain.

2 Error Resilient Embedded Video Coding Scheme

2.1 Overview

The whole the real-time key embedding and detecting process is divided into two parts: key embedded video coding part and key detecting & decoding part. In the key embedded video coding part, key embedding algorithm is added into the process of source coding of MPEG2 video. In this algorithm, key message will be modulated into the DCT coefficients. In order to improve the error resilience of the embedded key messages, we make use of FEC approach to conduct error control. Then, all messages will be encrypted by old key and sent out to another host via the network. In key detecting & decoding part, firstly we use the shared key to decrypt the incoming data packet, and decoding them. While decoding it, we detect the embedded key messages, which will be the shared key at the next communication interval and be used to decrypt the incoming packets.

2.2 Key Embedding and Key Detecting Algorithm

In this section, we use the ALV (Average Luminance Value) modulation in the DCT domain to implement this algorithm. When the MPEG2 bitstream arrives to the transcoder, the transcoding algorithm can be abstracted to perform in a way that first decodes the MPEG2 bitstream, then down-samples the YUV sequence and re-encodes the bitstream into MPEG4 or H.264 bitstream. It is the re-encoding process, specifically, the re-quantization process that makes the video signal different from the original content. As for the ALV of a field, since it is averaged by the number of DCT blocks, when such number is large enough and these blocks are independent, based on the "Law of Large Numbers", the displacement of the ALV of a field will be small. The detailed demonstration is shown in Appendix A. Fig.1 illustrates one kind of method to divide the 640×480 format picture into 10 fields which is composed of 640×480/8/8/10 = 480 8 by 8 blocks. The distance between any of the two blocks in the same field must be as far as possible to satisfy the independence requirement. Such a blocks partition philosophy is the same as cell allocation philosophy in cellular mobile communication system [3] and it is benefit for satisfying this independence requirement. By changing the ALV of the fields, we can embed 1 bit in each field. Since 480 are large enough to resist the "noise", the receiver can successfully detect the embedded bit with great probability.

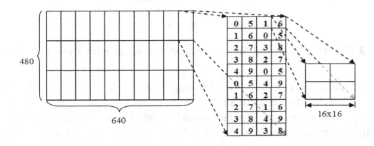

Fig. 1. One type of Block set partition mode in 640x480 format sequence

Although the adjustment can take place in both pixel domain and DCT domain, the DCT domain seems better because it is nearer to the output bitstream than the pixel domain and thus makes the embedding more precisely. In Appendix A, we have analysis the relationship between the ALV of a 8x8 DCT block (no matter residual block or intra block) and it's DC component after quantization then we have come to the conclusion: To increase the average value of a block by Δ in MPEG2 encoder, set

$$C_D^q = \left\lfloor (8\Delta + C_D + \frac{Q}{2})/Q \right\rfloor \tag{1}$$

Here the meanings of parameters in equation (1) are illustrated in Fig.2 which is the outline of DCT domain key embedding diagram using MPEG2 encoder. By using this DCT domain key embedding diagram, we can embed a key bit into each field of the picture.

The above processes have determined that the ALV of a field can be a carrier wave to bear the key data. Fig.3 illustrates the modulation scheme and detecting scheme we have proposed.

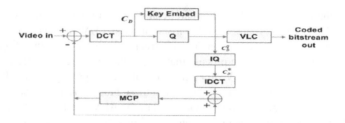

Fig. 2. MPEG2 encode diagram to change the average luminance value in the bitstream to embed data. MCP stands for motion-compensated prediction.

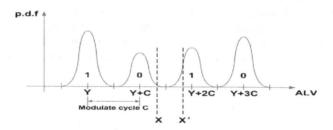

Fig. 3. Receiver's theoretical ALV distribution by using quantization index modulation

The horizontal coordinate is ALV (Average Luminance Value) of a field, Y is a real number arbitrarily selected between [0, 255] as an anchor value to prevent ALV value from being out of range and must be known by both the encoder and the receiver. C is the modulation cycle. Once Y is determined, the value of C depends on the distribution of ALV deviation after transcoding which is in inverse ration to the block set size N and in direct proportion ratio to transcoder's quantizers. In our experiments, C ranges from 4 to 16. Adding integer numbers of C to the datum mark Y will produce a series of modulation reference points Y+nC (n=0, 1...). Note that when n is an odd number, the reference point is for embedded bit '0', otherwise it is for embedded bit '1'. The reference points are the only values that the block sets' ALV can be after the embedding modulation. As shown in Fig.4, to embed a bit '1' in a region of a picture, we first compute the ALV value of this block set, assuming it is X, then we find '0' is the nearest reference point. So we change the ALV of this region to be Y+2C which stands for bit '1'. This ALV value might be slightly changed during the transmission. On the receiver side, decoder can compute the region's ALV value X', by judging the type of its nearest reference point, decoder can draw out the embedded bit easily. Here, the displacement of X' to Y+2C is due to the network handling and the transcoder. The probability of successfully detecting one bit key depends on modulation cycle C and the quantizers used in the transcoder.

2.3 Error Resilient Key Embedding Algorithm

The reliability of key data transmission can be improved by Forward Error Correction (FEC), thus lowering the key data missing probability in packet lossy environment. In this paper, we use Reed-Solomon (RS) codes [4]. For symbols composed of m bits, the encoder for an (n, k) RS code group the incoming data stream into blocks of k information symbols (km bits) and appends n-k parity symbols to each block. And n is the block length. For RS codes operating on m-bits symbols, the maximum block length is : $n_{max} = 2^m - 1$. For an (n, k) RS code, any error pattern resulting in less than

$$t_1 = \left\lfloor \frac{n-k}{2} \right\rfloor$$ symbol errors can be corrected. For symbol erasures (symbol loss or

known symbol errors), (n, k) RS code can correct $t_2 = n - k$ erasures. Generally, if

$$2t_1 + t_2 \leq n - k$$

the RS code can recover all the original symbols. In this paper, we choose m = 8, therefore a symbol corresponds to one byte.

2.4 Key Data Frame Format

To make the system more robust, a key data frame format can be designed for synchronization of key data detecting. The key data stream will be sent in the form of frames, and the key technique used in this procedure is called "bit stuffing". This technique makes the frame be able to contain any amount of bits. In this schema, each frame uses a binary sequence that consists of two '0' and eight '1', i.e., '01111110' to denote the place of its beginning and end, and the key data is placed between the two flags. Since the key data stream may also contain the same sequence, the sender should count the number of "1" in series in the data stream. When the number reaches 5, a bit of "0" will be inserted, by what means the sequence "01111110" existed in the data stream becomes "011111010". The receiver still counts the number of "1" in series. If a sequence of "01111110" is detected, the starting or end flag is met and the receiver determines to start or end storing a frame of data to its memory. Otherwise when "0111110" is detected, the receiver removes the last "0" automatically and saves the "011111" before it. In this scheme the border between two frames can be uniquely detected, since the flag sequence never exists in the data stream.

3 Simulation Experiments

As for source signals, we use two MPEG2 test sequences *dinosaur* and *Live-captured video* which are both encoded at 640x480 size and 20fps using 500frames. *Dinosaur* contains fast motion and scene change; while *Live-captured video* is derived from captured video, which contains slow motion and fixed scene. And our simulation platform is illustrated in Fig.4.

The source-coding distortion introduced by our key embedding algorithm is illustrated on Fig.5. Fig.5 (a) illustrates the PSNR of the dinosaur sequence at the receiver. We can find that when modulation cycle smaller than 4 can provide good performance and the distortion derived from key embedding can be neglected. Fig.5 (b) illustrates the probability of successfully detecting all the 10 bits in a frame changing with the modulation cycle C. Here we can see that when the successfully detecting probability is set to 0.98, the modulation cycle can be minimized with the maximum profit.

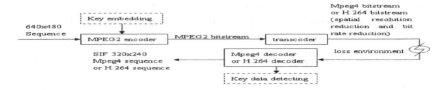

Fig. 4. Block diagram of key data embedding, transmission and key detecting

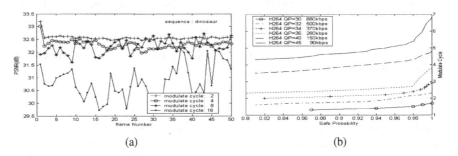

(a)   (b)

Fig. 5. PSNR of frames and the probability of successfully detecting 10 bits in a frame changing with the modulation cycle C at the receiver

Assuming that the probability of successively detect a bit from a region is α, and the packet loss rate is β, then the probability that there is no key bit error in a frame is

$$P_{framesafe} = \alpha^{10}$$

The value of $P_{framesafe}$ is determined by the luminance modulated scheme. Practically, trading off between safety and video quality, we usually set $P_{framesafe} = 0.98$. The probability that the parity bits can check out the key bit error in a frame is

$$P_{checked} = \sum_{i=0,1,3,5} \sum_{j=0,1,3,5} [P(i \text{ bits error in region } 1,2,3,4,9) \times P(j \text{ bits error in region } 5,6,7,8,10)] - P_{framesafe}$$

$$\approx C_{10}^1 \alpha^9 (1-\alpha) + C_{10}^2 \alpha^8 (1-\alpha)^2 \frac{1}{2} + C_{10}^3 \alpha^7 (1-\alpha)^3 \frac{1}{4} + C_{10}^4 \alpha^6 (1-\alpha)^4 \frac{1}{2}$$

(ignore the advent of > 5 key bit errors in one frame), thus comes the probability of "erasure" for a frame $P_{erasure} = \beta + P_{checked}$ and the probability of "error" for a frame is

$$P_{error} = (1 - P_{checked} - P_{framesafe})$$

Fig.6 illustrates the probability of safely received 128 bits key data *vs* the loss packet rate of the network. It can be seen that the key data error rate of a GOP (P_{unsafe}) increases with increasing packet loss rate (R_{lost}) for different value $p_{framesafe}$.

This RS code can only be used when the network transmission is extremely reliable and the value of $P_{framesafe}$ approach to ideal ($P_{framesafe} \rightarrow 1$). Increasing the number of redundant packet by 3, we get the results indicated in Fig.6(b). In this situation, the target value $p_{framesafe}$ is quite satisfied when packet loss rate is lower than 16% and $P_{framesafe} = 0.98$. As for the case when the value of $P_{framesafe}$ is especially high, we can again increase the number of redundant embedded frames, with results shown in Fig.6(c), to serve the high reliability of key drawing. The only flaw of such increasing is that the feasible rekey cycle becomes longer.

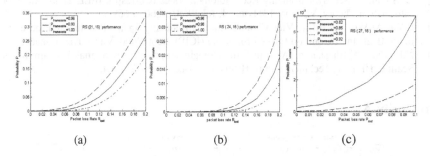

(a)   (b)   (c)

Fig. 6. The error rate of a GOP by using different packet loss rate and redundant packets

Table 1. Complexity of the proposed key embedding algorithm

Sequence	Dinosaur	Live-captured
Coding time without embedding	1.21f/s	1.28f/s
Coding time with embedding	1.12f/s	1.18f/s
Increased processing time	8.03%	8.47%

As for the embedding speed of the algorithm, table 1 presents comparison of coding times with/without key embedding. Note that the two sequences are all 500 frames with 640x480 pixel format and the CPU used is P4 2.0G.

4 Conclusion

In this paper, we propose a new key embedded video coding scheme, which is of error resilience and transparence for adaptation mechanism, and can be combined with existing key distribution mechanism to provide access control for video multicast applications. After a series of simulation experiments, we can see from the figures that when using more redundant embedded frames, the probability of successfully detecting the key data can be quite satisfied in a worse network environment.

References

[1]   Wade Trappe, Jie Song, Radha Poovendran, and K.J.Ray Liu, Key Management and Distribution for Secure Multimedia Multicast, IEEE Transaction on Multimedia, Vol. 5, No.4, December 2003, pp.544-557.
[2]   H. Yin, C. Lin, F. Qiu, B. Li, Z. Tan, A Media-Dependent Secure Multicast Protocol for Adaptive Video Applications, in Proc. of ACM SIGCOMM Asia Workshop 2005,Beijing China.
[3]   D. Everitt and D. Manfield, Performance analysis of cellular mobile communication systems with dynamic channel assignment, *IEEE J. Select. Areas Commun.*, vol. 7, pp. 1172-1180, Oct. 1989.
[4]   G. Solomon, Self-synchronizing Reed-Solomon codes (Corresp.), IEEE Transactions on Information Theory, Volume: 14, Issue: 4, Jul 1968, pp:608 - 609.
[5]   P.Yin, M.Wu, and B.Liu, Video Transcoding by Reducing Spatial Resolution, Proceeding of the IEEE Int'1 Conf. on Image Processing (ICIP), Sept. 2000, Vancouver, Canada.
[6]   N.Merhav, V.Bhaskaran, A Transform Domain Approach To Spatial Domain Image Scaling, HP Labs Technical report, HP-94-116, December 15, 1994.

Appendix A:

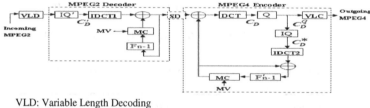

VLD: Variable Length Decoding
VLC: Variable Length Coding
MV: Motion Vectors   SD : spatial solution downscaling
Q: quantize   MC : Motion Compensation
IDCT: Inverse DCT   IQ: De-quantize
                                   F : Reconstructed Frame

Fig. 7. Simply Cascaded Pixel-Domain Transcoder (MPEG2 to MPEG4)

The module SD (spatial resolution downscaling) in the transcoder diagram is optional, it converts the $M \times N$ spatial resolution into a stream with smaller resolution, such as $M/2 \times N/2$ or $M/4 \times N/4$. Usually, the downscaling can assure the average luminance value in a 16×16 luminance block remain unchanged after downscale to 8×8 luminance block no mater the downscale is operating in the spatial domain or in the DCT domain. Details can be found in [5, 6].

The input sequence to the MPEG4 encoder is a YUV sequence decoded by the MPEG2 decoder. Let C_D be the DC coefficient of an 8×8 block after discrete cosine transform in MPEG4 encoder, C_D^q be the coefficient after being quantized by Q_D, and C_D^* be the reconstructed DC coefficient of C_D, we have:

$$C_D^q = \left\lfloor (C_D + \frac{Q_D}{2})/Q_D \right\rfloor, \quad C_D^* = C_D^q \times Q_D$$

Let $D_Q = C_D^* - C_D = \left\lfloor (C_D + \frac{Q_D}{2})/Q_D \right\rfloor \times Q_D - C_D$. Obviously, D_Q is uniform

distributed between $-\dfrac{Q_D}{2}$ and $\dfrac{Q_D}{2}$, and the expected value of D_Q is

$$E(D_Q) = 0, \tag{2}$$

and the variance of D_Q is

$$Var(D_Q) = \frac{1}{12}Q_D^2 \tag{3}$$

Suppose that there are N times of such different blocks in a same frame, with D_Q

marked as D_Q^i ($i = 1, 2...N$). Let $\overline{D} = \dfrac{\sum\limits_{i=1}^{N} D_Q^i}{N}$, then we also have:

$$E(\overline{D}) = E(\frac{\sum\limits_{i=1}^{N} D_Q^i}{N}) = \frac{1}{N}\sum\limits_{i=1}^{N} E(D_Q^i) = 0 \tag{4}$$

and

$$Var(\overline{D}) = E(\overline{D} - E(\overline{D}))^2 = E(\frac{\sum\limits_{i=1}^{N} D_Q^i}{N})^2 = \frac{1}{N^2}E(\sum\limits_{i=1}^{N} D_Q^i)^2 \tag{5}$$

if blocks are independent, then D_Q^i are independent, we have:

$$Var(\overline{D}) = \frac{1}{N^2}E(\sum\limits_{i=1}^{N} D_Q^i)^2 = \frac{1}{N^2}\sum\limits_{i=1}^{N} E(D_Q^i)^2 = \frac{Var(D_Q)}{N} = \frac{Q_D^2}{12N} \tag{6}$$

Equation (6) tells us that for a "region" composed of a certain large number of independent luminance blocks, the average luminance value of the pixels compound this region will be only little changed during the transcoding manipulation. The extent of this value alteration is in inverse proportion to the number of the blocks.

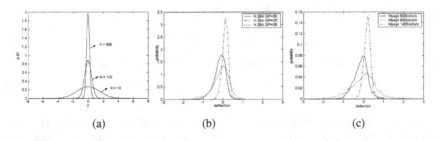

(a)   (b)   (c)

Fig. 8. ALV of the field during the transcoding manipulation with different number of blocks (a) shows the theoretical distribution of ALV displacement of a field composed of N macroblocks after transcoding with $Q_D = 16$. (b) and (c) illustrate the experimental distribution of ALV displacement after H.264 and MPEG4 transcoding respectively.

Appendix B: DCT Domain Luminance Alteration

A two-dimensional DCT is performed on small blocks (8 pixels *by* 8 lines) of each component of the picture to produce blocks of DCT coefficients. The coefficient corresponding to zero horizontal and vertical frequency is called the DC coefficient:

$$F(u,v) = \frac{2}{N}C(u)C(v) \sum_{x=0}^{N-1} \sum_{y=0}^{N-1} f(x,y)\cos\frac{(2x+1)u\pi}{2N}\cos\frac{(2y+1)v\pi}{2N} \quad (7)$$

Where:
$$C(u),C(v) = \begin{cases} \frac{1}{\sqrt{2}} & for \ u,v=0 \\ 1 & otherwise \end{cases} \quad (8)$$

Substitute N by 8, for the value of DC coefficient of block is

$$F(0,0) = \frac{1}{8} \sum_{x=0}^{7} \sum_{y=0}^{7} f(x,y) \quad (9)$$

From equation (9) we can come to the following conclusion:

Theorem 1: for 8 by 8 blocks, if each of the luminance pixel value is increased by ΔY, the DC coefficient will also increase by $8\,\Delta Y$. In other words, the increasing of DC coefficient by $8\,\Delta Y$ will lead to the average luminance value of an 8 by 8 block increasing by ΔY.

To change the average value of the block according to the volume of embedded data, operation can be performed on C_D^q which will be VLC coded in the MPEG2 bitstream. Here C_D^q is a DC coefficient value after alteration and quantization. Attention must be paid that the AC coefficients are not changed. As for the value of the reconstructed DC coefficient C_D^*, we can express it by:

$$C_D^* = Q \times C_D^q \quad (10)$$

According to theorem 1, the increase of the average luminance value of a block is:

$$\Delta = (C_D^* - C_D)/8 = (Q \times C_D^q - C_D)/8 \quad (11)$$

If we want to increase the average value of a block by Δ, we can set

$$C_D^q = \left\lfloor (8\Delta + C_D + \frac{Q}{2})/Q \right\rfloor \quad (12)$$

Although the average luminance pixel of a block could be changed easily after quantization, two troubles are still remained. First is that equation (12) does not promise to find out a C_D^q precisely change the average value we need unless $(8\Delta + C_D)/Q$ is an integer. Second is the limitation of the pixel value which prevents the exact change of the value even if $(8\Delta + C_D)/Q$ is an integer. For example, increasing a block's average luminance value by 1 will be ignored if the luminance values of the block are totally 255.

Fortunately, the rigorous demand is not for a block, but for a region. Because of the large number of blocks, if we come up against unsatisfied block value change, we can compensate from other blocks. In this section, we forward a simple scheme to control the value change of the blocks in a region as shown in Fig.9.

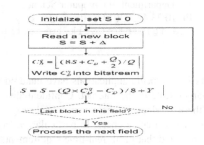

Fig. 9. Scheme to change the average luminance value of the blocks to embed data in the region. Δ is the average value increased in the region. Q is the quantizer of the DC coefficient. S is the residual ALV for all blocks that have been processed.

Puzzle - A Novel Video Encryption Algorithm

Fuwen Liu and Hartmut Koenig

Brandenburg University of Technology Cottbus,
Department of Computer Science,
PF 10 33 44, 03013 Cottbus, Germany
{lfw, koenig}@informatik.tu-cottbus.de

Abstract. Networked multimedia applications have matured in recent years to be deployed in a larger scale in the Internet. Confidentiality is one of the primary concerns of these services for their commercial usages, e.g. in video on demand services or in video conferences. In particular, video encryption algorithms are strongly required that fulfill real-time requirements. In this paper we present the video encryption algorithm *Puzzle* to encrypting video streams in software. It is fast enough to fulfill real-time constraints and to provide a sufficient security. *Puzzle* is a video compression independent algorithm which can be easily incorporated into existing multimedia systems.

1 Introduction

Due to significant advances in video compression and networking technologies, networked multimedia applications, e.g. video on demand or video conferences, are becoming increasingly popular. Confidentiality is one of the primary concerns for their commercial use. This issue is usually addressed by encryption. Only authorized parties who possess the decryption keys are able to access to the clear multimedia contents. While for text and audio encryption applicable algorithms are available, there is still a lack of appropriate video encryption algorithms. In particular, video encryption algorithms are strongly required that fulfill real-time requirements. The most straightforward approach is to encrypt the entire compressed video stream with conventional cryptographic algorithms such as AES [1]. This is called a *naive algorithm* approach [2]. This approach is simple to implement and easy to integrate into existing multimedia systems, since it is independent of certain video compression algorithms.

Nowadays, advanced computers are fast enough to encrypt a single channel MPEG2 video stream with a bit rate between 4 and 9 Mbps in real-time using the naive algorithm approach [3]. However, this evolution of the computer power does not completely eliminate the need to develop faster encryption algorithms for video data. Many multimedia applications such as video on demand and multiparty P2P video conferences always require specific algorithms for the video encryption because they usually support multi-channel video communication. The simultaneous encryption or decryption, respectively, of all streams causes a huge processing burden at the end systems. Appropriate encryption algorithms allow to alleviate these burdens and to enroll more users to the service.

J. Dittmann, S. Katzenbeisser, and A. Uhl (Eds.): CMS 2005, LNCS 3677, pp. 88–97, 2005.

Since mid 90's many research efforts have been devoted to designing specific video encryption algorithms. Several algorithms were proposed. These algorithms, however, are characterized by a considerable unbalance between security and efficiency. Some of them are efficient to fulfill the real-time requirements but with a limited security level, whilst others are vice versa strong enough to meet the security demands but with a limited encryption efficiency. Moreover, most of these algorithms are related to a certain video compression algorithm and implemented together in software. This makes them less practicable, because today video compression algorithms are standardized and mostly implemented in hardware.

In this paper we propose the video encryption algorithm *Puzzle* which is not only efficient but also sufficiently secure. *Puzzle* can be easily integrated into existing video systems regardless of their implementation (i.e. software or hardware). The paper is organized as follows. After addressing related work in Section 2 we describe the principle of the *Puzzle* algorithm in Section 3. Next in Section 4, we evaluate its performance and compare it with the standard cipher AES. In Section 5 we give a security analysis of *Puzzle*. Some final remarks conclude the paper.

2 Related Work

Existing video encryption methods have been comprehensively surveyed in [4], [5], where they are called *selective encryption* algorithms. This underlines the essence of these methods. They only partially encrypt relevant video information to reduce the computational complexity by exploiting compression and perceptual characteristics. The relationship between selective encryption algorithms and video compression algorithms is a key factor to decide whether an encryption algorithm can easily be integrated into a multimedia system. In this paper we therefore further classify the selective encryption algorithms into two categories according to their association with video compression algorithms: joint compression and encryption algorithms and compression- independent encryption algorithms.

The main idea of the *joint compression and encryption algorithms* is that encryption is applied to a certain step of the compression algorithm so that the output is significantly different from a video stream using a standard compression algorithm. The receivers cannot re-establish the original video without having the encryption key. Figure 1 illustrates the paradigm.

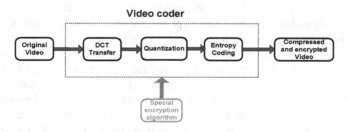

Fig. 1. Principle of *joint compression and encryption* algorithms

The approaches [6], [7], [8], [9] are well known examples of such kind of algorithms. The weakness of the joint compression and encryption techniques is that they cannot be integrated into multimedia systems whose video codecs are implemented in hardware. Certainly, these approaches can be combined with multimedia systems implemented in software, but they completely destroy the modular design of the original codec. Appropriate modifications of the standard video codecs must be made to accommodate these schemes. Therefore, *joint compression and encryption* algorithms preclude the use of standard video codecs in multimedia systems.

The basic idea of *compression-independent encryption algorithms* (see Fig.2) is that compression and encryption are carried out separately. Only parts of the compressed video streams are encrypted with conventional algorithms taking the particular characteristics of the compressed video streams into account.

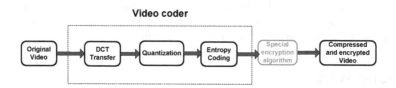

Fig. 2. Principle of *compression- independent encryption* algorithms

So Spanos and Maples [10] and Li [11] exploit the fact that B- and P-frames are predicted from I-frames in interframe compression algorithms. Both proposed encryption approaches in which only the I-frames are encrypted. In theory it should prevent an eavesdropper without encryption key from the reconstruction of the original video. However, Agi and Gong [2] demonstrated that some scene contents are still discernible by directly playing back the selectively encrypted video stream on a standard decoder, since the unencrypted I-macro blocks in the B- and P-frames can be fully decoded without any information from the I-frames. Moreover, this approach did not achieve a significant computational reduction with respect to the total encryption, because the I-frames make about 30~ 60 per cent of an MPEG video [2]. Qiao and Nahrstedt [12] introduced the *video encryption algorithm* VEA in which half of the bit stream is encrypted with a standard encryption algorithm. This half stream is exclusive-ORed with the other half stream. The statistical analysis shows that MPEG video streams are almost uniformly distributed. VEA takes advantage of this special statistical behaviour of MPEG video streams to achieve the sufficient security level. However, the algorithm reduces the encryption load only by 47 per cent, since a half bit stream has to be encrypted with conventional algorithms.

The inflexibility and confinement to deploying joint compression and encryption algorithms in current multimedia systems make them less practicable. Compression-independent encryption algorithms, in contrast, do not suffer from this weakness. They can be easily integrated into existing multimedia systems. Although several such kinds of algorithms are available, they do not achieve a noticeable encryption speed improvement compared to naive algorithms (only about a double speed-up). Moreover, some of them are not resistant to the simple perceptual attack (playing back an encrypted video stream on a standard video player).

In the sequel, we present an efficient and sufficiently secure video encryption algorithm. The outstanding benefit of this scheme is the drastic reduction of encryption overhead for the high resolution video. The algorithm we present here has been improved compared to the first sketch in [13] which appeared not strong enough to resist against sophisticated differential attacks [15]. The new version performs the encryption in reverse order to remove the suspected vulnerability. This reordering in part changed the encryption steps.

3 Principle of the *Puzzle* Algorithm

In this section we first give an overview on the basic idea of the *Puzzle* algorithm. After that the steps of the algorithm are described in detail.

3.1 Principle

The *Puzzle* algorithm is inspired by the children game puzzle which splits an entire picture into many small pieces and places them in disorder so that children cannot recognize the entire picture. When children play the game, they have to spend much time to put these pieces together to re-establish the original picture (see Figure 3).

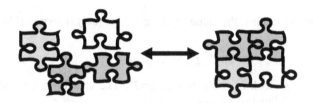

Fig. 3. Puzzle game

Children usually reconstruct the original picture using or comparing known fragments of the picture and referring them to the accompanied original picture. We cannot therefore straightforwardly apply the game to encrypt a video frame. If we, however, modify the rules of the game in the following way, it will be nearly impossible for children to recover the original picture. The children should be only allowed to view the reverse side of the pieces, so that they have to re-establish the picture without any hints to the original picture. It is manifested that $n!$ trials are required to re-establish the original, where n is the number of pieces. Basically, n needs not necessarily to be large. Assume that a picture is divided into 64 pieces, then the number of possible permutations is $64! = 1.27 \times 10^{89}$. It is unlikely that children reconstruct the original picture when having so many permutations. With this rule in mind we designed our *Puzzle* algorithm.

3.2 Encryption Steps

Puzzle consists of two steps: (1) *Puzzling* the compressed video data of each frame and (2) *Obscuring* the puzzled video data. In step (1) the video data are partitioned into many blocks which are randomly shuffled afterwards. Step (2) corresponds to the turning over the pieces to the reverse side.

3.2.1 Puzzling
A compressed video frame is puzzled by *partitioning* the frame into n blocks of same length b and *disordering* these blocks according to a random permutation list.

3.2.1.1 Partitioning
Given a L bytes long frame (excluding the frame header) of compressed video data V ($v_1v_2...v_L$). The partitioning of the compressed video data V of length L into n blocks of the same length b is a typical factoring problem, i.e. $L = n \times b$. This problem is easy to solve if one of two variables (n,b) is assumed as constant. Unfortunately, we cannot solve this problem this way. If we fix the value of b, the value of n may become very large in some frames or very small in other ones, since the length L varies for each frame. On the other hand, a too large value of n causes a larger computation overhead when exchanging the blocks. If the value of n is too small the scheme can be easily be broken. To solve the problem we put some constraints on the variables n,b. The length of a block b should be $b=2^m$, where m is an integer. The value of n is only allowed to vary in the range from mb to $2mb$, whereby mb is a predefined constant number. It indicates that the compressed video data V should be at least split into mb blocks.

Using these constraints, the value of m can be uniquely determined by the following formula:

$$mb \le L / 2^m < 2mb .$$

(1)

The length of a block is given through $b=2^m$. The actual block number n can be calculated by the following formula:

$$n = \begin{cases} pn & \text{if } pn \text{ is even} \\ pn-1 & \text{if } pn \text{ is odd} \end{cases}$$

(2)

Where pn is the quotient of L/b. Formula (2) makes the value of n always an even number. This operation is necessary to disorder the blocks in the next step. With formula (1) and (2), the product of n and b might be unequal to the video frame length L when pn is odd or the remainder of L/b is unequal to zero. The difference between both is determined using the following formula:

$$d = L - n \times b$$

(3)

Formula (3) implies that the d bytes video data at the beginning of the video frame will be excluded from the disordering procedure.

3.2.1.2 Disordering
The basic idea for the disordering of the blocks is that the n blocks of compressed video data $V(v_{d+1}v_{d+2}...v_L)$ are divided into two equal parts: an upper and the lower one. Each consists of $n/2$ blocks. Both parts are interchanged in accordance with a permutation list $P=p_1p_2...p_{n/2}$. This permutation list should be derived from a random se-

quence to resist an attacker to guess the original position of the blocks. We exploit a stream cipher with an key K, such as SEAL [16] or AES-CTR[17], to generate l bytes of random sequence, called key stream S ($s_1s_2...s_l$), for each video frame. Since the values of the key stream S vary for each video frame, the permutation lists of different frames are distinct. The algorithm to generate the permutation list is described in the *Appendix*. After deriving the permutation list we can generate the temporary cipher text $T=t_1t_2...t_{L-d}$ from the video data $V=v_{d+1}v_{d+2}...v_L$ by swapping the ith block of the upper part with the p_i^{th} block of the lower part of V. Figure 4 shows an example of this disordering process. It is assumed that a frame V is split into 256 blocks $B_1B_2...B_{256}$. The permutation list derived from the key stream S is $P=$ {256, 213, 216 ... 130}.

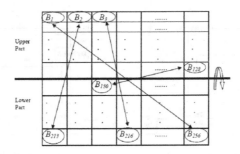

Fig. 4. A *Puzzle* scenario

3.2.2 Obscuring

The temporary cipher text T is obscured using a light-weight encryption. Its basic idea is to encrypt only a small portion of T (first l bytes) with a stream cipher. Every l bytes are grouped into a portion for the rest data of T. Each portion is encrypted by simply exclsive-ORing its preceding. The procedure is as follows. The first d bytes of the compressed video data $V(v_1v_2...v_d)$ that are not involved in the puzzling procedure are exclusive-ORed with d bytes of key stream $A(a_1 a_2...a_d)$ generated by a stream cipher with the encryption key K. The first l ($l<L$) bytes of T ($t_1t_2...t_l$) are exclusive-ORed with l bytes of the key stream S ($s_1s_2...s_l$) generated in the puzzling step. The sense of the reuse of key stream S is to make the algorithm more efficient. After that the first l bytes of T are used as key stream and exclusive-ORed with the second l

Input text	$v_1v_2...v_d$	t_1	t_2	...	t_l	t_{l+1}	t_{l+2}	...	t_{2l}	t_{2l+1}	t_{2l+2}	...	t_{3l}	... ...t_{L-d}
$\oplus$														
Key stream	$a_1a_2...a_d$	s_1	s_2	...	s_l	t_1	t_2	...	t_l	t_{l+1}	t_{l+2}	...	t_{2l}	... ...t_{L-d-l}
Cipher text	$c_1c_2...c_d$	c_{d+1}	$c_{d+2}...c_{d+l}$			c_{d+l+1}	$c_{d+l+2}...c_{d+2l}$			c_{d+2l+1}	$c_{d+2l+2}...c_{d+3l}$			... ... c_L

Note: v_i, s_i, a_i and t_i denote a data byte. The input text contains the temporary cipher text T and the first d bytes of the compressed video data.

Fig. 5. Obscuring algorithm

bytes. Then the second l bytes of T are exclusive-ORed with the third l byte and so on until the end of the frame is reached. As output we receive the L bytes long cipher text C ($c_1c_2.. .t_L$). Figure 5 shows the principle. Note that the frame header remains unencrypted, because it usually contains standard information.

3.3   Encoding and Decoding Procedures

The components of the *Puzzle* encoding procedure described above are summarized in Figure 6a). The original compressed video sequence can be recovered from the cipher text at the receiver's side by executing the encoding operations in reverse order (see Figure 6b)).

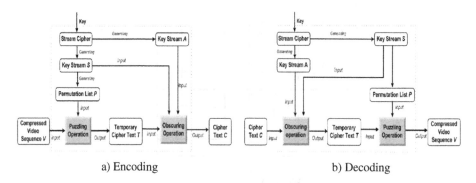

a) Encoding   b) Decoding

Fig. 6. Encoding and decoding procedures of *Puzzle*

4   Measurements

We run a series of experiments for different resolution videos to measure the speed of *Puzzle* in comparison with the standard cipher AES on a SUN ULTRA 10 platform. To make a trade-off between security and efficiency, the values of the variable l and mb in our algorithm are both set to 128. Further we used AES-CTR [17] as stream cipher. The measurement results are depicted in Figure 7.

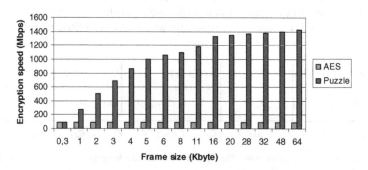

Fig. 7. Comparison of the encryption speed of AES and *Puzzle*

Figure 7 shows that the encryption speed of AES basically does not change for different frame sizes, whereas that of *Puzzle* noticeably increases for larger frames. AES and *Puzzle* only have a nearly equivalent encryption speed at a frame size of 300 byte. With increasing frame sizes the encryption speed of *Puzzle* becomes considerably higher than that of AES. This indicates that *Puzzle* is better suited for high resolution video streams which usually have a large frame size.

5 Security Analysis of the *Puzzle* Algorithm

In this section we evaluate the security properties of the *Puzzle* algorithm. A good crypto system should withstand the following most important attack classes [14]: *ciphertext-only attacks*, *known-plaintext attacks*, and *chosen-plaintext attacks*. Furthermore, the measure to defend against *differential attack* should be taken into account.

Ciphertext-only attacks: Based on the cipher text an adversary has two possibilities for trying to re-establish the original frame encrypted with *Puzzle* (see Figure 6b)). He/she can either attempt to break the puzzling and then the obscuring operation or to crack these steps in the reverse order. The first attack corresponds to the situation when the child first tries to put the disordered pieces to their correct position only looking at their backside and then turns the whole correctly reordered picture to the right side. In *Puzzle* each frame is split in at least 128 blocks in the puzzling operation, i.e. more than $64! = 1.27 \times 10^{89}$ trials to reconstruct a single original frame. This is obviously computationally infeasible to be broken, especially as a 128 bit key length standard block cipher is believed to be computationally secure enough today. The number of possible permutation for such standard block cipher is, however, only $2^{128} = 3.4 \times 10^{38}$.

The second attack resembles the situation when the child first turns the disordered pieces to the right side one by one and then re-establishes the picture using content information. In *Puzzle* the cipher text C is generated by connecting two puzzled plaintexts fragments using the exclusive OR operation except the first $l+d$ bytes of the obscuring operation. As shown in [12] the computation complexity to obtain a 10 bytes MPEG compressed video sequence by separating two 5 bytes long exclusive-ORed plaintext is equivalent to that of breaking a 64-bit key length block cipher which has 2^{64} combinations. As mentioned in Section 4, we recommend to applying *Puzzle* on video sequences with a frame length larger than 300 bytes. Accordingly the attacker has at least to try all $30 \times 2^{64} \approx 2^{69}$ combinations to obtain the plain texts of the disordered blocks for a single frame.

Known- plaintext attacks: Given a compressed video frame and its corresponding cipher text, as show in Figures 5 and 6b), it is not difficult for an attacker to get the l bytes long key stream S and the d bytes long key stream A. However, the attacker is unable to decrypt the other video frames using this key stream, since we utilize AES-CTR as the stream cipher to generate the distinct key streams S and A with encryption key K for each frame. It is further impossible to derive the encryption key K from a known key stream S, since AES-CTR is a confidentiality mode [17] which is secure against known-plaintext attacks. Therefore our algorithm can withstand these attacks.

Chosen-plaintext attacks: Our scheme is resistant against chosen-plaintext attacks for the same reasons given for known- plaintext attacks.

Differential attacks: The original goal of the differential cryptanalysis is to attempt to reconstruct the encryption key by studying the differences between the plaintext and the respective ciphertext pairs. The differential cryptanalysis can reduce the complexity of attacking a cipher by half. Generally speaking, it is a specific kind of a *chosen-plaintext attack*. As discussed above, such attack is not effective to our scheme. On the other hand, attackers might apply the basic idea of differential cryptanalysis to launch a *specific* ciphertext-only attack by analyzing the ciphertext of our scheme without the knowledge of the respective plaintext for the specific structure of our scheme. The order of encryption procedure in our scheme decides, whether our scheme is strong enough to withstand such a specific ciphertext-only attack. In [13] we first obscured the original frame and then puzzled the obscured one. This encryption order is suspect to be too weak for specific ciphertext-only attacks, because the edges values of the blocks of the original video frame tend to be very close. These close values are inherited to the obscured frame in this encryption order. The attacker might determine which blocks might be neighbors using this information. For that reason, we have changed the encryption order, i.e. first puzzling then obscuring. The edges of neighbor blocks will now have significantly different values so that such an attack is avoided.

6   Final Remarks

In this paper we presented the improved video encryption algorithm *Puzzle* for encrypting video communication in real-time. *Puzzle* is a compression-independent encryption algorithm which can be easily integrated into available multimedia applications. It provides a good trade-off between security demands and encryption efficiency. *Puzzle* achieves a sufficiently fast encryption speed to meet the real-time requirements of most used multimedia applications, especially for high resolution video streams. *Puzzle* withstands most important cryptanalysis attacks. By changing the order of the encryption steps the algorithm has become resistant against differential attacks. We use *Puzzle* as part of the security architecture of our multiparty P2P video conference system BRAVIS [18] to ensuring confidential talks over the Internet.

References

1. NIST: Advanced Encryption Standard. FIPS 197, 2001.
2. I. Agi and L. Gong: An Empirical Study of MPEG Video Transmission. NDSS'96, pp.137-144, 1996.
3. B. G. Haskell, A. Puri, and A. N. Netravali: Digital Video: An Introduction to MPEG-2. Kluwer Academic Publishers, 1996.
4. B. Fuhrt and D. Kirovski: Eds. Multimedia Security Handbook, CRC Press, 2004.
5. X. Liu and A. M. Eskicioglu: Selective Encryption of Multimedia Content in Distribution Networks: Challenges and New Directions. IASTED International Conference on Communications, Internet and Information Technology (CIIT), 2003.
6. L. Tang: Methods for Encrypting and Decrypting MPEG Video Data Efficiently. In Proceedings ACM International Conference on Multimedia, pp.219-229, 1996.

7. C. Shi, S. Y. Wang, and B. Bhargava: MPEG Video Encryption in Real-Time Using Secret Key Cryptography. PDATA'99, 1999.
8. W. Zeng and S. Lei: Efficient Frequency Domain Selective Scrambling of Digital Video. IEEE Transactions on Multimedia, 2002.
9. C.–P. Wu and C.-C. J. Kuo: Efficient Multimedia Encryption via Entropy Codec Design. SPIE Int. Symposium on Electronic Imaging 2001, Vol. 4314, 2001.
10. G. A. Spanos and T. B. Maples: Performance Study of a Selective Encryption Scheme for the Security of Networked Real-time Video. ICCCN, pp. 2-10, 1995.
11. Y. Li, Z. Chen, S. –M. Tan, and R. H. Campbell: Security Enhanced MPEG Player. IEEE 1st International Workshop on Multimedia Software, 1996.
12. L.Qiao and K. Nahrstedt: Comparison of MPEG Encryption Algorithms. Computer and Graphics 22 (1998) 4, pp.437-448.
13. F. Liu and H. Koenig: A Novel Encryption Algorithm for High Resolution Video. In Proceeding of ACM NOSSDAV'05, pp.69-74, 2005.
14. A. J. Menezes, P. C. van Oorschot, and S. A. Vanstone: Handbook of Applied Cryptography. CRC Press Series on Discrete Mathematics and its Applications. CRC Press, 1997.
15. E.Biham and A.Shamir: Differential Cryptanalysis of the Full 16-round DES. Advances in Cryptology-CRYPTO'92. Springer. pp.487-496, 1992.
16. P. Rogaway and D. Coppersmith: A software-optimized encryption algorithm. Proceedings of the 1st International Workshop on Fast Software Encryption, Springer, pp.56-63, 1993.
17. M. Dworkin: Recommendation for Block Cipher Modes of Operation, Methods, and Techniques. NIST Special Publication 800-38A, Dec.2001.
18. The BRAVIS video conference system. http://www.bravis.tu-cottbus.de.

Appendix: Generation of the Permutation List

Algorithm Permutation list generation
   Input: A key stream $S=s_1s_2...s_l$, n -- number of blocks in the compressed video data V
   Output: A permutation list $P=p_1p_2..p_{n/2}$.

---

   begin
      Let A be an auxiliary sequence $A=a_1a_2...a_{n/2}$, its value of an element is
      $a_i = i+n/2,\ 1\le i \le n/2$;

      Define D as another auxiliary sequence which is used to temporarily save the value selected from the key stream S;
      for $i=1$ **to** l **do**
         /* Make the value of every element in S ranging from 1+n/2 to n. */
         if $((s_i\ mod\ n)\le n/2)$ $s_i= (s_i\ mod\ n)+n/2$;
            else $s_i= s_i\ mod\ n$;
         end if
      Put s_i in the auxiliary sequence D without repetition;
      Extract s_i from the sequence A and build sequence $\{A\text{-}D\}$;
      end for;
         /* Get the permutation list P, || denotes the append operation. */
         $P=D||\{A\text{-}D\}$;
      end

Selective Image Encryption Using JBIG

Roman Pfarrhofer[1] and Andreas Uhl[1,2]

[1] School of Telematics & Network Engineering,
Carinthia Tech Institute (CTI),
A-9020 Klagenfurt, Austria
[2] Department of Scientific Computing,
Salzburg University,
A-5020 Salzburg, Austria

Abstract. Selective encryption techniques of JBIG encoded visual data are discussed. We are able to show attack resistance against common image processing attacks and replacement attacks even in case of restricting the amount of encryption to 1% – 2% of the data. The low encryption effort required is due to the exploitation of the interdependencies among resolution layers in the JBIG hierarchical progressive coding mode.

1 Introduction

Encryption schemes for multimedia data need to be specifically designed to protect multimedia content and fulfil the security requirements for a particular multimedia application [9]. For example, real-time encryption of an entire video stream using classical ciphers requires heavy computation due to the large amounts of data involved, but many multimedia applications require security on a much lower level (e.g. TV news broadcasting [17]). In this context, several selective encryption schemes have been proposed recently which do not strive for maximum security, but trade off security for computational complexity.

Several reviews have been published on image and video encryption including selective (or partial) encryption methods providing a more or less complete overview of the techniques proposed so far [24]. Kunkelmann [12, 11] and Qiao and Nahrstedt [22] provide overviews, comparisons, and assessments of classical encryption schemes for visual data with emphasis on MPEG proposed up to 1998. Bhargava et al. [1] review four MPEG encryption algorithms published by the authors themselves in the period 1997 – 1999. More recent MPEG encryption surveys are provided by But [2] (where the suitability of available MPEG-1 ciphers for streaming video is assessed) and Lookabaugh et al. [15] (who focus on a cryptanalysis of MPEG-2 ciphers; in [14] the authors discuss MPEG-2 encryption as an example for selective encryption in consumer applications, the paper having broader scope though).

Of course, other data formats have been discussed with respect to selective encryption as well (Liu and Eskicioglu [16] give an overview with focus on shortcomings of current schemes and future issues): coding schemes based on wavelets [21], quadtrees [4, 13], iterated function systems (fractal coding) [23], and vector quantization [3] have been used to create selective encryption schemes.

J. Dittmann, S. Katzenbeisser, and A. Uhl (Eds.): CMS 2005, LNCS 3677, pp. 98–107, 2005.

In case a selective encryption process requires a multimedia bitstream to be parsed in order to identify the parts to be subjected to encryption, the problem of high processing overhead occurs in general. For example, in order to selectively protect DC and large AC coefficients of a JPEG image (as suggested by some authors), the file needs to be parsed for the EOB symbols 0x00 to identify the start of a new 8×8 pixels block (with two exceptions: if 0xFF is followed by 0x00, 0x00 is used as a stuffbit and has to be ignored and if AC63 (the last AC-Coefficient) not equals 0 there will be no 0x00 and the AC coefficients have to be counted). Under such circumstances, selective encryption will not help to reduce the processing demands of the entire application [20].

A possible solution to this problem is to use the visual data in the form of progressive, scalable, or embedded bitstreams. In such bitstreams the data is already organized in layers according to its visual importance due to the compression procedure and the bitstreams do not have to be parsed to identify the parts that should be protected by the encryption process. In previous work, several suggestions have been made to exploit the base and enhancement layer structure of the MPEG-2/4 scalable profiles [5, 7, 8, 12, 25] as well as to use embedded bitstreams like SPIHT [4] and JPEG 2000 [10, 18] to construct efficient selective encryption schemes.

In this work we propose a selective encryption scheme with extremely low encryption demand focussed onto losslessly encoded imagery which is based on the hierarchical progressive coding mode of JBIG. In order to be able to process grayscale images with this JBIG based approach, we use a bitplane representation which has been discussed before in the context of selective bitplane encryption [6, 19]. The JBIG based approach improves the latter techniques significantly. Section 2 reviews the basic functionalities of the JBIG format. Section 3 explains how to exploit the JBIG format properties for selective encryption and provides experimental results showing evidence of our schemes' effectiveness and ability to withstand attacks. Concluding remarks are given in section 4.

2   JBIG Basics

Joint Binary Image Experts Group is an ITU standard (ITU recommendation T.82) finalized in 1993 for compressing binary images and was meant to improve the fax compression standards of that time especially with respect to the coding of halftoned images.

JBIGs core coding engine is a binary context-based adaptive arithmetic coder similar to the IBM Q-coder. In this section we will mainly focus on the hierarchical progressive coding mode of JBIG since the understanding of the associated techniques is crucial for the selective encryption technique described subsequently. As a first step a binary multiresultion hierarchy is being constructed as shown in Fig. 1.

Simple downsampling by two violates the Nyquist sampling theorem and leads to severe artifacts especially for typed documents and halftoned images. Therefore, a linear recursive IIR filter employing a 3×3 window in the higher re-

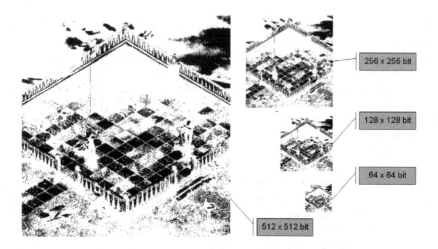

Fig. 1. Resolution layers of JBIGs hierarchical progressive mode

sulution level and 3 neighbouring samples from the already filtered low resolution image is used to create the low-pass filtered versions of the binary image.

When feeding these binary images into the arithmetic coder, for all resolution layers except the lowest one the context used within the coder consists of 6 neighbouring pixels of the currently encoded resolution layer and employs as well 4 neighbouring pixels of the already encoded layer with lower resolution to exploit the correlations among the resolution layers. This leads to significantly lower entropy values for the pixels to be coded in the higher resultion layers. Additionally, two strategies bypass the arithmetic coder if pixel values may be determined without encoding the actual values:

– Deterministic prediction (DP): based on knowledge about neighbouring pixel values of the current resolution layer, neighbouring pixel values of the layer with lower resolution, and the rule how the multiresolution hierarchy has been built, some pixel values are known without explicitly encoding them, the values may be derived from the other data.
– Typical prediction (TP): in the lowest resolution layer this means that identical lines are coded only once. A following identical line is labelled as being "typical" by setting a corresponding flag and the content is not fed into the coder. In the remaining layers, for a "typical" pixel being surrounded by pixels of the same colour follows that the corresponding four pixels in the next higher resolution layer have the same colour. A line is labelled as "typical" if it entirely consists of typical pixels and a corresponding flag is being set. Based on this technique, large homogeneous regions may be reconstructed without actually decoding a single pixel.

Note that by using cross-layer contexts, DP, and TP a high amount of dependency among resolution layers is used for encoding the data. As a consequence, if parts of the data are lost for some reason, the errors caused by the missing data are propagated into the other resolution layers originally not affected by data loss.

In addition to the hierarchical layer structure, JBIG supports to partition the input image and all lower resolution layers into equally sized horizontal stripes. Accordingly, the entities encoded independently into the bitstream are denoted "stripe data entities" (SDE) which may be ordered in different manners. This has to be synchronized between encoder and decoder of course.

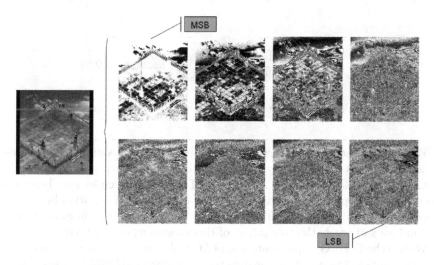

Fig. 2. Splitting an 8bpp image into its 8 bitplanes

In order to be able to compress grayscale images with JBIG, the grayscale images are split into a bitplane representation (e.g. 8 bitplanes for a 8bpp grayscale image as shown in Fig. 2), subsequently the bitplanes are JBIG compressed independently.

3   Selective Encryption Using JBIG

In previous work we have used the bitplane representation as described in the last section for selective encryption [19] – after splitting a grayscale image into its bitplanes, only a fraction of these planes (starting with the MSB) can be encrypted. It turns out that this approach is vulnerable by replacement and reconstruction attacks and therefore a secure setting requires up to 50% of the data to be encrypted. This approach is shown in the upper half of Fig. 3 (note that the processing of 4 bitplanes requires only the encryption of 35% of the JBIG encoded image in this case since planes close to the MSB can be compressed more efficiently of course).

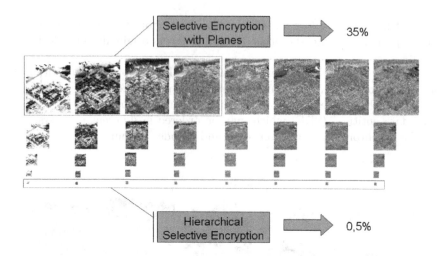

Fig. 3. Selective bitplane encryption vs. JBIG based encryption

When using the JBIG hierarchy for selective encryption only the lowest resolution of 5 layers may be encrypted, in this case for all bitplanes. This results in encrypting 0.5% of the original data only. These two principles may be mixed additionally: it is possible to limit encryption to a subset of reslution layers of a selected set of bitplanes only. In the following subsections, we will evaluate this idea and we will assess the robustness of this scheme against attacks.

We use the C JBIG implementation of M. Kuhn available via *anonymous ftp* from ftp.uni-erlangen.de in the directory pub/doc/ISO/JBIG/. This software has been extended to support encryption of arbitrary SDEs, for encryption we use the C++ AES implementation of B. Gladman[1] in CFB mode to avoid data padding for block completion. Our software avoids unwanted marker emulation by simply skipping parts of the encryption keystream in that case. For the subsequent experiments, we use 8bpp 512 × 512 grayscale images (see Fig. 4) and set the lowest resolution in JBIG to 32 × 32 pixels.

3.1   Reduction of Encryption Effort

The most extreme case in our setting is to encrypt the lowest resolution layer of the MSB only. This corresponds to encrypting 0.056% and 0.066% of the JBIG encoded Escher and Lena images, respectively. Fig. 5(a) shows the directly reconstructed Lena image where a significant amount of high frequency information is still visible (see Fig. 7 left for the Escher image case). Additionally, we know from analysis in [19] that encrypting MSB data only is highly insecure against attacks.

We know furthermore from previous results that restricting the encryption operation to a low number of bitplanes does not lead to satisfying results with

---

[1] http://fp.gladman.plus.com/AES/index.htm

(a) Lena   (b) Escher painting

Fig. 4. Test images

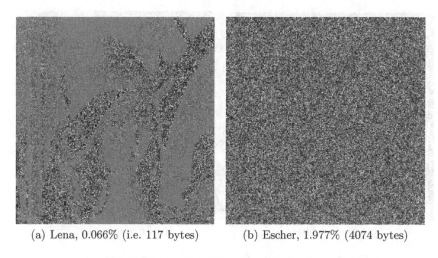

(a) Lena, 0.066% (i.e. 117 bytes)   (b) Escher, 1.977% (4074 bytes)

Fig. 5. Encrypting different amounts of data

respect to securtiy. Therefore, we slightly increase the amount of data subject to encryption by protecting the lowest resolution layer of 4 bitplanes, starting from the MSB. This results in encrypting 0.265% of the JBIG encoded Escher image (see Fig. 8 left for a visual impression of the directly reconstructed data where no structures related to the image are visible any more). As we shall see later, this setting is already almost satisfactory from the security standpoint.

Finally, we look at the most secure setting considered in this context where we encrypt the two lowest resolution layers of all bitplanes. This still limits the amount of encrypted data to 1.977% and 2.292% for the Escher and Lena images, respectively. We show an example of a directly reconstructed Escher image in Fig. 5(b).

3.2   Attack Resistance

For testing attack resistance, we apply the following operations to the selectively encrypted images:

– Median filtering
– Edge detection (for the latter two attacks, we use the corresponding default Paint Shop Pro© algorithms)
– Replacement attack: the encrypted data used in the reconstruction process introduces a noise like pattern into the image. Therefore, we replace the encrypted data by constant zero data. We compensate for the change in average luminance as described in [19].

We first investigate the most extreme setting where only the lowest layer of the MSB bitplane is encrypted (compare Fig. 5(a) for the Lena case and Fig. 7 left for Escher). Neither median filtering nor edge detection do reveal the content of the image to a satisfying extent (see Fig. 6).

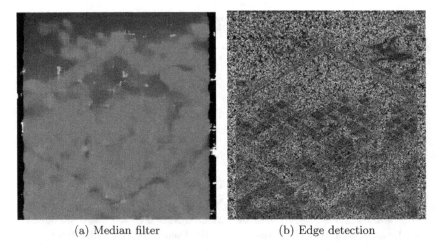

(a) Median filter   (b) Edge detection

Fig. 6. Attack results: Escher image, 0.056% encrypted

However, the replacement attack shows to be effective in this setting (based on the results in [19], this is not surprising of course) which means that this parameter choice is not secure enough – Fig. 7 clearly shows the main structures of the original image.

When increasing the amount of encryption to 0.265% (by encrypting the lowest resolution layer of 4 bitplanes), we realize that now not even the replacement attack is able to deliver results that give any detailed information about the encrypted image (see Fig. 8).

As a consequence, the scenario when encrypting the lowest two resolution layers of all bitplanes (as shown in Fig. 5(b)) can be considered secure in any case.

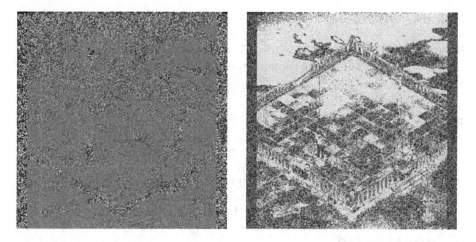

Fig. 7. Escher image (0.056% encrypted), direct reconstruction & replacement attack

Fig. 8. Escher image (0.265% encrypted), direct reconstruction & replacement attack

4   Conclusion

We have discussed selective encryption of JBIG encoded visual data exploiting the interdependencies among resolution layers in the JBIG hierarchical progressive coding mode. Contrasting to earlier ideas when selectively encrypting a subset of bitplanes, we are able to show attack resistance even in case of restricting the amount of encryption to 1% – 2% of the data only. The extremely low amount of data required to be protected in our technique also allows the use of public-key cryptography thereby simplifying key management issues.

Acknowledgements

Most of this work has been done at CTI in the context of a system security lab in summer term 2003. Partial support by the Austrian Science Fund, project no. 15170, is acknowledged.

References

[1] B. Bhargava, C. Shi, and Y. Wang. MPEG video encryption algorithms. *Multimedia Tools and Applications*, 24(1):57–79, 2004.

[2] Jason But. Limitations of existing MPEG-1 ciphers for streaming video. Technical Report CAIA 040429A, Swinburne University, Australia, April 2004.

[3] T. S. Chen, C. C. Chang, and M. S. Hwang. Virtual image cryptosystem based upon vector quantization. *IEEE Transactions on Image Processing*, 7(10):1485–1488, October 1998.

[4] H. Cheng and X. Li. Partial encryption of compressed images and videos. *IEEE Transactions on Signal Processing*, 48(8):2439–2451, 2000.

[5] Jana Dittmann and Ralf Steinmetz. Enabling technology for the trading of MPEG-encoded video. In *Information Security and Privacy: Second Australasian Conference, ACISP '97*, volume 1270, pages 314–324, July 1997.

[6] Marc Van Droogenbroeck and Raphaël Benedett. Techniques for a selective encryption of uncompressed and compressed images. In *Proceedings of ACIVS (Advanced Concepts for Intelligent Vision Systems)*, pages 90–97, Ghent University, Belgium, September 2002.

[7] Ahmet Eskicioglu and Edward J. Delp. An integrated approach to encrypting scalable video. In *Proceedings of the IEEE International Conference on Multimedia and Expo, ICME '02*, Laussanne, Switzerland, August 2002.

[8] Mark M. Fisch, Herbert Stögner, and Andreas Uhl. Layered encryption techniques for DCT-coded visual data. In *Proceedings (CD-ROM) of the European Signal Processing Conference, EUSIPCO '04*, Vienna, Austria, September 2004. paper cr1361.

[9] B. Furht and D. Kirovski, editors. *Multimedia Security Handbook*. CRC Press, Boca Raton, Florida, 2005.

[10] Raphaël Grosbois, Pierre Gerbelot, and Touradj Ebrahimi. Authentication and access control in the JPEG 2000 compressed domain. In A.G. Tescher, editor, *Applications of Digital Image Processing XXIV*, volume 4472 of *Proceedings of SPIE*, pages 95–104, San Diego, CA, USA, July 2001.

[11] T. Kunkelmann. *Sicherheit für Videodaten*. Vieweg Verlag, 1998.

[12] Thomas Kunkelmann. Applying encryption to video communication. In *Proceedings of the Multimedia and Security Workshop at ACM Multimedia '98*, pages 41–47, Bristol, England, September 1998.

[13] X. Li, J. Knipe, and H. Cheng. Image compression and encryption using tree structure. *Pattern Recognition Letters*, 18:1253–1259, 1997.

[14] T. D. Lookabaugh and D. C. Sicker. Selective encryption for consumer applications. *IEEE Communications Magazine*, 42(5):124–129, 2004.

[15] T. D. Lookabaugh, D. C. Sicker, D. M. Keaton, W. Y. Guo, and I. Vedula. Security analysis of selectiveley encrypted MPEG-2 streams. In *Multimedia Systems and Applications VI*, volume 5241 of *Proceedings of SPIE*, pages 10–21, September 2003.

[16] Xiliang Lu and Ahmet M. Eskicioglu. Selective encryption of multimedia content in distribution networks: Challenges and new directions. In *Proceedings of the IASTED International Conference on on Communications, Internet and Information Technology (CIIT 2003)*, Scottsdale, AZ, USA, November 2003.

[17] Benoit M. Macq and Jean-Jacques Quisquater. Cryptology for digital TV broadcasting. *Proceedings of the IEEE*, 83(6):944–957, June 1995.

[18] Roland Norcen and Andreas Uhl. Selective encryption of the JPEG2000 bitstream. In A. Lioy and D. Mazzocchi, editors, *Communications and Multimedia Security. Proceedings of the IFIP TC6/TC11 Sixth Joint Working Conference on Communications and Multimedia Security, CMS '03*, volume 2828 of *Lecture Notes on Computer Science*, pages 194 – 204, Turin, Italy, October 2003. Springer-Verlag.

[19] M. Podesser, H.-P. Schmidt, and A. Uhl. Selective bitplane encryption for secure transmission of image data in mobile environments. In *CD-ROM Proceedings of the 5th IEEE Nordic Signal Processing Symposium (NORSIG 2002)*, Tromso-Trondheim, Norway, October 2002. IEEE Norway Section. file cr1037.pdf.

[20] A. Pommer and A. Uhl. Application scenarios for selective encryption of visual data. In J. Dittmann, J. Fridrich, and P. Wohlmacher, editors, *Multimedia and Security Workshop, ACM Multimedia*, pages 71–74, Juan-les-Pins, France, December 2002.

[21] A. Pommer and A. Uhl. Selective encryption of wavelet-packet encoded image data — efficiency and security. *ACM Multimedia Systems (Special issue on Multimedia Security)*, 9(3):279–287, 2003.

[22] Lintian Qiao and Klara Nahrstedt. Comparison of MPEG encryption algorithms. *International Journal on Computers and Graphics (Special Issue on Data Security in Image Communication and Networks)*, 22(3):437–444, 1998.

[23] Stephane Roche, Jean-Luc Dugelay, and R. Molva. Multi-resolution access control algorithm based on fractal coding. In *Proceedings of the IEEE International Conference on Image Processing (ICIP'96)*, pages 235–238, Lausanne, Switzerland, September 1996. IEEE Signal Processing Society.

[24] A. Uhl and A. Pommer. *Image and Video Encryption. From Digital Rights Management to Secured Personal Communication*, volume 15 of *Advances in Information Security*. Springer-Verlag, 2005.

[25] C. Yuan, B. B. Zhu, Y. Wang, S. Li, and Y. Zhong. Efficient and fully scalable encryption for MPEG-4 FGS. In *IEEE International Symposium on Circuits and Systems (ISCAS'03)*, Bangkok, Thailand, May 2003.

On Reversibility of Random Binning Techniques: Multimedia Perspectives

Sviatoslav Voloshynovskiy[1], Oleksiy Koval[1], Emre Topak[1],
José Emilio Vila-Forcén[1], Pedro Comesaña Alfaro[2], and Thierry Pun[1]

[1] CUI-University of Geneva, Stochastic Image Processing Group,
24, rue du Général-Dufour, 1211 Genève 4, Switzerland
[2] Signal Processing in Communications Group,
Signal Theory & Communications Department, University of Vigo, 36200 Vigo, Spain
{svolos, Oleksiy.Koval, Emre.Topak, Jose.Vila, Thierry.Pun}@cui.unige.ch
pcomesan@gts.tsc.uvigo.es

Abstract. In this paper, we analyze a possibility of reversibility of data-hiding techniques based on random binning from multimedia perspectives. We demonstrate the capabilities of unauthorized users to perform hidden data removal using solely a signal processing approach based on optimal estimation as well as consider reversibility on the side of authorized users who have the knowledge of key used for the message hiding.

1 Introduction

Digital data-hiding appeared as an emerging tool for multimedia security, processing and management. A tremendous amount of possible applications have been recently reported that include copyright protection, tamper proofing, content integrity verification, steganography and watermark-assisted media processing such as multimedia indexing, retrieval and quality enhancement [1].

Most of these applications are facing an important problem of host interference. The related issue in communications under the assumption of a fixed channel was considered by Gel'fand and Pinsker [2]. Costa considered the Gel'fand-Pinsker problem in a Gaussian formulation and mean squared distortion criteria and demonstrated that the capacity of the Gaussian channel with the Gaussian interfering host can be equal to the capacity of interference-free communications using *random binning*-based codebook design [3]. Recent advantages in the design of practical capacity achieving codes makes this technique even more attractive for various purposes [4].

The wide practical use of the Gel'fand-Pinsker set-up has raised a number of problems related to its performance and reversibility in various multimedia applications. Although these aspects seem to be unrelated from the first point of view, there exist a lot in common among these issues that can throw more light on the optimal design of binning-based techniques.

Therefore, the goal of this paper is to reveal these relationships on the side of data-hider in multimedia applications. Similar framework for the case of descrete alphabets was considered by Eggers *et al.* [5].

J. Dittmann, S. Katzenbeisser, and A. Uhl (Eds.): CMS 2005, LNCS 3677, pp. 108–118, 2005.
© IFIP International Federation for Information Processing 2005

The paper has the following structure. The basic information-theoretic set-up of side information-assisted data-hiding is considered in Section 2. Section 3 presents the analysis of reversibility problem from multimedia perspectives for both unauthorized and authorized users. The experimental results demonstrating the validity of presented theoretical analysis are given in Section 4. Finally, Section 5 concludes the paper and presents some future research perspectives.

Notations. We use capital letters to denote scalar random variables X, bold capital letters to denote vector random variables $\mathbf{X}$, corresponding small letters x and $\mathbf{x}$ to denote the realizations of scalar and vector random variables, respectively. The superscript N is used to designate length-N vectors $\mathbf{x} = x^N = [x[1], x[2], ..., x[N]]^T$ with k^{th} element $x[k]$. We use $X \sim p_X(x)$ or simply $X \sim p(x)$ to indicate that a random variable X is distributed according to $p_X(x)$. The mathematical expectation of a random variable $X \sim p_X(x)$ is denoted by $E_{p_X}[X]$ or simply by $E[X]$ and $Var[X]$ denotes the variance of X. Calligraphic fonts $\mathcal{X}$ denote sets $X \in \mathcal{X}$ and $|\mathcal{X}|$ denotes the cardinality of set $\mathcal{X}$. $\mathbf{I}_N$ denotes the $N \times N$ identity matrix. We also define the watermark-to-image ratio (WIR) as WIR$=10\log_{10}\frac{\sigma_W^2}{\sigma_X^2}$ and the watermark-to-noise ratio (WNR) as WNR $= 10\log_{10}\frac{\sigma_W^2}{\sigma_Z^2}$, where σ_X^2, σ_W^2, σ_Z^2 represent the variances of host data, watermark and noise, respectively.

2 Gel'fand-Pinsker Set-Up: Random Binning in Data-Hiding

In this section we consider the Gel'fand-Pinsker problem in data-hiding formulation. The generalized block-diagram of this set-up is shown in Figure 1.

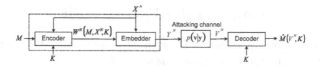

Fig. 1. Generalized Gel'fand-Pinsker channel coding with side information at the encoder: data-hiding formulation

In this scenario, the data-hider has access to the uniquely assigned secret key $K = k$, uniformly distributed over the set $\mathcal{K} = \{1, 2, ..., |\mathcal{K}|\}$ of cardinality $|\mathcal{K}|$, and to the non-causal interference $\mathbf{x} \in \mathcal{X}^N$. A message $m \in \mathcal{M}$ is uniformly distributed over $\mathcal{M} = \{1, 2, ..., |\mathcal{M}|\}$, with $|\mathcal{M}| = 2^{NR}$, where R is the data-hiding rate. It is assumed that the stego and attacked data are defined on $\mathbf{y} \in \mathcal{Y}^N$ and $\mathbf{v} \in \mathcal{V}^N$, respectively. The length N vector distortion function is defined as:

$$d^N(\mathbf{x}, \mathbf{y}) = \frac{1}{N}\sum_{i=1}^{N} d(x_i, y_i), \tag{1}$$

where $d(x_i, y_i)$ denotes element-wise distortion between x_i and y_i.

Definition 1: A *discrete memoryless data-hiding channel* consists of five alphabets $\mathcal{X}$, $\mathcal{K}$, $\mathcal{W}$, $\mathcal{Y}$, $\mathcal{V}$ and a transition probability matrix $p_{V|W,X}(v|w,x) = p_{Y|W,X}(y|w,x)p_{V|Y}(v|y)$. The attack channel is subject to the distortion constraint D^A:

$$\sum_{\mathbf{y} \in \mathcal{Y}^N} \sum_{\mathbf{v} \in \mathcal{V}^N} d^N(\mathbf{y},\mathbf{v}) p_{V|Y}(\mathbf{v}|\mathbf{y}) p_Y(\mathbf{y}) \leq D^A, \tag{2}$$

where $p_{V|Y}(\mathbf{v}|\mathbf{y}) = \prod_{i=1}^N p_{V|Y}p(v_i|y_i)$.

Definition 2: A $(2^{NR}, N)$ code for data-hiding channel consists of a *message set* $\mathcal{M} = \{1,2,...,2^{NR}\}$, an *encoding function:* $f^N : \mathcal{M} \times \mathcal{X}^N \times \mathcal{K} \rightarrow \mathcal{W}^N$, an *embedding function:* $\varphi^N : \mathcal{W}^N \times \mathcal{X}^N \rightarrow \mathcal{Y}^N$, subject to the embedding distortion constraint D^E: $\frac{1}{|\mathcal{K}||\mathcal{M}|} \sum_{k \in \mathcal{K}} \sum_{m \in \mathcal{M}} \sum_{\mathbf{x} \in \mathcal{X}^N} d^N(\mathbf{x}, \varphi^N(f^N(m,\mathbf{x},k),\mathbf{x})) p_{\mathbf{X}}(\mathbf{x}) \leq D^E$ and a *decoding function:* $g^N : \mathcal{V}^N \times \mathcal{K} \rightarrow \mathcal{M}$.

We define the *average probability of error* for a $(2^{NR}, N)$ code as:

$$P_e^{(N)} = \frac{1}{|\mathcal{M}|} \sum_{m \in \mathcal{M}} Pr[g^N(\mathbf{V},K) \neq m | M = m]. \tag{3}$$

Definition 3: A rate $R = \frac{1}{N} \log_2 |\mathcal{M}|$ is achievable for the distortions (D^E, D^A), if there exists a sequence $(2^{NR}, N)$ codes with $P_e^{(N)} \rightarrow 0$ as $N \rightarrow \infty$.

Definition 4: The capacity of the data-hiding channel is the supremum of all achievable rates.

Theorem 1 (Data-hiding capacity for the fixed channel): A rate R is achievable for the distortion D^E and the attack channel $p(v|y)$, with the bounded distortion D^A, iff $R < C$, where:

$$C = \max_{p(u,w|x,k)} [I(U;V|K) - I(U;X|K)], \tag{4}$$

and U to be a random variable $u \in \mathcal{U}$, with $|\mathcal{U}| \leq \min\{|\mathcal{W}|, |\mathcal{Y}|\} + |\mathcal{X}| - 1$. We also assume that $p(u,w|x,k) = p(u|x,k)p(w|u,x,k)$.

The details of this theorem proof in more general form of active attacker are provided in [6]. The main difference with our set-up is the codebook construction and the corresponding interpretation of the user key. In the scope of this paper, the key K is considered uniquely as the index that defines the codebook of a particular user. Contrarily, in [6] the key represents a side information shared between the encoder and the decoder and can be in some relationship with X. Therefore, we assume that K is solely an independent of X cryptographic key.

2.1   Costa Set-Up: Gaussian Assumption

Costa considered the Gel'fand-Pinsker problem for the Gaussian context and mean-square error distance [3]. The corresponding fixed channel $p_{V|W,X}(v|w,x)$ is the Gaussian one with $X \sim \mathcal{N}(0, \sigma_X^2)$ and additive $Z \sim \mathcal{N}(0, \sigma_Z^2)$ (Figure 2).

The auxiliary random variable was chosen in the form $U = W + \alpha X$ with optimization parameter α to maximize the rate:

$$R(\alpha) = \tfrac{1}{2} \log_2 \frac{\sigma_W^2 (\sigma_W^2 + \sigma_X^2 + \sigma_Z^2)}{\sigma_W^2 \sigma_X^2 (1-\alpha)^2 + \sigma_Z^2 (\sigma_W^2 + \alpha^2 \sigma_X^2)}. \tag{5}$$

Costa has shown that if $\alpha = \alpha_{opt} = \frac{\sigma_W^2}{\sigma_W^2 + \sigma_Z^2}$ that requires the knowledge of σ_Z^2 at the encoder, $R(\alpha_{opt})$ does not depend on the host variance and:

$$R(\alpha_{opt}) = C^{\text{AWGN}} = \tfrac{1}{2} \log_2 \left(1 + \frac{\sigma_W^2}{\sigma_Z^2} \right) \tag{6}$$

that corresponds to the capacity of AWGN channel without host interference.

It is important to note that the number of codewords in each message bin of the Gel'fand-Pinsker set-up is approximately equal to $2^{NI(U;X|K)}$. In the Costa set-up, $I(U; X|K) = \tfrac{1}{2} \log_2 \left(1 + \alpha^2 \frac{\sigma_X^2}{\sigma_W^2} \right)$. Thus, the larger variance of the host σ_X^2, the larger number of codewords is needed at the encoder at each bin.

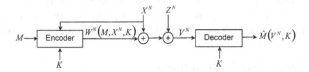

Fig. 2. Costa channel coding with the host state information at the encoder

3   Reversibility of Random Binning

3.1   Unauthorized User Reversibility

In multimedia applications, the unauthorized users are considered not to have access to the secret key used for the data-hiding. Nevertheless, these users might be motivated in certain circumstances [7] to estimate the original image $\mathbf{X}$ given noisy version of stego data $\mathbf{V}$ (Figure 3).

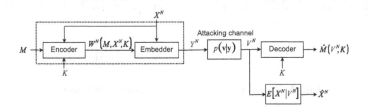

Fig. 3. Reversibility set-up for the unauthorized user

Assume that in this set-up $\mathbf{X} \sim \mathcal{N}(0, \sigma_X^2 \mathbf{I}_N)$, $\mathbf{W} \sim \mathcal{N}(0, \sigma_W^2 \mathbf{I}_N)$ and $\mathbf{Z} \sim \mathcal{N}(0, \sigma_Z^2 \mathbf{I}_N)$. In this case, the embedding distortion is $D^E = \sigma_W^2$ and the attacker distortion corresponds to the variance of AWGN, i.e., $D^A = \sigma_Z^2$.

To estimate **X**, one can use either minimum mean squared error (MMSE) or maximum a posteriori probability (MAP) estimators that coincide in the case of Gaussian set-up. The MMSE estimate of the unauthorized user is obtained as:

$$\hat{\mathbf{X}} = E[\mathbf{X}|\mathbf{V}]. \tag{7}$$

Assuming $\mathbf{v} = \mathbf{x} + \mathbf{w} + \mathbf{z}$, one obtains the following MMSE estimate [8]:

$$\hat{\mathbf{X}} = \frac{\sigma_X^2}{\sigma_X^2 + \sigma_W^2 + \sigma_Z^2} \mathbf{V}. \tag{8}$$

The variance of this estimate D_{MMSE}^r is given by:

$$D_{\mathrm{MMSE}}^r = E[d^N(\hat{\mathbf{X}}, \mathbf{X})] = \frac{\sigma_X^2(\sigma_W^2 + \sigma_Z^2)}{\sigma_X^2 + \sigma_W^2 + \sigma_Z^2}. \tag{9}$$

It is important to note that $\widehat{\mathbf{X}}$ depends on the variances of original image, watermark and noise. In the asymptotic case of infinitely large image variance ($\sigma_X^2 \rightarrow \infty$) that corresponds to the highly textured regions in images or edges, no reliable estimate is possible. Moreover, perfect host restoration is not possible in this set-up even in the noiseless case ($\sigma_Z^2 = 0$) due to the watermark presence that reflects the price of lack of information for the unauthorized users.

3.2 Authorized User Reversibility

In the case of authorized user, the secret key used for data-hiding at the encoder is available at the decoder side. The knowledge of the key considerably extends the possibilities of image restoration on the decoder side in comparison with the unauthorized user. The block-diagram of this set-up is shown in Figure 4.

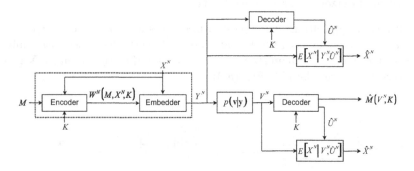

Fig. 4. Reversibility set-up for the authorized user

Several scenarios are possible. *Scenario (A) (noisy case)*. This scenario refers to the situation when the data-hider designs the scheme for a particular fixed channel $p(v|y)$, certain achievable rate and corresponding codebook construction. The decoder should properly estimate the sent message based on **V** and K. At the same time, the authorized user is interested to estimate the host based on the available possibly distorted data $\mathbf{V}$ using the mapping $\psi^N : \mathcal{V}^N \times \mathcal{K} \to \hat{\mathcal{X}}^N$. The criterion that judges the performance of above mapping is defined based on the mean-squared estimation error similarly to the previous case, i.e.:

$$D^r = E[d^N(\hat{\mathbf{X}}, \mathbf{X})]. \qquad (10)$$

Therefore, the problem is to design the estimator ψ that produces the minimum mean-squared estimation error.

Scenario (B) (Noiseless Case). The second scenario of interest (upper part of Figure 4) refers to the situation when the data-hider designs the codebook for a particular fixed channel $p(v|y)$, performs data-hiding procedure and stores the data in the form of $\mathbf{Y}$ for himself and at the same time makes it available via the channel $p(v|y)$. After certain time, the data-hider finds it necessary to recover the original host data due to some reasons caused by the loss of original data, its unavailability due to the time or access restrictions. In these circumstances, the authorized user knows the key and has the undistorted watermarked data $\mathbf{Y}$. The problem now is formulated as the design of a proper mapper ψ that can produce MMSE estimation of $\mathbf{X}$ based on $\mathbf{Y}$. Moreover, it is of particular interest to establish a possibility to perfectly restore the original data $\mathbf{X}$, i.e., to achieve restoration distortion equal to zero.

We split our analysis in two parts. Firstly, we consider the reversibility of Gel'fand-Pinsker problem for the authorized user. Secondly, we analyze the Costa set-up to have a fair comparison with the previously considered scenario of unauthorized user reversibility.

The problem formulation that will be a common basis for the set-ups below can be given as follows. In the case of authorized user it is supposed that the distorted version of the watermarked data $\mathbf{V}$ and the key K are available. The problem is to design the estimate $\hat{\mathbf{X}}$ of the original data $\mathbf{X}$ based on $\mathbf{V}$ using all information about the data-hiding scheme design and corresponding codebook of the user defined by the key K. The quality of the obtained estimate should be validated by the restoration distortion D^r.

Reversibility of the Gel'fand-Pinsker Set-Up. In the analysis of Gel'fand-Pinsker set-up, we assume that the conditions of reliable message communications provided by the Theorem 1 are satisfied and $\hat{m} = m$ with $P_e^{(N)} \to 0$ as $N \to \infty$. This implies that given the distorted data v^N and the key k, the decoder can uniquely find a jointly typical pair $(u^N(m,j,k), v^N) \in A_\delta^{*(N)}(U,V)$[1], where $j \in \{1, 2, ..., J\}, J = 2^{NR'}, R' = I(U; X)$ is the number of bits that are used to represent the host, and it can declare that $\hat{m} = m$ and $\hat{u}^N = u^N$, where $\hat{u}^N$ is the estimate of u^N.

---

[1] Here and in the following we assume that the set $A_\delta^{*(N)}(U, X)$ is defined for a particular realization of the key $K = k$. Typical and jointly typical sets are defined in the strong sense, see [9], pp. 288 and 434.

In the noisy case (scenario A) (Figure 4) one can design a proper estimator of $\hat{x}^N$ based on v^N for the fixed channel $p(v|y)$ and errorless knowledge of u^N. The decoder forms the MMSE estimate $\hat{x}^N$ given v^N and u^N:

$$\hat{\mathbf{X}} = E[\mathbf{X}|\mathbf{V}, \mathbf{U}(\mathbf{W}(M, \mathbf{X}, K), \mathbf{X})], \qquad (11)$$

where we emphasize that u^N is a function of the known message m, key k and the host realization x^N itself.

In the noiseless case (scenario B), $v^N = y^N$ and $y^N = \varphi^N(x^N, w^N)$. Since $w^N = f^N(m, x^N, k)$ and assuming that $\hat{m} = m$ is correctly decoded that is obviously a case for the noiseless transmission and k is known, one can substitute w^N into y^N obtaining $y^N = \varphi^N(x^N, f^N(m, x^N, k))$ and find $\hat{x}^N$ assuming invertibility of functions $\varphi^N(.)$ and $f^N(.)$. In this case, $\hat{x}^N = x^N$ and the authorized user can obtain the perfect estimate of the original data at the decoder.

Reversibility of the Costa Set-Up. To practically validate the above framework, we consider reversibility of the Costa set-up assuming $\mathbf{X} \sim \mathcal{N}(\mathbf{0}, \sigma_X^2 \mathbf{I}_N)$, $\mathbf{W} \sim \mathcal{N}(\mathbf{0}, \sigma_W^2 \mathbf{I}_N)$ and $\mathbf{Z} \sim \mathcal{N}(\mathbf{0}, \sigma_Z^2 \mathbf{I}_N)$. The distorted version of the watermarked data $\mathbf{v} = \mathbf{x} + \mathbf{w} + \mathbf{z}$ is available at the decoder as well as the authorized user key k. This makes possible to find $\hat{\mathbf{u}}$ based on the jointly typical decoding in the k-specified codebook. Moreover, we assume that $\hat{\mathbf{u}} = \mathbf{u}$ meaning that the sent codeword can be recovered at the decoder. From the Costa assumption about the auxiliary random variable, one can express the watermark as:

$$\mathbf{W} = \mathbf{U} - \alpha\mathbf{X}. \qquad (12)$$

Substituting $\mathbf{W}$ into $\mathbf{V}$, one obtains:

$$\mathbf{V} = (1 - \alpha)\mathbf{X} + \mathbf{U} + \mathbf{Z}, \qquad (13)$$

because of $\hat{\mathbf{u}} = \mathbf{u}$ according to our assumption. The MMSE estimate of $\mathbf{X}$, $\hat{\mathbf{X}} = E[\mathbf{X}|\mathbf{V}, \mathbf{U}]$, assuming Gaussian data statistics is given by:

$$\hat{\mathbf{X}} = a\mathbf{V} + b\mathbf{U}, \qquad (14)$$

where $a = \sigma_X^2 \sigma_W^2 (1-\alpha)(-2\alpha\sigma_W^2\sigma_X^2 + \sigma_X^2\sigma_W^2 + \alpha^2\sigma_W^2\sigma_X^2 + \alpha^2\sigma_Z^2\sigma_X^2 + \sigma_Z^2\sigma_W^2)^{-1}$, $b = \sigma_X^2 (\sigma_W^2\alpha + \alpha\sigma_Z^2 - \sigma_W^2)(-2\alpha\sigma_W^2\sigma_X^2 + \sigma_X^2\sigma_W^2 + \alpha^2\sigma_W^2\sigma_X^2 + \alpha^2\sigma_Z^2\sigma_X^2 + \sigma_Z^2\sigma_W^2)^{-1}$.
The variance of this estimator is:

$$D^r(\alpha) = E[d^N(\hat{\mathbf{X}}, \mathbf{X})] = \frac{\sigma_X^2\sigma_W^2\sigma_Z^2}{\alpha^2\sigma_X^2\sigma_Z^2 + \sigma_W^2(\sigma_X^2(1-\alpha)^2 + \sigma_Z^2)}. \qquad (15)$$

In the noiseless case (scenario B), $\sigma_Z^2 = 0$, using (12) and assuming that $\alpha \neq 1$ and $\mathbf{V} = \mathbf{Y} = \mathbf{X} + \mathbf{W}$, the estimate (14) is reduced to:

$$\hat{\mathbf{X}} = \tfrac{1}{1-\alpha}(\mathbf{V} - \mathbf{U}) = \tfrac{1}{1-\alpha}(\mathbf{Y} - \mathbf{U}) = \tfrac{1}{1-\alpha}(\mathbf{X} + \mathbf{W} - \alpha\mathbf{X} - \mathbf{W}) = \mathbf{X} \qquad (16)$$

that leads to $D^r = 0$ and provides the perfect reversibility.

In the above analysis we have referred to the generic selection of the parameter α. However, it depends on the variance of the watermark and the noise, i.e., maximum allowed embedding and attacking distortions. Normally in the practice of the digital data-hiding, the actual value of the applied attack variance is rarely known in advance at the encoder. Thus, α is selected keeping in mind some critical, the least favorable, or average conditions of system applications. This definitely provides the mismatch between the optimal parameter and the actual one that leads to some decrease in the system performance in terms of maximum achievable rate that will be shown by the results of our simulation.

Nevertheless, it is interesting to investigate the hypothetical system performance in terms of reversibility, if one assumes the perfect knowledge of the operational scenario at the encoder that makes possible to choose the optimal parameter $\alpha = \alpha_{opt}$ according to the Costa result. In this case, substituting $\alpha_{opt} = \frac{\sigma_W^2}{\sigma_W^2 + \sigma_Z^2}$ into (15), one obtains:

$$D^r(\alpha_{opt}) = \frac{\sigma_X^2 (\sigma_W^2 + \sigma_Z^2)}{\sigma_W^2 + \sigma_X^2 + \sigma_Z^2} \qquad (17)$$

that coincides with the estimation variance of the unauthorized user (9). The Gel'fand-Pinsker/Costa set-ups are designed to maximize the rate of reliable communications but not to minimize possible distortion of the host communicated via the noisy channel. This justifies that side information-assisted host estimation accuracy in this set-up cannot exceed one provided by estimation without side information. Thus, this scheme is not the optimal one when two constraints are imposed simultaneously. The option of reversibility was considered as a granted one along the main line of reliable message communications.

4   Results of Computer Simulation

To confirm the theoretical findings, we have performed the experimental validation of different reversibility scenarios for the Gaussian set-up. Figure 5 summarizes the known results for the achievable rates of the Costa set-up (6) with different values of optimization parameter α for the WIR equal to -6 dB and -16 dB to underline the critical dependence of the achievable rates on the selection of α. While capacity of the AWGN channel is achieved for α_{opt} (6), the fixed α is not optimal for all WNRs in terms of achievable rate and one observes the rate loss. It is a natural price for the lack of prior information about attack variance at the encoder.

To investigate the impact of α on the restoration distortion, we have performed a number of simulations for different types of users. Firstly, assuming unauthorized user, who is aware only of the host, watermark and noise statistics, we have applied the MMSE estimation (8). The variance of this estimate D^r_{MMSE} (9) equals to the variance of the authorized user $D^r(\alpha_{opt})$ (17) and is plotted in Figure 6 for both WIRs. Secondly, assuming the authorized user with the knowledge of the key (consequently, we suppose the knowledge of $\mathbf{U}$), we have computed the variance of the restored host $D^r(\alpha)$ according to (15) for various values of α (Figure 6).

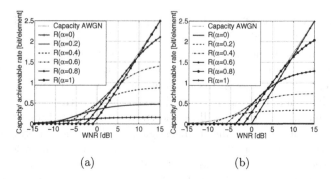

(a)   (b)

Fig. 5. Costa rate: WIR=-6 dB and WIR=-16 dB

The obtained results confirm the non-optimality of the optimal Costa α selection for host communications. They demonstrate the estimation accuracy improvement at low WNRs in comparison with unauthorized user/authorized user with $\alpha = \alpha_{opt}$ when α parameter increases. However, at high WNRs the situation is the opposite one. This behavior is justified by the fact that for $\alpha = 0$ (spread sprectrum communications) $\mathbf{U} = \mathbf{W}$ and it represents additional interference source for host communications. In this case the input for the optimal MMSE estimator of $\mathbf{X}$ will be $(\mathbf{V} - \mathbf{U})$. Therefore, $D(\alpha = 0) = \frac{\sigma_X^2 \sigma_Z^2}{\sigma_X^2 + \sigma_Z^2}$ and asymptotically perfect host recovery at high WNRs ($\sigma_Z^2 \to 0$) is possible.

When $\alpha = 1$, $\mathbf{V} = \mathbf{X} + \mathbf{W} + \mathbf{Z}$, $\mathbf{U} = \mathbf{X} + \mathbf{W}$ and the optimal MMSE estimate is obtained based on $\mathbf{U}$ only. Thus, $D(\alpha = 1) = \frac{\sigma_X^2 \sigma_W^2}{\sigma_X^2 + \sigma_W^2}$ and it is independent of σ_Z^2. Therefore, at low WNRs this selection of α provides the smallest possible variance of the host estimation while at the high WNRs presence of $\mathbf{W}$ leads to the performance loss in comparison with the previous case ($\alpha = 0$).

The performed analysis allows to conclude that knowledge of the auxiliary random variable plays a crucial role for accurate host estimation in the Costa communications set-up. However, in order to provide satisfactory solution for both high and low WNRs one needs to design a communications protocol for the properly selected value of α (for instance, $\alpha \in [0.4, 0.6]$, Figure 6).

Finally, it can be observed (Figure 6) that as WNR $\to \infty$ or $\sigma_Z^2 \to 0$ that corresponds to the noiseless case within the considered scenario B, D^r for the authorized user tends to 0 for all values of α. This corresponds to the case of perfect reversibility and confirms our theoretical analysis. At the same time, the unauthorized user distortion asymptotically tends to $\frac{\sigma_X^2 \sigma_W^2}{\sigma_X^2 + \sigma_W^2}$, i.e., it is non-decreasing with σ_Z^2 that prevents the perfect reversibility for the unauthorized user in this signal processing set-up.

5   Conclusions and Future Perspectives

In this paper, the problem of reversibility of random binning-based data-hiding was analyzed from multimedia perspectives. Estimation-based reversibility was

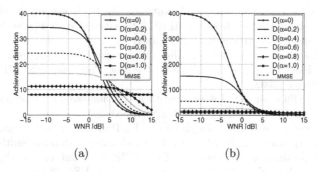

(a)   (b)

Fig. 6. Distortion: WIR=-6 dB and WIR=-16 dB

generally formulated within the Gel'fand-Pinsker framework and qualitatively analyzed in the Costa set-up. We demonstrated that in the noisy case the unauthorized user is capable to remove the hidden data using optimal MMSE with the same host reconstruction distortion than the authorized one with the perfect knowledge of the attacking noise variance. Contrarily, non-optimal in the communications sense selection of α together with the access to the proper codeword **U** provide significant estimation performance improvement. In the noiseless case $(\sigma_Z^2 \longrightarrow 0)$, the knowledge of **U** allows the authorized user to completely recover the host data $(\sigma_Z^2 = 0)$ that is never possible for the unauthorized user.

As a possible extension of the presented results we are going to consider the problem of maximization of the rate of reliable communications for a given target distortion D^{*r} and WNR regime that can be formulated as a joint optimization of achievable rate and restoration distortion. Finally, the same set-up will be analyzed from the security perspective.

Acknowledgements

This paper was partially supported by SNF Professeur Boursier grant PP002–68653, by the European Commission through the IST Programme under contract IST-2002-507932-ECRYPT and European Commission through sixth framework program under the number FP6-507609 (SIMILAR) and Swiss IM2 projects.

The information in this document reflects only the authors views, is provided as is and no guarantee or warranty is given that the it is fit for any particular purpose. The user thereof uses the information at its sole risk and liability.

References

1. Cox, I.J., Miller, M.L., Bloom, J.A.: Digital Watermarking. Morgan Kaufmann Publishers, Inc., San Francisco (2001)
2. Gel'fand, S., Pinsker, M.: Coding for channel with random parameters. Probl. Control and Inf. Theory **9** (1980) 19–31
3. Costa, M.: Writing on dirty paper. IEEE Trans. on Inf. Th. **29** (1983) 439–441

4. Perez-Freire, L., Perez-Gonzalez, F., Voloshynovskiy, S.: Revealing the true achievable rates of Scalar Costa Scheme. In: IEEE International Workshop on Multimedia Signal Processing (MMSP), Siena, Italy (2004) 235–238
5. Eggers, J., Buml, R., Tzschoppe, R., Girod, B.: Inverse mapping of scs-watermarked data. In: Eleventh European Signal Processing Conference (EUSIPCO'2002), Toulouse, France (2002)
6. Moulin, P., O'Sullivan, J.: Information-theoretic analysis of information hiding. IEEE Trans. on Information Theory **49** (2003) 563–593
7. Voloshynovskiy, S., Koval, O., Deguillaume, F., Pun, T.: Visual communications with side information via distributed printing channels: extended multimedia and security perspectives. In: Proceedings of the SPIE Int. Conf. on Security and Watermarking of Multimedia Contents III, San Jose, CA, USA (2004)
8. Kay, S.M.: Fundamentals of Statistical Signal Processing: Estimation Theory. Prentice Hall Signal Processing Series (1993)
9. Cover, T., Thomas, J.: Elements of Information Theory. Wiley and Sons, New York (1991)

A Graph–Theoretic Approach to Steganography

Stefan Hetzl[1] and Petra Mutzel[2]

[1] Institute of Computer Languages (E185),
Vienna University of Technology, Favoritenstraße 9,
A-1040 Vienna, Austria
hetzl@logic.at
[2] Institute of Algorithm Engineering, LS11,
University of Dortmund, Joseph-von-Fraunhofer Str. 20,
D-44221 Dortmund, Germany
petra.mutzel@cs.uni-dortmund.de

Abstract. We suggest a graph-theoretic approach to steganography based on the idea of exchanging rather than overwriting pixels. We construct a graph from the cover data and the secret message. Pixels that need to be modified are represented as vertices and possible partners of an exchange are connected by edges. An embedding is constructed by solving the combinatorial problem of calculating a maximum cardinality matching. The secret message is then embedded by exchanging those samples given by the matched edges. This embedding preserves first-order statistics. Additionally, the visual changes can be minimized by introducing edge weights.

We have implemented an algorithm based on this approach with support for several types of image and audio files and we have conducted computational studies to evaluate the performance of the algorithm.

Keywords: Steganography, graph theory, information hiding.

1 Introduction

The purpose of steganography is to conceal the fact that some communication is taking place. This is achieved by embedding a secret message in some cover data. This process – the embedding algorithm – produces stego data which must not raise suspicion that the secret message exists. The intended receiver extracts the secret message from the stego data. Typically, the sender and the receiver must share a common secret, like a secret key in cryptography.

This paper presents a new graph-theoretic approach to steganography based on the idea of exchanging rather than overwriting samples. By exchanging samples, the secret message can be embedded while preserving the color frequencies, thus automatically avoiding detection by tests based on first-order statistics. We construct a graph from the cover data and the secret message. A vertex in this graph will correspond to the necessity of making a change to the cover data. Two vertices that are potential partners for an exchange will be connected by an edge. This approach has the following advantages:

J. Dittmann, S. Katzenbeisser, and A. Uhl (Eds.): CMS 2005, LNCS 3677, pp. 119–128, 2005.
© IFIP International Federation for Information Processing 2005

1. It does not depend on the type of the cover data (e.g. image, audio,...).
2. It is easily extendable concerning the question which exchanges are allowed by defining additional restrictions on the set of edges. This allows for modular addition of visual and statistical criteria to the embedding algorithm.
3. It reduces the problem of finding a steganographic embedding to the well investigated combinatorial problem of finding a maximum matching in a graph (see e.g. [9,8]).

We have implemented an algorithm based on this approach in the system *steghide* [7]. Our computational experiments have shown that sufficiently large matchings can be found, so that first-order statistics are not changed substantially. Additionally, the visual differences can be minimized by introducing edge weights and minimizing the weights of all matched edges.

This paper is organized as follows. Section 2 contains a theoretical description of our new approach. In Section 3 we describe the implementation of an algorithm based on this approach. Section 4 contains a discussion of the steganographic security of our algorithm in comparison to other methods.

2   A Graph-Theoretic Approach

2.1   Terminology

The central concept for abstracting the embedding process from the underlying data format is that of a *sample*. A sample is the smallest data unit of a certain data format, e.g., the data making up a pixel in an image (a R/G/B triple in true-color bitmaps). The set of values a sample (of a certain data format) can have, is denoted as $\mathbb{S}$. A cover (or stego) file is an array of samples.

For cover (or stego) data $D = \langle s_1, \ldots, s_N \rangle$ and a set $P \subseteq \{1, \ldots, N\}$ the *frequency* of the sample value $x \in \mathbb{S}$ in the set P is $|\{i \in P \mid s_i = x\}|$. We define a function $v : \mathbb{S} \to \{0, \ldots, m-1\}$ assigning an *embedded value* to every sample value, where m can be varied for different data formats. For a traditional least significant bit (LSB) embedding, m would be 2 and $v(s) = \mathrm{LSB}(s)$. Additionally we use a construction mentioned in [1]: We do not embed a value in a single sample, but instead in a set of k samples, more precisely, as modulo m sum of their embedded values. This has the advantage that we have the freedom to choose one of these k samples for modification. Let $D = \langle s_1, \ldots, s_N \rangle$ be some cover (or stego) data. We define the value that is embedded in the i-th k-tuple of samples as: $V_i(D) = v(s_{k \cdot (i-1)+1}) \oplus_m \cdots \oplus_m v(s_{k \cdot (i-1)+k})$, where $1 \leq i \leq \lfloor \frac{N}{k} \rfloor$. The secret message will be denoted as $E_m = \langle e_1, \ldots, e_n \rangle$ where $e_i \in \{0, \ldots, m-1\}$ for $i \in \{1, \ldots, n\}$. The purpose of this notation is to make clear that the data that will be embedded is encoded in digits modulo m which is assumed for the construction of the graph. For $m = 2$, the values e_i are the bits of the secret message.

A graph G is a structure (V, E) where V is the set of vertices and $E \subseteq V \times V$ is the set of edges. We will only consider undirected graphs, so $(x, y) \in E$ and $(y, x) \in E$ are the same edge. Every edge can be assigned a weight which will be denoted by $c(e)$ for $e \in E$. A *matching* $M \subseteq E$ is a set vertex-disjoint edges, i.e. there do not exists two edges $e_1, e_2 \in M$ and a $v \in V$ such that both e_1 and e_2 are connected to v. A *maximum cardinality matching* on a given graph G is one largest (w.r.t. its cardinality) matching on G. A *maximum cardinality minimum weight matching* M is a maximum cardinality matching where $\sum_{e \in M} c(e)$ is minimal among all maximum cardinality matchings. An edge $e \in E$ is called *matched* with respect to some matching M if $e \in M$. A vertex $v \in V$ is called *matched* (in M) if there is an edge in M that is incident to v. We will sometimes write $v \in M$ for a vertex $v \in V$ to indicate that this vertex is matched in M, respectively $v \notin M$ to indicate that it is not matched. A *perfect matching* is a matching such that all vertices of the graph are matched.

2.2   Construction of the Graph

In this section we will describe the construction of the graph.

Definition 1. *Let $C = \langle s_1, \ldots, s_N \rangle$ be the cover data, $k \geq 1$. A **vertex** is a structure (P, T) where $P = \langle p_1, \ldots, p_k \rangle \in \{1, \ldots, N\}^k$ is a k-tuple of positions in the cover file, and $T = \langle t_1, \ldots, t_k \rangle \in \{0, \ldots, m-1\}^k$ is a k-tuple of target values.*

The precise meaning of a vertex is as follows: Exactly one of the samples s_{p_i}, $i \in \{1, \ldots, k\}$ needs to be changed to a sample value s_i^* for which $v(s_i^*) = t_i$ holds to embed a certain part of the secret message. The number k is fixed for a graph and will in the following also be called the *samples per vertex* ratio.

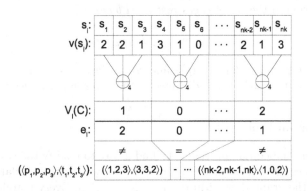

Fig. 1. Example for the vertex construction with $k = 3$ and $m = 4$

After having defined the structure of a single vertex it remains to describe the construction of the set of vertices: Basically we have to create a vertex for every k-tuple of samples of which one needs to be changed. Fig. 1 shows an example of our construction for cover data $C = \langle s_1, \ldots, s_N \rangle$ with $k = 3$, $m = 4$ and secret message $E_4 = \langle e_1, \ldots, e_n \rangle$. The first row contains the samples of the cover data.

The second row contains the values that are embedded in the (unmodified) cover data. Three (in general k) of these values are combined using addition modulo four (in general m) to form the value $V_l(C)$ which is compared to the l-th part of the secret message (e_l). If these two values are not equal (as in the first and last case but not in the second case) a vertex is created in the last line. The target values are computed by adding the difference $d = e_l \ominus_m V_l(C)$ to each $v(s_i)$. This has the effect that replacing one of the $v(s_i)$ with its corresponding target value t_1, t_2 or t_3 yields e_l as value of the vertex. This operation is called *embedding a vertex*.

Definition 2. *Let v and w be two vertices with $v = (\langle p_1, \ldots, p_k \rangle, \langle t_1, \ldots, t_k \rangle)$ and $w = (\langle q_1, \ldots, q_k \rangle, \langle u_1, \ldots, u_k \rangle)$ and let $i, j \in \{1, \ldots, k\}$. There is an **edge** connecting the i-ith sample value of v with the j-th sample value of w, written as $(v, w)_{i,j} \in E$ if*

$$v(s_{p_i}) = u_j \text{ and } v(s_{q_j}) = t_i$$

An edge connects two vertices and is labeled with the index of one sample value from each vertex. An exchange of these two sample values results in embedding both vertices. Note that it is possible that two vertices are connected by more than one edge. In this case a matching can contain only one of these edges.

The above definition alone does not prohibit exchanges that create visible distortions such as for example exchanging a black and a cyan pixel. We need to define a restriction on this set of edges that takes *visual similarity* into account. We define a distance function $d : \mathbb{S} \times \mathbb{S} \to \mathbb{R}$ meant to capture the notion of visual distance. We define a relation of visual similarity $\sim$ for $s_1, s_2 \in \mathbb{S}$ as: $s_1 \sim s_2 \Leftrightarrow d(s_1, s_2) \leq r$ for some neighborhood radius r. Now we can give the refined definition of the set of *edges restricted by $\sim$*:

$$E^{\sim} = \{(v, w)_{i,j} \in E \mid s_{p_i} \sim s_{q_j}\}$$

where $v = (\langle p_1, \ldots, p_k \rangle, \langle t_1, \ldots, t_k \rangle)$ and $w = (\langle q_1, \ldots, q_k \rangle, \langle u_1, \ldots, u_k \rangle)$. The cost $c : E \to \mathbb{R}$ of an edge is the distance of the two sample values $d(s_{p_i}, s_{q_j})$.

2.3   Finding an Embedding

The goal of the embedding process is to find a way to modify the cover file such that all vertices are embedded. For this purpose we try to calculate a perfect matching on the graph defined in the previous section. Every matching on this graph corresponds to a set of (disjoint) exchanges of sample values in the cover file. Conducting these exchanges has the effect that all matched vertices will be embedded. Of course we cannot except to reach a perfect matching for every cover file. To embed those vertices that can not be matched it is necessary to overwrite one sample per vertex. An operation like this will change the sample value frequencies, but this operation needs to be done only on the unmatched vertices and in Sec. 3.2 we show that for natural cover data we can find matchings of sufficient cardinality.

As an additional feature one can bias the algorithm towards choosing short (w.r.t. their cost) edges to minimize the overall visual impact by trying to find a minimal weight maximum matching.

3   Implementation

We have implemented an algorithm based on our new graph-theoretic approach in the system *steghide* [7]. Our implementation supports palette images, true-color images, jpeg images, waveform audio data and μ-law audio data. As additional security measure we permute the samples before embedding in a way determined by the secret key to guarantee a uniform distribution of stego samples in the stego file (as recommended e.g. in [12]).

3.1   Data Structures and Algorithms

The number of vertices in our graphs grows in $O(n)$, where n is the size of the secret message. The number of edges grows in $O(n^2)$. For example, a graph for a true-color image and embedding data of size 1KB has about $3,200$ vertices and $98,000$ edges (on average). If the size of the embedded data raises to 4KB, then the size of the graph gets up to $12,500$ vertices and $1,470,000$ edges. However, our aim is to embed an even greater amount of data. This huge size of the graphs has two important implications: First, it is impossible to store a graph using an adjacency list, because the number of edges simply becomes too high. And second, even if there are fast algorithms to solve the matching problem running in time $O(\sqrt{|V|} \cdot |E|)$ (see [8]) it is necessary to use simple heuristics that are even faster. Note that this does not result in a decrease of the quality of the obtained matchings because it is compensated by choosing data format specific values for the parameters m, k and r that result in graphs such that heuristics can find matchings of sufficient quality (see Sect. 3.2).

In our implementation, we have not stored the graph using an adjacency list, instead we use data structures that allow an on-the-fly construction of the edges: The *sample value adjacency list* is an array indexed by the sample values that for each sample value s contains a list of those sample values that have a distance $\leq r$ to s. These lists are sorted by distance in ascending order. We also need a data structure called *sample value occurrences* that is an array indexed by the sample values that for each sample value s contains a list of pointers to those vertices that contain s. Using these two data structures we can iterate through the edges of a given vertex in order of ascending distance without the need to store an adjacency list.

As mentioned above, we use heuristics to speed up the calculation of the maximum cardinality minimum weight matching. We use the greedy construction heuristic formally described in Algorithm 1 (see, e.g., [9]).

This heuristic adds vertices ordered by their degree[1] and - for equal degrees - with their shortest edge to the matching. Sorting by degree significantly increases

---

[1] The degree of a vertex is the number of edges incident to this vertex.

Input   : Graph $G = (V, E)$
Output   : Matching M on G

Sort all vertices by degree in ascending order into $\langle v_1, \ldots, v_n \rangle$;
Initialize $M = \emptyset$;
Mark all vertices as active;
for $i = 1, \ldots, n$ **do**
   | **if** v_i *is active and* $degree(v_i) > 0$ **then**
   | | Set $e = (v_i, w)$ = shortest edge of v_i;
   | | Set $M = M \cup \{e\}$;
   | | Mark v_i and w as inactive and delete all of their edges from E;
   | **end**
end
return M;

Algorithm 1. The static minimum degree construction heuristic (SMD)

the cardinality in comparison to a random selection because vertices that have a lower number of possible partners are matched first. Additionally sorting vertices with equal degrees by shortest edge biases the non-determinism in the algorithm towards choosing shorter edges.

After this construction heuristic, for some data formats we use a heuristic depth-first search for *augmenting paths* as postprocessing step. Augmenting paths then can be used to increase the cardinality of the matching. The interested reader is referred to [9] for details.

3.2   Computational Studies

To evaluate the performance of the implementation empirically, we created a test set of cover files for every data format. The image test sets have been created by digitizing 50 images showing natural scenes with an Epson flatbed scanner, which then have been converted to the appropriate file format: to bitmaps using 256 color palettes, to uncompressed true-color bitmaps (16.7 million colors) and to color jpeg images. The audio data has been taken from different CDs and then stored as 16 bit waveform data and converted to the μ-law format. The tests have been conducted with different amounts of random data as secret messages.

These test sets have been very useful to determine good values for the data format specific parameters: the samples per vertex ratio k, the modulus m and the radius r. As distance function we use the euclidean distance in the RGB cube for palette and true-color images, for the other formats we use the absolute distance between the sample values. Table 1 shows values for the parameters s.t. an embedding rate as high as possible is reached while still allowing nearly perfect matchings and thus preservation of first-order statistics. The embedding rate is the rate of the size of the secret message to the size of the cover file and can be calculated as $r = \frac{1}{\frac{2}{m} \cdot k \cdot s}$ where s is the size of a sample in bits. A sample in a jpeg file is a coefficient of the discrete cosine transform. Coefficients with the value 0 are not used to embed data, because setting a coefficient that is 0

Table 1. Data format specific definitions

	palette	true-color	jpeg	waveform	μ-law
radius r	20	10	1	20	1
samples/vertex k	3	2	3	2	2
modulus m	4	4	2	2	2
embedding rate	8.33%	4.16%	5.86%	3.13%	6.25%
algorithms	SMD	SMD	SMD	SMD,DFS	SMD,DFS

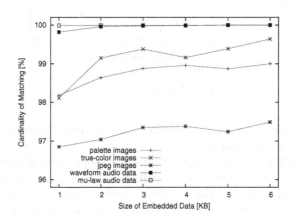

Fig. 2. Matching cardinality

in the cover file to 1 in the stego file can result in visually detectable distortion of the image. For this reason, the embedding rate of a jpeg file can be given only empirically, so the exact value given in the table is only valid for our image database, however for other natural images the value will be similar. The last row shows which algorithms are used on a specific file format. SMD refers to the static minimum degree construction heuristic (as described in Algorithm 1) and DFS refers to the heuristic depth first search for augmenting paths presented in [9]. For the audio data formats it is useful to apply the DFS postprocessing step, because the SMD heuristic already produced high quality solutions (98.2%–99.7% matched vertices for waveform data and 99.8%–99.9% for μ-law data) and the DFS postprocessing step is rather fast when applied to such high quality solutions but still yields even better solutions.

Fig. 2 shows the cardinalities of the calculated matchings. The cardinality of the obtained matchings is very high (more than 97% of the vertices have been matched). This is due to the high density of the graphs obtained using our parameter settings. For the audio data formats almost 100% of the vertices have been matched. In contrast to the audio data formats, for jpeg files only 97% can be reached. This data format is more difficult to handle, because the coefficients of the discrete cosine transform do not have a uniform distribution, instead sample values with smaller absolute values occur more often (see, e.g.

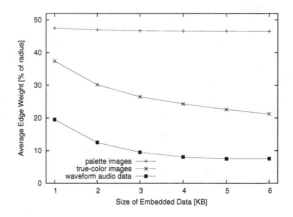

Fig. 3. Average edge weight

[12]). These results show that embeddings can be found that do not modify first-order statistics substantially.

Fig. 3 shows the average weight in % of the radius. An unbiased algorithm would choose edges with random weight with the result of an average edge weight of 50% of the radius. Biasing the algorithms towards choosing shorter edges has a significant effect for true-color images and waveform audio data.

We have observed that true-color images need considerable more running time than the other data formats, e.g. for embedding 6KB data the construction heuristic takes approximatly 12 seconds to complete compared to less than one second for the other data formats. This is due to the high number of different sample values. The problem is that, in general, creating the sample value adjacency list needs $O(|\mathbb{S}'|^2)$ time (where $\mathbb{S}'$ is the number of sample values actually occurring in the graph).

4   Steganalysis

The number of unmatched vertices is an upper bound on the number of changes to first-order statistics. Our experiments have shown that sufficiently good matchings ($< 3\%$ unmatched) can be reached for natural cover data. This makes our approach practically undetectable by tests that look only at first-order statistics such as the χ^2-attack [14]. Furthermore it is not possible to specify a set of groups partitioning $\mathbb{S}$ s.t. exchanges occur only inside a group making our approach also undetecable by the generalized χ^2-attacks in [10,4,13].

It would be interesting to run the blind steganalysis scheme [5] against our implementation to compare its detectability to the other tested algorithms [12,10,11], in particular to Salle's model-based approach. His algorithm does not only preserve the global histogram of jpeg files but also the frequencies of each individual DCT coefficent. Note that our approach could easily be extended by adding a restriction to the set of edges which allows only exchanges of sample within one DCT coefficient. This would have the effect that also the frequencies of the individual coefficients will be preserved. In fact, any restriction that can be expressed by allowing or disallowing single sample value exchanges can be added. It remains to be investigated how powerful this really is.

For a targeted steganalysis of our approach for jpeg files the blockiness measure seems to be a candidate. The blockiness measure gives an indication of the discontinuities at the 8x8 boundaries of jpeg blocks and was used in [6] to break outguess [10].

5   Summary and Outlook

We have presented a graph-theoretic approach to steganography that is based on exchanging rather than overwriting samples. Thus it preserves first-order statistics without the need for additional changes as in [10]. A graph is constructed from the cover data and the secret message where each vertex corresponds to the necessity of making a certain change and each edge represents a possible sample exchange. The embedding is found by solving the well-investigated combinatorial problem of finding a maximum cardinality minimum weight matching in this graph. The maximality of the cardinality ensures that a maximal amount of data is embedded by exchanges. The unmatched vertices need to be embedded in a way that does not preserve first-order statistics. However, as demonstrated in our computational studies, the number of unmatched vertices is negligibly low ($0\%-3\%$) for natural cover data. Additionally the minimality of the edge weights ensures that the visual changes introduced by the embedding are as small as possible. We have implemented the algorithm with support for true-color images, palette image and jpeg images as well as waveform and μ-law audio data.

Our approach can easily be extended by adding further restrictions on the set of edges (beyond the simple visual restriction $s_{p_i} \sim s_{q_j}$). An example would be a restriction for jpeg files to preserve also the frequencies for each individual DCT coefficient. Another example is the method described in [3] (and recently broken in [2]) to determine all pairs of stochastically independent sample values. Any restriction that can be expressed by allowing or disallowing single sample value exchanges can be added.

From the point of view of combinatorics the following two extension seem interesting: 1) to allow exchanging more than one sample per vertex and 2) to allow not only (disjoint) exchanges but arbitrary permutations. Both would provide more flexibility but would amount to more difficult combinatorial problems.

Acknowledgements

The authors would like to thank the anonymous referees for important suggestions for the improvement of this paper.

References

1. Ross J. Anderson. Stretching the Limits of Steganography. In Ross J. Anderson, editor, *Information Hiding, First International Workshop*, volume 1174 of *Lecture Notes in Computer Science*, pages 39–48. Springer, 1996.
2. Rainer Böhme and Andreas Westfeld. Exploiting Preserved Statistics for Steganalysis. In Jessica J. Fridrich, editor, *Information Hiding, 6th International Workshop*, volume 3200 of *Lecture Notes in Computer Science*. Springer, 2004.
3. Elke Franz. Steganography Preserving Statistical Properties. In F.A.P. Petitcolas, editor, *Information Hiding, 5th International Workshop*, volume 2578 of *Lecture Notes in Computer Science*, pages 278–294. Springer, 2003.
4. Jessica Fridrich, Miroslav Goljan, and David Soukal. Higher–order statistical steganalysis of palette images. In *Proceedings of the Electronic Imaging SPIE Santa Clara, CA, January 2003*, pages 178–190, 2003.
5. Jessica J. Fridrich. Feature-based Steganalysis for JPEG images and Its Implications for Future Design of Steganographic Schemes. In Jessica J. Fridrich, editor, *Information Hiding, 6th International Workshop*, volume 3200 of *Lecture Notes in Computer Science*, pages 67–81. Springer, 2004.
6. Jessica J. Fridrich, Miroslav Goljan, Dorin Hogea, and David Soukal. Quantitative steganalysis of digital images: estimating the secret message length. *Multimedia Systems*, 9(3):288–302, 2003.
7. Stefan Hetzl. Steghide, `http://steghide.sourceforge.net/`.
8. Silvio Micali and Vijay V. Vazirani. An $O(\sqrt{|V|}|E|)$ Algorithm for Finding Maximum Matching in General Graphs. In *21st Annual Symposium on Foundations of Computer Science*, pages 17–27, Syracuse, New York, October 1980. IEEE.
9. R. Möhring and M. Müller-Hannemann. Cardinality Matching: Heuristic Search for Augmenting Paths. Technical Report 439, Fachbereich Mathematik, Technische Universität Berlin, 1995.
10. Niels Provos. Defending Against Statistical Steganalysis. In *10th USENIX Security Symposium, Proceedings*, 2001.
11. Phil Sallee. Model-based Steganography. In Ton Kalker, Ingemar J. Cox, and Yong Man Ro, editors, *Digital Watermarking, Second International Workshop*, volume 2939 of *Lecture Notes in Computer Science*, pages 154–167. Springer, 2003.
12. Andreas Westfeld. F5–A Steganographic Algorithm: High Capacity Despite Better Steganalysis. In Ira S. Moskowitz, editor, *Information Hiding, 4th International Workshop*, volume 2137 of *Lecture Notes in Computer Science*, pages 289–302. Springer, 2001.
13. Andreas Westfeld. Detecting Low Embedding Rates. In F.A.P. Petitcolas, editor, *Information Hiding, 5th International Workshop*, volume 2578 of *Lecture Notes in Computer Science*, pages 324–339. Springer, 2003.
14. Andreas Westfeld and Andreas Pfitzmann. Attacks on Steganographic Systems. In Andreas Pfitzmann, editor, *Information Hiding, Third International Workshop, IH'99, Dresden, Germany, 1999, Proceedings*, volume 1768 of *Lecture Notes in Computer Science*, pages 61–76. Springer, 2000.

Non-interactive Watermark Detection for a Correlation-Based Watermarking Scheme

André Adelsbach, Markus Rohe, and Ahmad-Reza Sadeghi

Horst Görtz Institute for IT Security, Ruhr-Universität Bochum, Germany
andre.adelsbach@nds.rub.de
{rohe, sadeghi}@crypto.rub.de

Abstract. Cryptographic techniques have been deployed to securely prove the presence of a watermark in stego-data without disclosing any security critical information to the detecting party.

This paper presents a detailed practical construction and implementation results of a correlation-based non-blind watermarking scheme in the non-interactive zero-knowledge setting. We extensively describe the modifications and hurdles that had to be overcome to transform a well-known watermarking scheme – whose general detection principle is applied in many other known schemes – into a two-party setting where the critical detection input, i.e. the watermark vector and the original data is cryptographically concealed from the verifying party using a commitment scheme. Our prototype implementation is very efficient and is an evidence of the practical feasibility of zero-knowledge watermark detection.

Keywords: Watermark, detection, implementation, zero-knowledge.

1 Introduction

When using watermarks as evidence in applications, such as fingerprinting, dispute resolving or direct authorship proofs, the presence of a watermark, embedded by some party (e.g., a merchant or the author) has to be verifiable by another, not fully trusted party (e.g., a judge, a dispute resolver or a customer). Unfortunately, verifying the presence of a watermark in given data by means of the watermarking system's detection algorithm requires knowledge of the watermark, the watermarking key and, in non-blind watermarking systems, additionally the original data. Once this information was disclosed to a malicious party, it enables this party to perfectly remove the watermark without any perceptible quality degradation.

Adelsbach and Sadeghi [1] suggest to conceal the critical detection input from the potentially dishonest verifying party in commitments and to apply a zero-knowledge protocol in which a prover $\mathcal{P}$ proves to the verifying party $\mathcal{V}$ that the committed watermark is detectable in the alleged stego-data.[1] The protocol

---

[1] Other protocols have been proposed before, but these do not achieve the same level of security or have documented security flaws [2].

J. Dittmann, S. Katzenbeisser, and A. Uhl (Eds.): CMS 2005, LNCS 3677, pp. 129–139, 2005.

is zero-knowledge which guarantees that the verifier gains no knowledge on the embedded watermark.

In this paper we present the concrete construction of a zero-knowledge proof system for the watermarking scheme proposed by Cox et al. [3] as *one example* for the class of correlation-based and non-blind detectable watermarking schemes. Furthermore, we give a precise quantisation of the computation and communication complexities of the protocol. After minor transformations, the correlation value can be computed as a polynomial expression such that the entire zero-knowledge watermark detection protocol can be composed from elementary zero-knowledge sub-protocols and by using the commitment scheme's homomorphic property.

We want to stress that this zero-knowledge watermark detection paradigm can be applied to *any* watermarking scheme whose detection criterion can be expressed as a polynomial expression. This also includes more advanced embedding and detection strategies to improve robustness and imperceptibility with respect to the HVS as cited in [4]. We have chosen the scheme of Cox et al. [3], because it is a widely known example of correlation-based watermark detection and convenient to demonstrate the practical feasibility of strong zero-knowledge watermark detection.

Outline: Section 2 recapitulates the technical basics, i.e. the applied watermarking scheme and the cryptographic primitives. Section 3 treats all considerations and modifications of the original watermarking scheme when it is transformed into an efficient zero-knowledge protocol. In Section 4 we estimate the computation and communication complexities and present results of a prototype implementation.

2   Technical Preliminaries

2.1   Watermarking Scheme by Cox et al.

Here we shortly recall the major facts from the watermarking scheme by Cox et al. [3] for black and white still-images as the basis for our detection protocol.

Generation: The watermark vector WM consists of m (in the order of 1000) independently chosen $N(0,1)$-distributed coefficients.

Embedding: The discrete cosine transformation (DCT) is applied to the original image, resulting in $\hat{W}$. Let $\hat{W}^{[m]}$ denote the m coefficients carrying the watermark information which corresponds here to the m highest magnitude AC-coefficients in $\hat{W}$. Cox et al. originally propose three different equations to embed the watermark, yielding the m-dimensional vector $\hat{W'}^{[m]}$ of marked coefficients $\hat{W'}_i^{[m]}$ for $i = 0, \ldots, m-1$:

$$\hat{W'}_i^{[m]} = \hat{W}_i^{[m]} + \alpha \cdot WM_i \tag{1}$$

$$\hat{W'}_i^{[m]} = \hat{W}_i^{[m]} \cdot (1 + \alpha \cdot WM_i) \tag{2}$$

where the constant α denotes the strength of embedding. As the third equation $\hat{W}'^{[m]}_i = \hat{W}^{[m]}_i \cdot \left(e^{\alpha \cdot WM_i} \right)$ is practically not used, we omit its further discussion.

Substituting $\hat{W}'^{[m]}$ in $\hat{W}$ and applying the inverse discrete cosine transformation DCT^{-1} results in the watermarked image W'.

Detection: To decide whether a given watermark WM is contained in image W^* we extract a watermark candidate WM^* whose correlation value is computed against the watermark WM. In this extraction we first compute $\hat{W} = DCT(W)$ and $\hat{W}^* = DCT(W^*)$. Then set $\hat{W}^{[m]}$ to the m-highest magnitude coefficients of $\hat{W}$ and $\hat{W}^{*[m]}$ to the corresponding coefficients (same position) of $\hat{W}^*$. Then WM^* is obtained by inverting the embedding equation (see Section 3.1). Finally, we compute the correlation

$$corr = \frac{WM \cdot WM^*}{\| WM^* \|} \tag{3}$$

and compare it to some given threshold S. If $corr \geq S$ then WM is considered to be present. Otherwise it is considered to be absent.

2.2   Cryptographic Primitives

Commitment Scheme. A *commitment scheme* is a cryptographic protocol that allows one party, the so-called *committer* $\mathcal{C}$, to commit himself to a message $s \in \mathcal{M}$ from the message space $\mathcal{M}$, such that the *recipient* $\mathcal{R}$ of the commitment C_s is assured that $\mathcal{C}$ is unable to change the value of s afterwards (*binding property*). At the same time s is kept secret from the recipient $\mathcal{R}$ (*hiding property*).

Protocols: A commitment scheme consists of two main protocol steps:

1. Commit(): To commit to a certain message $s \in \mathcal{M}$, $\mathcal{C}$ runs the algorithm $(C_s, sk_{C_s}) \leftarrow \mathsf{commit}(s)$ to obtain the commitment C_s to s and the corresponding *secret key* sk_{C_s} that allows $\mathcal{C}$ to open C_s correctly in the Open() protocol. The committer passes C_s to the recipient who saves it for further use.
2. Open(): To open C_s to $\mathcal{R}$, $\mathcal{C}$ sends the message s and the corresponding secret key sk_{C_s} to the recipient. With this information $\mathcal{R}$ is able to verify s regarding the previously received commitment C_s. If the verification has been successful, $\mathcal{R}$ outputs the message s, otherwise he rejects. We denote such a successful protocol run as $(\mathcal{C} : -; \mathcal{R} : s) \leftarrow (\mathcal{C} : s, sk_{C_s}; \mathcal{R} : -; C_s)$

We refer to [5] for a detailed introduction to commitment schemes.

The Concrete Commitment Scheme: We use the Damgård-Fujisaki (DF) integer commitment scheme [6] in our protocol. A commitment to a message $s \in \mathbb{Z}$ is computed as $C_s := g^s h^{sk_{C_s}} \bmod n$, where n is the product of two safe primes, h is a random element of high order and its order has only large prime factors. g is a random element from $< h >$ and $\log_h g$ is unknown to $\mathcal{C}$. g, h

and n form together with some other public (security) parameters (cf. Section 4) the so-called *commitment description* $descr_{com}$. Instantiated in this manner, the DF commitment scheme is *statistically hiding* and *computationally binding* under the *strong RSA assumption*.

Homomorphic Property: The structure of the DF commitment scheme allows $\mathcal{R}$ to perform computations on secret values without knowledge of the corresponding opening information. This feature can be used to increase the efficiency of the watermark detection protocol. Let C_x and C_y be two commitments to the secret values x and y and γ be some publicly known integer. The committer $\mathcal{C}$, knowing sk_{C_x} and sk_{C_y}, can open the product $C_x \cdot C_y$ as $x + y$: $(\mathcal{C} : -; \mathcal{R} : x + y) \leftarrow (\mathcal{C} : x + y, sk_{C_x} + sk_{C_y}; \mathcal{R} : -; C_x \cdot C_y)$. Furthermore, $(C_x)^\gamma$ can be opened as $\gamma \cdot x$: $(\mathcal{C} : -; \mathcal{R} : \gamma \cdot x) \leftarrow (\mathcal{C} : \gamma \cdot x, \gamma \cdot sk_{C_x}; \mathcal{R} : -; (C_x)^\gamma)$ and $C_x \cdot g^\gamma$ can be opened as $\gamma + x$: $(\mathcal{C} : -; \mathcal{R} : \gamma + x) \leftarrow (\mathcal{C} : \gamma + x, sk_{C_x}; \mathcal{R} : -; C_x \cdot g^\gamma)$. Consequently, $\mathcal{R}$ can autonomously compute C_{x+y}, $C_{\gamma \cdot x}$ and $C_{\gamma + x}$, which can be opened accordingly by $\mathcal{C}$.

Elementary Zero-Knowledge Proof Systems. Interactive two-party proof systems involve a so-called *prover* $\mathcal{P}$ and a so-called *verifier* $\mathcal{V}$ where each of them has its own *private input* and both have access to some given *common input*. In our context, the common input consists of commitments of which $\mathcal{P}$ is aware of the secret messages and the corresponding secret keys as its private input. Applying such proof systems $\mathcal{P}$ convinces $\mathcal{V}$ that he is indeed able to open the commitments, provided as common input, correctly and that certain relations hold among their secret messages. There exist three security requirements for these proof systems: *Completeness:* If $\mathcal{P}$ and $\mathcal{V}$ act honestly, every run of the proof system will be accepted by $\mathcal{V}$. *Soundness* guarantees that a cheating prover (e.g. $\mathcal{P}$ has no opening information for the commitments) can trick $\mathcal{V}$ to accept the proof protocol only with a negligible probability. Finally, the *zero-knowledge* requirement guarantees that $\mathcal{V}$ gains no new knowledge from a protocol run beyond the assertion that has been proven.

We will make use of several elementary zero-knowledge proof protocols, which prove the multiplicative relation ($\mathsf{PoK}_{mult}()$), the square relation ($\mathsf{PoK}_{sq}()$) and the equality relation on committed values ($\mathsf{PoK}_{eq}()$).[2] We use the multiplication protocol proposed by Damgård and Fujisaki [6], while the square and the equality proof are adapted from Boudot [7]. Finally, we use a proof system $\mathsf{PoK}_{\geq 0}()$ which proves that a committed value is greater or equal to zero. An elegant proof system has been suggested by Lipmaa [8] and is based on a number theoretical result by Lagrange, which states that every positive integer x can be represented as a sum of four squares, i.e. $x = x_1^2 + x_2^2 + x_3^2 + x_4^2$. Hence, the proof system $\mathsf{PoK}_{\geq 0}()$ can be composed by 4 square proofs, the homomorphic addition of $C_{x_1^2}, \ldots, C_{x_4^2}$ and the proof of an equality relation for $C_{x_1^2 + x_2^2 + x_3^2 + x_4^2}$ and C_x.

Typically, zero-knowledge proofs are executed as interactive challenge-response protocols. However, there exists an efficient transformation to convert

---

[2] For example, $\mathsf{PoK}_{mult}(C_c; C_a, C_b)$ denotes a zero-knowledge proof that $\mathcal{P}$ can open C_a, C_b and C_c, such that $a \cdot b = c$ holds.

the interactive version of a proof protocol into a non-interactive version in the random oracle model [9] where the prover performs a complete precomputation of a proof and passes it to the verifier. Our implementation uses the elementary sub-proofs in this efficient proof mode.

We will give the computational complexity of all protocols in terms of modular exponentiations (E), modular inversions (I) and modular multiplications (M), as these operations dominate their complexities. With $\mathsf{Comp}_{\mathcal{P}}$ we denote the *computational complexity* of the prover, whereas $\mathsf{Comp}_{\mathcal{V}}$ refers to that of the verifier. L denotes the computation expense of a 4-square Lagrange decomposition, for which an efficient probabilistic algorithm can be found in [10]. With $\mathsf{Comm}_{(\mathcal{P},\mathcal{V})}$ we denote the *communication complexity*, measured as the number of bits exchanged between $\mathcal{P}$ and $\mathcal{V}$.

The complexities of the basic protocols mainly depend on the security parameters of the DF commitment scheme, namely $|n|$, k, T, B and $C(k)$ (which we will denote as F). Here, $|n|$ denotes the binary length of the strong RSA modulus. B is an estimator for the upper bound of the order of $< h >$, such that $ord(< h >) \le 2^B$, while T specifies the message space $\mathcal{M} = [-T, T]$. We use the parameter k to limit the maximum statistical distance (statistical zero knowledge property) between an accepting real and a simulated protocol view which is less than 2^{-k}. F (aka $C(k)$ in [6]) determines the challenge size and therefore the security parameter for the proof's soundness. As such, it limits the probability that a cheating prover is able to carry out an accepting proof to $< 2^{-|F|}$. For further details regarding these parameters we refer to [6]. Table 1 gives an overview of $\mathsf{Comp}_{\mathcal{P}}$, $\mathsf{Comp}_{\mathcal{V}}$ and $\mathsf{Comm}_{(\mathcal{P},\mathcal{V})}$, including the communication complexity for reasonably chosen security parameters (cf. Section 4).

Technical Remark: Watermarking schemes require computations on real numbers, while the applied DF commitment scheme supports integers. However, by scaling all real values by an appropriate factor λ (e.g. $\lambda = 10^{10}$ or 10^{20}) we can perform all required computations in the integer domain. For instance, the relation $a \cdot b = c$ is scaled as $(\lambda_a a) \cdot (\lambda_b b) = (\lambda_a \lambda_b) c$.

Table 1. Communication and computation complexities in the non-interactive proof mode

Relation	$\mathsf{Comp}_{\mathcal{P}}$	$\mathsf{Comp}_{\mathcal{V}}$	$\mathsf{Comm}_{(\mathcal{P},\mathcal{V})}$	[KBytes]
$\mathsf{PoK}_{mult}()$	$6E + 9M$	$9E + 3I + 6M$	$6|F| + 3|T| + 8k + 3B + 5$	0.66
$\mathsf{PoK}_{sq}()$	$4E + 6M$	$6E + 2I + 4M$	$4|F| + 2|T| + 5k + 2B + 3$	0.44
$\mathsf{PoK}_{eq}()$	$4E + 5M$	$6E + 2I + 4M$	$4|F| + |T| + 5k + 2B + 3$	0.38
$\mathsf{PoK}_{\ge 0}()$	$38E + 42M + L$	$30E + 10I + 23M$	$8|n| + 20|F| + 9|T| + 25k$ $+10B + 15$	3.13

3   Transformation into the ZK-Setting

For each embedding equation (1) and (2) we consider its inversion, yielding WM^* and rate its usability. Furthermore, we address the problem how $\mathcal{V}$ chooses the detection coefficients $\hat{W}*_i^{[m]}$ as he is only aware of the committed version of $\hat{W}$.

3.1   Embedding Equations

The first step of the detection algorithm is to extract WM^* from the alleged stego-image $\hat{W}^*$, which, in non-blind detection, additionally involves the original image $\hat{W}$. In zero-knowledge watermark detection, $\mathcal{V}$ is only aware of the committed version $C_{\hat{W}^{[m]}} := (C_{\hat{W}_1^{[m]}}, \ldots, C_{\hat{W}_m^{[m]}})$ of $\hat{W}$ such that, after the extraction, he has to be convinced in zero-knowledge that the content of $C_{WM^*} := (C_{WM^*_1}, \ldots, C_{WM^*_m})$ has been obtained correctly.

Equation 1: In case WM was embedded according to Equation (1) then WM^* is obtained[3] as

$$\Delta_i := \alpha \cdot WM^*_i = \hat{W}*_i^{[m]} - \hat{W}_i^{[m]}. \tag{4}$$

such that Δ_i is a difference of committed values, which can be easily computed in the committed domain by taking advantage of the homomorphic property of the commitment scheme.

Equation 2: In this case Δ_i is obtained as the quotient

$$\Delta_i := \alpha \cdot WM^*_i = \left(\hat{W}*_i^{[m]} - \hat{W}_i^{[m]} \right) / \hat{W}_i^{[m]}. \tag{5}$$

To convince $\mathcal{V}$ in the committed domain that Δ_i in C_{Δ_i} has been computed correctly as $\Delta_i = \hat{W}*_i^{[m]} \cdot \left(\hat{W}_i^{[m]} \right)^{-1} - 1$ an additional zero-knowledge proof has to be performed. Therefore, the computation of C_{Δ_i} at the beginning of the detection protocol described in Section 3.4 has to be extended by an additional multiplication subproof and a proof that $\left(\hat{W}_i^{[m]} \right)^{-1}$ was computed correctly.[4] Clearly, the entire detection protocol can be extended by the described subproofs, but this introduces additional overhead. Hence, embedding the watermark with Equation (1) yields a more efficient zero-knowledge watermark detection protocol.

3.2   How Verifier Determines $\hat{W}*^{[m]}$

The original heuristic in Cox's watermarking scheme (see Section 2.1) requires to select the coefficients of $\hat{W}$ with the m-highest magnitudes to construct $\hat{W}*^{[m]}$

---

[3] We invert to $\Delta_i := \alpha \cdot WM^*_i$ instead of WM^*_i, because with Δ_i in the detection inequality the construction of an efficient protocol is easier to achieve, cf. Sec. 3.3.

[4] This can be achieved by proving the multiplicative relation $\mathsf{PoK}_{mult}(C_z; C_{\left(\hat{W}_i^{[m]} \right)^{-1}}, C_{\hat{W}_i^{[m]}})$ and that z is close enough to 1. The latter can be proven by an interval proof [7] that $z \in [1 - \delta, 1 + \delta]$ for a reasonable small δ.

and $\hat{W}^{[m]}$. In the context of zero-knowledge watermark detection, this heuristic cannot be done in a straightforward way, since $\mathcal{V}$ only knows the committed version $C_{\hat{W}^{[m]}}$ of the original transformed image $\hat{W}$. We describe two (among several other) viable solutions to overcome this problem:

Solution 1: This method provides a generic solution which is applicable to *every* correlation-based watermarking scheme whose detection criterion can be expressed as a polynomial. The general idea of this solution is that WM is chosen as large as the image size (e.g., $m = N \cdot N$) and that all positions i, not supposed to be marked, are set to value $WM_i := 0$. In this case no selection for $\hat{W}*^{[m]}$ and $\hat{W}^{[m]}$ is required at all and *corr* remains unaffected as well. Unfortunately, this general approach involves a significant overhead, as the number m of coefficients that have to be processed becomes quite large.

Solution 2: Here we consider the *special case* where the embedding positions are public parameters of the watermarking scheme and, therefore, can be given as common input to both parties, thus yielding more efficient detection protocols. One possibility to obtain these fixed embedding positions has been proposed by Piva et al [11] and works as follows: Embed WM along a zig-zag scan of the AC coefficients similar to the walk in the JPEG compression algorithm (but on the entire $N \times N$ DCT-transformed image). Embedding of the watermark begins at a predetermined diagonal l, which becomes part of the common input. l is chosen such that a sufficient number of low-frequency AC coefficients is used for embedding. This methodology matches the required choice of significant coefficients in $\hat{W}$ for embedding WM, since for most images the low-frequency coefficients mainly coincide with the highest magnitude coefficients of $\hat{W}$. The result is a compatible efficient zero-knowledge version of Cox's watermarking scheme.

3.3 Adaption of the Detection Inequality

We have to transform the detection criterion $corr \geq S$ respectively $corr - S \geq 0$ such that the computation of $corr$ can be expressed as a polynomial term. Inserting Equation (3) into $corr - S \geq 0$ leads to $\sum_{i=0}^{m-1} WM_i \cdot WM^*_i - S \cdot \sqrt{\sum_{i=0}^{m-1}(WM^*_i)^2} \geq 0$. The detection threshold S is chosen as $S \geq 0$ [3]. If WM is present, then $\sum_{i=0}^{m-1} WM_i \cdot WM^*_i \geq 0$ also holds. In this case we are allowed to square the inequality in order to eliminate the root term which would require additional zero-knowledge subproofs. Otherwise, we are already assured in this stage that WM is not present and can omit further computations (cf. Section 3.4).

Now the resulting term has a polynomial form which allows us to apply the zero-knowledge protocol primitives. A multiplication with α^2 allows us to use $\Delta_i := \alpha \cdot WM_i$ directly from Equation (4) or (5) which leads to the detection criterion

$$\underbrace{\left(\sum_{i=0}^{m-1} WM_i \cdot \Delta_i\right)^2}_{=:A} - \underbrace{S^2 \cdot \sum_{i=0}^{m-1} \Delta_i^2}_{=:B} \geq 0. \qquad (6)$$

An intermediate computation of C_{Δ_i}, C_{A^2} and C_B and a proof that $A^2 - B \geq 0$ in C_{A^2-B} convinces a verifier that a given committed watermark C_{WM} is present in W^*.

Certainly, the entire protocol becomes less sophisticated if one assumes a detection criterion $S \geq WM \cdot WM^*$ without any denominator. However, in the zero-knowledge setting, one cannot simply multiply Equation (3) by $\|WM^*\|$ because this value is obtained from $\hat{W}^{[m]}$, which is cryptographically concealed from the verifier by $C_{\hat{W}^{[m]}}$. Making it public as a new detection threshold $S \cdot \|WM^*\|$ would leak knowledge about WM^* and, hence, about $\hat{W}^{[m]}$.

3.4   The Entire Detection Protocol

The common input to the protocol (a graphical illustration can be found in [12]) consists of the commitments C_{WM}, $C_{\hat{W}^{[m]}}$, the commitment description $descr_{com}$, W^*, the watermark position l and the detection threshold S. Furthermore, $\mathcal{P}$ knows the plain-text version of WM and $\hat{W}^{[m]}$ as well as the corresponding secret opening information of the commitments.

First, $\mathcal{P}$ and $\mathcal{V}$ compute $\hat{W}*^{[m]}$ according to the JPEG-analog zig-zag heuristic, starting at diagonal l. In several stages, $\mathcal{P}$ and $\mathcal{V}$ interactively compute the required committed intermediate results C_Δ, C_{A^2} and C_B. Finally, $\mathcal{P}$ proves to $\mathcal{V}$ that the detection equation (6) is satisfied.

$\mathcal{V}$ computes all m components C_{Δ_i} of C_Δ homomorphically as $C_{\Delta_i} := g^{\hat{W}*_i^{[m]}}$. $\left(C_{\hat{W}_i^{[m]}}\right)^{-1}$. The committed addends for C_A, i.e., $C_{WM_i \cdot \Delta_i}$, have to be provided by $\mathcal{P}$ and $\mathcal{P}$ initiates m subproofs $\mathsf{PoK}_{mult}()$ to convince $\mathcal{V}$ that the products contained in $C_{WM_i \cdot \Delta_i}$ are correct. Afterwards, $\mathcal{V}$ can compute C_A homomorphically on his own as $C_A := \prod_{i=0}^{m-1} C_{WM_i \cdot \Delta_i}$. Before the squaring step, $\mathcal{P}$ has to prove that A contained in C_A is greater or equal to zero. Otherwise, this would imply that $corr$ in Equation (3) is < 0 and $\mathcal{V}$ would be assured already in this stage of the protocol that WM is not present in W^* and aborts the protocol. Finally, $\mathcal{P}$ generates C_{A^2}, sends it to $\mathcal{V}$ and proves in zero-knowledge that C_{A^2} indeed contains the square of the value A contained in C_A.

In the next protocol section, value B of Equation (6) is determined: $\mathcal{P}$ provides $C_{\Delta_i^2}$ and proves that $C_{\Delta_i^2}$ indeed contains the square of the value Δ_i contained in C_{Δ_i}. Then $\mathcal{V}$ can compute C_B and C_{A^2-B} by making use of the commitment scheme's homomorphic property. The watermark detection protocol is finished by a proof that the value $A^2 - B$, contained in C_{A^2-B}, is greater or equal to 0.

Completeness of the protocol follows from the completeness of all subprotocols and the homomorphic property of the commitment scheme. The *soundness* of the entire protocol holds, because $\mathcal{P}$ would either have to break the soundness of at least one sub-protocol or the binding property of the commitment scheme. As both is assumed to be computationally infeasible, soundness of the overall protocol follows. The *zero-knowledge* property follows from the zero-knowledge property of the sub-protocols and from the fact that additional communication consists of commitments, which are statistically hiding.

4   Implementation Results

Theoretical Bounds: We discuss the communication complexity for the sequential composition of non-interactive elementary sub-protocols. The generation of $\hat{W}*^{[m]}$ will be neglected in computation complexity as it is not part of the very zero-knowledge watermark detection protocol. All in all, in addition to the protocol communication of the sub-proofs, $\mathcal{P}$ transfers $2m + 1$ commitments (namely $C_{WM_i \cdot \Delta_i}$, C_{A^2} and $C_{\Delta_i^2}$; $i = 0, \ldots, m - 1$), which corresponds to approximately $(2m + 1) \cdot |n|$ bits of traffic. $\mathsf{Comm}_{(\mathcal{P},\mathcal{V})}^{WMCox} = m \cdot \mathsf{Comm}_{(\mathcal{P},\mathcal{V})}^{\mathsf{PoK}_{mult}()} + 2 \cdot \mathsf{Comm}_{(\mathcal{P},\mathcal{V})}^{\mathsf{PoK}_{\geq 0}()} + (m + 1) \cdot \mathsf{Comm}_{(\mathcal{P},\mathcal{V})}^{\mathsf{PoK}_{sq}()} + (2m + 1) \cdot |n| = (2m+17)|n|+(10m+44)|F|+(5m+20)|T|+(13m+55)k+(5m+22)B+8m+33$.

Next we consider $\mathcal{V}$'s computation complexity: The homomorphic computations which provide the intermediate committed results require the following operations: The computation of $C_{\Delta_i} : m \cdot E + m \cdot I + m \cdot M$, $C_A : (m - 1) \cdot M$, $C_B : E + (m - 1) \cdot M$, and the computation of $C_{A^2-B} : I + M$ such that we obtain a computation complexity of $(m + 1) \cdot E + (m + 1) \cdot I + (3m - 1) \cdot M$. Together with the sub-protocols, we get $\mathsf{Comp}_{\mathcal{V}}^{WMCox} = m \cdot \mathsf{Comp}_{\mathcal{V}}^{\mathsf{PoK}_{mult}()} + 2 \cdot \mathsf{Comp}_{\mathcal{V}}^{\mathsf{PoK}_{\geq 0}()} + (m+1) \cdot \mathsf{Comp}_{\mathcal{V}}^{\mathsf{PoK}_{sq}()} + (m+1) \cdot E + (m+1) \cdot I + (3m-1) \cdot M = (16m + 67) \cdot E + (6m + 23) \cdot I + (13m + 49) \cdot M$.

$\mathcal{P}$ is able to follow $\mathcal{V}$'s homomorphic operations directly on the secret values and secret keys of the corresponding commitments. Therefore, we obtain a computation complexity of $(4m + 4) \cdot E + (4m + 5) \cdot M$. Hence, $\mathcal{P}$'s computation complexity including all sub-protocols is: $\mathsf{Comp}_{\mathcal{P}}^{WMCox} = m \cdot \mathsf{Comp}_{\mathcal{P}}^{\mathsf{PoK}_{mult}()} + 2 \cdot \mathsf{Comp}_{\mathcal{P}}^{\mathsf{PoK}_{\geq 0}()} + (m + 1) \cdot \mathsf{Comp}_{\mathcal{P}}^{\mathsf{PoK}_{sq}()} + (4m + 4) \cdot E + (4m + 5) \cdot M = (14m + 84) \cdot E + (19m + 95) \cdot M + 2 \cdot L$.

This leads to a total computation complexity of $\mathsf{Comp}_{(\mathcal{P},\mathcal{V})}^{WMCox} = (30m + 151) \cdot E + (6m + 23) \cdot I + (32m + 144) \cdot M + 2 \cdot L$.

Practical Results: A prototype implementation was done in JAVA to achieve a proof of concept of the practicability of zero-knowledge watermark detection. Table 2 shows the results for different numbers of coefficients while the security parameters were chosen as follows: $|n| = 1024$, $B = 1024$, $T = 2^{512}$, $|F| = 80$ and $k = 40$. The runtime was measured for a prover and a verifier process, running simultaneously on one Athlon 1200 desktop PC. The estimated lower bound for the communication complexity $\mathsf{Comm}_{(\mathcal{P},\mathcal{V})}$ – without any implementation or network overhead – is obtained by summarising the theoretical results from Table 1 together with the transmission of the supplementary commitments. The last column of Table 2 shows that if the communication traffic exchanged by our implementation is compressed by a zip-packer, we come very close to the expected theoretical bound $\mathsf{Comm}_{(\mathcal{P},\mathcal{V})}$.

Since the same bases g and h are used in all subproofs and intermediate commitments, the use of fixed-base exponentiation algorithms (see Chapter 14 of [13]), achieved a speed up of factor 3 for the modular exponentiations. The precomputation required by these exponentiation algorithms took 4 : 20 minutes

Table 2. time [min:sec] and $\mathsf{Comm}_{(\mathcal{P},\mathcal{V})}$ [Bytes], precomputation time excluded

Coeffs	time	$\mathsf{Comm}_{(\mathcal{P},\mathcal{V})}$	measured $\mathsf{Comm}_{(\mathcal{P},\mathcal{V})}$	zip $(\mathsf{Comm}_{(\mathcal{P},\mathcal{V})})$	$\frac{\mathsf{Comm}_{(\mathcal{P},\mathcal{V})}}{\mathrm{zip}(\mathsf{Comm}_{(\mathcal{P},\mathcal{V})})}$ in %
100	0:58	152,360	221,614	161,879	5.6
200	1:53	290,560	413,808	303,825	4.4
400	3:42	566,960	801,080	587,493	3.5
800	7:19	1,119,760	1,572,529	1,154,695	3.0
1000	9:09	1,396,160	1,958,554	1,438,377	2.9

and can be done during the setup of the commitment scheme and has to be done only once for all further executions of watermark detection protocol.

5 Conclusion

We presented the entire technical details how to construct a non-interactive zero-knowledge watermark detection protocol for the watermarking scheme by Cox et al [3] chosen as an established correlation-based scheme for many similar derivatives. The obtained results of a prototype implementation state that this secure methodology is indeed applicable in practice and not just a theoretical construction.

References

1. Adelsbach, A., Sadeghi, A.R.: Zero-knowledge watermark detection and proof of ownership. In: Information Hiding, IHW 2001. Volume 2137 of LNCS., Springer, Germany (2001) 273–288
2. Adelsbach, A., Katzenbeisser, S., Sadeghi, A.R.: Watermark detection with zero-knowledge disclosure. ACM Multimedia Systems Journal, Special Issue on Multimedia Security **9** (2003) 266–278
3. Cox, I., Kilian, J., Leighton, T., Shamoon, T.: A secure, robust watermark for multimedia. In: Information Hiding—First International Workshop, IH'96. Volume 1174 of LNCS., Springer Verlag (1996) 175–190
4. Hernandez, J., Perez-Gonzales, F.: Statistical analysis of watermarking schemes for copyright protection of images. In: Proceedings of the IEEE. Volume 87. (1999) 1142–1166
5. Damgård, I.: Commitment schemes and zero-knowledge protocols. In Damgård, I., ed.: Lectures on data security: modern cryptology in theory and practise. Volume 1561 of LNCS. Springer Verlag (1998) 63–86
6. Damgård, I., Fujisaki, E.: A statistically-hiding integer commitment scheme based on groups with hidden order. In: ASIACRYPT. Volume 2501 of LNCS., Springer (2002) 125–142
7. Boudot, F.: Efficient proofs that a committed number lies in an interval. In: Advances in Cryptology – EUROCRYPT '2000. Volume 1807 of LNCS., Springer Verlag (2000) 431–444
8. Lipmaa, H.: On diophantine complexity and statistical zero-knowledge arguments. In: ASIACRYPT. Volume 2894 of LNCS., Springer (2003) 398–415

9. Bellare, M., Rogaway, P.: Random oracles are practical: A paradigm for designing efficient protocols. In: Proceedings of the ACM CCS, ACM Press (1993) 62–73
10. Rabin, M.O., Shallit, J.O.: Randomized Algorithms in Number Theory. Communications on Pure and Applied Mathematics **39** (1986) S 239– S 256
11. Piva, A., Barni, M., Bartolini, F., Cappellini, V.: Dct-based watermark recovering without resorting to the uncorrupted original image. In: Proceedings of ICIP97. Volume I., Santa Barbara, CA, USA, IEEE (1997) 520–523
12. Adelsbach, A., Rohe, M., Sadeghi, A.R.:   Full   version   of   this   paper. http://www.prosec.rub.de/publications.html (2005)
13. Menezes, A.J., van Oorschot, P.C., Vanstone, S.A.: Handbook of Applied Cryptography. CRC Press series on discrete mathematics and its applications. CRC Press (1997) ISBN 0-8493-8523-7.

Video Surveillance:
A Distributed Approach to Protect Privacy

Martin Schaffer and Peter Schartner

University of Klagenfurt, Austria
Computer Science · System Security
{m.schaffer, p.schartner}@syssec.at

Abstract. The topmost concern of users who are kept under surveillance by a CCTV-System is the loss of their privacy. To gain a high acceptance by the monitored users, we have to assure, that the recorded video-material is only available to a subset of authorized users under exactly previously defined circumstances. In this paper we propose a CCTV video surveillance system providing privacy in a distributed way using threshold multi-party computation. Due to the flexibility of the access structure, we can handle the problem of loosing private-key-shares that are necessary for reconstructing video-material as well as adding new users to the system. If a pre-defined threshold is reached, a shared update of the master secret and the according re-encryption of previously stored ciphertext without revealing the plaintext is provided.

1 Introduction

The major concern of users monitored by a CCTV video surveillance system is the loss of their privacy. It is obvious, that encrypting the recorded material raises the acceptance by the monitored users. But what about unauthorized decryption? In this paper we propose several mechanisms concerning the setup, the recording and the retrieval of videos, and the key management during all these phases. Some of the mechanisms involve multi-party computation (MPC, see [18,6,8]), so that we can enforce dual control. A trusted third party (TTP) may also be used to enforce dual control. But if this TTP is compromised, a single unauthorized person may be able to decrypt the whole video-material. The main requirements for our system include:

- Privacy-protection of the monitored users.
- Shared generation and update of keys and key components.
- Tree-based access structure to provide a mechanism for substitution.
- Dual control (4-eyes principle) within the video retrieval process.
- Minimal access of authorized people to monitored information.

Several papers about video surveillance exist, most of which focus on the ability to detect and identify moving targets. Only a few discuss the privacy protection of recorded material. The authors in [9] for example describe a cooperative, multi-sensor video surveillance system that provides continuous coverage

J. Dittmann, S. Katzenbeisser, and A. Uhl (Eds.): CMS 2005, LNCS 3677, pp. 140–149, 2005.

over battlefield areas. In [10] the emphasis lies on face recognition – a solution to protect privacy by de-identifying facial images is given. A similar approach can be found in [2] concentrating on videos in general. The most general solution to cover privacy in coherence to monitoring targets seems to be presented in [16]. However the system in [16] uses a privacy preserving video console providing access control lists. Once the console has been compromised videos may be decrypted without any restrictions.

In our paper we focus on video surveillance where real-time reactions are *not* necessary like in private organisations where staff has to be monitored. In case of criminal behaviour recorded video material can be decrypted if sufficiently enough instances agree – this e.g. is not provided in [10]. Our approach can certainly be combined with the general solution proposed in [16] but also used for other applications such as key escrow as proposed in [15].

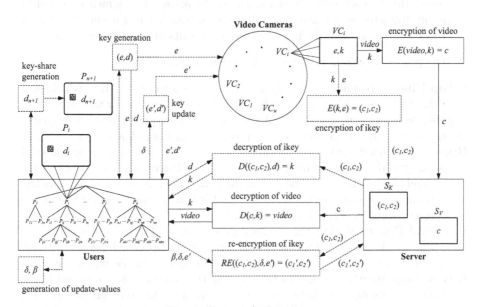

Fig. 1. System Architecture

Figure 1 shows the system architecture of the proposed system including all components and interactions within the setup phase, recording phase, retrieval phase and key management. Computations within dotted boxes represent MPCs whereas undotted boxes are performed by a single instance. Labelled arrows show which instance(s) deliver(s) or receive(s) which value(s).

The proposed system employs the following hardware-components and users:

Video Cameras. According to the monitored processes, video cameras record either single pictures or videos. Since we want to guarantee privacy of the monitored users, we have to encrypt the video material. After encrypting the video, it is sent to the video server S_V, whereas the key used for this encryption is (encrypted and) sent to the key server S_K.

Video Server S_V. Here the received encrypted video material is stored in a suitable database so that it can be easily retrieved, if required.

Key Server S_K. Keys that are used for encrypting videos are chosen interval-wise (so we provide minimal access to videos). Therefore, we call them interval-keys (ikeys) and store them encrypted at S_K.

Users. In this paper, the term *user* always means an instance retrieving videos, not a person monitored by the system. Within strict regulations (e.g. dual control), these users are authorized to decrypt the stored videos. Due to the fact that enterprises are often hierarchically structured, we have to provide easy deputy-mechanisms. If a user is not available, he may be simply replaced by a qualified set of users of the next lower level in the hierarchy.

Smartcards. In order to enforce the cooperation of several users in the decryption process, the corresponding private key d is shared among a group of users. Hence, each user holds a share of the private key, which is stored in a pin-protected smartcard. Note that the private key d is never available in the system or present during intermediate results of the decryption process.

The proposed system consists of the following procedures:

Setup Phase. To initialize the system, the users perform a MPC which provides each user with a random share of private key d in a fair way. Additionally, the users generate shares of the corresponding public key. These shares are sent to the video cameras which reconstruct the public key e.

Recording Phase. Due to performance reasons, the recorded video-material is encrypted by use of a hybrid cryptosystem. Hence, each video camera has to hold the public key e. The ikey is then encrypted by use of an asymmetric scheme (employing the public key e) and is finally sent to S_K, whereas the symmetrically encrypted video is sent to S_V.

Retrieval Phase. Within the retrieval phase, the authorized users perform a MPC which provides them with the ikey of the specific interval, without direct usage of the private key d (which corresponds to the public key e).

Key Management. In order to take part in the system, a new user has to retrieve a share of the private key d. To achieve this, the users already enrolled in the system perform a MPC which finally provides the new user with his share. Since the decryption process involves threshold cryptography, some smartcards (and the shares stored there) may be lost, without any danger for the privacy of the stored video material. Additionally, we employ a mechanism which regularly updates the remaining shares (without changing the shared private key) and hence makes the shares on the lost (or stolen) smartcards useless. Finally, we propose a mechanism to perform a shared update of d and the corresponding public key e. It is obvious that in this case, all encrypted ikeys have to be re-encrypted, whereas the encrypted video material remains unchanged since the ikeys have not been compromised.

In the remainder of the paper we will give a more formal description of the processes briefly discussed by now. Note that within the proposed mechanisms we will only care about passive adversaries (see [6,8]) from inside the system and we will assume that there exist pair-wise protected links between the individual parties participating in the surveillance process.

2 Fundamentals

Every computation in the following sections – except symmetric algorithms – is reduced modulo p (within bases) or modulo q (within exponents, sharing polynomials and interpolation formulas). The direct successors of the root of the tree-based access structure are called first-level-users and united in the set $\mathcal{U}$. To reduce complexity, we will only consider one video camera called VC.

2.1 Shamir's Secret Sharing

To share a secret $s \in \mathbb{Z}_q^*$ among n users resulting in the shares $s_1, \ldots, s_n$ (short: $s \mapsto (s_1, \ldots, s_n)$) we use the following randomly chosen t-degree polynomial according to [17]:

$$s_i = g(i), \quad g(x) = s + \sum_{j=1}^{t} r_j \cdot x^j, \quad r_j \in_R \mathbb{Z}_q^* \tag{1}$$

In order to reconstruct the secret s (short: $(s_1, \ldots, s_n) \mapsto s$) we need at least $t+1$ shares, because there are $t+1$ unknown values in a t-degree polynomial. For efficiency reasons we use the interpolation formula of Lagrange (see e.g. [12]):

$$s = g(0), \quad g(x) = \sum_{i=1}^{n} s_i \cdot \lambda_{x,i}^s, \quad \lambda_{x,i}^s = \prod_{\substack{j=1 \\ j \neq i}}^{n} (x - j) \cdot (i - j)^{-1} \tag{2}$$

Several computations of the upcoming sections use the following transformation:

$$z = y^s \overset{(2)}{=} y^{\sum_{i=1}^{n} s_i \cdot \lambda_{0,i}^s} = \prod_{i=1}^{n} y^{s_i \cdot \lambda_{0,i}^s} \tag{3}$$

2.2 Symmetric Cryptosystem

Recording videos causes a lot of data. Hence, we apply a symmetric algorithm (e.g. AES, see [1]) to encrypt the video-material. We simply define the encryption function $E_S(m, k) = c$ and decryption function $D_S(c, k) = m$.

2.3 ElGamal Cryptosystem

We suppose that the reader is familiar with the basic ElGamal cryptosystem [4]. Assuming the key generation has already taken place resulting in the public key e and the private key d, the encryption E and decryption D can be performed as follows (with g a generator of $\mathbb{Z}_q^*$):

$$E(m, e) = (g^\alpha, m \cdot e^\alpha) = (c_1, c_2), \quad e = g^d, \quad \alpha \in_R \mathbb{Z}_q^* \tag{4}$$

$$D((c_1, c_2), d) = c_2 \cdot \left(c_1^d\right)^{-1} = m \tag{5}$$

3   ElGamal Threshold Decryption and Re-encryption

A public key cryptosystem can be shared in several ways. The plaintext, the public key, the ciphertext as well as the private key can be used in a distributed way. For a video surveillance system sharing the encryption process does not make sense. However, sharing the decryption process enables us to realize dual-control. To increase the security it is very useful to share the ciphertext as well. For lack of space we decided not to describe this variation. Instead we focus on how to share the decryption process emphasizing on selected aspects of the corresponding management of key-shares. Due to its simplicity we use ElGamal threshold decryption firstly proposed in [3]. The basic ElGamal decryption can be divided into two parts so that its computation only uses shares of private key d. Therefore d has to be shared using a t-degree polynomial: $d \mapsto (d_1, \ldots, d_n)$. The ElGamal decryption function can be modified replacing d with its Lagrange-representation over the shares:

$$D((c_1, c_2), d) = c_2 \cdot \left(c_1^d\right)^{-1} \overset{(3)}{=} c_2 \cdot \left(\prod_{i=1}^{n} c_{1i}^{\lambda_{0,i}^d}\right)^{-1} \overset{(5)}{=} m, \quad c_{1i} = c_1^{d_i} \qquad (6)$$

Now we can divide this computation into the following two sub-functions:

Decryption Step 1. This step has to be done by at least $t + 1$ shareowners.

$$D_1(c_1, d_i) = c_1^{d_i} \overset{(6)}{=} c_{1i}$$

Decryption Step 2. To compute m at least $t + 1$ outputs of D_1 are required.

$$D_2((c_{11}, \ldots, c_{1n}), c_2) = c_2 \cdot \left(\prod_{i=1}^{n} c_{1i}^{\lambda_{0,i}^d}\right)^{-1} \overset{(6)}{=} m$$

If the private key d has been compromised we have to provide an update of d and a re-encryption of the corresponding ciphertext without revealing plaintext. In [19] an approach based on distributed blinding is given. There, a ciphertext is first blinded by a randomly chosen and encrypted value. After having decrypted the blinded ciphertext in a particular way the resulting blinded plaintext is encrypted with the new public key and finally unblinded. The advantage of this approach is that the instances that blind the ciphertext do not know anything about the private key. This is useful for transferring a ciphertext from one instance to another one (with different keys). In our case we need a mechanism that provides an update of the private key and the corresponding ciphertext. In our scenario the solution in [19] would require a distributed blinding, a distributed decryption and a distributed unblinding. As a consequence we propose a different variation based on the distance δ between the old private key d and the new private key d'. The advantage of our re-encryption is that we only modify the old ciphertext and do not perform decryptions and encryptions respectively.

Theorem 1. *Assume (c_1, c_2) is a ciphertext performed over m and e. Then a ciphertext based on $e' = e \cdot g^\delta$ and decryptable by $d' = d + \delta$ can be computed by doing the following random transformation of (c_1, c_2) without intermediately revealing the corresponding plaintext m:*

$$RE((c_1, c_2), \delta, e') = (c_1 \cdot g^\beta, c_2 \cdot c_1^\delta \cdot e'^\beta) = (c_1', c_2'), \quad \beta \in_R \mathbb{Z}_q^* \qquad (7)$$

$$d' = d + \delta, \quad e' = e \cdot g^\delta \qquad (8)$$

Proof. Let (c_1', c_2') be a transformed ciphertext according to (7). Then the basic ElGamal decryption with new private key d' results in m because:

$$D((c_1', c_2'), d') \stackrel{(5)}{=} c_2' \cdot (c_1'^{d'})^{-1} \stackrel{(7)}{=} c_2 \cdot c_1^\delta \cdot e'^\beta \cdot ((c_1 \cdot g^\beta)^{d'})^{-1}$$

$$\stackrel{(8)}{=} c_2 \cdot c_1^\delta \cdot (e \cdot g^\delta)^\beta \cdot ((c_1 \cdot g^\beta)^{d+\delta})^{-1}$$

$$\stackrel{(4)}{=} m \cdot e^\alpha \cdot g^{\alpha \cdot \delta} \cdot (g^d \cdot g^\delta)^\beta \cdot ((g^\alpha \cdot g^\beta)^{d+\delta})^{-1}$$

$$\stackrel{(4)}{=} m \cdot g^{\alpha(d+\delta)} \cdot g^{\beta(d+\delta)} \cdot (g^{(\alpha+\beta)(d+\delta)})^{-1} = m$$

$\square$

The re-encryption process in (7) can also be divided into two sub-functions so that it can be performed in a distributed way (assume: δ and β are shared):

Re-encryption Step 1. The first step is done locally by every user P_i.

$$RE_1(c_1, \delta_i, e', \beta_i) = (g^{\beta_i}, c_1^{\delta_i}, e'^{\beta_i}) = (\tilde{c}_{1i}, c_{1i}, e_i')$$

Re-encryption Step 2. The second step uses all outputs of RE_1 and the old ciphertext.

$$RE_2(c_1, (\tilde{c}_{11}, \ldots, \tilde{c}_{1n}), (c_{11}, \ldots, c_{1n}), (e_1', \ldots, e_n'), c_2) = (c_1', c_2')$$

$$c_1' = c_1 \cdot \prod_{i=1}^{n} \tilde{c}_{1i}^{\lambda_{0,i}^\beta}, \quad c_2' = c_2 \cdot \left(\prod_{i=1}^{n} c_{1i}^{\lambda_{0,i}^\delta} \right) \cdot \prod_{i=1}^{n} e_i'^{\lambda_{0,i}^\beta}$$

If there is no need to mask the correspondence between old and new ciphertext, the modifications of the original randomness α by use of β can be removed.

4   Video Surveillance

4.1   Setup Phase

During the initialization of the system, a key-pair (e, d) for the ElGamal cryptosystem has to be generated in a shared way. To achieve this, all users cooperatively generate shares of the private key d without reconstructing it. Then they compute shares of e without any interaction and send them to the video camera which interpolates e. The distributed key generation proposed in [11] is very useful to generate a private key without reconstructing it. A more secure version is proposed in [5]. However, we need a fair tree-structured generation of the private key. Based on this fact we modify the original protocol in order to be able to build such a tree. A detailed description of a tree-shared generation of secret values can be found in [14] – we refer to it for lack of space.

4.2   Recording Phase

Within this phase VC uses local hybrid encryption. First of all VC generates an interval-key k at random and encrypts the interval-video using symmetric encryption described in section 2.2: $E_S(video, k) = c$. For encryption of k the camera uses asymmetric encryption described in section 2.3 with public key e: $E(k, e) = (c_1, c_2)$. Within each interval the camera sends the encrypted video to S_V and its corresponding encrypted ikey to S_K. Both server store the ciphertext in a particular database.

4.3   Retrieval Phase

The retrieval of a particular video can be done in two steps:

Decryption of ikey. S_K has to send (c_1, c_2) to every user in $\mathcal{U}$ who agrees to reconstruct the video. Then each user P_i performs $D_1(c_1, d_i) = c_{1i}$ and broadcasts the result within $\mathcal{U}$. Finally every user P_i decrypts ikey k by computing $D_2((c_{11}, \ldots, c_{1n}), c_2) = k$.

Decryption of Video. S_V has to send the encrypted video c (corresponding to k) to every user P_i who decrypts it by performing $D_S(c, k) = video$.

5   Managing Private-Key-Shares

Generally, an access structure has to be very flexible within an organisation. The more users exist the sooner it might occur that a user is leaving or joining the system.

5.1   Registration of a New User

When registering a new user P_{n+1} we have to distinguish users of the first level who do not have a predecessor and users of lower levels who always have predecessors.

New First-Level-User. Every existing first-level-user P_i shares his share $d_i \mapsto (d_{i1}, \ldots, d_{in+1})$ among $\mathcal{U}' = \mathcal{U} \cup \{P_{n+1}\}$. Then every user P_j in $\mathcal{U}'$ interpolates the received shares $(d_{1j}, \ldots, d_{nj}) \mapsto d_j$. Due to the fact, that every share changes, an update of successor-shares has to be performed.

Others. Every user P_i of a lower level always has a predecessor P who is responsible for registering his new successor P_{n+1}. If P does not know the shares of his existing successors they have to send him their shares. Owning at least $t + 1$ shares of his successor enables P to generate a share $d_{n+1} = \sum_{i=1}^{n} d_i \cdot \lambda_{n+1,i}^d$ for P_{n+1} without provoking a recursive update of successor-shares. After importing d_{n+1} to P_{n+1}'s smartcard P removes $d_1, \ldots, d_n$ form his smartcard.

Generation of new shares can be done in several ways. An important fact is to keep side effects minimal which we cannot guarantee with the solution described above when registering a first-level-user. For more efficient but also some more complex variations we refer to our technical report [13].

5.2   Loss of Smartcards

If a user collects at least $t + 1$ previously lost smartcards he might be able to compromise the private key d. Regularly updates of shares without changing d make the collector's shares unusable. Such updates can be very time-consuming because all users of the access structure have to participate in the update process at the same time (except if centralized updates are used). If a user looses his smartcard his share can be reconstructed using the computations in section 5.1. We always have to consider the worst case which is that another user of the access structure finds the smartcard. Then the threshold is decreased which we want to avoid. Due to this fact we propose to run an update-protocol first and then generate a new share for the user who lost his smartcard.

5.3   Proactive Behaviour

Collecting lost smartcards can be used to decrease the threshold. So we have to update the private-key-shares without changing the private key (as proposed in [7]). This should be done in case of loosing a smartcard but can also be performed proactively regularly. Using short intervals can be very time-consuming if updates are done in a distributed way because users have to be online at the same time. In this case the update could be initiated by a central trusted authority. A big advantage of this variation is that updates could be run in batch-mode.

What happens if threshold t is vulnerable within one interval? In this case we propose to update the private key in a shared way in sufficient time which forces a re-encryption of ciphertext that corresponds to the compromised private key (see section 6). Until the re-encryption process has been finished S_K has to be protected against availability-compromising attacks. To handle this problem we propose to share the ciphertext-pairs (c_1, c_2) among several server. This would lead to several modifications of the basic system which we do not describe here.

5.4   De-registration of Users

If a user leaves the organisation his smartcard (holding the share) should be securely destroyed. If a new user takes over his tasks the protocol described in section 5.1 has to be run.

6   Update of Private Key and Corresponding Ciphertext

First of all (e, d) has to be updated by all cameras and all shareowners of d. Before destroying the update-values a re-encryption of every ciphertext (c_1, c_2) generated using e has to be done.

Shared Generation of Update-Values. All the users in $\mathcal{U}$ run the tree-based key generation mentioned in section 4.1 to get shares $\delta_1, \ldots, \delta_n$ of a private-key-update δ and shares $\beta_1, \ldots, \beta_n$ of randomness-update β.

Update of Private-Key-Shares. Every user P_i computes $d'_i = d_i + \delta_i$ which is a share of private key $d' = d + \delta$.

Shared Update of Public Key. All users perform the updated public key $e' = e \cdot \prod_{i=1}^{n} g^{\delta_i \cdot \lambda^\delta_{0,i}}$ in a distributed way and send e' to VC.

Re-encryption of Encrypted ikeys. S_K has to send the old ciphertext-part c_1 to every user P_i participating in the re-encryption processes. Then each P_i has to perform $RE_1(c_1, \delta_i, e', \beta_i) = (\tilde{c}_{1i}, c_{1i}, e'_i)$. Finally, each output of RE_1 has to be sent to S_K which then replaces the old ciphertext (c_1, c_2) by the output of $RE_2(c_1, (\tilde{c}_{11}, \ldots, \tilde{c}_{1n}), (c_{11}, \ldots, c_{1n}), (e'_1, \ldots, e'_n), c_2) = (c'_1, c'_2)$.

7   Security Analysis

We now briefly analyse the power of each instance of the system to retrieve any secret information. However, we do not consider the tree-structure – the analysis can be interpreted recursively.

As long as video cameras are not able to solve the discrete logarithm problem and do not compromise at least $t + 1$ first-level-users, they are not able to get any information about the private key d, update-values δ and β or any shares of the users. To decrypt video-material S_V needs the corresponding ikey. But to get access to it he has to compromise at least $t + 1$ first-level-users and S_K. A first-level-user needs at least t other shares to reconstruct d or update-values δ and β. Moreover, he has to compromise S_K and S_V to be able to decrypt videos. Up to t smartcards of first-level-users can be stolen and compromised without revealing any information about d. Regularly updates of shares increase the security of the private key. Moreover, the smartcards are secured by a Personal Identification Number. To preserve resistance against active malicious behaviour (e.g. sending wrong intermediate results), extensions according to secure multi-party computation with active adversaries are required (see [6,8]).

8   Conclusion and Future Research

Considering the requirements stated in section 1, it can be seen that all of them have been realized.

Privacy-protection of the monitored users is provided by encryption of video-material and interval-keys. 4-eyes principle (dual control) is provided by a tree-based access structure. Minimal access of authorized people to monitored information is guaranteed by scaling monitored intervals to a minimum so that many ikeys are generated. Keys and key components are generated tree-based in a fair distributed way according to [14]. Update of keys and key components is realized by tree-based update-value generation and threshold re-encryption. Tree-based secret sharing provides the possibility to replace any user by his successors.

The discussed distributed version of ElGamal is well known since [3] and only one-out-of many. Discussing how public key cryptosystems can be distributed can lead to many more applications than access structures to monitored information.

When sharing functions the management of key-shares appears to be much more difficult than the "normal" key management. So our future research work will emphasize on managing keys in distributed public-key cryptosystems keeping the number of local shares minimal not limiting to the ElGamal cryptosystem.

References

1. Advanced Encryption Standard (AES). FIPS-Pub 197, NIST, 2001.
2. M. Boyle, C. Edwards, S. Greenberg. The Effects on Filtered Video on Awareness and Privacy. CSCW'00: Proceed. of the 2000 ACM conference on Computer supported cooperative work, Philadephia, PA, USA, 2000, pages 1–10.
3. Y. Desmedt, Y. Frankel. Threshold Cryptosystems. Adv. in Crypt.: Proceed. of CRYPTO'89, Springer-Verlag, pp. 307–315, 1990.
4. T. ElGamal. A Public-Key Cryptosystem and a Signature Scheme Based on Discrete Logarithms. Adv. in Crypt.: CRYPTO'84, Springer-Verlag, pp. 10–18, 1985.
5. R. Gennaro et al. Secure Distributed Key Generation for Discrete-Log Based Cryptosystems. Proceed. of EUROCRYPT'99, Springer LNCS 1592, pp. 295-310.
6. O. Goldreich et al. How to play any mental game – a completeness theorem for protocols with honest majority. Proc. 19th ACM STOC, p. 218–229, 1987.
7. A. Herzberg et al. Proactive secret sharing or: how to cope with perpetual leakage. In Adv. in Crypt.: CRYPTO'95, vol. 963 of LNCS, Springer-Verlag, pp. 339–352.
8. M. Hirt. Multi-Party Computation: Efficient Protocols, General Adversaries, and Voting. Ph.D. thesis, ETH Zurich, 2001 Reprint as vol. 3 of ETH Series in Information Security and Cryptography, Hartung-Gorre Verlag, Konstanz, 2001.
9. R.T. Collins et al. A System for Video Surveillance and Monitoring. Proceedings of the American Nuclear Society (ANS) Eighth International Topical Meeting on Robotics and Remote Systems, 1999.
10. E. Newton, L. Sweeney, B. Malin. Preserving Privacy by De-identifying Facial Images. IEEE Transactions on Knowledge and Data Engineering, vol. 17, no. 2, pp. 232–243, February 2005.
11. T. Pedersen. A threshold cryptosystem without a trusted party. Adv. in Crypt.: EUROCRYPT'91, vol. 547 of LNCS, Springer-Verlag, pp. 522–526, 1991.
12. J. Pieprzyka, T. Hardjono, J. Seberry. Fundamentals of Computer Security. Springer-Verlag, 2003.
13. M. Schaffer. Managing Key-Shares in Distributed Public-Key Cryptosystems. Technical Report TR-syssec-05-04, University of Klagenfurt, Austria, August 2005.
14. M. Schaffer. Tree-shared Generation of a Secret Value. Technical Report TR-syssec-05-01, University of Klagenfurt, Austria, June 2005.
15. M. Schaffer, P. Schartner. Hierarchical Key Escrow with Passive Adversaries. Technical Report TR-syssec-05-02, University of Klagenfurt, Austria, June 2005.
16. A. Senior et al. Blinkering Surveillance: Enabling Video Privacy through Computer Vision. IBM Research Report RC22886 (W0308-109), August 28, 2003.
17. A. Shamir. How to share a secret. Comm. of the ACM, vol. 11, pp. 612–613, 1979.
18. A.C. Yao. Protocols for secure computation. In Proceed. of the 23rd IEEE Symposium on Foundations of Computer Security, 1982.
19. L. Zhou et al. Distributed Blinding for ElGamal Re-encryption. Proceed. 25th IEEE Int. Conf. on Distributed Computing Systems. Ohio, June 2005, p. 815–824.

Privacy-Preserving Electronic Health Records

Liesje Demuynck* and Bart De Decker

Department of Computer Science, K.U.Leuven,
Celestijnenlaan 200A, B-3001 Leuven, Belgium
{Liesje.Demuynck, Bart.DeDecker}@cs.kuleuven.be
http://www.cs.kuleuven.ac.be

Abstract. Electronic health records enable the global availability of medical data. This has numerous benefits for the quality of offered services. However, privacy concerns may arise as now both the patient's medical history as well as the doctor's activities can be tracked. In this paper, we propose an electronic health record system which allows the patient to control who has access to her health records. Furthermore, provided she does not misuse the system, a doctor will remain anonymous with respect to any central authority.

1 Introduction

In e-health, new information and communication technologies are used to improve the quality of healthcare services while at the same time reducing the corresponding costs. This is, for example, achieved by electronic health records (EHRs), which allow for global availability of medical information in a standardized format. EHRs enable efficient communication of medical information, and thus reduce costs and administrative overhead. Furthermore, medical errors can be reduced significantly. In current healthcare systems, medical data can be interpreted in ambiguous ways. Moreover, a patient's health records can be dispersed over multiple sites without the healthcare professional having access to (or even knowledge of) this data. EHRs provide a solution to these problems.

There are, however, serious privacy concerns associated with the move towards electronic health records. Medical data should not only be protected against outsiders, but also against insiders. Studies have shown that patients do not trust central authorities with their medical data. They want to decide themselves who is entrusted with this data and who is not. These concerns are justified, as unauthorized secondary use of medical information, for example by an employer or for advertising purposes, can easily be achieved.

Next to patients, healthcare providers want their privacy to be protected. A central repository of medical data controlled by strong access regulations allows for the monitoring of a doctor's actions. Central authorities can track down who is treated by which doctor, how, and for what reasons. Hence, patient-doctor autonomy is disrupted.

Unfortunately, current technologies abstract away from privacy concerns in order to obtain both secure and efficient health record systems. In this paper,

---

* Research Assistant of the Research Foundation - Flanders (FWO - Vlaanderen).

J. Dittmann, S. Katzenbeisser, and A. Uhl (Eds.): CMS 2005, LNCS 3677, pp. 150–159, 2005.

we propose a system which is both secure and privacy-preserving. The system protects the patient's privacy by allowing her to control who has access to her medical information. However, no personal information can be hidden from the doctor entrusted with this access. Furthermore, a doctor's privacy is conditionally preserved: unless abuse is detected, no central authority knows which patient is treated by which doctor and for what purposes.

The remainder of this paper is structured as follows. First, the building blocks used in the system are introduced. Afterwards, we describe the system itself and evaluate its properties. Finally, we conclude the paper with a brief discussion of related work and a summary containing the major conclusions and future work.

2   Basic Building Blocks

2.1   Cryptographic Hash Functions

A good hash function $\mathcal{H}$ resembles a random function as much as possible. It takes an input of arbitrary length and maps it to an output of fixed length. Hash functions are efficiently computable but hard to invert. Also, it is difficult to find two inputs mapping onto the same output.

2.2   The RSA Function

The RSA function [11] for an instance (n, v) is a trapdoor one-way permutation in $\mathbb{Z}_n^*$ defined as $\mathrm{RSA}_{(n,v)} : w \mapsto w^v \bmod n$. Here, value n is constructed as the product of two random primes p and q with binary length $|p| = |q| = |n|/2$. Value v is randomly chosen and relative prime to $\phi(n) = (p-1)(q-1)$.

The function is efficiently computable and easy to invert if $v^{-1} \bmod \phi(n)$ is known. It is assumed that in all other cases, the RSA function is hard to invert.

In the remainder of this paper, we will denote the execution of i subsequent applications of $\mathrm{RSA}_{(n,v)}$ to an initial value w as $\mathrm{RSA}^i_{(n,v)}(w)$, with $\mathrm{RSA}^0_{(n,v)}(w) = w$. Note that $\mathrm{RSA}^i_{(n,v)}(w) = \mathrm{RSA}_{(n,v^i)}(w)$ for each $i \in \mathbb{N}$.

2.3   The Guillou-Quisquater Proof of Knowledge

A Guillou-Quisquater proof of knowledge [7] is an interactive protocol between a prover P and a verifier V. The inputs to the protocol are public values x and (n, v). After successful execution, V is convinced that P knows a value w such that $w = \mathrm{RSA}^{-1}_{(n,v)}(x)$. In addition, the only thing V can learn from this protocol execution is whether or not P knows such a w.

In the remainder of this paper, we will denote the Guillou-Quisquater proof for an instance (n, v^i) with $i \in \mathbb{N} \setminus \{0\}$ as $\mathrm{GQProof}\{\mathrm{RSA}^{-i}_{(n,v)}(x)\}$.

2.4   Verifiable Encryption

A verifiable encryption scheme [13,1,3] is an interactive two-party protocol between a prover P and a verifier V. The public input of the protocol is a public encryption key pk and a value x with $(w, x) \in \mathcal{R}$ for a one-way relation $\mathcal{R}$

and a secret value w only known to P. After successful execution, V obtains an encryption of w under public key pk.

A verifiable encryption ensures the verifier that the encrypted value w is as such that $(w, x) \in \mathcal{R}$ for the specified relation $\mathcal{R}$ and public value x. As a consequence, it also convinces V that the prover knows a secret value w corresponding to x. Moreover, the protocol does not reveal any additional information about w to V than what she already knew beforehand. In particular, if V does not know the private key sk corresponding to pk, then she cannot find out w.

A verifiable encryption protocol can be created for the RSA relation $(w, x = \mathrm{RSA}^i_{(n,v)}(w))$. In the remainder of the paper, this encryption will be denoted as $\mathrm{VEncrypt}_{pk}\{w, w = \mathrm{RSA}^{-i}_{(n,v)}(x)\}$.

2.5   Anonymous Credential Systems

Anonymous credentials [4,2] allow for anonymous yet accountable transactions between users and organizations. Here, a simplified version of the system is presented. In particular, not all functionality is described and abstraction is made of the use of pseudonyms. Also, note that anonymous credential systems should be built on top of anonymous communication channels [5,10].

Credential Issuing. An organization can issue a credential to a user. This credential may contain attributes such as a name, address or expiration date. After successful execution of the issue protocol, the user receives a non-transferable credential *Cred* and the organization receives an issue transcript. The issue protocol will be denoted as getCred(*attrlist*) → *Cred*; *GetTrans*.

Credential Showing. The user proves to an organization that she is in possession of a credential *Cred*. In addition, she selectively discloses some attributes to the verifier. The result of the protocol is a transcript *ShowTrans* for the verifier. Different transcripts (and thus different shows) of the same credential cannot be linked to each other or to their corresponding *GetTrans*. During a show protocol, the user may decide to enable some additional options; she may sign a message *Msg* with her credential, which provides a provable link between *ShowTrans* and this message. In addition, she might enable *ShowTrans* to be deanonymizable. Upon fulfillment of the condition *DeanCond*, this allows for a trusted deanonymizer to recover the corresponding transcript *GetTrans*, which might then be used to identify the user. In the sequel, the show protocol will be denoted as showCred(*Cred*, [*attrs*], [*DeanCond*)], [*Msg*]) → *ShowTrans*.

Credential Revocation. A credential can be revoked by its issuer. This is denoted as revokeCred(*GetTrans*).

3   Description of the System

We first give an overview of the system's requirements, roles and protocols. Afterwards, the construction of these protocols is described in detail.

3.1 Requirements, Roles and Protocols

Requirements. The system consists of anonymized electronic health records, which are stored in a central database. Each record contains medical information about a patient, signed by an approved but unknown healthcare professional.

To protect the patient's privacy, only authorized doctors may access the database. These doctors can read and inspect all the health records. However, unless they have gained the patient's trust, doctors should not be able to link different records of a patient to each other or to the patient. This trust must be complete, i.e. the patient must not be able to hide partial medical information towards a trusted doctor.

Doctors must enjoy full anonymity with respect to the system. It must not be possible for any central authority to track down which patient is treated by which doctor and for what purposes. However, when abuse of anonymity is detected, this anonymity should be revoked and appropriate actions should be taken. Types of abuse are, for example, illegal requests for a patient's health records or the submitting of incorrect health records.

Roles. An individual using the system is either a *doctor D* or a *patient P*. A doctor is assumed to live up to a deontological code and does not share any medical information about a patient with another doctor, unless both are entrusted with the care of this person. A special type of doctor is an *emergency doctor ED*. An emergency doctor works at an emergency room (ER) and hence needs special privileges.

The system itself consists of a *registrar R*, a *database manager DBMan*, and an *emergency service ES*. Next to this, a number of *deanonymizers* may be present. Deanonymizers judge and perform deanonymizations when abuse is detected. The registrar stores bookkeeping information and registers both patients and doctors. The database manager guides the retrieval and addition of health records from and to the database by performing the necessary access controls. Finally, the emergency service performs emergency retrieval of health records when the patient is unconscious and her doctor is unreachable.

Protocols. A patient entering the system first performs a *patientRegistration* with R. As a result, she obtains a list of private keys $sk_p(i)$ ($i \in \{1, \ldots, t\}$), which will be used at successive moments in time. P can now entrust a doctor D with her medical information by executing a *visitDoctor* protocol with D. From then on this doctor will be able to manage all of her health records. If P wants to end this trust relation, she enables a new private key $sk_p(i+1)$ by performing the *changePrivateKey* protocol with R. As a consequence, D will no longer be able to add or retrieve any *new* health records concerning P.

A doctor registers with the system by executing the *doctorRegistration* protocol with R. This provides her with an access credential to the record database. Once entrusted by a patient, D can manage her health records by means of the *addHealthRecord* and *retrieveHealthRecords* protocols. Finally, a doctor working at ER may perform an emergency retrieval of a patient's medical data by using the *emergencyRetrieval* protocol.

3.2   Practical Construction

System Setup. A trusted third party TTP generates a strong hash function $\mathcal{H}$ and system parameters (n, v) for the RSA-function. Furthermore, the emergency service ES generates an encryption keypair (pk_{es}, sk_{es}). Private key sk_{es} is kept secret by ES, while values (n, v), $\mathcal{H}$ and pk_{es} are made public to all participants. As no participant may invert the RSA-function, TTP must make sure the factors p and q of $n = pq$ are discarded immediately after parameter generation.

Health Records. A health record is a show transcript $ShowTrans$ generated as a result of a deanonymizable credential show by a doctor. The content of the record is a message of the form $(ID, medical\ data)$, signed during the show protocol. *Medical data* is a text string representing the health information and *ID* is a unique identification tag created as $ID = \mathcal{H}(sk_p(i) \parallel j)$ for a counter value j and a patient's temporal private key $sk_p(i)$. To ensure the uniqueness of *ID*, each counter value is used only once for a temporal private key.

PatientRegistration. A patient entering the system first generates her (private keys, public key) pair $((sk_p(1), \ldots, sk_p(t)), pk_p)$. This is done in a preprocessing stage. Patient P chooses a suitable t and random value $x \in_{\mathcal{R}} \mathbb{Z}_n^*$. She then sets $sk_p(i) = RSA_{(n,v)}^{t-i}(x)$ for $i \in \{1, \ldots, t\}$ and $pk_p = RSA_{(n,v)}^t(x)$. Each of the private keys will be used at successive moments in time. Note that, given private key $sk_p(i)$, all previous keys $sk_p(j)$ with $j \in \{1, \ldots, i-1\}$ can be computed, but none of the future keys $sk_p(k)$ with $k \in \{i+1, \ldots, t\}$.

P then starts the registration procedure with R. In a first step, she identifies herself to R and provides her with a verifiable encryption $\omega_{sk_p(1)}$ of $sk_p(1)$, encrypted under the emergency service's public key. Note that $\omega_{sk_p(1)}$ implicitly proves her knowledge of $sk_p(1)$. Afterwards, P retrieves a credential binding her identity with her current private key $sk_p(1)$.

The registrar additionally stores some bookkeeping information for later use. In particular, she stores a specification $i = 1$ of the current private key $sk_p(i)$, a verifiable encryption of $sk_p(1)$ and the current value n_1 for the counter used when creating a new record *ID*. She also stores the credential's issue transcript.

---

1. P : $((sk_p(1), \ldots, sk_p(t)), pk_p) = \text{generatekeys}(t)$
2. $P \leftrightarrow R$: verification of P's identity
3. $P \rightarrow R$: send(pk_p)
4. $P \leftrightarrow R$: $\omega_{sk_p(1)} = \text{VEncrypt}_{pk_{es}}\{sk_p(1), sk_p(1) = RSA_{(n,v)}^{-1}(pk_p)\}$
5. $P \leftrightarrow R$: getCred($\{$'patient'$, P, pk_p, 1\}) \rightarrow Cred_{sk_p(1)}; GetTrans_{sk_p(1)}$
6. R : store$(P, pk_p, \{1, \omega_{sk_p(1)}, GetTrans_{sk_p(1)}\}, \{1, n_1 = 0\})$

DoctorRegistration. A doctor registering with the system provides her identity and relevant university diplomas to R. The registrar checks this information, and, if approved, issues a doctor credential. This credential contains the doctor's specialties, such as, for example, the fact that she is an emergency physician.

1. $D \leftrightarrow R$: verification of identity and diplomas
2. $D \leftrightarrow R$: getCred($\{$'doctor', specialties$\}$) $\rightarrow$ $Cred_d$; $GetTrans_d$
3. R : store($GetTrans_d$)

VisitDoctor. Although a patient can visit her doctor anonymously, she must allow D to access her complete list of health records. Therefore, she gives D her private key $sk_p(i)$ and additionally proves that this is her current private key by showing both her credential and her public key pk_p. The resulting show transcript is then stored by D as a proof of the patient's trust. The private key $sk_p(i)$ can now be used by D to access the patient's health records.

1. $P \rightarrow D$: send($i, sk_p(i), pk_p$)
2. $P \leftrightarrow D$: showCred($Cred_{sk_p(1)}, \{$'patient', $pk_p, i\}, null, null$) $\rightarrow$ $ShowTrans$
3. D : check($\mathrm{RSA}^i_{(n,v)}(sk_p(i)) = pk_p$)
4. D : store($ShowTrans$)

AddHealthRecord(P). In order to add a patient's health record to the system, a new counter value must be obtained from R. Using this value, a doctor can create an identifier ID for the record. The record itself is then signed by a deanonymizable credential show and stored by $DBMan$ in the database.

The communication between D and both central authorities should be anonymous. Furthermore, for accountability reasons, D must prove to the registrar that she is a valid doctor knowing the private key $sk_p(i)$. This is done by a deanonymizable credential show combined with a GQ proof of knowledge.

1. D : $(sk_p(i), pk_p)$ =retrieveKeypair(P)
2. $D \leftrightarrow R$: showCred($Cred_d, \{$'doctor'$\}, AddReqCond, pk_p$) $\rightarrow$ $ShowTrans$
3. $D \leftrightarrow R$: GQProof$\{RSA^{-i}_{(n,v)}(pk_p)\}$
4. R : set $n_i = n_i + 1$
5. $D \leftarrow R$: send(n_i)
6. D : create $ID = \mathcal{H}(sk_p(i) \parallel n_i)$
7. $D \leftrightarrow DBMan$: showCred($Cred_d, \{$'doctor', [specialties]$\}, AddCond$, ($ID, data$$)) \rightarrow ShowTrans_{ID} = record_{ID}$
8. $DBMan$: add $record_{ID}$ to database

RetrieveHealthRecords(P). To retrieve all health records of a patient, D requests from R all counter values for all of the patient's current and previous private keys. Once these are retrieved, D can compute the corresponding record IDs and hence request P's records from the database.

Again, communication between D and the central authorities should be anonymous. Also, $DBMan$ logs the retrieval transcripts for accountability purposes.

1.	D	: $(sk_p(i), pk_p) =$ retrieveKeypair(P)
2.	$D \to R$	: indexRequest(pk_p)
3.	$D \leftarrow R$	: send$(\{1, n_1\}, \ldots, \{i, n_i\})$

repeat step 4: $\forall j \in \{0, \ldots, i-1\}, \forall k \in \{1, \ldots, n_{(i-j)}\}$:

4.1.	D	: create $ID_{jk} = \mathcal{H}(RSA^j_{(n,v)}(sk_p(i)) \parallel k)$
4.2.	$D \leftrightarrow DBMan$	: showCred$(Cred_d, \{\text{'doctor'}\}, RetrCond, ID_{jk}) \to ShowTrans$
4.3.	$D \leftarrow DBMan$	: send$(record_{ID_{jk}})$
4.4.	$DBMan$	: log$(ShowTrans)$

ChangePrivateKey. A patient changing her temporal key $sk_p(i)$ into $sk_p(i+1)$, reports this change to the registrar. She provides R with a verifiable encryption of her new private key and retrieves a credential $Cred_{sk_p(i+1)}$ for her new secret key. In addition, the patient's old credential is revoked.

1.	$P \leftrightarrow R$:	showCred$(Cred_{sk_p(i)}, \{\text{'patient'}, P, pk_p, i\}, null, null) \to ShowTrans$
2.	$P \leftrightarrow R$:	$\omega_{sk_p(i+1)} = $ VEncrypt$_{pk_{es}}\{sk_p(i+1), sk_p(i+1) = RSA^{-(i+1)}_{(n,v)}(pk_p)\}$
3.	R	: revokeCred$(GetTrans_{sk_p(i)})$
4.	$P \leftrightarrow R$:	getCred$(\{\text{'patient'}, P, pk_p, (i+1)\}) \to$ $Cred_{sk_p(i+1)}; GetTrans_{sk_p(i+1)}$
5.	R	: replace $\{i, \omega_{sk_p(i)}, GetTrans_{sk_p(i)}\}$ with $\{(i+1), \omega_{sk_p(i+1)},$ $GetTrans_{sk_p(i+1)}\}$, append $\{(i+1), n_{(i+1)} = 0\}$ to stored data

EmergencyRetrieval(P). An emergency doctor ED may in emergencies request the patient's private key. This is done by anonymously filing a deanonymizable request with the emergency service ES. By decrypting the verifiable encryption of $sk_p(i)$, ES can recover the patient's private key.

1.	$ED \leftrightarrow ES$	: showCred$(Cred_d, \{\text{'doctor'},\text{'ER'}\}, ERCond, \{P, motivation\})$ $\to ShowTrans_{ED}$
2.	ES	: evaluate and store request
3.	$ES \leftrightarrow R$	: request$(\omega_{sk_p(i)})$
4.	ES	: $sk_p(i) = $ decrypt$_{sk_{es}}(\omega_{sk_p(i)})$
5.	$ED \leftarrow ES$	: send$(sk_p(i))$

4   Evaluation

Both patients as well as doctors have privacy concerns regarding electronic health records. First of all, patients do not want their medical history to be publicly available. Also, in order to maintain their autonomy, doctors do not want their activities to be centrally trackable.

4.1 Privacy Control for the Patient

Because of the strong hash function $\mathcal{H}$ and secret input $sk_p(i)$, different health records belonging to the same patient are unlinkable. As a consequence, only authorized doctors being in possession of $sk_p(i)$ can access and link the patient's medical information. As these doctors know $sk_p(i)$, they must either enjoy the patient's trust, or be working at an emergency room.

By updating her private key, a patient prohibits all doctors from adding or retrieving any of her new health records. She can then renew her trust relation with some of these doctors by providing them with her new private key. All other doctors, however, will no longer be able to manage the patient's new health records. A key update is executed, for example, when a patient changes doctors or after an emergency retrieval.

Timing analysis may allow the database manager to estimate linkabilities between health records. To solve this problem, a doctor should not retrieve all of her patient's health records at once. Also, it is advisable to use anonymous communication channels and to store a cache of previously retrieved health records.

In case of an emergency, the emergency service ES can recover a patient's private key $sk_p(i)$. Hence, ES can retrieve and link all of the patient's health records. This is necessary to allow for a good service, for example when the patient is unconscious and her regular doctor is not available. However, the service must be trusted not to abuse her recovering powers. In order to minimize this trust, arbiters can inspect the recovery process. Also, trust can be distributed over multiple emergency services, who then have to cooperate to retrieve $sk_p(i)$.

When a patient detects abuse such as unauthorized access to her health records or the addition of wrong information, she can file a complaint. The doctor responsible for the abuse can then be identified and appropriate actions can be taken. (e.g. the doctor's credential could be revoked)

Although a patient can decide which doctor to trust, she cannot hide any medical information from this doctor. Indeed, a doctor can only accept a patient's trust, if she is shown a valid credential containing the patient's current private key $sk_p(i)$.

4.2 Autonomy of the Doctor

A health record in a database is actually a transcript *ShowTrans* of an anonymous credential. Therefore, the record does not reveal anything more about its creating doctor than her status as an authorized doctor with the specified specialties

Apart from the doctor registration procedure, all communication between a doctor and the central authorities (*R,DBMan* and *ES*) is anonymous. Hence, the only doctor information known to a central authority, is whether or not this doctor is registered with the system.

The anonymity received by a doctor is conditional, and can be revoked if abuse is detected. This revocation is performed by a third party trusted not to perform arbitrary deanonymizations. This trust can be minimized by using arbiters and by distributing the power to deanonymize over multiple organizations.

A doctor might want to know the identity of a health record creator. This is useful when she wants to share advice or when she needs extra information about the patient. Doctors can achieve this by anonymously filing a deanonymizable request to a trusted deanonymization organization. An alternative is the use of health records which contain no medical data but a reference to, and access information for another database. This may for example be a hospital's database containing all health records created by doctors affiliated with this hospital.

4.3   Scalability

An important issue when regarding a practical implementation is the scalability of the system. If more people use the system, a shift from a single central database towards multiple databases will be necessary. The registrar will then need to keep extra bookkeeping information about where each record is situated. Another potential problem is the possibility for collisions of hashfunctions. This can be countered by using multiple hashfunctions in order to create a unique record *ID*. Also, multiple RSA instances (n, v) can be used.

5   Related Work

The Health Insurance Portability and Accountability Act [9] imposes the development of national standards for electronic healthcare transactions. Next to this, it states strong requirements concerning security and data protection safeguards for medical information. The most important of these security safeguards is access control. The first proposals to solve this issue made use of public key infrastructures (PKIs). However, PKI technology was not designed for implementing access control. Rather, it was designed for public key cryptosystems to provide for confidentiality and integrity protection of data, and authentication of users. This authentication property can be used to implement access control. However, as each certificate is unconditionally linked to a (possibly pseudonymous) identity, all the user's transactional data can be collected. This has devastating consequences for user privacy.

Another solution is role based access control [12,6] in combination with anonymous communication [5,10]. It enables access control based on contextual information rather than on identity. However, anonymity is unconditional and abusive behaviour cannot be punished.

To allow for patient control, a shift towards patient-involvement, for example by the use of smartcards [8], is required. Such a shift allows the patient to view and control her own information. A complete shift is undesirable though, as this would allow the patient to add, delete or modify her own information.

6   Conclusions and Future Work

In this paper we have described a secure and privacy-preserving electronic health record system. The system protects the patient's privacy by allowing her to control who has access to her medical information. However, no personal information can be hidden from the medical practitioner entrusted with this access. Furthermore, the doctor's anonymity is conditionally preserved.

Future work includes research on how to combine the system with smartcard technology. These smartcards could contain, for example, the patient's private keys or medical certificates stating her blood group or a particular disease. Note though, that our setting requires the private keys to leave the smartcard, which is an alteration of the traditional smartcard setting.

Other work includes the usage of health records for statistical analysis. Such usage will require a transformation from the original database without linkabilities to a new anonymized database with linkabilities. Finally, a framework for handling disputes and abuses will be developed.

References

1. N. Asokan, V. Shoup, and M. Waidner. Optimistic fair exchange of digital signatures (extended abstract). In *EUROCRYPT*, pages 591–606, 1998.
2. S. A. Brands. *Rethinking Public Key Infrastructures and Digital Certificates: Building in Privacy*. MIT Press, Cambridge, MA, USA, 2000.
3. J. Camenisch and I. Damgård. Verifiable encryption, group encryption, and their applications to separable group signatures and signature sharing schemes. In T. Okamoto, editor, *ASIACRYPT*, volume 1976 of *Lecture Notes in Computer Science*, pages 331–345. Springer, 2000.
4. J. Camenisch and A. Lysyanskaya. An efficient system for non-transferable anonymous credentials with optional anonymity revocation. In *EUROCRYPT*, pages 93–118, 2001.
5. D. Chaum. Untraceable electronic mail, return addresses, and digital pseudonyms. In *Communications of the ACM*, volume 24, pages 84–88, February 1981.
6. D. F. Ferraiolo, J. F. Barkley, and D. R. Kuhn. A role-based access control model and reference implementation within a corporate intranet. *ACM Transactions on Information Systems Security*, 2(1):34–64, 1999.
7. L. C. Guillou and J-J. Quisquater. A practical zero-knowledge protocol fitted to security microprocessor minimizing both trasmission and memory. In *EUROCRYPT*, pages 123–128, 1988.
8. Health card technologies. http://www.hct.com.
9. Health insurance portability and accountability act. http://www.hipaa.org/.
10. A. Pfitzmann and M. Waidner. Networks without user observability: Design options. In *Advances in Cryptology- EUROCRYPT '85: Proceedings of a Workshop on the Theory and Application of Cryptographic Techniques*, pages 245–253, 1985.
11. R. L. Rivest, A. Shamir, and L. M. Adleman. A method for obtaining digital signatures and public-key cryptosystems. *Commun. ACM*, 21(2):120–126, 1978.
12. R. S. Sandhu, E. J. Coyne, H. L. Feinstein, and C. E. Youman. Role-based access control models. *IEEE Computer*, 29(2):38–47, 1996.
13. M. Stadler. Publicly verifiable secret sharing. In *EUROCRYPT*, pages 190–199, 1996.

Using XACML for Privacy Control in SAML-Based Identity Federations

Wolfgang Hommel

Munich Network Management Team,
Leibniz Computing Center Munich
`hommel@lrz.de`

Abstract. With Federated Identity Management (FIM) protocols, service providers can request user attributes, such as the billing address, from the user's identity provider. Access to this information is managed using so-called Attribute Release Policies (ARPs). In this paper, we first analyze various shortcomings of existing ARP implementations; then, we demonstrate that the eXtensible Access Control Markup Language (XACML) is very suitable for the task. We present an architecture for the integration of XACML ARPs into SAML-based identity providers and specify the policy evaluation workflows. We also introduce our implementation and its integration into the Shibboleth architecture.

1   Introduction

With Identity & Access Management (I&AM) systems, organizations are able to efficiently manage their employees' and customers' Personally Identifiable Information (PII) and access rights to local services, typically by storing them in a central enterprise directory or relational database.

To support cross-organizational business processes, I&AM has developed into Federated Identity Management (FIM); FIM standards, such as the Security Assertion Markup Language (SAML, [1]), enable cross-domain Web single sign-on, i.e. users are being authenticated by their so-called identity provider (IDP) and may then use external service providers (SPs) without requiring separate accounts there. Instead, the SPs trust the IDP, and the IDP vouches that the user has successfully been authenticated. A set of SPs and IDPs with such trust relationships established is called an identity federation.

The FIM protocols do not only provide single sign-on capabilities, i.e. the transmission of authentication information, but also support the exchange of user attributes between SP and IDP. For example, a SP could request a user's billing address and credit card information from the IDP. In business-to-business (B2B) scenarios, the IDP typically is the organization the user is working for, while in business-to-customer (B2C) scenarios it could be the user's ISP or credit card company.

Obviously, access to sensitive data such as Personally Identifiable Information (PII) must be restricted, i.e. there must be a way to control which attributes

J. Dittmann, S. Katzenbeisser, and A. Uhl (Eds.): CMS 2005, LNCS 3677, pp. 160–169, 2005.

the IDP hands out to the SPs, in order to protect the user's privacy and thus gain the user's acceptance. While the necessity for such a control mechanism is well-known under the term *Attribute Release Policies* (ARPs), none of the three major FIM standards — SAML [1], Liberty Alliance [2] and WS-Federation [3] — addresses this issue concretely and instead leaves it up to actual implementations.

Fortunately, although not required for standards compliance, some FIM implementations offer ARP support; e.g., Shibboleth [4] is the most advanced and wide-spread open source FIM software currently in use, with its focus on privacy clearly being one of the major reasons for its popularity. However, even Shibboleth only provides rudimentary ARPs in a proprietary format, and the development of more sophisticated ARPs is explicitly encouraged. We analyze existing ARP implementations and their deficiencies in section 2.

The *eXtensible Access Control Markup Language* (XACML, [5]) is a generic and very flexible language for modeling access rights. In section 3, we derive XACML's suitability for the formulation and enforcement of ARPs and demonstrate how it fulfills an advanced set of ARP design criteria and goals. We present an architecture for the integration of XACML ARPs into SAML-based identity providers and then introduce our implementation for Shibboleth in section 4.

2   Related Work and State of the Art

Privacy on the internet and in e-commerce scenarios is a well-studied field and several solutions have found many adopters. To clarify the scope of our work, we first demonstrate how our intents differ from and complement those found in the established privacy standard P3P [6]. We then analyze two ARP implementations and show their limits by means of an e-commerce scenario.

Independent from the development of the FIM standards, the *Platform for Privacy Preferences* (P3P) has been standardized by the W3C for the use in web sites. P3P-enabled web browsers automatically fetch a web site's privacy policies; by comparing them with the user's locally specified preferences, they can decide whether the user agrees to use the site under the given privacy conditions. P3P is neither intended nor suitable for modeling FIM ARPs, because it is an SP-side-only mechanism which does not specify how user preferences shall be stored on the browser or IDP side. It also is limited to web sites and defines an e-commerce specific user profile, whereas FIM protocols work for any kind of web service and support federation-specific user attributes. However, our XACML approach to FIM ARPs leverages the rationale behind P3P and the P3P Preference Exchange Language (APPEL, [7]).

Shibboleth [4] is based on SAML and due to its origin, the higher education institutions in the USA, privacy is an important aspect, so its built-in support for fine-grained ARPs comes at no surprise. Shibboleth distinguishes between *site ARPs*, which are used by IDP administrators to specify defaults for all users, and individual *user ARPs*. Shibboleth ARPs consist of *rules*. Each rule specifies one *target*, i.e. a tuple *(service provider, service)*, which allows to differentiate between multiple services offered by the same SP. For each *attribute* in the rule, this target's access can be granted or denied, optionally based on the attribute's current value. In the following example access to the user's surname is granted to every SP (XML namespaces have been removed to enhance readability):

```
<AttributeReleasePolicy>
    <Rule>
        <Target> <AnyTarget/> </Target>
        <Attribute name="surname">
            <AnyValue release="permit"/>
        </Attribute>
    </Rule>
</AttributeReleasePolicy>
```

Shibboleth combines the site ARP and the user ARP to form the *effective ARP*; if there is a conflict, i.e. one ARP allows access to an attribute while the other does not, or if the SP requests an attribute for which no ARP has been defined, access to the attribute will be denied.

To support distributed management of site ARPs and to distinguish between multiple roles a user can be acting in, Nazareth and Smith suggested an alternative implementation, which uses public key based ARPs [8]. They are choosing the simple public key infrastructure (SPKI, [9]) and the simple distributed security infrastructure (SDSI, [10]) as a base for their ARPs. This approach features hierarchical ARPs, so, for example, a department's ARP can be intersected with the whole company's ARP to form the resulting site ARP, which in turn is intersected with the user ARP. Opposed to Shibboleth's built-in ARPs, no conditions on an attribute's current value can be specified.

Both implementations lack functionality which is demanded in many real world scenarios; those deficiencies are:

- The ARPs are not context sensitive. For example, users typically are willing to grant access to more attributes, such as their credit card data, when they purchase something from a web site than when they are just looking for information; i.e., the purpose why the SP requests the attribute is not considered at all.
- No obligations can be specified. As an example, a user might want to be informed whenever an SP accesses the credit card data, e.g. by means of a logfile or by email.
- Access must be granted or denied to each attribute separately, i.e. there is no way to group attributes. For example, a delivery address may consist of the attributes *given name, surname, street, postal code* and *city*. It is cumbersome having to set up five rules per target instead of one.
- The access conditions are not flexible enough. For example, only the currently requested attribute's value can be part of a Shibboleth ARP condition and there are no environmental functions available; so, if credit card number and expiry date are stored in separate attributes, there is no way to release the credit card number only if it is still valid.

Both approaches also use proprietary formats, leading to the typical implications such as lacking interoperability and the need for dedicated tools as well as additional implementation work.

3 XACML-Based Attribute Release Policies

We will now demonstrate that XACML is an excellent choice to model and enforce ARPs; our architecture, which integrates XACML components into a SAML-based IDP, is introduced in section 3.2. We tailor XACML to specify the ARP syntax and semantics in section 3.3 and define the policy evaluation workflow in section 3.4.

3.1 XACML's Suitability

There are many organizational and technical reasons to use XACML:

1. *Interoperability.* XACML is an OASIS-ratified standard which has successfully been employed in distributed access control before, for example in combination with SAML ([11], [12]) and PERMIS [13]. Its relationship to P3P has been outlined in [14]. Developers and administrators do not need to learn yet another policy language, and GUIs for end users might be re-used with only minor modifications.
2. *Compatibility.* As both are XML-based, Shibboleth ARPs can easily be converted to XACML ARPs. The algorithm is outlined in section 4.
3. *Extensibility.* As requirements are known to change over time and as users will be more familiar with ARP concepts, the language used for ARPs must be flexible enough to allow later extensions; XACML clearly is.
4. *Schema independency.* Opposed to e.g. P3P, XACML has not been designed for a fixed schema; instead, each identity federation can select a suitable data schema or create a dedicated new one. Due to XACML's support for XPath expressions, attributes need not be flat key/value pairs, but structured attributes are also supported. Note that a standardized format for ARPs is independent of the arbitrary format of the data protected by ARPs.
5. *Multiple roles.* IDPs may allow a user to store several profiles, e.g. one used at work and one used in spare time; XACML ARPs can easily be applied to each of them.
6. *Grouping of attributes.* XACML allows the definition of variables, which can be used to group attributes, so access rules need not be specified for each attribute separately. An example is given below.
7. *Decentralized management.* Besides distinguishing between *user ARPs* and *site ARPs*, it is possible to split ARPs into multiple distributed parts, each of which can be maintained on its own. The distribution optionally can reflect hierarchical structures, but priority based and other policy conflict resolution mechanisms are supported as well. The total number of rules required even for sophisticated policies can be kept low. Policy evaluation is easy to understand for the users, and the results are comprehensible.

8. *Conditions.* XACML is very flexible regarding the formulation of conditions under which an attribute can be accessed. Primarily, this includes the specification of a) the *service provider* who requests the data, b) the actual *service* being used, in case an SP offers more than one service, and c) the *purpose* the data is being collected for. Furthermore, all attributes' current values and environmental information, e.g. the current date and time, can be used.

9. *Obligations.* XACML features the specification of obligations, such as sending an email or writing to a logfile when a positive or negative decision about an access attempt has been made.

10. *Optional use of PKI.* While it is possible to use an existing public key infrastructure (PKI) to assure the integrity of user ARPs, it is not a prerequisite for the use of ARPs. In particular, users are not required to handle client-side certificates with their web browser, as this is often error-prone and constrains the use of different machines, devices and browsers. Note that this only affects how ARPs are stored and is independent of whether the released attributes are transmitted to the service provider encrypted or not.

11. *Existing implementation.* XACML ARPs can be evaluated by any standard compliant XACML implementation. An excellent open source implementation is available [15].

Yet, XACML is a generic access control language and must be tailored to our purpose. After an architectural overview, we specify the XACML elements, which are necessary for ARPs, along with their syntax and semantics.

3.2 Architectural Overview

We have integrated an XACML component into a SAML-based IDP, which is minimally invasive and maintains full SAML compatibility. Our XACML component consists of a policy enforcement point (PEP) which we have designed and implemented as described below, and an out-of-the-box XACML policy decision point (PDP).

Figure 1 shows a high-level overview of the relevant components:

− Attribute requests are received by the SAML PDP, which passes them on to our XACML PEP.
− The XACML PEP converts attribute requests into appropriate XACML requests, which the XACML PDP evaluates. Details are given below.
− The attribute values and ARPs are kept in dedicated stores, such as LDAP servers or relational database management systems.
− Administrators and users use dedicated interfaces to maintain the site and user ARPs, respectively. For users, the ARP editing frontend could be combined with the usual self services, i.e. the web site where they can change their passwords, set up their e-mail addresses, update their personal information, etc. The realization of a suitable web interface will be part of our future work.

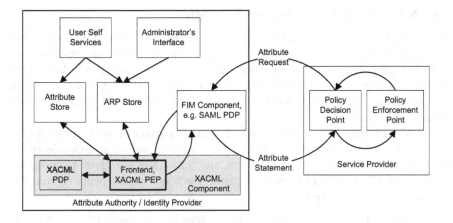

Fig. 1. Overview of components involved in ARP processing

The ARP processing workflow for new attribute requests is as follows:

1. Several parts of the attribute request are extracted by the SAML PDP and forwarded to the XACML PEP: a) The list of the requested attributes, and b) meta-data, such as an identifier of the service provider, the actual service being used and the purpose as stated by the requester.
2. The XACML PEP creates one XACML request per requested attribute, which is then evaluated by the XACML PDP. This is necessary for the following reason: if the complete list of requested attributes would be passed on to the XACML PDP in a single XACML request, the result would be an "all or nothing" response. This means that if just one attribute was not allowed to be released, none of the requested attributes would be released. However, in practice many SPs are greedy and request more attributes than would be required for service provision. Thus, we have to decide about the access to each of the attributes separately.
3. To provide everything the XACML PDP needs, the PEP fetches the necessary ARPs and attributes from the appropriate stores:
   - Multiple ARPs may have to be evaluated; typically, there is at least one site and one user ARP involved. Their combination and evaluation is specified in section 3.4.
   - Besides the attributes which have been requested, additional attributes for the evaluation of conditions within ARPs may be required. Those attribute values are included in the XACML request as ResourceContent, see section 3.3.
4. Each attribute request is then evaluated by the XACML PDP; its response is composed of the release decision and optional XACML obligations. The XACML PEP fulfills these obligations before returning the attributes, whose release was permitted, to the SAML PDP.
5. The SAML PDP delivers the attributes to the SP.

The next section describes the elements available within each XACML ARP.

3.3   XACML ARP Syntax and Semantics

In general, each XACML `policy` consists of `rules`. Rule combining algorithms such as "first applicable" or "deny overrides" control how rules are evaluated and when rule processing stops. Both rules and whole policies can specify `targets`; if the policy's targets do not match the actual attribute requester, none of its rules are considered. An empty `target` definition makes sure that the whole policy is always considered.

Each `rule` must have an effect, which is either `permit` or `deny`. It can declare its own target by specifying the protected resources, one or more subjects and the actions attempted by these subjects, and optionally also have a condition.

An XACML ARP will typically contain the following elements (a complete example can be found below):

1. *Priority specification.* The policy's priority is specified as XACML `CombinerParameter` element. Typically, user ARPs will have higher priorities than site ARPs, so users can override the default settings made by the IDP administrator. The combination of multiple ARPs during the evaluation of a request is described in section 3.4. Lines 2–6 demonstrate the priority declaration in the example.

2. *Rule precedence specification.* Each policy must choose one rule combining algorithm. XACML's built-in "first applicable" algorithm, which stops rule evaluation after the first matching rule has been found, is suitable for most tasks and easy to comprehend by the users (see line 1 in the example).

3. *Grouping of attributes.* To group attributes, the names of any number of attributes can be concatenated to form a regular expression, e.g. `Street|-ZIP|City`, and assigned to a variable using a `VariableDefinition` element.

4. *Attribute specification.* XACML `resource` elements specify the user attribute identifiers. Each attribute identifier is an URI, which shall be composed of the IDP identifier, the user identifier, the user role and the attribute name. XACML `VariableReference` elements can be used to speficy attribute groups. Wildcards can also be used. In the example, lines 11–20 show how a user's *creditCardNumber* attribute is selected.

5. *Requester specification.* The triple (*service provider, service, purpose*) is specified as a a a conjunctive sequence of three `SubjectMatch` elements within an XACML `subject` node-set as shown in lines 21–33 of the example.

6. *Action specification.* The obligatory XACML `action` is always `read`, as SAML does not allow write operations by the SP yet (see lines 34–40).

7. *Conditions.* XACML conditions may be used to achieve even finer-grained restrictions. All user attributes are included as `ResourceContent` in the XACML request. A description of the powerful XACML functions which can be used within conditions is out of the scope of this paper.

8. *Obligations.* XACML provides the `Obligation` element; writing to a text file and sending an email are part of the standard, but arbitrary other obligations can be implemented as well (see lines 42–49 in the example).

If a PKI is available, the integrity of ARPs can be protected by applying XML signatures as described in [16]. Below is an example which grants access to the user's credit card number to an online shop only if an actual book order is placed; an obligation specifies that each allowed release must be logged.

```
1  <Policy id="xacmlARP1" RuleCombiningAlg="first-applicable">
2    <CombinerParameters>
3      <CombinerParameter ParameterName="ARPpriority">
4        100
5      </CombinerParameter>
6    </CombinerParameters>
7    <Description> ARP by user John Doe </Description>
8    <Rule id="CreditCardToBookShop" effect="permit">
9      <Description> Release credit card number to bookshop </Description>
10     <Target>
11       <Resources>
12         <Resource>
13           <ResourceMatch MatchId="string-equal">
14             <AttributeValue>
15               idp.example.com/johndoe/defaultrole/creditCardNumber
16             </AttributeValue>
17             <ResourceAttributeDesignator AttributeId="resource-id" />
18           </ResourceMatch>
19         </Resource>
20       </Resources>
21       <Subjects>
22         <Subject>
23           <SubjectMatch MatchId="string-equal" AttributeValue="shop.example.com">
24             <SubjectAttributeDesignator AttributeId="service_provider" />
25           </SubjectMatch>
26           <SubjectMatch MatchId="string-equal" AttributeValue="bookshop">
27             <SubjectAttributeDesignator AttributeId="service" />
28           </SubjectMatch>
29           <SubjectMatch MatchId="string-equal" AttributeValue="purchase">
30             <SubjectAttributeDesignator AttributeId="purpose" />
31           </SubjectMatch>
32         </Subject>
33       </Subjects>
34       <Actions>
35         <Action>
36           <ActionMatch MatchId="string-equal" AttributeValue="read">
37             <ActionAttributeDesignator AttributeId="action-id" />
38           </ActionMatch>
39         </Action>
40       </Actions>
41     </Target>
42     <Obligations>
43       <Obligation Id="Log" FulfillOn="Permit">
44         <AttributeAssignment Id="text">
45           Your credit card number has been released to:
46           <SubjectAttributeDesignator AttributeId="service_provider" />
47         </AttributeAssignment>
48       </Obligation>
49     </Obligations>
50   </Rule>
51   <Rule id="DoNotReleaseAnythingElse" effect="deny"/>
52 </Policy>
```

3.4   Policy Evaluation Workflow

For the evaluation of an attribute request, an XACML PolicySet is created by combining all relevant ARPs, i.e. those ARPs whose target element matches the requester. This is handled by our XACML PEP.

Each ARP has a priority, and the XACML PolicySet is built by including the ARPs ordered by decreasing priority; the "first-applicable" algorithm is then used for the evaluation of the PolicySet. If multiple ARPs have the same priority, the inner order of their inclusion in the policy set is indeterminate; this should be avoided to achieve deterministic evaluation results, unless other techniques are applied to ensure that those ARPs have disjunctive target sets. The resulting PolicySet can be evaluated by any standard compliant XACML PDP.

Obviously, the complexity of XACML policies and XACML implementations can lead to security vulnerabilities; we address these issues by using Sun's reference XACML PDP implementation and working on easy and intuitive graphical user interfaces, as outlined in the next sections.

4   Implementation and Integration into Shibboleth

We have implemented the XACML component in Java, using Sun's XACML PDP implementation [15], which does not support XACML variables yet, so attribute grouping has to be done by our XACML PEP if necessary.

A standalone version is command line driven and creates the XACML request which is evaluated by the PDP. It also creates the XACML `PolicySet` as described in section 3.4; future versions will take the more elegant approach of implementing a custom XACML policy combiner which supports policy priorities because XACML itself does not yet, but it provides the necessary extension hooks. Besides its usefulness for development, we will use the standalone version to enable users to test and debug their ARPs through a web interface.

An integration into Shibboleth's IDP component (called Origin) is possible by replacing two methods in the build-in attribute resolver: first, `list-PossibleReleaseAttributes()` must return the names of the user attributes which should be retrieved, and afterwards `filterAttributes()` has to remove all attributes whose release is not permitted by the ARPs. The user's and service provider's ids are passed to both methods, which provides sufficient information for identifying, combining and evaluating the relevant XACML-based ARPs.

Shibboleth's built-in ARPs can be lossless converted to XACML-based ARPs. Basically, Shibboleth ARP `targets` become XACML `subjects` and Shibboleth ARP `attribute` elements turn into XACML `resources`. As release decisions are made on `attribute` and not on `rule` level in Shibboleth ARPs, each Shibboleth `attribute` is converted into a dedicated XACML `rule`. We have successfully automated this transformation using an XSLT stylesheet.

5   Summary and Outlook

In this paper, we first analyzed existing implementations of Attribute Release Policies (ARPs), which are the core privacy management tool in today's identity federation standards. We have found several shortcomings and described their consequences for real world applications and user acceptance. We then provided arguments to use XACML as base for ARPs, a well-established access control language standard, which has been successfully used in the field of distributed access control before. We presented an architecture for the integration of XACML ARPs into SAML-based identity providers, which remains fully compliant to the SAML standard. The syntax and semantics of XACML ARPs have been specified along with the policy evaluation workflow, which makes use of an out-of-the-box XACML policy decision point. Finally, we introduced our implementation, the way to integrate it into Shibboleth, a popular open source identity federation software, and outlined an algorithm which converts existing Shibboleth ARPs lossless to XACML ARPs.

We are planning to integrate this ARP engine into the next major version of Shibboleth, but for use in a production environment, intuitive graphical user interfaces for the creation, testing and maintenance of these ARPs must be conceived and implemented to hide the complexity from the end users. We will also investigate the use of XACML for the so-called Attribute Acceptance Policies, which are the counterpart to ARPs on the service provider side; similar deficiencies such as yet another proprietary format can be found there presently.

Acknowledgment. The author would like to thank the members of the Munich Network Management (MNM) Team (http://www.mnm-team.org/), directed by Prof. Dr. Hegering, for helpful discussions and valuable comments on earlier drafts of this paper.

References

1. Cantor, S., Kemp, J., Philpott, R., Maler, E.: Security Assertion Markup Language v2.0. OASIS Security Services Technical Committee Standard (2005)
2. Varney, C.: Liberty Alliance — Privacy and Security Best Practices 2.0. http://project-liberty.org/specs/ (2003)
3. Kaler, C., Nadalin, A.: Web Services Federation Language (WS-Federation). http://www-106.ibm.com/developerworks/webservices/library/ws-fed/ (2003)
4. Erdos, M., Cantor, S.: Shibboleth architecture (v05). http://shibboleth.internet2.edu/docs/ (2002)
5. Moses, T.: OASIS eXtensible Access Control Markup Language 2.0, core specification. OASIS XACML Technical Committee Standard (2005)
6. Reagle, J., Cranor, L.F.: The Platform for Privacy Preferences. In: Communications of the ACM. Volume 42., ACM Press (1999) 48–55
7. Langheinrich, M.: A P3P Preference Exchange Language — APPEL 1.0. http://www.w3.org/TR/P3P-preferences/ (2002)
8. Nazareth, S., Smith, S.: Using SPKI/SDSI for Distributed Maintenance of Attribute Release Policies in Shibboleth. Technical Report TR2004-485, Department of Computer Science, Dartmouth College, Hanover, HN 03744 USA (2004)
9. Ellison, C., Frantz, B., Lampson, B., Rivest, R., Thomas, B., Ylnen, T.: SPKI Certificate Theory. IETF Proposed Standard, RFC 2693 (1999)
10. Rivest, R., Lampson, B.: SDSI — A Simple Distributed Security Infrastructure. Presented at CRYPTO'96 Rumpsession (1996)
11. Lepro, R.: Cardea: Dynamic Access Control in Distributed Systems. Technical Report TR NAS–03–020, NASA Advanced Supercomputing Division, Ames (2003)
12. Mazzuca, P.: Access Control in a Distributed Decentralized Network: An XML Approach to Network Security. Honors Thesis, Dartmouth College (2004)
13. Chadwick, D., Otenko, A.: The PERMIS X.509 Role Based Privilege Management Infrastructure. In: Proceedings of the 7th ACM Symposium on Access Control Models and Technologies. SACMAT, ACM Press (2002) 135–140
14. Anderson, A.H.: The Relationship Between XACML and P3P Privacy Policies. http://research.sun.com/projects/xacml/ (2004)
15. Proctor, S.: Sun's XACML implementation. http://sunxacml.sf.net/ (2004)
16. Anderson, A.: XML Digital Signature profile of XACML 2.0. OASIS TC Committee draft, 16. September 2004 (2004)

Verifier-Tuple as a Classifier for Biometric Handwriting Authentication - Combination of Syntax and Semantics

Andrea Oermann, Jana Dittmann, and Claus Vielhauer

Otto-von-Guericke-University of Magdeburg,
Universitaetsplatz 2, 39106 Magdeburg, Germany
{andrea.oermann, jana.dittmann, claus.vielhauer}@iti.cs.uni-magdeburg.de

Abstract. In this paper, a new concept for classifying handwriting data and its analysis for biometric user authentication is presented. The concept's characteristic is the combination of syntax and semantics. It implies a determination of four distinct levels of syntax and semantics to lower complexity and structure information. We demonstrate the concept's impacts on on-line handwritings and the user verification, and clarify the benefit of applying information of higher levels of semantics within the authentication methods. As a result we are able to evaluate techniques for biometric user authentication. Furthermore, we precisely outline and reason a more accurate biometric user authentication system, due to the classification given by the Verifier-Tuple concept.

Keywords: Biometrics, Security of Multimedia Content, Identification and Authentication.

1 Motivation

The Verifier-Tuple (VT) is a new concept for classifying information to determine its origin and authenticity as it was originally presented for audio in [1]. It enables a scalable evaluation of techniques for biometric user authentication. The idea of the VT is originated in the field of forensics where the identification, localization and verification of an author of information are focus of recent research. Since there is a great degree of overlap in the goals on the methods between forensics and biometric user authentication, an application of VT appears adequate.

The goal of biometric user authentication is the automated verification of a living human beings identity. Biometric user authentication is becoming increasingly relevant for academic and industrial research. Biometrics will soon be generally implemented in different areas and applications from ID cards to security to applications of insurance companies. Therefore, biometrics improve the level of security in infrastructures and applications.

Two classes of biometric modalities exist. The first class includes behavioral-based modalities such as speech and handwriting. The second class includes physiological modalities such as fingerprint, face, iris, retina, or hand geometry.

J. Dittmann, S. Katzenbeisser, and A. Uhl (Eds.): CMS 2005, LNCS 3677, pp. 170–179, 2005.

We confine our study to the first class as we base our work on previous evaluations for another behavioral modality, speech authentication, in [1]. In this paper, handwriting is the focus. Because of its individual uniqueness and its usage as a deliberate declaration of consent, especially for signing contracts and agreements, handwriting is generally accepted and preferred as a method for biometric user authentication.

The major benefit of the VT is its ability to structure information into detail and combine different levels of information. Three distinct goals can be outlined when connecting levels of syntax and semantics. The first goal is obtaining more accurate results for biometric user authentication by incorporating information of a higher semantic level in the authentication process. The second goal is reducing complexity by restructuring information, and the third goal is using the tuple's function as a design criterion for future handwriting based biometric applications.

The paper is structured as follows: In section 2, the concept of the VT is introduced implying four levels of syntax and semantics. Section 3 gives a brief overview of sampling and data representation for handwriting biometrics from a signal processing perspective. This is followed by the tuple's application to handwriting including a detailed classification of the handwriting information in section 4. Furthermore, results of combinations of syntax and semantics levels are outlined. Results based on experimental evaluations will underline the correctness of the VT and provide the tuple's conceptual proof in section 5. Finally, section 6 concludes by summarizing the paper and providing a perspective on future work.

2   Concept of the Verifier-Tuple

As introduced in [1], we define the Verifier-Tuple (VT) as a concept for classifying information. Based on this, we are able to structurally analyze information by detail, classify features of interest, and evaluate existing techniques. The following descriptions and specifications are also presented in [1].

The idea of our VT is derived from the general concept of the explanation of programming languages [2]. The VT consists of four parts as it is shown in the formula below: the syntax, the executive semantics, the functional semantics and the interpretative semantics. Each part can be seen as a level of information which has to be analyzed to retrieve the whole context.

$$VT = \{SY, SE_E, SE_F, SE_I\} \tag{1}$$

SY = syntax
SE_E = executive semantics
SE_F = functional semantics
SE_I = interpretative semantics

The syntax is defined as the composition of certain signs within a selected alphabet. It is a systematic, orderly arrangement and it is rooted in linguistics.

In order to analyze the syntax of languages, formal logic is applied as presented in [3] and [4]. The syntax describes the processing of the elements of an alphabet by following certain rules, structures and regulations. The syntax functions to define valid and permitted constructs within an alphabet.

Semantics is the study or science of meaning in language. Semantics implies the connection of characters, tokens or symbols and their relation to the meant object or information [5]. Semantics is associated with the interpretation of the facts given by the syntax. Thus, semantics enables to draw conclusions about the author of information and his or her intention. The interpretative characteristic of semantics is differentiated in three successive levels, the executive semantics, the functional semantics and the interpretative semantics.

The executive semantics can be defined as an application of a particular operation which determines a particular process sequence. Based on a certain input the operation effectively generates an output [2]. This level of semantics extracts connected, abstract syntactic elements as an output. The functional semantics includes a semantic algebra and evaluation functions as a further interpretative enhancement [2]. The functional semantics analyzes the impact of allocations of variables. Deriving from the syntax and the executive semantics, applied functions within the functional semantics specify measurement categories for analyzing the meaning of the information presented by the medium. The interpretative semantics is mostly provided by a human being but can also be integrated in a digital, automatic system. It is based on background knowledge and can be abstractly explained through methods of formal logic as presented in [2].

This concept of the VT enables a more detailed analysis and classification of information. With this structured division of information, it is not only possible to extract particular features, but also manipulations or attacks can be recognized and localized. Further, it allows drawing conclusions about the context which is not directly presented within the analyzed information such as certain metadata as we refer to later in this paper. A specified application of the VT for handwriting is demonstrated in section 4.

3   Sampling and Data Representation for Handwriting

The characteristics of the generation of a particular handwriting can be specified by the movement of the pen tip during the writing process. The main dimensions of this movement are pen position (horizontal/vertical), pen tip pressure and pen angle. Digitizer tablets provide sensor technology for the analog-digital conversion of these kinds of dynamics. PDAs or Tablet PCs as types of computers provide position information, represented as sequences of pen position points at discrete and continuous time intervals.

This representation of continuous information is also denoted as sampled signals, and for the case of position signal, we use the notation $x(t)$ for horizontal pen position signals and $y(t)$ for vertical pen position signals. The pen tip pressure signal can be either a binary pen-up/pen-down signal or describe pressure resolutions at a higher quantization level (typically up to 1024 levels) which is denoted as $p(t)$. Finally, some current commercial digitizer tablets provide pen azimuth signals, denoted as $\Theta(t)$, the orientation of the vertical projection of the pen onto the writing surface, similar to a compass, as well as pen altitude signals $\Phi(t)$, describing the angle of the pen above the writing surface.

The goal of biometric user authentication using handwriting is the determination of similarities based on features derived from these sampled signals. For this purpose, different algorithms are applied [15] to bind the biometric data to an identity in order to authenticate a certain user.

4 Verifier-Tuple for Handwriting

The architecture of a biometric user authentication system is generally structured as follows: Initially, reference data is sampled during enrollment and stored in a database. Later, handwriting signals are sampled and analyzed for subsequent authentications. Authentication algorithms require certain parameters and reference data from the reference storage. In [7], [8], and [9], an overview of the variety of these authentication algorithms is provided. Well known algorithms are for example Dynamic time Warping (DTW), Hidden-Markov-Models (HMM), Neural Networks, Multi Level Approaches, or statistical approaches such as the Biometric Hash [10].

Two different goals of authentication can be outlined. The first goal is the verification of one particular known user of the reference storage. This implies a comparison of n signal samplings to 1 particular reference storage sampling ($1:1$ comparison). The second goal is the identification of a particular not known user which implicates a comparison of 1 signal samplings to n particular reference storage sampling ($1:n$ comparison). Depending on the desired authentication mode, the system parameters may change.

The application of the VT to handwriting biometrics results in the feature classification as demonstrated in the listing below. Features are differentiated and assigned to a particular level of the VT. Level 1 marks the syntactical properties of handwriting, level 2 the executive semantics, level 3 the functional semantics, and level 4 the interpretative semantics. Level 1 includes the original signal features, as provided from the sampling process. Level 2 classifies features derived from the original signals by applying feature extraction algorithms which lead to various abstraction levels. For this purpose, the biometric algorithm requires input from level 1 in any case but may additionally consider parameters from level 3 or 4. Level 3 presents the textual or visual presentation of information. In the particular case of handwriting, level 3 describes the content of the written sequence and its individual shape. Level 4 abstracts information about the context and background knowledge of the writing process. This may include for example environmental information, such as time and location of the sampling, as well as information about the hardware involved.

Table 1 summarizes the application of the VT concept to different levels of features found in handwriting biometrics:

Table 1. Classification of Handwriting features

Level 1: Syntax	Dynamic features which are:
	o Horizontal pen position signal $x(t)$
	o Vertical pen position signal $y(t)$
	o Pen tip pressure signal $p(t)$
	o Pen azimuth signal $\Theta(t)$
	o Pen altitude signal $\Phi(t)$
Additional:	o Horizontal pen acceleration signal $a_x(t)$
	(via horizontal pen force)
	o Vertical pen acceleration signal $a_y(t)$
	(via vertical pen force)
Level 2: Executive semantics	Features resulting from different classes of algorithms for verifying handwriting such as:
	o Dynamic Time Warping (DTW)
	o Hidden-Markov-Models (HMM)
	o Neural Networks
	o Multi Level Approaches
	o BioHash with distance measures for extracting
	certain statistical parameters
In Particular:	o Set of k statistical parameters
	derived from the syntax
Level 3: Functional semantics	Textual and visual information (what is written)
	o Word + its individual shape
	o Passphrase + its individual shape
	o Symbol + its individual shape
	o Number + its individual shape
	o Signature + its individual shape
Level 4: Interpretational semantics	Information about the context and background knowledge
	o Tablet
	o Pen
	o Device
	o Environment
	o Emotions
	o Metadata [11], [12] or Soft Biometrics [13], [14]
	o Acceptance

This new classification of handwritings for biometric user authentication is restructuring the authentication parameters. Parameters are now further differentiated according to the levels of syntax and semantics. The major benefit of this concept is the precise analysis of information. Certain defined classes pool information features. Thus, information can hardly get lost without being recognized. Compared to other approaches of feature classification, that punctually and arbitrarily pick a particular feature to extract, our approach can structurally analyze more than one feature at the same time. Hence, with this structure the complexity of information and its analysis for user authentication can be reduced. Furthermore, the accuracy of techniques for verifying handwritings can be evaluated. The VT implies the assumption that, the more information can be applied to the technique, the better and more reliable results can be achieved for authentication.

The different levels and their relation to each other will now been explained into more detail. Level 1, the class of syntax, has already been elaborated in section 3. Especially level 2, the class of executive semantics is focus of current research investigations. Figure 1 demonstrates an example for the generation of information of level 2 by applying the biometric hash algorithm to information of level 1. Signals are used as the input as it can be seen on the left side.

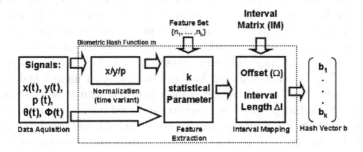

Fig. 1. Example for Level 1 and 2: Syntax and executive semantics [6], statistical representation.

Based on these signals, k statistical parameters are extracted such as the total writing time in ms, the total number of event pixels, the total absolute path length in pixels, or the total number of sample values. A complete description of the currently supported set of statistical parameters is provided in [6]. By applying an interval mapping function which implies the process parameter Interval Matrix IM, the Biometric Hash Vector b is generated which includes particular features. For authentication, this Biometric Hash Vector b will be compared with stored vectors of the database. Certain distance measures decide whether a user will be verified or not. These distance measures also belong to the class of level 2, the executive Semantics.

The class of level 3, the functional semantics is illustrated in Figure 2. This level 3 includes the classification of varying textual contexts used by the writers such as signatures, pin codes, passphrases, symbols, or numbers. Certain information such as "Sauerstoffgefäß" [oxygen container], as exemplified in Figure 2, written by two different writers is semantically equal within this level 3 of the VT model, while it differs from each other in level 1 and subsequently level 2. The meaning of the information is the same even if the signal distribution

Fig. 2. Handwriting examples of the German word "Sauerstoffgefäß" from two different writers [6].

is varying. This observation is a justification of our model with respect to the possibility to discriminate different writers, even if they write identical text.

Beside others, the interpretative semantics in level 4 classifies tablet categories or the interpretation of certain metadata [12] or soft biometrics [13], [14] such as cultural aspects [11] for the usage and acceptance of handwriting for biometric user authentication. The inclusion of this level 4 of information in biometric user authentication systems is a major subject of ongoing research.

There are two kinds of impact the interpretative semantics in level 4 can have for an analysis of information. One impact can be outlined as follows: Based on the three preceding levels, one is able to derive assumptions about not particularly in the original handwriting sample included information within level 4 of the VT model such as soft biometrics. The other impact is determined through the additional consideration of information within in the interpretative semantics of level 4 as parameter input to processed operations in lower levels such as the authentication algorithms. Tests in section 5 will provide conceptual proof that, by this means of level 4 features, a more accurate result for biometric user authentication can be achieved.

These examples lead to the assumption that the more parameters can be applied to the analysis of handwriting information, the more accurate and reliable results can be achieved for biometric user authentication. Better recognition results can be achieved with the combination of signal analysis and metadata or soft biometrics, respectively the combination of syntax and semantics.

5   Tests for Evaluating the Verifier-Tuple

For evaluating the Verifier-Tuple we refer to some test results presented in [6]. Our goal is the exemplary demonstration of the tuple's benefits as a new classification of information and hence, showing the advantages of the combination of different classified levels of syntax and semantics.

The tests include algorithms for handwriting as a biometric user authentication. Evaluations of those algorithms are based on the Equal Error Rate (ERR), the point where False Match Rate (FMR) and False Non-Match Rate (FNMR) are identical [6], [15]. FNMR is the percentage probability of rejections by a biometric system of authentic user while FMR is the percentage probability of rejections of non-authentic user. Thus, ERR is one decision measure value at a specific operating point of a biometric system and implies the probability of great similarities as presented in Table 2 and 3.

Table 2. EER for different tablet categories, textual content Signature (n/a = not available) [6], MQED

Tablet Category	Equal Error Rate (EER)			
	EER$_{Random}$	EER$_{Blind}$	EER$_{Low Force}$	EER$_{Brute Force}$
StepOver+PRESS	0.1	0.26	n/a	0.34
Cintiq15	0.12	0.2	0.34	0.38
All	0.18	0.3	0.4	0.42
Midres-PQ	0.15	0.25	0.4	0.42

Table 3. EER for different tablet categories, textual content Signature (n/a = not available) [6], BioHash

Tablet Category	Equal Error Rate (EER)			
	Random	Blind	Low-Force	Brute-Force
All	15 %	14 %	11 %	18 %
Cintiq15	5 %	12 %	10 %	13%
Midres PQ	22 %	34 %	33 %	33 %
StepOver+PRESS	5 %	29 %	n/a	16 %

For our evaluation, we refer to those handwritings from the database, presented in [6] that have been collected with three classes of digitizer tablets: StepOver+PRESS, Cintiq15, Midres-PQ (collection of different tablets with a medium spatial resolution) and the joint set of all tablets, denoted as "All". Further, the MQED algorithm is applied for authentication in Table 2 and the BioHash algorithm in Table 3. For evaluating the VT, our focus is on the EER$_{Random}$, shown in the second column from right of both tables. Table 2 and Table 3 both represent Equal Error Rates for different tablet categories and the textual content *Signature*, but results shown in Table 3 are more accurate than in Table 2. In comparison to Table 2, the BioHash algorithm, whose test results are presented in Table 3, applies additional information of level 2, the executive semantics, since it abstracts to statistical features. Information of level 4, the interpretative semantics, is reflected by the four table rows, where each row represents a different scenario with respect to the hardware used for sampling of the handwriting signals. In particular, the algorithms consider knowledge about the used tablet in all cases except row "All". We observe that for both algorithms, the recognition accuracy improves, if the specific type of tablet is known to the authentication systems, i.e StepOver+PRESS and Cintiq15 have lower error rates than Midres-PQ and All. That is, knowing the type of digitizer (interpretative semantics level 4 in the VT model) can improve accuracy as compared to conditions, where there is uncertainty about the hardware.

We interpret this demonstration as a first proof of the concept of the VT as a classifier for biometric handwriting authentication. The approach of [6] has shown that considering more knowledge of semantics for analyzing handwritings more accurate and reliable results for user authentication can be achieved.

6   Conclusion and Future Work

This paper has shown the usability of the concept of the Verifier-Tuple as a new classifier for biometric handwriting authentication and the following aspects can be summarized:

The VT is a new concept to classify biometric information in a structured manner. Its major benefit is the ability to pool information together into one level of syntax and three levels of semantics. The concept enables an efficient combination of information of these levels in biometric applications. By applying our developed concept more accurate and reliable results for biometric user authentication can be achieved.

While in the test scenario discussed in this paper, information of a higher semantic level, such as the type of digitizer tablet was known a-prior, it might be of interest in future investigations to perform analysis of signals and classes of algorithms towards determination of such higher level of information. For example, to identify the type of sampling device used during recording of the biometric data. Furthermore, by applying and evaluating metadata and soft biometric features such as the cultural origin, ethnicity and education, hypotheses of the user acceptance of a biometric user authentication system can be possibly derived in future. Future work will also include the analysis of compression of data by its entropy in order to figure out how far the data can be compressed and still discriminative features of interest can be extracted to grant accurate and secure authentication systems.

Comprising our earlier work on the forensic background, we can conclude that Verifier-Tuples are not only adequate to analyze an on-line handwriting into detail but also we can give more reliable assumptions about user authentication in general. With this paper we have shown the Verifier-Tuple's characteristics as a scalable concept for different media.

Acknowledgements

The information in this document is provided as is, and no guarantee or warranty is given or implied that the information is fit for any particular purpose. The user thereof uses the information at its sole risk and liability. The work described in this paper has been supported in part by the Federal Office for Information Security (BSI), Germany, in particular the development of the tuple, and partly by the EU-India project CultureTech, especially the hardware independency tests. The German Government is authorized to reproduce and distribute reprints for Governmental purposes notwithstanding any copyright notation there on. The views and conclusions contained herein are those of the authors and should not be interpreted as necessarily representing the official policies, either expressed or implied, of the Federal Office for Information Security (BSI), or the German Government.

References

1. A. Oermann et al.: Verifyer-Tupel for Audio-Forensic to determine speaker environment, accepted at ACM Multimedia and Security (2005)
2. H.R. Nielson, F. Nielson: Semantics with Applications: A Formal Introduction, revised edition, John Wiley & Sons, original 1992 (1999)
3. N. Chomsky: Syntactic Structures, Mouton and Co., Den Haag (1957)
4. N. Chomsky: Aspects of the Theory of Syntax, MIT Press, Massachusetts Institute of Technology, Cambridge, MA (1965)
5. S. Löbner: Semantik: eine Einführung, De Gruyter Studienbuch Berlin (2003)
6. C. Vielhauer: Biometric User Authentication For IT Security: From Fundamentals to Handwriting, Springer, New York, U.S.A., to appear 2006 (2006)
7. R. Plamandon, G. Lorette: Automatic Signature Verification and Writer Identification - the State of the Art, Pergamon Press plc., Pattern Recognition, 22, Vol. 2 (1989) 107 - 131
8. F. Leclerc, R. Plamondon: Automatic Verifictaion and Writer Identification: The State of the Art 1989-1993, International Journal of Pattern Recognition and Artificial Intelligence, Vol. 8 (1994) 643 - 660
9. J. Gupta, A. McCabe: A Review of Dynamic Handwritten Signature Verification, Technical report at James Cook University, Australia (1997)
10. C. Vielhauer, R. Steinmetz, A. Mayerhöfer, Biometric Hash based on Statistical Features of Online Signatures, In: Proceedings of the IEEE International Conference on Pattern Recognition (ICPR), Canada, Vol. 1 (2002) 123 - 126
11. S. Schimke, C. Vielhauer, P.K. Dutta, T.K. Basu, A. De Rosa, J. Hansen, B. Yegnanarayana, J. Dittmann: Cross Cultural Aspects of Biometrics, in Proceedings of Biometrics: Challenges arising from Theory to Practice (2004) 27-30
12. C. Vielhauer, T. Basu, J. Dittmann, P.K. Dutta: Finding Meta Data in Speech and Handwriting Biometrics, to appear in: Proceedings of SPIE (2005)
13. A. K. Jain, S. C. Dass and K. Nandakumar: Soft Biometric Traits for Personal Recognition Systems, in Proceedings of International Conference on Biometric Authentication (ICBA), LNCS 3072, Hong Kong, July (2004) 731-738
14. A. K. Jain, S. C. Dass and K. Nandakumar: Can soft biometric traits assist user recognition?, in Proceedings of SPIE Vol. 5404, Biometric Technology for Human Identification, Orlando, FL, April (2004) 561-572
15. C. Vielhauer, T. Scheidat: Fusion von biometrischen Verfahren zur Benutzerauthentifikation, In: P. Horster (Ed.), D-A-CH Security 2005 - Bestandsaufnahme, Konzepte, Anwendungen, Perspektiven (2005) 82 - 97

Decentralised Access Control in 802.11 Networks

Marco Domenico Aime, Antonio Lioy, and Gianluca Ramunno

Politecnico di Torino, Dipartimento di Automatica e Informatica,
Corso Duca degli Abruzzi 24, 10129 Torino, Italy
{M.Aime, Lioy, Ramunno}@Polito.it

Abstract. The current WiFi access control framework descends from solutions conceived in the past for dial-up scenarios. A key difference between the two worlds is mobility: dial-up handles nomadic users, while modern wireless networks support continuous mobility through always-on personal devices. Not surprisingly, WiFi authentication does not exploit mobility in any way; on the contrary, mobility is perceived as a problem to be fixed by some fast-handoff solution. Though fast-handoff is indeed an open issue, mobility may even help to build security systems. The paper describes a decentralised access control framework for WiFi networks that exploits mobility to avoid a central authority to be always online.

1 Motivation

WiFi authentication and access control infrastructure, as defined in [1], relies on a central authority, the Authentication Server, to be always on-line as it is directly involved in each authentication attempt. A host of proposals have outlined changes to improve scalability and performance of this basic solution. [2] uses peer interaction among Access Points (APs) to move security contexts rather than creating new ones. Unfortunately, it is limited to APs within the same network segment and again requires the AP to interact with a remote entity (now another AP instead of the Authentication Server) for every authentication attempt. [3] brilliantly solves the network segment limitation and allows interactions with the Authentication Server to occur before the actual authentication attempts. Most interesting, in [4] the same authors propose a decentralised solution to let APs discriminate which authentication attempts they should expect. An AP learns which APs its users come from by tracking the source AP in each authentication attempt directly experimented: APs can thus foresee authentication attempts and proactively query the Authentication Server for proper credentials. The only limitation of [3] is the Authentication Server itself: though a central authority is a cornerstone in current network authentication architectures, it has some clear drawbacks. In particular, it is a single point of failure: when it falls, no authentication attempt can occur and the whole wireless network is stuck. This is perfectly acceptable when security is more important than availability, but it looks draconian in scenarios where availability plays a key role. Many modern applications of wireless networks do present this characteristic. For instance, in a museum where a wireless network delivers information only to paying visitors, the availability of the service is far more important than an eventual unauthorised access. Similar arguments apply to a road access control system

J. Dittmann, S. Katzenbeisser, and A. Uhl (Eds.): CMS 2005, LNCS 3677, pp. 180–190, 2005.
© IFIP International Federation for Information Processing 2005

for vehicles: the cost of a false alarm (eventually triggering police intervention) is far more expensive than latency/failure in fraud detection. Nevertheless, in both examples efficient mechanisms are needed to revoke authorisation, for example when a customer definitely leaves the facility or the controlled area in general.

Recently, [5] has shown that mobility can be perceived as an aid to build security systems rather than a problem to be solved. We propose a decentralised access control solution that does not require a central authority to be always online and exploits node mobility to update authorisation status within the network. We recognise the main limit in that it requires advanced cryptographic techniques to be implemented both at client terminals and APs, and we will analyse the actual scope of this limit.

2 A Decentralised Access Control Framework

Here we investigate a novel framework where a central authority still exists but acts as a group manager rather than an authentication server. Its task is to admit and expel users from the group of authorised users, but it is not directly involved in each authentication attempt and access control decision. Fresh information on group membership is propagated by terminals as they roam within the network of APs. Recently admitted users will propagate their visa by their own, while membership revocation requires an ad-hoc transfer of information from the central authority to at least one AP. Revocation information can be either pushed by a remote network connection to a randomly chosen AP, or entrusted to a special terminal, or eventually delayed and given to a newly admitted terminal. In order to enable mutual authentication APs are equipped with the same class of credentials as the mobiles.

A straightforward way to implement our framework is a Public Key Infrastructure (PKI) based on digital certificates. The central authority would act as a Certification Authority (CA) and emit a certificate to every admitted user. Ownership of a valid certificate testifies group membership: APs may verify group admission by asking users for a certificate signed by the central authority. The overloading of public key certificates (PKC) with authorisation beyond identity information is a common practice even if more specialised techniques exist such as the attribute certificates (AC). However, revocation is the Achilles' heal of classic PKIs when deployed in fully decentralised scenarios. Revocation information is not propagated inside the certificates and should be retrieved by other means to correctly validate a certificate. In practice, a verifier must either query an online OCSP server or download an updated Certificate Revocation List (CRL) signed by the CA [6]. We deem both these solutions unsatisfactory because they involve the connection with an online authority that we aim to avoid. Note that CRLs could be propagated by terminals as for certificates, but there is no connection between admission and revocation information and thus no guarantee that they will be propagated with the same care. The relevance of this unsolved issue is clearly stated in [7].

As already observed, our task can be interpreted as a group membership problem, a well-established subject in security literature. In Sect. 3, we propose a simple extension to standard X.509 certificates able to satisfy our requirements. We then identify in the dynamic accumulator concept proposed in [8] an advanced cryptographic technique able to enhance our solution. Both solutions require fixed cryptographic burden for all involved operations despite the current size of the group. In our framework this is a precondition to grant perfect scalability to large numbers of users. It also helps to estimate the requirements imposed on APs by cryptographic tools far more complex than current ones (even in latest security extensions [1], APs support only symmetric cryptography). The solutions rely on mobile terminals to propagate group membership information: to model it we referred to the literature about diffusion processes and epidemiological processes (see [9] for a broad spectrum review). In particular, in Sect. 4, we extend part of the analysis in [10] and adapt it to the peculiar requirements of our scenario. The involved dynamics are sensibly different since we want propagation to encompass the whole network while studies on viral spreading aim to limit the propagation of the infection. Moreover, we investigated the connection between terminal mobility patterns and the resulting propagation dynamics. Finally, in Sect. 5, we investigate how the system heavily depends on how information to be propagated is distributed within the mobile node population.

3   The Protocol

We propose two mechanisms that can actually implement our framework, the former based on traditional PKIs and thus keener to current WiFi authentication system, the latter exploiting the advanced cryptographic techniques proposed in [11]. Both solutions entrust mobile terminals with the propagation of access control information as long as they travel within the AP network.

3.1   Basic Solution

WiFi authentication infrastructure can already rely on digital certificates, though in a rather centralised fashion. The first step towards decentralisation is delegating the Authentication Server functionality to the APs. We argue that asymmetric cryptography's burden at APs is not a serious issue as it should be supported in any case to secure remote management. Nevertheless, it would be more problematic in environments experiencing fast mobility and strict authentication time constraints: in this case [3] may remain the best choice.

The Central Authority is in fact a Certification Authority and emits certificates to mobiles as they enter the community: schemes such as [12] can make this phase both secure and practical. Also APs are given certificates from the CA: they can be installed at deployment time through manual configuration or an imprinting mechanism as in [13]. Then, mobiles use their certificates to authenticate against APs through EAP-TLS or similar methods. Still, the main issue is revocation. We thus extend classic certificates to make revocation information easier to be spread by mobile nodes. The aim is twofold: (1) we eliminate the burden of transmitting huge membership information lists and (2) admission and revocation information are tightly joined.

Mobiles could propagate revocation information as CRLs. The CRL size would be a problem specially if revocation is frequent and/or certificate validity is long. For instance, in the museum example certificates could be revoked as customers exit the museum. Even worst, there is no guarantee that mobiles would propagate CRLs since there is no connection between admission and revocation information. Thus, CRL emission should be frequent and APs should categorically refuse authentication if an updated CRL is not available: this imposes uncomfortable time constraints on the information spreading mechanism. Admission and revocation data may be linked simply by embedding CRLs within the certificates, but this is prevented by the size CRLs can grow to. We thus split revocation information within newly emitted certificates. Delta-CRLs [14] are a classic mechanism to limit the overhead due to CRL update. We extend this concept by having standard certificates to embed a subset of revocation data. This partial information is then spread by mobiles' movements and reconstructed at APs. The choice of a proper strategy to select which subset of information should be embedded in a particular certificate is addressed later in Sect. 5. Different embedding strategies may influence dramatically the security of the system. In fact, they determine the "information gap" probability, that is the probability that some revocation data is missing at APs. In this basic solution an information gap directly results in exposure to unauthorised access.

The above scheme fits scenarios where admissions are fairly frequent. For instance, it may work well in our museum example. We identify a key conceptual limit of this approach in that the nodes are obliged to spread fixed chunks of revocation data, but have no incentive to spread latest information: only recent certificates actually do valuable propagation job. An enhanced solution thus requires additional mechanisms able to push all members to look for fresh information and propagate it.

3.2 Enhanced Solution

We further extend our proposal with the concept of dynamic accumulators. One-way accumulators are a novel cryptographic tool first introduced in [15]. A one-way accumulator allows to securely test the presence of a particular value within a set of values previously accumulated in a single fixed-size accumulator value. [8] extends the original construction to make the set of accumulated values to be dynamically changed.

We exploit a dynamic accumulator to build a compact representation of group membership. From [8], we retain the concept and implementation of a dynamic accumulator while renouncing to anonymous verification to avoid zero-knowledge proofs and their cryptographic burden. The Central Authority (let's identify it as CA) maintains a public key for a membership accumulator besides its usual public key. The accumulator public key consists in a RSA modulus $n = pq$ of length k, where p and q are safe primes ($p = 2p' + 1$ and $q = 2q' + 1$). During admission, the CA assigns to every mobile a prime e drown from a range $[A, B]$ where $2 < A < B < A^2 < n/4$. [1] The CA computes the new accumulator values as $z' = z^{e_a} \bmod n$, where z is the current accumulator value and e_a is the value assigned to the new member. Then the CA embeds $(e_a, u = z, z')$ within the terminal's certificate. When revoking a membership, the CA update the accumulator as $z' = z^{e_r^{-1} \bmod (p-1)(q-1)} \bmod n$, where z is the current accumulator value and e_r is the value inserted in the certificate being revoked.

To verify admission, an AP should both validate the mobile's certificate and check that the value e embedded within the certificate is still present in the latest accumulator value. To prove presence in the accumulator, a node associated to the prime e should

---

[1] Refer to [8] for a discussion on the choice of the range $[A, B]$.

show the witness u that satisfies $z = u^e \bmod n$ where z is the latest accumulator value. Updated accumulator values z are spread by mobiles while filing their certificates.

The actual complexity in managing this scheme is updating the witness u. As [8] shows, a node should update its witness u for every change of the accumulator value. For every e_a added to the accumulator, the witness of every node must be updated as $u' = u^{e_a} \bmod n$; while for every e_r removed from the accumulator, the new witness is $u' = u^b z^a$ where z is the new accumulator value, and a, b satisfy $ae + be_r = 1$ and are computed through the extended GCD algorithm. Hence, not only the fresh accumulator values but also the e added/removed from the accumulator should be propagated.

We argue that mobile-driven propagation may be exploited not only for accumulator values but also for accumulator change information. For instance, this can be achieved by having the CA to embed a subset of past changes (the e added/removed to/from the accumulator) in newly emitted certificate as done with revocation information in the basic solution of Sect. 3.1.

It's quite interesting to notice that a gap in the information being propagated has now quite different implications. As long as an AP knows the latest accumulator value it can safely prevent any unauthorised access. However, a legitimate terminal may not be able to prove its membership since it lacks data required to update its witness. Symmetrically, a terminal having updated credentials may not be able to authenticate an AP that has missed recent membership evolutions. These conditions are particularly scary in our reference scenarios where security must coexist with reliability. However, we notice that we have gained a lot of flexibility:

- *in policies*: nodes (APs or terminals) can flexibly choose between security and usability by accepting authentication attempts based on dated accumulator values
- *in resources*: nodes (APs or terminals) can tune the storage they reserve to accumulator history based on their policy
- *in fallbacks*: APs (and with more complex schemes also terminals) can fall back to expensive retrieval mechanisms just when needed and only for missing information chunks: alternatives are an online central directory or a peer-to-peer query system among APs

Related to the last point, note that the access to an online repository is going to be less frequent than in a classic CRL-based solution: once retrieved by a particular AP, missing information can then be propagated by terminals' movements.

Now, mobiles have additional incentive to propagate up-to-date information. In fact, a mobile will propagate the last known accumulator value to avoid storing multiple credential generations. This implies it will also tend to propagate membership changes that are needed to let APs update their own credentials. In practice, nodes will: (1) receive recent accumulator values from the APs they visit in the form of fresh certificates emitted by the CA, (2) update their own credentials, and (3) propagate fresh certificates containing the updated information.

The above schema is prone to further extensions. First, the terminal-driven propagation can be sided with a push mechanism among APs. At random intervals APs may send random chunks of information to a random selected peer (once again, information on AP community can be easily propagated by mobile terminals). A very low pushing probability can speed up propagation tremendously when mobility patterns are too much constrained: this is granted by the famous work of Watts and Strogatz [16].

Moreover, the anonymous credential system defined in [11] (the framework which dynamic accumulators where originally defined for) could further extend our framework and provide a key additional feature, namely untraceability of mobiles through anonymous authentication. In practice, the authentication process allows to verify the user authorisation without identifying her. If long-term terminal identifiers are hidden and node's movements are disguised, this ensures that the mobile presence, location and movements cannot be tracked within the covered area. Untraceability may be a key feature in public services covering large areas. Embracing the above anonymous credential system would require to drop standard certificates and would impose far higher cryptographic requirements to terminals and APs. However, the above construction would hold and terminal mobility could still be used to diffuse accumulator changes. An exhaustive analysis of the opportunities offered by an anonymous credential system and the relative performance impact are left for further investigation.

4   Terminal Mobility and Information Propagation

Both our basic and enhanced solutions rely on terminal mobility to propagate information. Let us analyse their behaviour of our solutions in terms of information spreading.

We model the network of APs as a graph $G = (N, E)$ where N is the set of APs and E is the set of acquaintances. In other words, an edge $e_{j,i} \in E$ if $n_j, n_i \in N$, and a terminal can physically move from the AP n_j to the AP n_i. Then we refer to the viral spreading model presented in [10] and adapt it to our though different problem. This model aims to predict the dynamics of virus spreading in a computer network. We notice strong analogies with our propagation mechanism, where update information can only move from an aware AP to an unaware one thanks to the passage of a mobile between them. A main difference, that we will have to cope with, is that the probability of transmission cannot be assumed equal for all links as in [10], but heavily depends on the topology of the AP network and the terminal mobility patterns.

From the model described in [10], we retain some key quantities and overload them with different semantic:

$p_{i,t}$ – probability that the AP i has updated information at time t

$\beta_{j,i}$ – probability that updated information is propagated by any terminal from AP j to AP i

$\zeta_{i,t}$ – probability that AP i does not receive updated information from its neighbours at time t

Note that $\beta_{j,i}$ may now vary for each link. The quantity $\zeta_{i,t}$ is redefined as the probability that at time t an AP i has no updated information and will not receive it from any terminal coming from any of its neighbouring APs:

$$\zeta_{i,t} = \prod_{j:e_{j,i} \in E} (p_{j,t-1}(1 - \beta_{j,i}) + (1 - p_{j,t-1})) = \prod_{j:e_{j,i} \in E} (1 - \beta_{j,i} * p_{j,t-1}) \quad (1)$$

We then use $\zeta_{i,t}$ to define $p_{i,t}$. In spite of the original model, in our case the "infected" status is irreversible: that is, once an AP has received a particular information chunk it can retain it indefinitely.[2] The quantity $p_{i,t}$ is thus computed as:

$$p_{i,t} = 1 - (1 - p_{i,t-1})\zeta_{i,t} \tag{2}$$

The probability $\beta_{j,i}$ is related to terminal mobility patterns. We model terminal mobility as a discrete Markov chain $M = (N, E^*)$ where N is the usual set of APs and E^* is the set E of links between APs weighted with the rate of terminals that transits along each link. We thus introduce two new quantities:

$a_{j,i}$ – probability that a terminal connected to AP j moves to AP i

π_i – probability that at a given time a given terminal is connected to AP i

Under ergodic conditions, using matrix notation we can compute $\boldsymbol{\Pi} = \boldsymbol{A}\boldsymbol{\Pi}$ as the principal eigenvector of the matrix $\boldsymbol{A}$, that is the eigenvector associated to the eigenvalue $\lambda = 1$. From theory, since each column of $\boldsymbol{A}$ adds up to one, at least one positive unitary eigenvalue exists, and for the ergodic assumption all other eigenvalues will be less than one.

Clearly, this mobility model is very simple. First, the model is discrete and thus the terminals are allowed to move only at discrete times. Second, it allows to model only constant numbers of terminals roaming within the network in a completely independent way. Third, the Markov assumption implies a memoryless behaviour of terminals, namely it is impossible to catch multiple highly-preferred directional paths along the network. Nevertheless, this model suffices to investigate relations between node mobility and information dissemination. In Sect. 4.1 we use it to analyse the behaviour of our access control framework against simple network topologies and highly guided mobility patterns. For instance, this may be the case in a wireless-enabled museum.

We can now define the probability $\beta_{j,i}^*$ that a given terminal propagates updated information from AP j to AP i as

$$\beta_{j,i}^* = a_{j,i}\pi_j \tag{3}$$

Assuming the same roaming pattern for all mobiles, we can finally compute the probability $\beta_{j,i}$ that some terminal propagates updated information from AP j to AP i:

$$\beta_{j,i} = 1 - (1 - \beta_{j,i}^*)^M \tag{4}$$

where M is the number of terminals present in the network, constant in time. Handling multiple roaming patterns requires to define a different matrix $\boldsymbol{A}$ per each pattern to determine a different β^* per each pattern.

4.1 Information Propagation Analysis

Rather than focusing on a particular AP topology, we chose to experiment our framework against a set of schematic topologies somehow related to typical architectonic structures. In particular, we selected the four topologies shown in Fig. 1:

---

[2] Actually, APs may purge obsolete information once the certificate it refers to is expired, but this lies outside the spreading analysis.

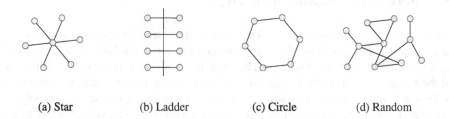

<table>
<tr><td>(a) Star</td><td>(b) Ladder</td><td>(c) Circle</td><td>(d) Random</td></tr>
</table>

Fig. 1. Different AP topologies

- star – this represents an hall/square surrounded by a set of places; the square is a common building as well as city architectural module since ancient Greece
- ladder – represents a corridor/street with a sequence of places on both its sides; this is a module made famous by Roman cities
- circle – in our simple mobility model, this is the best representative of a guided corridor/street; this may model a museum as well as an highway
- random mesh – this is mainly used for comparison but it may model for example a large exposition ambient

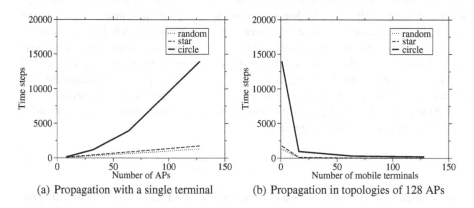

(a) Propagation with a single terminal   (b) Propagation in topologies of 128 APs

Fig. 2. Propagation in different AP topologies

Figure 2(a) shows how the number of discrete time steps t needed to have $p_{i,t} > 0.99$ for all APs changes based on the number of APs. Figure 2(b) shows instead how t changes based on the number of mobile terminals in different topologies of 128 APs. As expected, propagation may perform poorly when mobility paths are particularly constrained (as in the circle topology). However, as the number of mobiles grows the probability of a jump between two given APs rapidly increases and so does the propagation speed.

5   Information Embedding Strategy

Both the solutions discussed in Sect. 3 rely on mobile terminals to carry some chunks of information, either revocation data under the certificate-based solution or accumulator updates within the enhanced solution. However, In Sect. 3 we have put off the definition of the actual embedding strategy, that is the choice of what subset of information has to be included in each newly emitted certificate for propagation. To complete the analysis of our proposal, we present an initial investigation on the tremendous effects embedding strategies may have on its global behaviour.

Following the idea behind Delta-CRLs, a sliding window selection mechanism may be used. In other words, a newly emitted certificate includes all and only the changes occurred from the immediately previous certificate. In this case, the probability P_{gap} that some block of information gets permanently lost can be computed as:

$$P_{gap}(T) = 1 - (1 - P_m)^T \qquad (5)$$

where P_m is the probability that a single certificate gets lost and T is the number of emitted certificates. P_m highly depends on the specific scenario: for instance, it is effected by the probability that users subscribe to the service but do not use it, and the threat of sabotage attempts. We argue that a careful analysis of proper values of P_m is crucial and leave it to future investigation. Nevertheless, from (5) it is evident that P_{gap} will rapidly approach 1 even for low values of P_m. The problem is that a single missing certificate is sufficient to create a permanent gap in the information being propagated.

To overcome the poor performance of the sliding window approach, we propose to randomly choose the subset of information to be embedded. To limit the size of embedded information, the probability that a specific information gets embedded is decreased as its freshness. Assuming membership change events are fully ordered,[3] we define the probability P_e that the information chunk at ordinal number t gets embedded in a new certificate emitted at time T as

$$P_e(t, T) = \frac{1}{(T - t)^\alpha} \qquad (6)$$

The parameter α determines the size of the embedded information in a single certificate, as well as the expected number of certificates that a particular information is embedded in. Table 1 shows the expected number of information chunks embedded in a certificate with different values of α and different sizes T of information history. Note that the behaviour with T approaching infinity is not relevant since old information sooner or later can be dropped because of certificate expiration.

To analyse the performance of our probabilistic embedding strategy, we start computing the probability that the t-th information is not lost at time T when supposing that all the successive certificates are not lost:

$$P_{presence}(t, T) = 1 - (P_m * \prod_{2 < s < (T-t)} (1 - P_e(s, T))) \qquad (7)$$

---

[3] Full orderability is obviously guaranteed by allowing a single entity, the CA, to modify the set.

Table 1. Expected number of embedded information chunks

	$T = 10$	$T = 100$	$T = 1000$	$T = 10000$
$\alpha = 0.9$	2.68	4.28	5.57	6.60
$\alpha = 1$	2.93	5.19	7.49	9.79
$\alpha = 1.1$	3.22	6.43	10.52	15.69

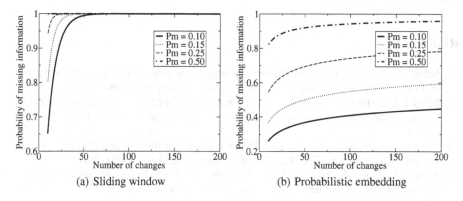

(a) Sliding window   (b) Probabilistic embedding

Fig. 3. Comparison of different embedding strategies

The above equation states that the t-th information chunk is present if the t-th certificate is not lost or if it has been embedded in some of the successive certificates. Now we can compute P_{gap} at time T as:

$$P_{gap}(T) = 1 - ((1 - P_m) * \prod_{2 < t < T} (P_{presence}(t, T))) \tag{8}$$

This states that we face a gap when not all the information is somehow present, either in its native certificate or embedded in successive ones.

Figures 3(a) and 3(b) show how the two discussed strategies behave with different values of the probability P_m that a single certificate gets lost: as expected, with the sliding window the gap probability rapidly tends to one, while the probabilistic embedding leaves additional space to recovering.

6   Final Remarks

The analysis presented here suggests further investigation. First, a more realistic mobility model could help to better understand how our approach fits in real environments. In particular, it could prove interesting to understand when the integration of terminal-based propagation with push mechanisms by APs may be useful and the achievable efficiency. Our probabilistic embedding strategy should be tested against coalition of adversaries trying to prevent or manipulate the information spreading. We argue that a detailed comparison among different strategies could help to measure the actual robustness of our solution. As already observed, a major extension is related to the integration of an anonymous credential system. This could boost the value of our construction in environments where privacy is a concern. A careful performance analysis of the specific credential system is a key step towards this opportunity. Finally, we argue that an implementation of the specific mechanisms we have described could help to gain additional insight in the whole system behaviour. Actually, this step is unavoidable to understand whether fully decentralised authentication frameworks may challenge traditional ones in future wireless networks.

References

1. IEEE: Std 802.11i/d7.0, part 11: Wireless medium access control (MAC) and physical layer (PHY) specifications: Medium access control (MAC) security enhancements (2003)
2. IEEE: P802.11f/d5, recommended practice for multi-vendor access point interoperability via an inter-access point protocol across distribution systems supporting IEEE 802.11 operation (2003)
3. Mishra, A., Shin, M., Arbaugh, W.A.: Proactive key distribution to support fast and secure roaming. Submission to IEEE 802.11 Working Group 802.11-03/084r0 (2003)
4. Mishra, A., Shin, M., Arbaugh, W.A.: Pro-active key distribution using neighbor graphs. Technical report, Department of Computer Science, University of Maryland College Park (MD, USA) (2003)
5. Capkun, S., Hubaux, J.P., Buttyan, L.: Mobility helps security in ad hoc networks. In: Proc. of the 4th ACM international symposium on Mobile Ad Hoc Networking & Computing (MobiHoc). (2003) 46–56
6. Wohlmacher, P.: Digital certificates: a survey of revocation methods. In: Proc. of the 2000 ACM workshops on Multimedia. (2000) 111–114
7. Rivest, R.L.: Can we eliminate certificate revocations lists? In: Proc. of Financial Cryptography (FC). (1998) 178–183
8. Camenisch, J., Lysyanskaya, A.: Dynamic accumulators and application to efficient revocation of anonymous credentials. In: Crypto # 2002. (2002) 61–76
9. Newman, M.E.J.: The structure and function of complex networks. In: SIAM Review. Volume 45(2). (2003) 167–256
10. Wang, Y., Chakrabarti, D., Wang, C., Faloutsos, C.: Epidemic spreading in real networks: An eigenvalue viewpoint. In: 22nd Symposium on Reliable Distributed Systems (SRDS). (2003) 25–34
11. Camenisch, J., Lysyanskaya, A.: An efficient system for non-transferable anonymous credentials with optional anonymity revocation. In: EuroCr # 2001. (2001) 93–117
12. Balfanz, D., Smetters, D.K., Stewart, P., Wong, H.C.: Talking to strangers: Authentication in ad-hoc wireless networks. In: Proc. of Network and Distributed System Security Symposium (NDSS), San Diego (CA, USA) (2002)
13. Stajano, F., Anderson, R.: The resurrecting duckling: Security issues for ad-hoc wireless networks. In: Proc. of the 7th International Workshop on Security Protocols, Cambridge (UK) (2000) 172–194
14. Cooper, D.A.: A more efficient use of delta-CRLs. In: IEEE Symposium on Security and Privacy (S&P). (2000) 190–202
15. Benaloh, J., de Mare, M.: One-way accumulators: A decentralized alternative to digital signatures. In: EuroCr # 93. (1994) 274–285
16. Watts, D., Strogatz, S.: Collective dynamics of 'small-world' networks. Nature **393** (1998) 440–442

Multimodal Biometrics for Voice and Handwriting

Claus Vielhauer and Tobias Scheidat

School of Computer Science, Department of Technical and Business Information Systems,
Advanced Multimedia and Security Lab, Otto-von-Guericke University Magdeburg,
Universitätsplatz 2, D-39106 Magdeburg, Germany
{claus.vielhauer, tobias.scheidat}@iti.cs.uni-magdeburg.de
http://wwwiti.cs.uni-magdeburg.de/iti_amsl/

Abstract. In this paper a novel fusion approach for combining voice and online signature verification will be introduced. While the matching algorithm for the speaker identification modality is based on a single Gaussian Mixture Model (GMM) algorithm, the signature verification strategy is based on four different distance measurement functions, combined by multialgorithmic fusion. Together with a feature extraction method presented in our earlier work, the Biometric Hash algorithm, they result in four verification experts for the handwriting subsystem. The fusion results of our new subsystem on the multimodal level are elaborated by enhancements to a system, which was previously introduced by us for biometric authentication in HCI scenarios. Tests have been performed on identical data sets for the original and the enhanced system and the first results presented in this paper show that an increase of recognition accuracy can be achieved by our new multialgorithmic approach for the handwriting modality.

Keywords: biometrics, combination, distance, fusion, handwriting, identification, matching score level, multialgorithmic, multimodal, voice.

1 Introduction

The necessity for user authentication rose strongly in the last years. In the today's digital world it is no longer possible for humans to determine the identity of the other one mutually from face to face, for example due to the distance between two parties, which may be virtually linked by a computer network (e.g. the World-Wide Web). The task of ensuring the identity of participants of a process is made increasingly often by automatic systems, e.g. by user verification. Verification is the confirmation of the identity of a person. The three fundamental methods of user verification are based on secret knowledge, personal possession and biometrics. An important advantage of biometrics is that it identifies the person neither by knowledge, nor by an object, which can be lost or handed over to other persons. In contrast to knowledge and possession, biometric characteristics are intrinsically conjoined to their owners. Prominent modalities for biometrics are passive traits like iris and fingerprint on one side and behavioral properties such as voice and handwriting on the other. Voice and handwriting, especially signature, are very intuitive behavioral and ubiquitous

J. Dittmann, S. Katzenbeisser, and A. Uhl (Eds.): CMS 2005, LNCS 3677, pp. 191–199, 2005.

biometrics. They can be captured by modern personal computers, as well as by Personal Digital Assistants (PDA) or even some pen-enabled smart phones. Further, no expensive special hardware is required. Only a microphone and a graphical tablet or touch sensitive display are necessary.

One of the problems with biometrics is the lack of recognition accuracy of single systems, reflected for example by the error characteristics of false identifications. In order to increase the accuracy of biometric systems, some approaches try to reach a better performance by combination of various biometric modalities (e.g. fingerprint and iris). These approaches are called multimodal or multibiometric verification systems. These multimodal biometrics can be advantageous also for persons, who cannot exhibit one or several of the required characteristics. For example, a missing modality could be ignored and those characteristics available could be increasingly significant for subjects lacking one ore more features.

Given a biometric system of only one single modality, another possibility to improve the verification performance is the fusion of different algorithms of this individual biometrics. Systems of this category are denoted as multialgorithmic systems. In this paper we analyze the effects of replacement of a subsystem of an existing multimodal system to the recognition accuracy. While the original subsystem is based on a single distance measurement algorithm for handwriting, the new subsystem is a multialgorithmic signature verification expert. For our analysis, we first give an overview of the original multimodal system and the underlying fusion strategy. We then summarize the multialgorithmic approach for signature verification. This multialgorithmic approach is then used as a replacement for the subsystem for handwriting, which is introduced by our novel fusion model. In our experimental evaluation we then compare the multimodal recognition results of the original and the new subsystem.

This paper is structured as follows. In section 2, we give a short description of the original multimodal system. Section 3 provides an overview of the fusion methods for combining multimodal or multialgorithmic biometric systems. Further, it describes our new approach based on the fusion of four signature verification experts. We present first experimental results of this new subsystem alone, and at the end of the third section for the entire multimodal system with and without the new subsystem. In section 4 we summarize this article, draw some conclusions for our research and discuss further activities in this area.

2 Multimodal Fusion on the Example of Voice and Handwriting

In the multimodal approach presented in [2], the biometrics speech and signature are fused with one another. The focus here is on the use of pen-based mobile devices for Human to Computer Interaction (HCI), where the authors concentrate on spoken and hand-written input. The problem with the use of speech is the influence of the results by noises and consequently, the fusion idea is to compensate this influence by a complimentary biometric modality, the handwriting.

Figure 1 outlines the multimodal biometric system model from [2]. The Fusion is accomplished on the matching score level (see chapter 3). In this perspective, the multimodal biometric system contains two separate biometric subsystems until the fusion process. Both subsystems have their own modality dependent input data. As from this point of view it is irrelevant whether the subsystems consist of one or more algorithms, the usage of multialgorithmic schemes for one or more of the subsystems generally fits in this multimodal layout.

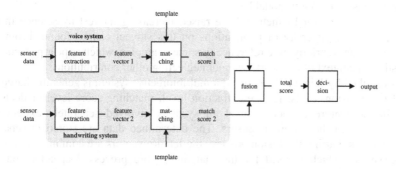

Fig. 1. Multimodal fusion for voice and handwriting on matching score level

For the actual design of the fusion strategy, a variety of alternatives exist, based on linear and non-linear weighting, user-specific and global weighting models et cetera. For the sake of simplicity, in [2] a global, linear weighting based on the modified z-score distance measures of each modality has been implemented. Here, separately for each modality the non-normalized distance measure x is normalized to the modified z-score z according to the following equation:

$$z = \frac{x - \min(x)}{\sigma} .$$ (1)

σ and $\min(x)$ denote the standard deviation and the minimum above all observed distance measures in a test. The fusion of z-scores is then simply given by the summation of the individual scores for the two modalities, z_{HW} for handwriting and z_{SR} for speaker recognition:

$$z_{final} = z_{SR} + z_{HW} .$$ (2)

The reference data and test data descended from ten persons for both, speech and handwriting. The spoken inputs are German. They were captured in a soundproofed environment. Later two kinds of noises, generated white Gaussian noise and recorded laptop fan noise, were added in order to simulate a mobile setup. Each person had to read 15 sentences for training and one different sentence for testing and for the signature part, each person had to write her or his signature six to eleven times. One of these samples was used as test sample. The samples remained were used for the reference data set. The handwriting data were acquired on a graphical tablet, Wacom Cintiq15, which output the same kind of signals as those digitizers used in tablet PCs.

A disadvantage of this original system is the missing weighting. These could use advantages of a person during speaking or writing by higher weight.

3 Fusion of Handwriting Algorithms

In order to increase the verification performance of the multimodal system described in section 2, we propose to use a multialgorithmic combination of handwriting verification methods in the signature part in order to achieve overall recognition improvements on the multimodal level.

Fusion strategies for biometrics have raised increasing interest by science in the recent past and a diversity of publications on this subject can be found. From the variety we want to briefly give reference to some examples, which appear particularly interesting in context of our work, without neglecting other contributions.

As described by Jain and Ross in [3] a multibiometric system is generally based on one of three fusion levels: feature extraction level, matching score level or decision level. In the feature extraction level all systems involved separately extract the information from the different sensors. The determined data are stored in separate feature vectors. During the fusion process, the feature vectors are combined to a joint feature vector, which is used for the matching score process. Dependent on the number of subsystems involved and the dimension of each individual feature vector, the resulting joint feature vector may be high dimensional, which can make its further processing cumbersome. The fusion on matching score level is based on the mixture of matching scores after the comparison between reference data and test data. Additionally, a normalization and weighting of the matching scores of the different modalities is possible, for example by relevance. The fusion results in a new matching score, which is the basis for decision. In decision based systems, each biometric subsystem involved is completed separately. Here, the individual decisions are combined to a final decision, e.g. by boolean operations like AND/OR. Because this fusion is accomplished at the latest point in time of the overall process, it cannot be controlled and parameterized as granularly as the other two approaches.

Matching score level based approaches have been successfully applied for a number of multimodal systems, for example in [3], a multibiometric system is presented by Jain and Ross, that uses face, fingerprint and hand geometry characteristics of a person for authentication. This system applies an user adapted weighting tactic. Ly-Van et al. [4] combine signature verification (based on HMM's) with text dependent (based on DTW) and text independent (based on Gaussian Mixture Model) speech verification, at a time. They report that fusion increases the performance by a factor 2 relatively to the best single system. Czyz et al. ([5]) propose combination strategies of face verification algorithms. The authors show that the combination based on simple sum rule can reach a better result than the best individual expert.

Because of the good characteristics, like simple normalization and weighting, and the encouraging results subscribed in [3] and [5] we decided for a fusion on matching score level in our multialgorithmic system for the handwriting modality.

3.1 New Approach

Our goal is to improve the verification performance of the multimodal system described in section 2 by use of multialgorithmic handwriting verification algorithm. If the handwriting modality itself reaches a better identification rate, the performance of the entire multimodal system should become better, which we want to demonstrate experimentally.

In [6] we have shown that in principle, multialgorithmic fusion can be achieved by multimodal fusion methods and because of the very encouraging test results in our work on handwriting, we choose the matching score level for combining the individual handwriting algorithms. Another argument for the matching score is that normalization and weighting can to be accomplished here relatively simple. Each algorithm (expert) produces a distance value, which expresses the similarity of reference data and test data. Normalization then makes the values of the different experts comparable to each other. In the last step before the decision process, weighting is applied to each matching score, where the definition of the weight parameters is part of the system configuration. Such a multialgorithmic fusion on matching score level is shown in figure 2. In difference to the multimodal fusion, the procedures involved use the same sensor data and reference data.

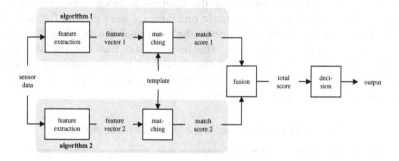

Fig. 2. Multialgorithmic matching score level fusion

At this time all algorithms in our system use the Biometric Hash method introduced in [1] for feature extraction from the handwriting samples. Only the similarity of input data and reference data is determined by different distance measurement functions. The used alternative distance measures are Canberra Distance, City Block (Manhattan) Distance, Euclidean Distance and Hamming Distance. Note that with a small distance, the feature vectors are each other more similar than with a larger.

In [7] we have shown that a well weighted fusion of different distance measure algorithms can result in a better verification performance than the best individual algorithm. These results were experimentally determined from a database of 1761 genuine enrollments (with 4 signatures per enrollment), 1101 genuine verification signatures and 431 well skilled forgeries by 22 persons. All samples have been captured on the same device, a Wacom Cintiq15. We have chosen this tablet since it has an active display. Through this not only the quality of the enrollments and verifications improves but also the quality of the forgeries becomes better. The reason for it is that the written text appears in the place in which it is produced. This corresponds to the natural writing behavior of human beings. We were able to show that the best fusion strategy of signatures results in a decrease of the EER of 12.1% in comparison to the best individual algorithm. Additional investigations with other trays and other semantic classes, as published in [6], led to similar results.

3.2 Multialgorithmic Fusion: Experimental Results

In our new approach we now want to use these improved concepts for the combination of voice and signature. In the first step we created a fusion of four distance measure algorithms within a biometric system as described above. In the second we combined the voice system and the handwriting system by the matching score level.

In order to show the increase in identification performance of the system described in [2], our tests based on the same signature test sets. Due to the functional properties of our evaluation program we used four out of five to ten signature samples for enrollments and the remaining one to six samples are used as test data for each user. In case that more than one test data are available for one enrollment per user, our system selects those enrollments having the smallest distance value. In our earlier work [7] in single tests of the four distance functions we have created five weighting strategies, based on the respective value of the individual distances for the test set. The weighting strategy, which led to the best results, was adapted also on the handwriting data from [2]. By using the described transformation function we determined a modified z-score. The identification rate for the signature amounts to 80% and the rate amounted to 50% before.

Table 1. Modified z-scores of the multialgorithmic method

	1	2	3	4	5	6	7	8	9	10
1	0,6	3,7	2,5	2,4	3,0	2,1	1,7	0,0	3,0	3,7
2	1,3	1,0	2,3	1,9	1,7	1,3	1,5	0,7	2,2	3,1
3	0,6	2,5	0,3	1,1	1,4	0,9	1,6	0,2	2,2	3,2
4	0,5	3,2	2,0	0,5	1,9	0,5	0,9	0,3	1,5	3,2
5	1,9	2,5	1,3	1,7	1,1	1,4	1,9	1,7	2,6	2,9
6	1,6	2,9	2,6	1,8	2,0	0,0	0,9	0,5	0,8	3,4
7	2,6	2,9	1,6	2,2	2,3	1,7	0,4	1,9	3,3	3,5
8	1,4	4,0	2,6	2,3	2,8	1,9	1,8	0,0	1,5	3,5
9	1,1	3,2	2,3	1,9	2,2	1,7	1,3	0,4	0,4	3,4
10	1,3	3,5	2,9	1,3	1,6	0,8	1,0	0,7	1,3	0,7

Table 1 shows the results of the identification tests. For each user an identification attempt was accomplished. The similarity of the test data of a person was determined in each case to their reference data and the reference data of all other persons. The matching scores of the individual algorithms were normalized, if necessary, to the interval [0-68]. The number results from the number of 69 of statistical features extracted by the Biometric Hash algorithm as suggested in [8]. In the next step, we determined the modified z-score as described in section 2. Identification is then performed by the nearest neighbor strategy. In case there are more then one matches for an assignment of a reference data to a test data, we consider an identification failure. With our new subsystem, we reached an identification rate of 80%. Table 1 shows the observed z-scores after the fusion. Columns show the enrollments for each user and rows show the verification data for each user, consequently, the marked diagonal shows the genuine z-scores of each user. The first column and the first row represent the user IDs.

We are confident that with a larger number of persons and/or test data and optimized parameterization of the fusion weights, identification rates could be improved, but we assume that with these first test results, we may conceptually prove the qualification of our approach for usage in multimodal systems.

3.3 Multimodal Fusion: Experimental Results

The next step is to bring together the speech-based subsystem and the multialgorithmic signature-based subsystem to form the multimodal system. To ensure that the results are comparable, we have selected the same proceeding for the multimodal fusion of the speech and the handwriting subsystems, which was used also with the original system, as described in [2]. This fusion consists of a non-weighted addition of the z-scores. In addition, we assume an uniform distribution of z-scores.

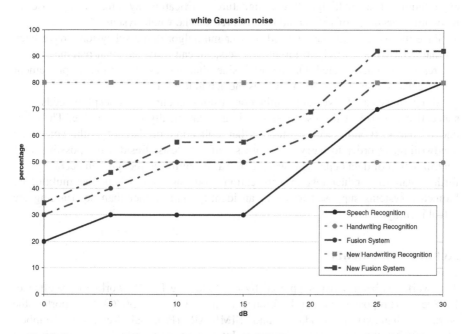

Fig. 3. Adapted identification rates and original identification rates as function of noise

As an overall improvement of 30% for the identification rate for the subsystem has been observed (originally 50%, now 80%), we can estimate the effect of accuracy of the multialgorithmic subsystem to 15% on the entire multimodal system. The improvement arises from the participation of both subsystems with equal weights. In figure 3 the improvement of the modified system is graphically represented in the comparison to the original system. In comparison to the original fusion, our improved approach has shown for example an identification rate improvement from 30% to 34.5% at a zero Signal-to-Noise-Ratio (SNR) and from 80% to 92% for an SNR of 25dB. Similarly, for all intermediate SNR values, we observe a significant improvement of the recognition rate.

4 Conclusions and Future Work

To best of our knowledge, so far no research results on the combination of multimodal and multialgorithmic experts concerning speech and handwriting has been published and in this work we implemented and evaluated this approach by enhancing an existing system [2]. The original system consisted of one speech-based subsystem and one signature-based subsystem and in our modification the signature-based subsystem was replaced by a multialgorithmic subsystem. Our examinations, based on identical data set as in the original publication, show that an improvement of the verification performance of the originally multimodal approach is feasible. By exploitation of a multialgorithmic signature verification system, an increase in recognition accuracy of 15% could be observed for the whole system.

Since the weight parameters used for our multialgorithmic subsystems have been estimated based on entirely different data sets, we can truly state that parameters and test results are uncorrelated. On the other side, this implies that further improvement can be achieved by optimization towards the actual test set.

Although we can derive some initial conclusions on our new concept, it needs to be stated that the size of the used test sets is not statistically representative. Therefore one of our next aims will be the further collection of data of both, voice and handwriting, in order to carry out more significant tests. Besides the possibility of determination of data dependent weights towards optimized recognition accuracy, we further plan to conduct test in verification mode as well, where the multimodal biometric systems supposed to verify an identity claim rather than determining the actual identity.

Acknowledgements

This work has been partly supported by the following EU Networks of Excellence: BioSecure (Proposal/Contract Reference number IST-2002-507634) supported the work on handwriting modality and SIMILAR (Proposal Reference Number: FP6–507609) the Human to Computer Interaction part activities on multimodal fusion. The contents of this publication are the sole responsibility of the authors and can in no way be taken to reflect the views of the European Union.

We would particularly like to thank Jana Dittmann for her support and fruitful discussions in the context of our work.

References

1. Vielhauer, C., Steinmetz, R., Mayerhöfer, A.: Biometric Hash based on Statistical Features of Online Signature, Proceedings of the International Conference on Pattern Recognition (ICPR), Conference on Pattern Recognition (ICPR), August, Quebec City, Canada, Vol. 1, (2002) 123-126, ISBN 0-7695-1696-3
2. Vielhauer, C., Schimke, S., Thanassis, V., Stylianou, Y.: Fusion Strategies for Speech and Handwriting Modalities in HCI, to appear in: SPIE Proceedings - Electronic Imaging, Security and Watermarking of Multimedia Contents VII (2005)
3. Jain, A.K., Ross, A.: Multibiometric Systems, Communications Of The ACM, Vol. 47, No. 1 (2004) 34-40
4. Ly-Van, B., Blouet, R., Renouard, S., Garcia-Salicetti, S., Dorizzi, B., Chollet, G.: Signature with Text-Dependent and Text-Independent Speech for Robust Identity Verification, Proceedings, IEEE Workshop on Multimodal User Authentication (2003) 13-18
5. Czyz, J., Kittler, J., Vandendorpe, L.: Combining face verification experts, Proceedings of ICPR 2002 – Intl. Conference on Pattern Recognition; Quebec; Canada (2002)
6. Scheidat, T.: Fusion von Klassifikationsverfahren für handschriftbasierte Benutzerauthentifikation, M. Sc. Thesis, University Magdeburg (2005) (in German)
7. Vielhauer, C., Scheidat, T.: Fusion von biometrischen Verfahren zur Benutzerauthentifikation, In: P. Horster (Ed.), D-A-CH Security 2005 – Bestandsaufnahme, Konzepte, Anwendungen, Perspektiven (2005) 82-97, ISBN 3-00-015548-1 (in German)
8. Vielhauer, C.: Biometric User Authentication for IT Security: From Fundamentals to Handwriting, Springer New York, to appear 2006

Compact Stimulation Mechanism for Routing Discovery Protocols in Civilian Ad-Hoc Networks

Huafei Zhu, Feng Bao, and Tieyan Li

Department of Information Security, Institute for Infocomm Research, A-Star
{huafei, baofeng, litieyan} @i2r.a-star.edu.sg

Abstract. In this paper, a refined sequential aggregate signature scheme from RSA that works for any modulus is presented, then a compact stimulation mechanism without a central, trusted authority for routing discovery in civilian ad hoc networks is proposed as an immediate application of this cryptographic primitive. Our protocol forces selfish nodes to cooperate and report actions honestly, thus enables our routing discovery protocol to resist selfish actions within our model.

Keywords: Network security, Routing discovery protocol, Sequential aggregate signature.

1 Introduction

Civilian ad hoc networks have been a very attractive field of academic and industrial research in recent years due to their potential applications and the proliferation of mobile devices. Unfortunately, ad hoc networks are vulnerable and subject to a wide range of attacks due to the open medium, dynamically changing topology, possible node compromise, difficulty in physical protection, absence of infrastructure and lack of trust among nodes. As a result, nodes in these networks can be faulty/malicious or selfish. Although the problems of faulty/malicious nodes can be important in multi-authority applications, the focus of this paper is on selfish nodes. We expect that selfish nodes are the dominant type of nodes in a civilian Ad hoc network, where the nodes do not belong to a single authority and forwarding a message will incur a cost to a node, thus a selfish node will need incentive in order to forward others' messages. A series works of Michiardi and Molva [12] and [13] have already shown that a selfish behavior can be as harmful, in terms of the network throughput, as a malicious one. Consequently, practical incentive to stimulate cooperative behaviors such as forwarding each other's message in such emerging civilian applications are certainly welcome.

1.1 Related Works

Incentives/stimulating cooperation is a serious issue in many protocols, including mobile ad hoc networks, peer-to-peer or overlay network systems, and even in traditional BGP Internet routing. This paper, however, is restrict to study the

J. Dittmann, S. Katzenbeisser, and A. Uhl (Eds.): CMS 2005, LNCS 3677, pp. 200–209, 2005.

incentive issues in routing discovery protocols and the incentive issues from these other fields are completely neglected. We thus sketch the following works that are closely related to this paper:

-In [14], Marti et al. proposed a reputation system for ad hoc networks. In their system, a node monitors the transmission of a neighbor to make sure that the neighbor forwards others' traffic. If the neighbor does not forward others' traffic, it is considered as uncooperative, and this uncooperative reputation is propagated throughout the network. Such reputation systems have several issues since there is no formal specification and analysis of the type of incentive provided by such systems and the system has not considered the possibility that even selfish nodes can collude with each other in order to maximize their welfare.

-Buttyan and Hubaux [4] proposed a stimulation approach that is based on a virtual currency, called nuglets, which is used as payments for packet forwarding. To implement the payment models, a tamper-proof hardware is required at each node to ensure the correct amount of nuglets is deducted or credited at each node. Besides the nuglets approach, the authors also proposed a scheme based on credit counter [5]. Although, this new scheme is simple and elegant, it still requires a tamper-proof hardware at each node so that the correct amount of credit credited or deducted.

- In [8], Jakobsson et al. proposed a micro-payment scheme for mobile ad hoc networks that encourages collaboration in packet forwarding by letting users benefit from relaying other's packets. The proposal is somewhat similar to [15] in that the originators of packet are charged per packet while users performing packet forwarding are paid per winning ticket. Although, the architecture for fostering collaboration is attractive, their approach is heuristic. Consequently, a less heuristic approach would be a great step forward. The recent work of Sprite (a simple, cheat-proof, credit-based system for mobile ad hoc networks [18]) can be viewed as such a forward step.

-The basic idea of Sprite is that [18]: suppose an initiator node n_0 is to send message payload m with sequence number $seq_0(0, d)$ to a destination node n_d, through path p which is generated by routing discovery protocol DSR (Dynamic Source Routing in ad hoc wireless networks [9]). Node n_0 first computes a signature s on $(H(m), p, seq_0(0, d))$. Then, n_0 transfers $(m, p, seq_0(0, d), s)$ to the next hop and increases $seq_0(0, d)$. Suppose that node n_i receives (m, p, seq, s). It first checks three conditions: 1) n_i is on the path; 2) the message has a sequence number greater than $seq_i(0, d)$; and 3) the signature is valid. If any of the conditions is not satisfied, the message is dropped. Otherwise, it saves $(H(m), p, seq, s)$ as a receipt. If n_i is not the destination and decides to forward the message, it sends (m, p, seq, s) to the next hop. In order to get credit for forwarding other's messages, a node needs to report to a Credit Clearance Service (CCS) the messages it has helped forward whenever it switches to a fast connection and has backup power (to implement this idea, Sprite assumes that a mobile node can also use a desktop computer as a proxy to report to the CCS). The CCS then determines the charge and credits to each node involved in the transmission of a message, depending on the reported receipts of a message. The contribution of

Sprite lies in that they avoid assumptions on the tamper proof hardware and the receipt submission is proved cheat-proof. Sprite works well on message forwarding protocols assuming that an originator has a path connected a destination node prior to the communication. To simulate cooperation for routing discovery, the authors further proposed the following mechanism based on DSR: when a node starts to broadcast a route request, the node signs (e.g., using RSA signature scheme) and broadcasts the message, and increases its sequence number counter by 1. Suppose a node receives a route request, it first decides whether the message is a replay by looking at the sequence number. The node saves the received route request for getting payment in the future. When the node decides to rebroadcast the route request, it appends its own address to the route request and signs the extended message. In this way, the signatures' size of a routing request may grow linearly with the inputs and increase communication overheads. Thus we need a cryptographic primitive that provides the functionality of a signature scheme and at the same time reduces the overall signature sizes.

1.2   Problem Statement

Normally what makes mobile ad hoc networks interesting is that they are generally operating with extremely limited memory and CPU resources. Most serious MANET protocols completely avoid public key cryptography. It is just too expensive. However, in energy limited networks, the energy consumed to compute 1000 32-bit additive operations is approximate to that of transmission of 1 bit. Thus, the communication complexity is clearly a dominate concern in energy-consumed networks. Thus, it is not surprising, many incentive based network systems are built on top of the public key cryptography, e.g., Nuglets [4] and Sprite [18]. We will follow the public key cryptography approach throughout the paper. Although the idea for designing Sprite is interesting and attractive [18], it still suffers from the problems stated below. That is

-Problem 1: In [18], the incentive system consists of a central, trusted authority called Credit Clearance Service (CCS) and a collection of mobile nodes. Each node n_i has a pair of public/secret key (PK_i, SK_i) which is certificated by a scalable certificate authority. The nodes are equipped with network interfaces that allow them to send and receive messages through a wireless overlay network, using GPRS or 3G in a wide-area environment while switching to IEEE 802.11 or Bluetooth in an indoor environment. Normally, what makes MANETs interesting is its distributed property, thus a central, trusted authority CCS may not be available. The same problem occurs also in the recent work of Martinelli, Petrocchi, and Vaccarelli [16]. As a result, any compact stimulation mechanism without a central authority is certainly welcome.

-Problem 2: The signatures' size of a routing message (request/reply) grows linearly with the inputs and increase communication overheads since each intermediate node should signs its routing messages in [18]. Thus how to reduce the line size of signatures to the constant size of is definitely an important research problem (communication complexity), i.e., the signature size should be independent of the number of intermediate nodes.

1.3 Our Works

At a high level, our approach to simulate cooperation for routing discovery can be addressed below:

-Stimulating cooperation in route discovery phase: we propose a new approach, called compact stimulation mechanism for routing discovery protocol to stimulate cooperation in routing discovery in an aggregate manner. This approach is based on endairA [6] and [3]. In endairA, the initiator of the route discovery process generates a route request, which contains the identifiers of the initiator and the target, and a randomly generated query identifier. Each intermediate node that receives the request for the first time appends its identifier to the route accumulated so far, and re-broadcasts the request. When the request arrives to the target, it generates a route reply. The route reply contains the identifiers of the initiator and the target, the accumulated route obtained from the request, and a digital signature of the target on these elements. The reply is sent back to the initiator on the reverse of the route found in the request. Each intermediate node that receives the reply verifies that its identifier is in the route carried by the reply, and that the preceding and following identifiers on the route belong to neighboring nodes. If these verifications fail, then the reply is dropped. Otherwise, it is signed by the intermediate node, and passed to the next node on the route (towards the initiator). When the initiator receives the route reply, it verifies if the first identifier in the route carried by the reply belongs to a neighbor. If so, then it verifies all the signatures in the reply. If all these verifications are successful, then the initiator accepts the route.

-Payment protocol for routing discovery: our payment protocol consists of two kinds of fees − on one hand, n_0 and n_d should pay SMALL amount fees to all intermediates nodes who are cooperated to establish multi-path from n_0 to n_d; on the other hand n_0 or n_d should pay LARGE amount fees to all intermediate nodes in a path which is uniquely selected by n_d since this path will be used to transform data between n_0 and n_d. Since the later case is dependent on the amount of data transmitted along the path thus we ignore this case. In the rest of our works we only consider the selfish actions in the routing discovery case.

A selfish node in civilian ad hoc networks is an economically rational node whose objective is to maximize its own welfare. As a result, a selfish node can exhibit selfish actions below:

-Type-1 selfish action: after receiving a message, the node saves a receipt but not forward the message;

-Type-2 selfish action: the destination node has received a message but does not report the receipt to the initiator;

-Type-3 selfish action: the node does not receive a message but falsely claim that it has received a message;

To protect our payment protocol from selfish actions, we force a destination node n_d to report back all participating nodes $(n_d, \cdots, n_0)$ to the initial node n_0. Since each intermediate node n_i who helped to propagate routing request is explicitly listed in the aggregate signature, it follows that any node who contributed to discover routing will be credited (which is determined by n_0 as well as n_d, possibly with the help of other auxiliary information, say, the number of hop). If a intermediate node n_i who contributed to establish a path successfully from n_0 to n_d, does not receive its credit, it can report its witness (a valid aggregate signature from n_d to n_0) to the n_0 and then obtains its credit from n_0. In this case, n_0 will be over charged by means of the punishment policy.

In summary, the contributions of this paper are follows. We first propose a new solution framework for designing compact stimulation routing discovery protocols in civilian ad hoc networks based on our newly constructed sequential aggregate signature schemes and then show that our incentive mechanism is secure against selfish actions within our model.

2   Building Block

Our compact stimulation mechanism for routing discovery protocol heavily relies on our newly constructed sequential aggregate signature scheme. The application of (sequential) aggregate signatures to other settings can be found in [1], [2], [11] and [17].

2.1   Syntax and Security Definition

A sequential signature scheme (KG, AggSign, AggVf) consists of the following algorithms [11]:

-A Key generation algorithm (KG): On input 1^k, KG outputs system parameters param (including an initial value $\mathcal{IV}$, without loss of generality, we assume that $\mathcal{IV}$ is a zero strings with length l-bit), on input param and user index $i \in \mathcal{I}$, it outputs a public key and secret key pair (PK_i, SK_i) for a user i.

-Aggregate signing algorithm (AggSign): Given a message m_i to sign, and a sequential aggregate σ_{i-1} on messages $\{m_1, \cdots, m_{i-1}\}$ under respective public keys PK_1, $\cdots$, PK_{i-1}, where m_1 is the inmost message. All of m_1, $\cdots$, m_{i-1} and PK_1, $\cdots$, PK_{i-1} must be provided as inputs. AggSign first verifies that σ_{i-1} is a valid aggregate for messages $\{m_1, \cdots, m_{i-1}\}$ using the verification algorithm defined below (if $i=1$, the aggregate σ_0 is taken to be zero strings 0^l). If not, it outputs $\perp$, otherwise, it then adds a signature on m_i under SK_i to the aggregate and outputs a sequential aggregate σ_i on all i messages $m_1, \cdots, m_i$.

-Aggregate verifying algorithm (AggVf): Given a sequential aggregate signature σ_i on the messages $\{m_1, \cdots, m_i\}$ under the respective public keys $\{PK_1, \cdots, PK_i\}$. If any key appears twice, if any element PK_i does not describe a permutation or if the size of the messages is different from the size of the respective public keys reject. Otherwise, for $j = i, \cdots, 1$, set $\sigma_{j-1} = $ Evaluate$(PK_1, \cdots, PK_j, \sigma_j)$. The verification of σ_{i-1} is processed recursively. The base case for recursion is $i = 0$, in which case simply check that σ_0. Accepts if σ_0 equals the zero strings.

To define the security of sequential aggregate signature scheme, we allow the adversary to play the following game [11].

-The aggregate forger $\mathcal{A}$ is provided with a initial value $\mathcal{IV}$, a set of public keys PK_1, $\cdots$, PK_{i-1} and PK, generated at random. The adversary also is provided with $SK_1, \cdots, SK_{i-1}$; PK is called target public key.

-$\mathcal{A}$ requests sequential aggregate signatures with PK on messages of his choice. For each query, he supplies a sequential aggregate signature σ_{i-1} on some messages $m_1, \cdots, m_{i-1}$ under the distinct public keys $PK_1, \cdots, PK_{i-1}$, and an additional message m_i to be signed by the signing oracle under public key PK.

-Finally, $\mathcal{A}$ outputs a valid signature σ_i of a message m_i which is associated with the aggregate σ_{i-1}. The forger wins if $\mathcal{A}$ did not request (m_i, σ_{i-1}) in the previous signing oracle queries.

By AdvAggSign$_\mathcal{A}$, we denote the probability of success of an adversary. We say a sequential aggregate signature scheme is secure against adaptive chosen-message attack if for every polynomial time Turing machine $\mathcal{A}$, the probability AdvAggSign$_\mathcal{A}$ that it wins the game is at most a negligible amount, where the probability is taken over coin tosses of KG and AggSign and $\mathcal{A}$.

2.2   Construction and the Proof of Security

We further propose a refined scheme that works for any RSA moduli, and is provably secure in the sense of [11] and thus can be applied for our compact incentive routing discovery protocol. More precisely,

Let $H: \{0,1\}^* \rightarrow \{0,1\}^l$ be a cryptographic hash function and $\mathcal{IV}$ be the initial vector that should be pre-described by a sequential aggregate signature scheme. The initial value could be a random l-bit string or an empty string. Without loss of generality, we assume that the initial value $\mathcal{IV}$ is 0^l. Our sequential aggregate signature scheme is described as follows:

- Key generation: Each user i generates an RSA public key (N_i, e_i) and secret key (N_i, d_i), ensuring that $|N_i| = k_i$ and that $e_i > N_i$ is a prime. Let G_i: $\{0,1\}^{t_i} \rightarrow \{0,1\}^{k_i}$, be cryptographic hash function specified by each user i, $t_i = l - k_i$.
- Signing: User i is given an aggregate signature g_{i-1} and $(b_1, \cdots, b_{i-1})$, a sequence of messages $m_1, \cdots, m_{i-1}$, and the corresponding keys (N_1, e_1), $\cdots, (N_{i-1}, e_{i-1})$. User i first verifies σ_{i-1}, using the verification procedure below, where $\sigma_0 = 0^l$. If this succeeds, user i computes $H_i = H(m_1, \cdots, m_i, (N_1, e_1), \cdots, (N_i, e_i))$ and computes $x_i = H_i \oplus g_{i-1}$. Then it separates $x_i = y_i \| z_i$, where $y_i \in \{0,1\}^{k_i}$ and $z_i \in \{0,1\}^{t_i}$, $t_i = l - k_i$. Finally, it computes $g_i = f_i^{-1}(y_i \oplus G_i(z_i)) \| z_i$. By $\sigma_i \leftarrow (g_i, b_i)$, we denote the aggregate signature(if $y_i \oplus G_i(z_i) > N_i$, then $b_i = 1$, if $y_i \oplus G_i(z_i) < N_i$, then $b_i = 0$; again we do not define the case $y_i \oplus G_i(z_i) = N_i$ since the probability the event happens is negligible), where $f_i^{-1}(y) = y^{d_i} \bmod N_i$, the inverse of the RSA function $f_i(y) = y^{e_i} \bmod N_i$ defined over the domain $Z_{N_i}^*$.
- Verifying: The verification is given as input an aggregate signature g_i, $(b_1, \cdots, b_i)$, the messages $m_1, \cdots, m_i$, the correspondent public keys (N_1, e_1), $\cdots, (N_i, e_i)$ and proceeds as follows. Check that no keys appears twice, that $e_i > N_i$ is a prime. Then it computes:
  - $H_i = H(m_1, \cdots, m_i, (N_1, e_1), \cdots, (N_i, e_i))$;
  - Separating $g_i = v_i \| w_i$;

- Recovering x_i form the trapdoor one-way permutation by computing $z_i \leftarrow w_i$, $y_i = \mathcal{B}_i(f_i(v_i) + b_i N_i) \oplus G_i(z_i)$, and $x_i = y_i || z_i$, where $\mathcal{B}_i(x)$ is the binary representation of $x \in \mathcal{Z}$ (with k_i bits).
- Recovering g_{i-1} by computing $x_i \oplus H_i$. The verification of (g_{i-1}, b_{i-1}) is processed recursively. The base case for recursion is $i = 0$, in which case simply check that $\sigma_0 = 0^l$.

Lemma [17]: The sequential aggregate signature scheme described above is provable secure in the sense of [11] in the random oracle model.

2.3   Comparison and Open Problem

We compare our sequential aggregate signature schemes with Kawauchi, Komano, Ohta and Tada's (KKOT) scheme [10], and Lysyanskaya et al's scheme [11] below;

-All three signatures are based on the hardness of RSA problem. For the i-th users, each signing processing needs one exponent computation while the verification processing needs $(i - 1)$ exponent computations. Thus all three schemes have approximate computational complexity;

-Lysyanskaya et al's first scheme can be viewed as improvement of of KKOT scheme [10]. The restriction of modulus in the KKOT's scheme $|N_i| - |N_{i-1}| = 1 + k_1 + k_2$ is replaced by users's moduli to be arranged in increasing order: $N_1 < N_2 < \cdots < N_t$ in Lysyanskaya et al's scheme.

-The second approach of Lysyanskaya et al's scheme does not require the modulus to be arranged in increasing order, however they are required to be of the same length. The signature will expanded by n bits $b_1, \cdots, b_n$, where n is the total number of users. Namely, during signing, if $\sigma_i \geq N_{i+1}$, let $b_i = 1$; else, let $b_i = 0$. In our scheme, the modulus are not required to be of the same length. We emphasize that in our scheme N_i is chosen by each user independently, thus our construction is the first scheme from RSA that works for any modulus. However as Lysyanskaya et al's scheme, our sequential aggregate signature is expanded by n bits $b_1, \cdots, b_n$, where n is the total number of users.

Following from the above discussion, we here present an interesting open problem: can we propose a sequential aggregate signature scheme such that N_i is chosen by each user independently, and at the same time no single bit of signature size will be expanded?

3   Stimulating Cooperation for Routing Discovery

In this section, we propose a compact stimulation mechanism for routing discovery in ad hoc networks. Suppose that a source node n_0 sends a routing request message $RREQ$ (it may include the maximum number of hops that is allowed to reach the destination node) to the destination n_d, where $RREQ$ is formatted by the endairA protocol (this protocol has nice features, for example, it ensures that once a path is outputted by endairA, it is always correct one). When the initiator n_0 starts to broadcast a route request, it signs and broadcasts route request message by an ordinary signature scheme specified [1]. When an intermediate node n_i decides to rebroadcast the routing request message if the signature of $RREQ$ is valid, it then appends its own address/identity to the received routing request and then rebroadcasts the $RREQ$ until the the destination node n_d is reached.

When multi routing pathes associated with the original request messages $RREQ$ arrive to the target node, it chooses a proper route path (e.g., with least hope number). Then it sends back the route reply to the initiator node. Each routing reply message $RREP$ contains identifiers of the initiator and the target, as well as that of all intermediate nodes, together with a sequential aggregate signature on $RREP$ which starts to sign from the target node n_d. Each intermediate node that receives the reply first check that its identifier is listed in the $RREP$ and then verifies the correctness of the received sequential aggregate signature on the message $RREP$. If both checks are valid, the message $RREQ$ is further signed by this intermediate node using its own secret key, and then send it to its successive node; Otherwise, the reply is dropped. When the initiator receives the route reply message, it verifies the correctness of sequential aggregate signature scheme, and if the verification is successful, then the initiator accepts the route and then pays the credential to each intermediate node according to its payment strategy [2].

3.1   Secure Against Selfish Actions

We now consider three types of selfish actions in our routing discovery protocol below:

-In the Type-1 selfish action, a node say n_i saves a valid aggregate signature (the receipt or the witness) but does not sign and forward the signature. In this case, each node along the path cannot be credited as there is no actual routing from n_d to n_0 (and hence from n_0 to n_d is established), thus violates the selfish action of n_i.

-In the Type-2 selfish action, the destination node n_d has received a valid $RREQ$ from n_{d-1}, but it does not send back the routing reply message $RREP$ (including its signature to $RREQ$) to the initiator n_{d-1}. In this case, there is no routing path available from n_0 to n_d. Thus, such a selfish behavior is completely avoided by n_d unless n_d refuses to receive any message from n_0.

-In the Type-3 selfish action, a node n_i does not receive a message but falsely claims it has signed and forwarded the aggregate signature to its successor; In this case the identity of n_i is not listed in the routing reply message $RRER$. Since the underlying sequential aggregate signature scheme is secure in the sense of

---

[1] To resist DoS attack, we assume that the initiator signs the routing request message $RREQ$ and the intermediate nodes to verify this signature. Notice that the ordinary signature of $RREQ$ can be absorbed by the underlying sequential aggregate signature

[2] How to specify the payment strategy is a complex issue, possibly the credential may be related to n_0 and n_d as well as the number of hop in a given routing, however we ignore the details of the payment protocol in this paper.

[11], the selfish node can forge a valid signature with at most negligible amount. Thus, the selfish action of can be captured.

In summary, we have the desired statement − assuming the underlying sequential aggregate signature scheme is secure in the sense of [11], our routing discovery is secure against selfish actions defined in Section 1.

3.2 Unsolved Problems

Notice that the reply attack does not work in our setting. The reply attack means that n_i stores a $RREP$ and reuses it later when it receives a new $RREQ$ and n_0 is fooled to think there exists a path with n_d. Since a $RREP$ message in our formate must contain the request message $RREQ$ and its signature which is signed by n_0. As a result, the replay attack does not work in our model. However we should point out the fact that our routing discovery protocol does not resist a selfish node n_i to introduce more intermediate nodes in a routing path explicitly. We therefore classify two potential selfish actions below.

-Greedy attack: for example, instead n_i broadcasts and forwards the $RREQ$ to n_{i+1}, it may intended to insert a set of redundant nodes, say $n_{i,1}$, $n_{i,2}$, $\cdots$, $n_{i,k}$, between n_i and n_{i+1}. This selfish action does not always work since the destination node is allowed to choose a path with less hop number. Thus, a remedy scheme maybe insert the maximum hop number in each $RREQ$ message. This is a possible solution to resist such a greedy attack.

-Collude attack: for example, a intermediate node n_{i-1}, n_i and the destination node n_d are collude to foolish n_0. In this case, n_d intends to insert a set of redundant intermediate nodes $n_{i,1}$, $n_{i,2}$, $\cdots$, $n_{i,k}$ between n_{i-1} and n_i. This collude is powerful and our routing discovery protocol fails in such an attack.

To best of our knowledge, all incentive based routing discovery protocol, say, [16] and [18] also suffer from the above attacks, we thus leave two open problems to the research community.

4   Conclusion

In this paper, we have presented a new solution to improve incentive-compatible routing discovery protocols in civilian networks based on our sequential aggregate signature scheme and have shown that our compact stimulation mechanism for routing discovery protocol resist certain selfish actions within our model.

References

1. Dan Boneh, Craig Gentry, Ben Lynn, Hovav Shacham: Aggregate and Verifiably Encrypted Signatures from Bilinear Maps. EUROCRYPT 2003: 416-432.
2. Dan Boneh, Craig Gentry, Ben Lynn, Hovav Shacham: A Survey of Two Signature Aggregation Techniques. In CryptoBytes Vol. 6, No. 2, 2003.
3. L. Buttyán and I. Vajda, Towards Provable Security for Ad Hoc Routing Protocols, 2nd ACM Workshop on Security in Ad Hoc and Sensor Networks (SASN 2004) Washington DC, USA, October 25, 2004.

4. L. Buttyán and J. P. Hubaux. Enforcing service availability in mobile ad hoc WANs, in IEEE/ACM Workshop on Mobile Ad hoc Networking and Computing (Mobi-HOC), Boston, MA, August 2000.
5. L. Buttyán and J. P. Hubaux, Stimulating cooperation in self-organizing mobile Ad hoc networks, ACM Journal for Mobile Networks (MONET), special issue on Mobile Ad hoc Networks, summer 2002.
6. Yih-Chun Hu, Adrian Perrig, David B. Johnson: Ariadne: a secure on-demand routing protocol for ad hoc networks. MOBICOM 2002: 12-23
7. J. Coron: On the Exact Security of Full Domain Hash. CRYPTO 2000: 229-235
8. M. Jakobsson, J. P. Hubaux, and L. Buttyan. A micropayment scheme encouraging collaboration in multi-hop cellular networks, in Proceedings of Financial Crypto 2003, La Guadeloupe, January 2003.
9. D. B. Johnson and D. A. Malt, Mobile Computing. Kluwer Academic Publishers, 1996, Dynamic Source Routing in Ad hoc Wireless Networks, Chapter 5.
10. K. Kawauchi, Y. Komano, K. Ohta and M. Tada: Probabilistic multi-signature schemes using a one-way trapdoor permutation, IEICE transactions on fundamentals, vol.E87-A, no5, pp.1141-1153, 2004.
11. Anna Lysyanskaya, Silvio Micali, Leonid Reyzin, Hovav Shacham: Sequential Aggregate Signatures from trapdoor one-way permutations. EUROCRYPT 2004: 74-90.
12. P. Michiardi, and R. Molva. Core: A Collaborative Reputation Mechanism to Enforce Node Cooperation in Mobile Ad Hoc Networks. In Proc. of CMS'02.
13. P.Michiardi, and R. Molva. A Game Theoretical Approach to Evaluate Cooperation Enforcement Mechanisms in Mobile Ad hoc Networks. In Proc. of WiOpt03 of the IEEE Computer Society.
14. S. Marti, T. Giuli, K. Lai, and M. Baker. Mitigating routing misbehavior in mobile Ad hoc networks, in Proceedings of The Sixth International Conference on Mobile Computing and Networking 2000, Boston, MA, Aug. 2000.
15. Silvio Micali, Ronald L. Rivest: Micropayments Revisited. CT-RSA 2002: 149-163.
16. F. Martinelli, M. Petrocchi, and A. Vaccarelli, Local management of credits and debits in mobile ad hoc networks. Conference on Communications and Multimedia Security, CMS 2004.
17. Huafei Zhu et al, Constructing Sequential Aggregate Signatures for Secure Wireless Routing Protocols, IEEE WCNC'05, New Orleans, 13-17 March, 2005, New Orleans, LA, USA.
18. Sheng Zhong, Jiang Chen, and Yang Richard Yang. Sprite: A Simple, Cheat-Proof, Credit-Based System for Mobile Ad hoc Networks.Proceedings of IEEE INFOCOM '03, San Francisco, CA, April 2003.

Polymorphic Code Detection with GA Optimized Markov Models

Udo Payer[1] and Stefan Kraxberger[2]

[1] Institute for Applied Information Processing and Communications (IAIK),
University of Technology Graz
[2] Stiftung - Secure Information and Communication Technologies (SIC),
Graz, Austria

Abstract. This paper presents our progression in the search for reliable anomaly-based intrusion detection mechanisms. We investigated different options of stochastic techniques. We started our investigations with Markov chains to detect abnormal traffic. The main aspect in our prior work was the optimization of transition matrices to obtain better detection accuracy. First, we tried to automatically train the transition matrix with *normal* traffic. Then, this transition matrix was used to calculate the probabilities of a dedicated Markov sequence. This transition matrix was used to find differences between the trained normal traffic and characteristic parts of a polymorphic shellcode. To improve the efficiency of this automatically trained transition matrix, we modified some entries in a way that byte-sequences of typical shellcodes substantially differs from normal network behavior. But this approach did not meet our requirements concerning generalization. Therefore we searched for automatic methods to improve the matrix. Genetic algorithms are adequate tools if just little knowledge about the search space is available and the complexity of the problem is very hard (NP-complete).

Keywords: intrusion detection, polymorphic shellcode detection, markov models, genetic algorithms, optimization.

1   Introduction

During the past years, different polymorphic shellcode engines have shown up in the internet. The concept of polymorphism is not new in the field of viruses, but it took about 10 years that these polymorphic mechanisms were also used in the field of polymorphic shellcodes. The most popular representatives are CLET and ADMmutate. Especially on the example of CLET, the authors of [CLET03] used a spectrum analysis mechanism to defeat data mining methods. The problem was to develop an engine which is capable to generate shellcodes which will be considered as normal by NIDSs. The basic idea of this approach was to analyze it usual traffic generated by the *usual use* of network services. This mechanism is described in [ADM03] and [CLET03] in more detail. The knowledge about bytes

J. Dittmann, S. Katzenbeisser, and A. Uhl (Eds.): CMS 2005, LNCS 3677, pp. 210–219, 2005.
© IFIP International Federation for Information Processing 2005

and byte-sequences can then be used to generate shellcode-sequences, depending on the probability of each occurring byte in the it normal traffic.

CLET and some other polymorphic engines try to be as similar to the *normal* traffic as possible. The *problem* with known shellcode-engines is that just single parts of the generated codes are used to adjust the generated byte-spectrum to the byte-spectrum of the overall network traffic. All other parts remains unchanged and can therefore be detected by using statistical methods. As shown in [Yn01],[YEZ02],[Yn00],[JTM01],[JV99] Markov models and HMMs are stochastic methods which can be used if an statistical relation between events and intrusion is given. Therefore it also must be able to use these methods to make decisions directly upon network traffic.

2 Markov Models

2.1 Overview

A Markov chain is a sequence of random values whose probabilities at a given time depends upon conditional probabilities of the recent past. The controlling factor in a Markov chain is the transition matrix which is used to calculate the conditional probabilities of dedicated state sequences and lengths.

2.2 Definition

There are three items involved to specify a general markov chain:

- State space S.

  S is a finite set of states. Let us label the states as $S = \{1, 2, 3, ..., N\}$ for some finite N.
- Initial distribution a_0.

  This is the probability distribution of the Markov chain at time 0. For each state $i \in S$, we denote by $a_0(i)$ the probability $P = \{X_0 = i\}$ that the Markov chain starts in state i. Formally, a_0 is a function taking S into the interval $[0,1]$ such that

$$a_0(i) \geq 0 \text{ for all } i \in S \tag{1}$$

and

$$\sum_{i \in S} a(i) = 1. \tag{2}$$

- Probability transition matrix P.

  If S is the finite set $\{1, 2, ..., N\}$, then P is an $N \times N$ Matrix. The interpretation of the number p_{ij} is the conditional probability, given that the chain is in state i at time n, and that the chain jumps to the state j at time $n + 1$. That is,

$$p_{ij} = P\{q_{n+1} = j | q_n = i\}. \tag{3}$$

We can also express the probability of a certain sequence $\{q_1, q_2, \ldots, q_n\}$ (the joint probability of the recent past and current observations) using the Markov assumption:

$$P(q_1, \ldots, q_n) = \prod_{i=1}^{n} P(q_i | q_{i-1}) \tag{4}$$

3   Transition Matrix

In our first approach we trained the transition matrix automatically from a given traffic data. This given network traffic was real network traffic captured, and stored in a file. Thereafter, this file was used to train a Markov model. But before training, this Markov model has to be initialized. Therefore, we have to specify and initialize the following items:

- State space S
  Because every character is coded as 1 byte, the possible state space for network traffic would be $S = \{0, 1, 2, \ldots, 255\}$. Due to the fact that Markov models are not intended to use zero as a state, we shifted the state space by 1. Therefore we used $S = \{1, 2, 3, \ldots, 256\}$ as state vector.
- Initial distribution a_0.
  For the first version we used an initial distribution of equal probability for every state to be the first state.

$$a_0(i) = 0,00390625 \text{ for all } i \in S \tag{5}$$

- Probability transition matrix P.
  As stated in section 2.1 it is crucial to determine an appropriate transition matrix to get good results. This is the main part of our work. In our first approach we learned the transition matrix automatically from a given traffic data. Therefore we collected the probabilities for all transitions from one character to another. By using this information it is possible to detect something which is not *normal* in relation to the learned traffic. The training data is represented as an array **b** with elements from the state space S. Then we counted all transitions from one particular character to another (e.g. 129 to 192) and divided the sum by the whole number of transitions for this character. The transition probability p_{ij} for one possible transition $i \rightarrow j$ requires the computation of

$$r_{ij} = \# \{k \in \{1, \ldots, N-1\} : \mathbf{b}_k = i \wedge \mathbf{b}_{k+1} = j\} \tag{6}$$

where N specifies the length of the data **b** from which we learn the transition matrix. Then, p_{ij} can be written as

$$p_{ij} = \frac{r_{ij}}{\sum_{j=1}^{N} r_{ij}}. \tag{7}$$

Figure 1 shows the probability distribution of a CLET polymorphic shellcode calculated with a Markov sequence length of 30 using the Markov assumption. The x-axis shows the byte length (position) and the y-axis represents the probability value for the sequence. To proof if a sequence is a polymorphic shellcode we used a threshold which we got from probability observations of many real shellcodes. With the learned transition matrix it was possible to detect the decipher engine and the enciphered code.

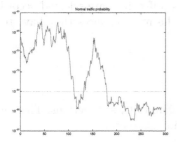 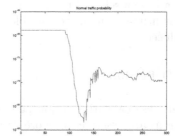

Fig. 1. Learned transition matrix   **Fig. 2.** Designed transition matrix

Since we did not get just *one* significant pike, causing more false positives, we decided to *improve* the distribution matrix. We used the knowledge that some byte-sequences are more likely in shellcodes than in normal traffic and modified the corresponding values manually. This modified matrix applied to shellcodes resulted in a substantial difference compared with normal network traffic. With the created transition matrix we are able to obtain the requested probability distribution (Figure 2). The First 100 Bytes show the probability of the NOP zone and then the significant pike represents the decipher engine. Afterwards the ciphered shellcode itself is displayed.

4   Optimizing the Transition Matrix

Since it is very hard to manually modify a transition matrix and take all important parameters into account, we searched for new solutions to this problem. Possible modifications are manifold and we just know very little about the values (instructions) and their influence on the result. Therefore, we decided to give an automated (optimization) search algorithm a chance. There are many methods which can be used to find a suitable solution, but all these methods do not necessarily show the best solution [RN95],[PJ84]. The solutions found by these methods are often considered as *good solutions*. One reason is that it is often very hard to prove the correctness of possible optimal solutions. Therefore, we decided to give the genetic algorithm a try.

5   Genetic Algorithms

Genetic algorithms are inspired by Darwin's theory of evolution. Solution to a problem solved by genetic algorithms uses an evolutionary process (it is evolved). The algorithm starts with a set of solutions (represented by chromosomes) called population. Solutions from one population are selected and used to form a new population through mutation and cross-over. This is motivated by a hope, that the new population will be better (yield better) than the old one. Solutions which are then selected to form new solutions (offspring) are selected according to their fitness - the more suitable they are the more chances they have to be reproduced.

5.1   Definitions

GAs always deal with solutions, goals, criteria, and fitness functions. These general terms are described in more details within this section.

- Solution

  In our case a solution is a representation of a specific transition matrix representing a set of possible offsprings. Due to the fact that our GA-implementation could not handle matrices, we converted the transition matrix into a vector where the rows of the matrix are appended consecutively. So we got a vector with 65536 values.

- Goal

  To measure the fitness of the solutions we have to compare the calculated probability distribution of an distinct shellcode with a desired probability distribution. This desired distribution is called **goal**.

- Evaluation criteria

  Since a genetic algorithm demands a single value as a measure for the fitness, we subtract the probability distribution of the solution from the goal, squared them, summed it up and divided by the length of the goal vector.

$$fitnessvalue = -\frac{\sum_{i=1}^{N}(R_i - G_i)^2}{N} \qquad (8)$$

  where R is the result and G the goal vector for the probability distribution of a single solution. N specifies the length of the distribution vector.

- GA parameters

  We used the GAOT Matlab package from the North Carolina State University with their default settings for *floatGA* [HJK95]. The options we used where *[1e-2 1 1 0.1]*.

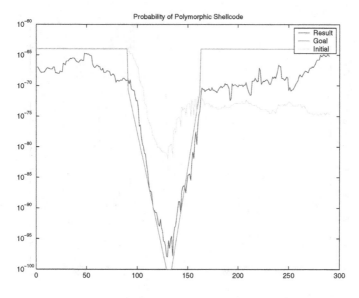

Fig. 3. Optimization result for an arbitrary shellcode

5.2 Optimizing the Detection for One Specific Shellcode

First we tried to use just one shellcode for our evaluation function to see if it is possible to optimize the transition matrix. By using just a single shellcode, it was possible to generate a transition matrix nearly reaching the preferred goal (figure 3). The preferred goal in this case shows a very significant peak at the position where the decipher engine appears in the evaluation function.

But due to the fact that we just used a single shellcode, the obtained transition matrix is very specialized and just qualified to find this single shellcode. All other shellcodes (generated by the same engine) seems to be to different and cannot be detected by this "improved" transition matrix. In figure 4 you can see five deciphering engines with a sequence-probability of 10^{-70}, whereas the second one shows a a small peak in the middle of the shellcode where we expect the deciphering engine. All other shellcodes just show that shellcodes are more unlikely that normal network traffic, but the significant peak in the middle of the shellcode is missing. The strong peaks at the top of the figure came from 0 bytes in the network traffic. Since no 0's are allowed in a polymorphic shellcode we do not calculate the sequence probability of such a sequence and assign a value of 1 instead. This very much depends on the selection of the boundaries. So we need another approach.

5.3 Applying the Evaluation Function to 10 Shellcode Instances

Since always a single fitness value decides about success or failure of a dedicated solution it is quite obvious that more samples would lead to better results. We

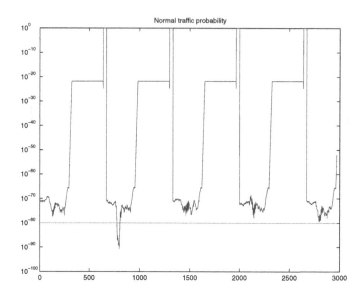

Fig. 4. Detection result for 5 shellcodes

started with a sequence of just 10 shellcodes packed-up back-to-back to evaluate our solutions. All used shellcodes were generated randomly and can even be a mix of different shellcode generators (Clet, ADMmutate, JempiScode).

After this preparation phase, the evaluation function is applied to the result of a dedicated solution (solution-vector). In doing so, the fitness-values are calculated for each single shellcode (according to 8) and the arithmetic median on all fitness values is calculated and returned to the genetic algorithm.

In figure 5 the sequence of 10 different shellcodes, the best initial solution, the goal, and the best found solution is shown. Here we see that calculating the arithmetic median on several shellcode instances and the use of this value as fitness value to train the GA yields much better than 5.2. In figure 5, you still can see the difference between normal traffic and shellcodes. But the most interesting point is the existence of the conspicuous peak in the middle of all shellcodes.

5.4 40 Decipher Engines and Similar Traffic as Evaluation Function

The next idea was to use shellcode-data from different decipher engines. No longer we are dealing with the whole shellcode. From now we just look at the most interesting part of the shellcode - the decipher engine (the *peaks*). To get a goal-function, we had to add some other traffic at the beginning and at the end of our evaluation example. To get better results, we used normal traffic data detected as false positives, by the captured method described in 5.3. And once again - in figure 6 the best initial solution the goal and the best found solution is displayed.

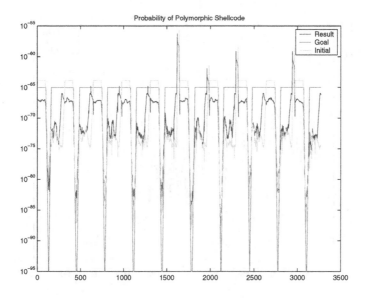

Fig. 5. Optimization result for 10 different shellcodes

The green line represents the untrained, initial behavior. Since the shown diagram is an enlarged picture of the interesting part of the diagram, we can se no difference between the deciphering engine and the rest of the shellcode.

The blue line is the trained result, showing significant differences 10^{10} between the deciphering engine and byte sequences looking very similar to decipher engines. By careful threshold-selection, we are now able to distinguish between real shellcode and false positives detected by 5.3, since peaks detected by 5.3 at 400 and 600 are eliminated by the improved transition matrix.

6 Experimental Results

At least we present the detection results for all transition matrices we produced. We have tested our implementation with real data from the hard disk. The amount of data we used was 126 MB, which we collected from different locations to get fair distributed data. The data itself contains no shellcodes but decipher engine similar code. We used a threshold for the detection with which could detect all the shellcodes from our test set. We are using only sequence calculation without any additional improvements like:

- NOP-zone detection
- Prefilter- or preprocessing-techniques
- Abstract Payload Execution
- Assembler command improvement

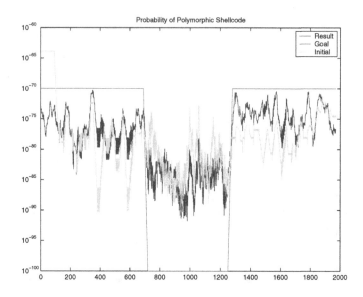

Fig. 6. Optimization result for 40 decipher engines and similar traffic data

We calculated the probability of Markov sequences with a length of 30 for the whole data by using a sliding window. The sliding window was shifted by one for every new sequence.

Table 1. Markov model detection performance with different transition matrices

	P1	P2	P3	P4
False negatives	0	0	0	0
False positives	33540	2540	652	13

- P1 - Learned transition matrix from normal traffic.
- P2 - Manually created transition matrix.
- P3 - Transition matrix obtained as solution from approach 5.3
- P4 - Transition matrix obtained as solution from approach 5.4

7   Conclusions

Since we did not know a good algorithms to modify a Markov model, trained with normal network traffic (to be able to detect any deviations from normal traffic) we used GAs to solve this problem. Starting with the evaluation of a single shellcode-instance, we proofed the concept of MM-adaptation by GAs to make MMs more significant in the special case of polymorphic shellcode.

We learned quick that a single shellcode-sample was insufficient to be used in our GA-fitness function. Thus, we increased the number of shellcode-probes and we used 10 instances to train the MM. We know that 10 instances are still insufficient to be able to detect a broader spectrum of polymorphic code (generated by different polymorphic generators). But the main idea of this paper was just to give a proof of concept.

References

[Cj04]   Chang, J.: *Stochastic Processes*. (http://pantheon.yale.edu/ jtc5/251/) (Accessed 2004/11/17).

[CLET03]   CLET Team: Polymorphic shellcode engine. *Phrack Magazine* 49(14).

[ADM03]   ADMmutate: ADMmutate shellcode engine. (http://www.ktwo.ca) (Accessed 2004/11/24).

[Mm03]   Mahoney, M.: *Network traffic anomaly detection based on packet bytes*. In Proc. ACM-SAC. 2003.

[KL04]   Kolesnikov, O.; Lee, W.: *Advanced Polymorphic Worms: Evading IDS by blending in with normal traffic*. (http://www.cc.gatech.edu/ ok/) (Accessed 2004/11/16)

[Oe02]   Oswald, E.: *Enhancing Simple Power-Analysis Attacks on Elliptic Curve Cryptosystems*. (CHES 2002). 4th International Workshop on Cryptographic Hardware and Embedded Systems. Redwood Shores. CA. USA.

[DHS00]   Duda O., Richard; Hart E., Peter; Stork G., David: *Pattern Classification*. Wiley Intersience. New York.

[RN95]   Russell A.; Norvig, P.: *Artificial Intelligence: A Modern Approach*. Prentice-Hall.

[PJ84]   Pearl, J.: *Heuristics: Intelligent search strategies for computer problem solving*. Addison-Wesley.

[HJK95]   Houck, Chris; Joines, Chris; Kay, Mike: *A Genetic Algorithm for Function Optimization - A Matlab Implementation*. NCSU-IE TR 95-09.

[Yn01]   Nong Ye et al.: *Probabilistic Techniques for Intrusion Detection Based on Computer Audit Data*. IEEE Transactions on Systems, man and cybernetics - Part A: Systems and Humans. Vol. 31. No. 4. July 2001.

[YEZ02]   Ye, N.; Ehiabor, T.; Zhang, Y.: *First-order versus high-order stochastic models for computer intrusion detection*. Quality and realiability engineering international. 2002.

[Yn00]   e, N.: *A Markov chain model of temporal behavior for anomaly detection*. In: Proc. of the 2000 IEEE Systems, Man, and Cybernetics Information Assurance and Security Workshop. New York

[JTM01]   Jha, S.; Tan, K.; Maxion, R.A.: *Markov Chains, Classifiers, and Intrusion Detection*.(CSFW 01) 14th IEEE Computer Security Foundations Workshop. Cape Breton. Novia Scotia. Canada.

[JV99]   u, W.H.; Vardi, Y.: *A hybrid high-order Markov chain model for computer intrusion detection*. Technical Report. TR92. National Institute of Statistical Sciences. 1999.

A Secure Context Management for QoS-Aware Vertical Handovers in 4G Networks*

Minsoo Lee and Sehyun Park

School of Electrical and Electronics Engineering, Chung-Ang University,
221, Heukseok-Dong, Dongjak-Gu, Seoul 156-756, Korea
lemins@wm.cau.ac.kr, shpark@cau.ac.kr

Abstract. In the 4G mobile networks which are expected to be very complex systems interconnecting various technologies, new intelligent services will need to be aware of various contexts. In this paper, we present the context management framework that exploits the agent technology in mobile communications and services. We focus mainly on the seamless secure handover which uses context information regarding location privacy, security, network environment, and QoS priority. We designed QoS Broker that can perform the autonomous decision making for context-aware handover without the direct intervention of users. To minimize the signaling overhead, we present an efficient context transfer mechanism among the Brokers. We also designed the context model for the seamless vertical handovers so that the Brokers could ensure the right context is available in the right place at right time. We developed the testbed and analyzed the performance of QoS-aware secure roaming with context transfer. Analytical results show that our context-aware vertical handover provides better performance and security with lower latency.

Keywords: 4G, context-aware, home network, QoS, vertical handover, mobile networks, security.

1   Introduction

The some key features in the vision of fourth generation (4G) wireless networks are high usability at anytime, anywhere, and with any technology, to support for intelligent services at low transmission cost[1]. The core component towards 4G architecture is system integration [2], where a unified wireless access system is to be established through the convergence of the services offered by current access technologies such as of wireless LANs (WLANs) with third-generation (3G) mobile networks including Universal Mobile Telecommunications System (UMTS) and CDMA2000. In these heterogeneous networks, providing seamless

---

* This research was supported by the MIC(Ministry of Information and Communication), Korea, under the Chung-Ang University HNRC(Home Network Research Center)-ITRC support program supervised by the IITA(Institute of Information Technology Assessment).

J. Dittmann, S. Katzenbeisser, and A. Uhl (Eds.): CMS 2005, LNCS 3677, pp. 220–229, 2005.

roaming services, as well as preserving security and privacy, is the most challenging problems in the integrated services. The seamless communication environments require a variety of context such as user identity, current physical location, weather conditions, time of day, date or season, and whether the user is driving or walking. The pervasive systems need to adapt to context changes, including mobility, network condition, security level and quality of service (QoS).

However, the context information is difficult to manage, because the its amount can be enormous. The context information is distributed in both network and mobile terminal. The context information can be either static or dynamic, location dependent. Wireless link is the bottle neck for context exchange. Furthermore, mobility management is more complicated in the integrated networks. A mobile node (MN) is equipped with multi-mode wireless interfaces to connect to one, multiple or all wireless access networks anytime anywhere. In security management for the vertical handovers (handovers between heterogeneous networks) encryption keys and authentication data may need to be exchanged at every handover, which further complicates and slows down the handover procedure.

A context management framework with intelligent tools can assist the users and applications in delivering the required QoS. Agent technology is expected to become the tool for development of future computing environments such as mobile computing, e-commerce, telecommunication network management, etc. [3]. In this paper, we present the context management framework that exploit the agent technology in communications with more emphasis on QoS-aware mobile agents. We focuse mainly on the QoS-awareness in seamless handover. QoS-aware vertical handover between heterogeneous networks is one of many possible adaptation methods for seamless services.

We designed *QoS Broker* and enhanced Location Manager that perform the autonomous decision making for context-aware handover without the direct intervention of users. When the secure vertical handover occurs, the MN and the access router need to exchange keys and authenticate each other. This process is time-consuming and creates a significant amount of signaling. To minimize the need to signal over the wireless link, context transfer mechanism could be one solution. We present an efficient context transfer mechanism among QoS Broker and Location Manager. AAA servers in different domains forward the AAA preestablished information to the new AAA servers. We also designed the context model for QoS-aware vertical handover for 3G/WMAN/WLAN interworking systems. With our context model the Brokers could ensure that the right context is available in the right place at right time. We have been developed the testbed and analyze the handover performance of location-aware secure roaming with context transfer in an IP-based 4G network with UMTS and WLAN access networks.

The rest of this paper is organized as follows. Section 2 describes the context model used in our solution. Section 3 presents our context management framework in the 3G/WLAN/WMAN interworking system. Section 4 describes our prototype for QoS-aware vertical handover. Section 5 describes our testbed and experimental result for QoS-aware vertical handover with context transfer. Section 7 concludes this paper.

2   A Context Model for QoS-Aware Services

Toward seamless services in 4G networks, a simple set of information is insufficient and a rich set of context is required [5]. In this paper we focused mainly on QoS and location context which is needed to support seamless vertical handovers. The entire context model is shown in Fig. 1. We propose the classified profiles[4] and the dynamic context to accommodate more adaptive and optimal service environments. A key advantage of the classified profiles is that QoS-aware and location-aware services can be customized to fit user's specific needs. Users and QoS Brokers adaptively modify the profile usages for the heterogeneous wireless networks. This mechanism could bring the maximized QoS and security as well as minimized leakage of privacy information. The layout of the context features could be identified according to the profile types(User, Nobile Node, Service, QoS Policy and Network Profiles). Profile types would be registered with Policy Servers, and each specification would lay out fields for use by the context transfer protocol. Default values, if specified, are already indicated by the profile type. The dynamic context provides current information about users and networks such as current user location, current user device, current QoS and service parameters. The dynamic context also includes the handover parameters that indicate to which network handover is most likely. This information changes dynamically when the user location or the network QoS changes.

3   Context Management Framework for Seamless Services in Future Mobile Networks

In this section, we propose the context management framework which is designed to meet the QoS and security requirements. The main objective of our framework is to ease the integration of heterogeneous networks by providing customized context profiles with QoS Brokers and Location Managers which can be assembled to create future seamless services. The Fig. 2 shows the proposed context management framework. The QoS and location-aware 3G/WMAN/WLAN interworking system is designed for satisfying the key requirements of 4G wireless networks. We assume that a MN is a triple-mode terminal with three interfaces 3G, WLAN and WMAN. For secure interworking we considered that authentication and key management should be based on the UMTS authentication and key agreement (AKA) and EAP-AKA or EAP-SIM for WLAN [6]. On the 3G/WLAN interworking a feasibility study [7] was conducted by the 3GPP with the loosely and tightly coupled solutions. The loose coupling solution allows a customer to access 3G packet-switched (PS) services over WLAN and to change access between 3G and WLAN networks during a service session. QoS is a critical issue for the service continuity.

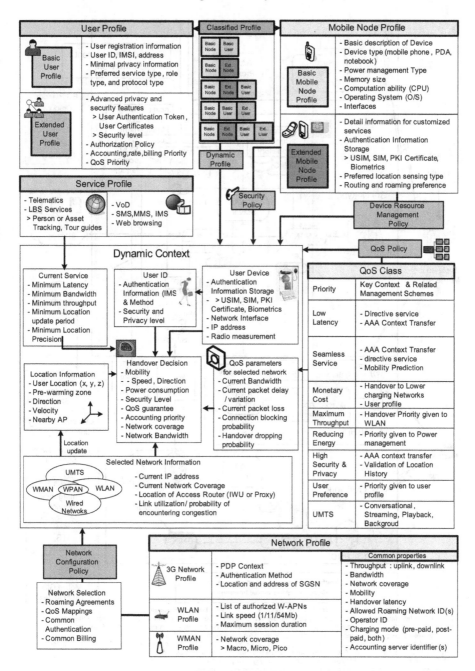

Fig. 1. Context Model used in Location and QoS-aware Interworking System

Tight Coupling refers to the alignment of WLAN interfaces with the access interfaces of the 3G network. WLAN is connected to Gateway GPRS support

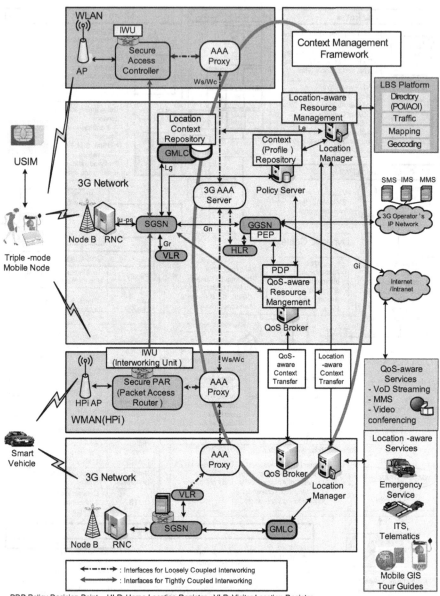

PDP. Policy Decision Point, HLR: Home Location Register, VLR: Visitor Location Register
Wr/Wb: This interface carries AAA signaling between the WLAN and the 3G visited or home PLMN in a secure manner
Ws/Wc: This interface provides the same functionality as Wr/Wb but runs between a AAA proxy and a3G AAA server
Wx: This reference point provides communication between AAA infrastructure and HSS
Wg: An AAA interface between 3GPP AAA proxy and WAGfor provisioning of routing enforcement functions for authorized users
Wα: This is used by a 3GPP AAA server to communicate with the online charging system
Wf: The interface between 3GPP AAA server and charging gateway function
Wi: Reference point between the packet data gateway and a packet data network
D'/Gr': This optional interface is used for exchanging subscription information between the 3G AAA server and the HLR

Fig. 2. The 3G/WLAN/WMAN Interworking System for QoS-aware Mobile Services

node (GGSN) via GSM Serving GPRS Support Node (SGSN) in the 3G network. The principle advantage of this solution is that the mechanisms for mobility, QoS, and security in the UMTS core network can be directly reused. We have also considered the interworking of the wireless metropolitan area networks (WMANs) with IEEE 802.16[8]. For several networking interfaces we adopt the notation and functionality specified in [9]. Location Managers get location information directly from Gateway Mobile Location Center (GMLC) [10].

The framework supporting context-aware vertical handovers includes QoS Brokers which evaluate QoS parameters makes decisions about adaptations to context changes. Policy server which gathers, manages profiles and policies as the result of service level agreement (SLA). Location Managers help QoS Brokers to make decision about location-aware resource management. AAA Proxies are responsible for the secure AAA information exchanges in executing handovers.

4   QoS-Aware Vertical Handover

4.1   Context Evaluation for Location-Aware Vertical Handover

In the traditional handover process, a MN seeks its nearest access points (APs) as candidates for the next handover. However with the variety of node densities, network coverage, and QoS guarantees of the interworking systems, the paradigm of handover through nearest AP must be reconsidered. Furthermore, an efficient QoS and location-aware scheme should allow the MN to consume less power to extend the battery life by minimizing the cryptographic operation during the secure handover. In the case of vertical handovers, we designed the QoS setup procedures supporting QoS-aware vertical handover. Our vertical handovers are based on the evaluation of dynamic context and decision priorities. We extended the concept of the context evaluation matrix [14].The evaluation matrix can be as follows (1):

$$AP_i = L_i \sum_{j=1}^{M} S_j \sum_{k=1}^{N} c_k q_k p_k \qquad (1)$$

- L_i is the parameter which will affect the location-aware handover decision. L_i represents the possibility of handover based on mobility prediction of the MN.
- S_i is the service which is both supported by the network and the mobile node.
- c_i is the coefficient of different parameters which represent user preference or operator specific parameters.
- q_i is parameter which will affect the QoS-aware handover decision. For example, q_1 can be the QoS priority and p_2 handover dropping probability.
- p_i are parameters which will affect the decision. For example, p_1 can be the currently available bandwidth of different APs and p_2 could be the signal strength of different APs.

In this evaluation matrix, AP_1, AP_2... are the access points. Each AP is evaluated by context information and the highest one is chosen.

4.2   QoS Management with QoS Broker

In our framework the QoS management procedure with QoS Broker includes the following three major steps.

> *Step1*: QoS Specification and QoS Profile Setting
> - Candidate application configurations and their resource assignments
> - Application adaptation policies, Application state template
> *Step2*: Service registration
> *Step3*: QoS Setup Procedure with QoS Broker
> - Service Discovery and authorization
> - Location-aware resource control with Location Manager
> - Application Configuration Selection
> - QoS Profile Downloading
> - Resource Allocation

We designed QoS Broker as shown in Fig. 3, the enhanced the model of [15][16]. QoS Broker plays key roles in QoS-aware handover with core modules like Application specific Control, QoS Service Management, QoS-aware resource Management and interworking interfaces to SGSN, Secure Access Router, AAA Broker and QoS Broker. QoS Broker acts as a Policy Administration Point (PAP) in service level agreement step and a Policy Decision Point(PDP) in QoS-aware service step. As a PAP, it creates a policy set to Service Level Agreements (SLAs) with users. The policy includes user profiles and other QoS parameters like QoS priority class, network preferences.

The QoS Brokers and Location Managers can support end-to-end QoS. Fig. 4 shows the location-aware end-to-end QoS support in vertical handover of UMTS-to-WLAN. The MN initiates the handover procedure and sending a handover request to its new Access Controller(AC) in WLAN (message 1). The request is then forwarded to the AAA server (message 2). AAA server sends QoS setup request to QoS Broker (3a). QoS Broker dumps the profile and performs QoS-aware resource configuration (3b). Then, QoS Broker interacts with Location Manager for location-aware resource management (3c). Upon successful authentication, AAA server performing the required association between user and MN, and informs the MN via the AR (3e+4). The messages 5∼8 represent the authorization procedure for the QoS setup in the vertical handover.

5   The Implementation Testbed

We developed the core components of our framework in Fig. 2 and we analyzed the performance of QoS-aware secure roaming with context transfer in an IP-based 4G network with UMTS and WLANs. Table 1 summarizes the parameters underlying the performance experiments. QoS Broker and Policy Server are running on SUN workstations with Solaris 8 operating system (O/S). AAA Servers are running on SUN workstations with Linux O/S and the modified FreeRADIUS library for RADIUS functionality. MNs are running on Pentium III machines and Lucent Orinoco 802.11b WLAN cards.

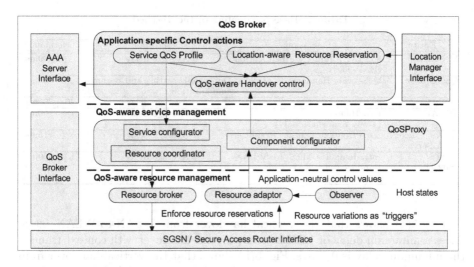

Fig. 3. QoS Broker Architecture

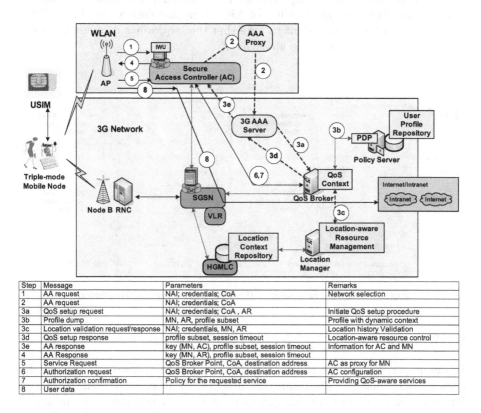

Step	Message	Parameters	Remarks
1	AA request	NAI; credentials; CoA	Network selection
2	AA request	NAI; credentials; CoA	
3a	QoS setup request	NAI; credentials; CoA , AR	Initiate QoS setup procedure
3b	Profile dump	MN, AR, profile subset	Profile with dynamic context
3c	Location validation request/response	NAI; credentials, MN, AR	Location history Validation
3d	QoS setup response	profile subset, session timeout	Location-aware resource control
3e	AA response	key (MN, AC), profile subset, session timeout	Information for AC and MN
4	AA Response	key (MN, AR), profile subset, session timeout	
5	Service Request	QoS Broker Point, CoA, destination address	AC as proxy for MN
6	Authorization request	QoS Broker Point, CoA, destination address	AC configuration
7	Authorization confirmation	Policy for the requested service	Providing QoS-aware services
8	User data		

Fig. 4. QoS-aware End-to-End Support in vertical handover of UMTS-to-WLAN

Table 1. Base parameters of the Testbed

Entity	Operation	Description	Performance
MN-AAA	802.1X full authentication (EAP-TLS)	Average delay	1,600ms
QoS Broker	QoS-aware Handover Control	QoS profile setting and resource configuration	80ms
MN-AP	802.11 scan (active)	Average delay	40∼ 300ms
MN-AP	Fast Handover (4-way handshake only)	Average delay	60ms
AAA Proxy-AAA Server	AAA Context Transfer Response	Average delay	15ms
UMTS /802.11	Intradomain UMTS to WLAN Handover with EAP-SIM authentication	Average delay	9,300ms

Fig. 5(a) shows that the vertical handover from WLAN-to-WLAN introduces a minimum delay of $1.2360s$, while for our handover with context transfer the minimum delay is $0.7161s$. Fig. 5(b) shows that the vertical handover from UMTS-to-WLAN introduces a minimum delay of $1.9484s$, while for our handover with context transfer the minimum delay is $0.8915s$. The modified AP represent that We modified the state machine of APs to support context caching in AAA context transfer. It is important to note that the improvement of our handover scheme with context transfer is about 54.3%.

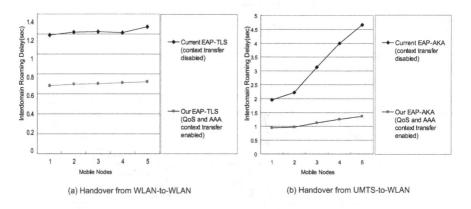

(a) Handover from WLAN-to-WLAN   (b) Handover from UMTS-to-WLAN

Fig. 5. Delay performance of the QoS-aware Vertical Handovers

6   Conclusions

In this paper, we analyze the context-aware computing issues and present the context-aware management framework designed to maximize the efficiency and interoperability for the desired QoS guarantee in 4G networks. The proposed framework can integrate a variety of wireless technologies (3G, WLAN and WMAN) into a seamless communication environment. We design QoS Broker to meet the various QoS requirement and Location Manager to effectively solve location-aware resource management problems. The experimental results of the fast QoS-aware handover with context transfer have been presented. The proposed QoS-aware handover mechanism is being integrated with the secure Web Services infrastructure[4] and new 3GPP/WLAN interworking systems[11].

References

1. Suk Yu Hui, Kai Hau Yeung: Challenges in the Migration to 4G Mobile Systems. IEEE Communications Magazine, vol 41. Dec. 2003. pp.54-59.
2. A. K. Salkintzis: Interworking Techniques and Architectures for WLAN/3G Integration toward 4G Mobile Data Networks. IEEE Wireless Communications, June 2004.
3. S.S. Manvi, P. Venkataram: Applications of agent technology in communications: a review. Computer Communications Vol 27, Number 8, Sept.2004. pp.1493-1508.
4. Minsoo Lee, Jintaek Kim, Sehyun Park, Jaeil Lee and Seoklae Lee: A Secure Web Services for Location Based Services in Wireless Networks. Lecture Notes in Computer Science, vol 3042. May 2004, pp. 332-344.
5. Sasitharan Balasubramaniam, et. al: Vertical handover supporting pervasive computing in future wireless networks. Computer Communications, May 2004.
6. Koien, G.M.; Haslestad, T.: Security aspects of 3G-WLAN interworking. IEEE Communications, November 2003.
7. 3GPP TR 22.934 v6.2.0: Feasibility Study on 3GPP System to WLAN Interworking. R6.
8. IEEE Std. 802.16-2001, IEEE Standard for Local and Metropolitan Area Networks, part 16, Air Interface for Fixed Broadband Wireless Access Systems. IEEE 2001.
9. 3GPP TS 23.234 v6.0.0:3G System to WLAN Interworking;System Description.
10. 3GPP TS 23.271 v6.8.0: Functional stage 2 description of Location Services(LCS).
11. Minsoo Lee, Jintaek Kim, Sehyun Park, Ohyoung Song and Sungik Jun: A Location-Aware Secure Interworking Architecture Between 3GPP and WLAN Systems. Lecture Notes in Computer Science, vol. 3506, May 2005, pp. 394-406.
12. Feng, V. W.-S., et. al: WGSN: WLAN-based GPRS Environment Support Node with Push Mechanism. The Computer Journal, vol. 47, no. 4, 2004. pp. 405-417.
13. Minghui Shi, et.al: IEEE 802.11 roaming and authentication in wireless LAN/cellular mobile networks. IEEE Wireless Communications, Aug 2004.
14. Wei, C. Prehofer: Context Management in Mobile Networks. in Proc. of ANwire Workshop, Nov. 2003.
15. Marques, V.et. al,: An IP-based QoS architecture for 4G operator scenarios. IEEE Wireless Communications, vol 10, June 2003. pp.54-62.
16. Nahrstedt, K.et. al: QoS-Aware Middleware for Ubiquitous and Heterogeneous Environments. IEEE Communications Magazine, Nov. 2001. pp.140-148.

Security Analysis of the Secure Authentication Protocol by Means of Coloured Petri Nets

Wiebke Dresp

Department of Business Information Systems,
University of Regensburg
wiebke.dresp@arcor.de

Abstract. Wireless communication demands for specialized protocols secure against attacks on the radio path while fitting the limited calculation and memory capabilities of mobile terminals. To ensure accessibility of mobile services beyond a user's home network, signing on a foreign network should be possible. The latter must be able to authenticate a user without learning any secret registration data. Chouinard et al. [DBC01] introduce the Secure Authentication Protocol for this purpose.

In this paper, an exhaustive security analysis of the protocol is presented. First, it is mapped to a coloured petri net. Then, two different intruder models are developed and integrated separately into it. The state spaces of the two nets are calculated; they each contain a set of nodes representing all reachable states. Both are examined to detect states where any security objective is violated indicating a security flaw in the protocol. As there are no such states in both nets, the protocol is proven secure.

Keywords: Secure Authentication Protocol, Coloured Petri Nets, Formal Protocol Verification, State Space Analysis, Security Analysis.

1 Security in Wireless Communication Networks

To gain access to mobile communication services such as telephony or data transfer, users (or their mobile terminals, respectively) have to be registered at a service provider called a user's home agent. He represents the union of a network infrastructure and a registration database where the users' data including authentication data is stored. It is to be kept secret for privacy reasons.

User and home agent usually communicate via the radio path. As radio waves spread out into all directions, all radio receivers within transmission range can obtain the exchanged data and it is easy to send spurious data to the communicating entities as well. Thus communication over the radio path has to be secured by cryptographic techniques. With respect to limited calculation and memory capabilities of mobile terminals, use of public key cryptography has to be cut down to an absolute minimum. The low bandwith of the radio path has also to be taken into account for appropriate protocol design.

Due to terminal mobility it is probable that a user leaves the range of his home agent making direct communication infeasible. To have nonetheless access

J. Dittmann, S. Katzenbeisser, and A. Uhl (Eds.): CMS 2005, LNCS 3677, pp. 230–239, 2005.

to mobile services, it should be possible for such a user to contact a network (called foreign agent) available at his current location. This scenario of logging on a foreign network is widely called roaming.

At first, the foreign agent does not have any information about the user but, to prevent fraud, needs to find out if the user is authentic. Only if he is sure about this, he is willing to provide services with cost. The authenticity of a user can be confirmed only by his home agent; on that account, the foreign agent has to contact him and ask for authentication on the basis of data provided by the user. Only if the response is positive, the foreign agent approves the user's logon. Note that each user only trusts his home agent and will never submit any of his secret registration data to a foreign agent. Therefore, the foreign agent has to trust the home agent that his answers are right.

A relevant task in protocol design is assuring the privacy of the registration data between the user and his home agent while communication between them can only be realized with the foreign agent as intermediate.

2   Secure Authentication Protocol

2.1   Entities and Security Objectives

The Secure Authentication Protocol presented in [DBC01] is tailored to the security demands of the entities participating in a roaming situation. Three regular entities with different security objectives participate:

- **User A (Alice)** wants to be sure that she is properly informed about HA's answer. Note that person and mobile terminal form a combined entity.
- **HA (Home Agent)** holding A's registration data; there is a strong trust relationship between A and HA. HA wants to be sure that the authentication request with A's data was genuinely generated and sent by A.
- **FA (Foreign Agent)** in proximity to the mobile handset. FA does not know any of A's data and there is no trust relationship between these two entities. FA wants to be sure that A is properly authenticated since he wants to limit the risk of being bilked of the invoice for services requested by A. This objective is met if FA receives a positive answer by HA if A has submitted correct data and a negative one otherwise.

2.2   Protocol

Symmetric and asymmetric encryption and decryption techniques referred to as $E_{asymm}(x; pk_X)$, $D_{asymm}(y; sk_X)$ and $E_{symm}(x; sesk_1)$, $D_{symm}(y; sesk_1)$ with plain text x and cipher text y are used with pairs of public and secret[1] keys (denoted pk_X, sk_X for entity X) and symmetric keys (serially numbered $sesk_1, ...$). H names a collision resistant hash function. $S(x, sk_X)$ and $V(y, pk_X)$ form a corresponding pair of signature and verification functions.

---

[1] To keep abbreviations distinguishable, the term "private key" is not used in this paper.

There is a certificate-based trust relationship between FA and HA^2. A secure channel can thus be established between them based on their public keys. To simplify matters, messages x sent via this channel are denoted $SecChannel(x)$ and in the following treated as plain text. A and HA share a secret password pwd_A as part of A's registration data. A protocol run[3] is carried out as follows:

1. FA sends a broadcast $broadc_{FA} = (pk_{FA}, loc_{FA})$ for all users in the transmission range. With FA's public key pk_{FA}, everybody can encrypt data for FA. loc_{FA} is some location information.

2. A creates a session key $sesk_1$ and calculates $encsesk_A = E_{asymm}(sesk_1; pk_{FA})$. Then she encrypts her request:

$$encreq_A = E_{symm}((id_A, pk_A, n_1, dp_A, hv_A); sesk_1)$$

with nonce n_1, A's mobile device profile dp_A and a hash value hv_A built with HA's domain name dn_{HA_A}[4]: $hv_A = H(id_A, n_1, dn_{HA_A}, dp_A, pk_A, pwd_A)$. A sends $encsesk_A$ and $encreq_A$ to FA.

3. FA subsequently calculates $sesk_1 = D_{asymm}(encsesk_A; sk_{FA})$ and from that $D_{symm}(encreq_A; sesk_1)$. The resulting values id_A, pk_A, n_1, dp_A and $sesk_1$ are stored. FA derives dn_{HA_A} from id_A and establishes a secure channel with HA. He submits $authreqfw = SecChannel(id_A, pk_A, n_1, dp_A, hv_A)$.

4. HA checks

$$hv_A \overset{?}{=} H(id_A, n_1, dn_{HA}, dp_A, pk_A, pwd_{A_{HA}}) = hv_{HA}.$$

HA takes dn_{HA} and $pwd_{A_{HA}}$ from the registration database. It is also checked if n_1 was used in a previous run in order to prevent replay attacks. In case of $hv_A = hv_{HA}$, HA sends a positive authentication response

$$authresp_{ACK} = SecChannel(id_A, ACK, hv_{HA}, sesk_2, n_2, n_3, cert_A)$$

to FA. ACK is a string of acknowledgement which possibly contains further details, e.g. the generation time of the response. The nonces n_2 and n_3 will later be used by A to generate session keys. $sesk_2 = H(n_1, n_2, pwd_A)$ is included so that FA can communicate securely with A without reusing $sesk_1$. HA also calculates and stores $sesk_3 = H(n_1, n_3, pwd_A)$. The certificate $cert_A = S((id_A, pk_A); sk_{HA})$ is submitted to A so that she can authenticate to other mobile terminals and service providers without involving HA in the future. Note that the certificate is modeled in a very simple way as there is no more detail given in [DBC01].

In case of $hv_A \neq hv_{HA}$ or replayed n_1, HA's authentication response is

$$authresp_{NACK} = SecChannel(id_A, NACK, hv_A, hv_2, n_2)$$

---

[2] Each entity is sure about the authenticity of the public key belonging to the couterpart's identity due to a certificate issued by a trusted third party.

[3] taken from [DBC01] with correction of a misprint discussed in personal correspondence with the authors

[4] Due to the format $userX@domainHA$, dn_{HA_A} can also be derived from A's ID.

with $hv_2 = H(pwd_A, n_2, hv_A)$. hv_2 proves that the negative authentication response was actually generated by HA. $NACK$ is a string with information on the rejection.

5. FA submits to A

$$authrespfw_{ACK} = E_{symm}((id_A, ACK, hv_{HA}, n_3, cert_A); sesk_2), n_2$$

or

$$authrespfw_{NACK} = E_{symm}((id_A, NACK, hv_A, hv_2, n_2); sesk_1), n_1.$$

6. A calculates $sesk_2 = H(n_1, n_2, pwd_A)$. If she has received a positive response, the message can be decrypted with it. id_A and hv_{HA} are checked; in case of a positive outcome, $cert_A$ is stored[5] and $sesk_3 = H(n_1, n_3, pwd_A)$ calculated. If A has received a negative answer $authrespfw_{NACK}$, she can decrypt it with $sesk_1$ and compares id_A and hv_A to her stored values. She also checks $hv_{2_A} = (pwd_A, n_2, hv_A) \overset{?}{=} hv_2$. If this is the case, she accepts the rejection.

3   Modeling the Protocol

In protocol analysis, cryptography is treated as a secure black box. This means it is assumed an intruder cannot compromise any cryptographic technique.

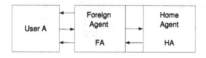

Fig. 1. Entities and Communication Paths in the Secure Authentication Protocol

3.1   Coloured Petri Net

Coloured petri nets [Jen92] have already proven suitable as a modeling technique for analysis of cryptographic protocols [DTM95] [DTM96] [Dre04]. They follow an elaborated mathematical syntax and provide a clear, intuitive and demonstrative graphical representation of the model thus facilitating its simulation and analysis which is a basic strength compared to other verification methods.

Data is modeled by tokens each belonging to a special data type called the colour set of a token. The token colour is the actual assignment of values to this token[6]. Figures 2 and 3 show the coloured petri net model of the Secure Authentication Protocol.

---

[5] Note that A does not verify the certificate herself.

[6] There is an analogy with object-oriented programming languages where objects carry certain attributes with attribute values.

3.2   Intruder Models

Following the intruder model of Dolev and Yao [DoY81], the intruder has to be
modeled with the highest imaginable strength so that *all* possible attacks on the
protocol can be identified. Considering the radio path insecure, the intruder has
full control over it. According to the model, he can then carry out the following
actions:

– Tapping and storage of all messages exchanged via the radio path
– Forwarding, rerouting and blocking of messages
– Generation of forged messages using tapped, randomly generated and obso-
  lete data and encryption techniques
– Decryption of ciphertext if the intruder has a matching key

There are two different intruder models conceivable for this protocol:

– An intruder can try to intervene on the radio path and thus deceive all
  regular entities.

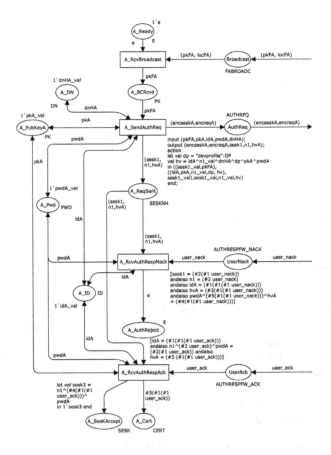

Fig. 2. Petri Net Model of the Secure Authentication Protocol (Entity *A*, Radio Path)

- Since *A* does not trust any entity except *HA*, it must as well be considered
  that *FA* might be malicious.

The second case considers a much stronger intruder. But as *FA* is not an honest
protocol participant in that case, the compliance of *his* security objectives should
be checked in the first model only. In both cases, the intruder may conspire with
a registered user.

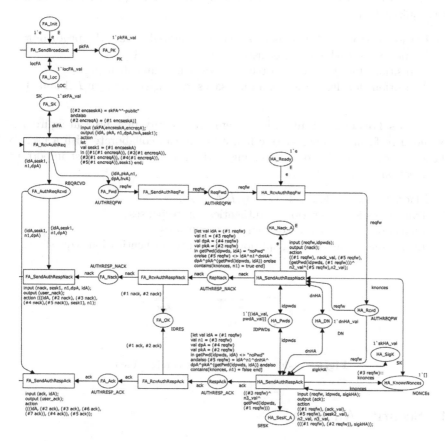

Fig. 3. Petri Net Model of the Secure Authentication Protocol (Entities *FA*, *HA*)

To perform an exhaustive security analysis, two different coloured petri nets
have to be modeled, each including one of the identified intruders.

Intruder on the Radio Path. This model assumes an intruder on the radio
path indicating *FA* is reliable. He can thus act as a foreign agent to *A* and
as a user to *FA* or collaborate with a user cheating only *FA*. The intruder is
integrated into the petri net as presented in figure 4.

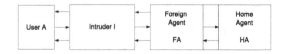

Fig. 4. Model with Intruder on the Radio Path

The entity mirrors A's and FA's sending and receiving transitions. Further, it is equipped with

- Places for storing all tokens received or generated during the protocol run, i.e. places for each colour set used by either A or FA
- Transitions for generation of requests, responses and their parts
- Transitions for decryption of all messages exchanged between FA and A

Malicious Foreign Agent. The foreign agent entity presented in figure 3 is extended to form an intruder (see figure 5). He can collaborate with a user to cheat HA or act on his own deceiving both A and HA. The most important modifications are:

- Places for each colour set used by HA or A
- Transitions for generation of authentication responses
- Transition for generation of spurious certificates
- Transitions for assembling spurious forwarded authentication requests

Fig. 5. Model with a Malicious Foreign Agent

4   Security Analysis

4.1   Relevant States in State Space

The state of a net is the assignment of all places with tokens. It changes when the number, positions, types and / or colours of tokens in the net are modified by transition firing. States are nodes in a digraph connected with edges each representing the firing of a binding element, i.e. a pair (t, b) with transition t and binding b (the assignment of token colours to each of the transition's variables). The *state space* represents the states reachable from the initial marking as a result of every possible permutation of transition firings. It is thus the exhaustive enumeration of all potential states and can be used to examine the security of a protocol as proposed in [DTM95], [DTM96] and [Dre04]. If any successful attack can be carried out, there has to be at least one state where any security objective is violated, and there is a path of fired binding elements from the initial state to the respective state describing the attack. If no such states exist, it is proven that the protocol is in fact secure concerning the specified objectives.

For the Secure Authentication Protocol, states violating the security objectives described in 2.1 are:

1. Incorrect *user_ack*: HA has built and sent a positive answer though A did not initiate the authentication process. These are all states with a token in HA_SesK_A (i.e. HA generated a positive response) but with a token in A_Ready or A_BCRcvd implying A did not send any request.
2. Incorrect certificate: I holds a certificate legally signed with HA's secret key. It contains id_A bound to a public key different from pk_A.
3. Compromised *sesk_3*: I has found out the $sesk_3$. These are all states where I holds a token with the same colour as the token in HA_SesK_A.
4. Forged *user_ack* or *user_nack*: A has accepted a positive or negative response although HA did not send the respective message. This includes scenarios where I has generated a response without involvement of HA as well as those where I has intercepted HA's response and generated a converse message.

The security objectives of FA are contained implicitly in 1. As message integrity between HA and FA cannot be attacked due to the secure channel, FA can be cheated only if an intruder makes HA produce wrong responses.

4.2   Determination of the Optimal Initial Marking

The initial knowledge of the intruder has to be chosen carefully. Due to the state explosion problem [Val98], an initial marking containing too many tokens can cause problems regarding the computability of the net's state space. It has, on the other hand, to be avoided that the initial marking is improperly small so that tokens allowing for successful attacks are missing. In this case, the state space analysis might claim security of a protocol which is *not* secure against *all* possible attacks.

To determine the optimal initial marking, the maximum number of tokens to be used in *one* protocol run is identified and then reduced with a semi-formal rationale; multiple runs will be discussed later in this paper.

First, random tokens generated by the intruder himself are addressed. This number can be derived from examination of the transitions for sending and encrypting messages. Note that only those tokens that cannot help to perform a successful attack - e.g. because they can never pass a specified check by a regular entity - are sorted out in the reduction steps. The following principles apply:

– An intruder can send out broadcasts needing a key pair and a true location information for this purpose.
– An intruder cannot guess any secret key to sign a certificate that could be accepted by any other entity[7].

---

[7] Although A does not verify a received $cert_A$ herself, she will use it communicating with others who surely will.

- Messages generated by means of public key cryptography always have to be created with the public key of the receiver. Random public keys and encrypted messages cannot be used.
- No intruder can guess a password or retrieve it otherwise as it is sent by A or HA only after applying the one-way hash function. Accordingly, he cannot generate hash values as this requires knowledge of a password.
- The session keys $sesk_2$ and $sesk_3$ are calculated using a password and can hence not be generated by then intruder. Session key $sesk_1$ is chosen by A and could also be made up by the intruder, but this is not necessary: he will receive a session key from A after sending out a public key broadcast. Random encrypted values cannot be used either as they lack a matching session key.
- Random IDs lead to rejection as HA only accepts requests with a known ID and a matching hash value (which I cannot create). Device profiles and domain names can also be useful only if they match a hash value which does not hold for random tokens.
- Nonces have to match a certain hash value or session key. This claim cannot be met as the intruder cannot generate valid hash values.

Thus, the initial marking concerning random tokens is reduced to pk_I, sk_I, loc_I for both intruder models.

As stated in 3.2, the intruder could also plot with a regular user X^8 to login as A and receive a certificate $cert_{A_I} = E_{asymm}((id_A, pk_X); sk_{HA})$. But as HA always calculates hv_{HA} depending on the password pwd_A associated with id_A in the database, he will not accept requests built with pwd_X.

Now, multiple protocol runs are considered: they can be simulated by equipping the model with data collected in previous protocol runs. It has to be determined if the intruder can use such old messages anywhere. As a nonce is included in each request and checked by HA, old requests will be detected leading to a negative authentication answer. Old authentication answers are useless as they can only be decrypted by A if generated with $sesk_1$ (chosen by A in the current protocol run) or $sesk_2 = H(n_1, n_2, pwd_A)$ (with n_1 chosen by A in the current run). This leads to the conclusion that no old tokens can be used for a successful attack on the protocol i.e. that multiple protocol runs cannot lead to better attack results.

4.3   State Space Analysis Results

The models were generated with the *CPN Tools* software developed at the University of Aarhus [CPN]. Its State Space Tool was used for calculation and analysis of the state spaces. Table 1 shows the results: there are no illegal states according to 4.1.

Since both intruders cannot succeed in compromising the security objectives, **the petri net verification technique attests that the Secure Authentication Protocol does not possess any protocol flaws.**

---

[8] X is registered at HA and that HA therefore contains a pair of ID and password (id_X, pwd_X) in his database.

Table 1. State Space Details

Intruder Model	Initial Marking	State Space Size	Illegal States
Intruder on radio path	pk_I, sk_I, loc_I	523	0
Malicious foreign agent	pk_I, sk_I, loc_I	136	0

5   Conclusion

A coloured petri net modeling the Secure Authentication Protocol has been presented. Two different intruder models have been integrated separately. The optimal initial markings have been derived to cope with the state explosion problem without influencing completeness and accuracy of the analysis. Evaluation of the nets' state spaces has shown the absence of illegal states so that the Secure Authentication Protocol is evidently secure against attacks on the protocol level.

References

[CPN]   CPN Tools Homepage: http://wiki.daimi.au.dk/cpntools/cpntools.wiki

[DBC01]   Dupré la Tour I., Bochmann G. v., Chouinard J.-Y.: A Secure Authentication Infrastructure for Mobile Communication Services over the Internet. Proceedings IFIP Working Conference CMS'01, 2001, pp. 405 - 416.

[DoY81]   Dolev D., Yao A.: On the Security of Public Key Protocols. Proceedings IEEE Symposium on Foundations of Computer Science, 1981, pp. 350 - 357.

[Dre04]   Dresp W.: Computer-gestützte Analyse von kryptographischen Protokollen mittels gefärbter Petrinetze. Diploma Thesis, Department of Business Information Systems, University of Regensburg, 2004.

[DTM95]   Doyle E., Tavares S., Meijer H.: Automated Security Analysis of Cryptographic Protocols Using Coloured Petri Net Specifications. Workshop on Selected Areas in Cryptography, SAC '95 Workshop Record, 1995, pp. 35-48.

[DTM96]   Doyle E., Tavares S., Meijer H.: Computer Analysis of Cryptographic Protocols Using Coloured Petri Nets. 18th Biennial Symposium on Communication, Kingston, Ontario, 1996, pp. 194-199.

[Jen92]   Jensen K.: Coloured Petri nets. Basic concepts, analysis methods and practical use, Vol. 1. Monographs in Theoretical Computer Science, Springer, 1992.

[Val98]   Valmari A.: The State Explosion Problem. Lecture Notes in Computer Science, Vol. 1491: Lectures on Petri Nets I: Basic Models, Springer, 1998, pp. 429-528.

Assessment of Palm OS Susceptibility to Malicious Code Threats

Tom Goovaerts, Bart De Win, Bart De Decker, and Wouter Joosen

DistriNet Research Group, Katholieke Universiteit Leuven,
Celestijnenlaan 200A, 3001 Leuven, Belgium
{tomg, bartd, bart, wouter}@cs.kuleuven.ac.be

Abstract. The Palm OS operating system for Personal Digital Assistants (PDAs) and mobile phones has a weak security architecture, which introduces all sorts of security problems. This paper specifically targets the problem of malicious code. The main contribution of this work is the in-depth analysis of different vulnerabilities in Palm OS and the ways in which they can be exploited by malicious code. Furthermore, the key reasons for this problem are discussed and some suggestions for improvement are formulated.

Keywords: malicious code, worms, mobile operating systems, Palm OS.

1 Introduction

PDAs have become very popular devices that appear in day to day life. They have evolved from simple electronic agendas to powerful connected mini-computers that use wireless communication technologies such as IrDA, Bluetooth, WiFi and GSM. These devices can hold sensitive information such as confidential documents and passwords or they can participate in commercial transactions. However, it has already been documented that the operating systems found on PDAs do not pay much attention to security [1,2].

One important class of security problems is malicious code such as viruses, Trojan horses, worms or backdoors. Except for the weak security architecture of PDA operating systems, there are two reasons why these devices are at risk of being targeted by malicious code. First of all, PDA applications are easily downloaded from the Internet and exchanged between devices. This encourages passive infection strategies, and it leads to a situation that is somewhat comparable to the old PC era where viruses were propagated on floppies. Secondly, new wireless communication technologies introduce new threats for actively propagating forms of malicious code. Imagine a worm that wirelessly propagates from PDA to PDA in rush hour traffic or in a full auditorium. When PDAs are being used for critical tasks such as mobile payment or as advanced security tokens, the malicious code problem is a risk that is completely unacceptable [3,4]. So far, a few PDA viruses have effectively been reported [5,6,7].

In this paper, the security problems of Palm OS with respect to malicious code are discussed. We have carried out an in-depth vulnerability assessment of

J. Dittmann, S. Katzenbeisser, and A. Uhl (Eds.): CMS 2005, LNCS 3677, pp. 240–249, 2005.
© IFIP International Federation for Information Processing 2005

Palm OS and discuss how vulnerabilities in the operating system can be exploited by malicious code. All of these vulnerabilities have been tested in practice in a prototypical worm. Some suggestions are proposed to tackle the problems and the security architecture of the future version of the operating system is evaluated shortly. The implementation and verification of the vulnerabilities has been carried out in a master's thesis [8].

The rest of this paper is structured as follows. Section 2 gives a short introduction to Palm OS. Section 3 discusses the vulnerabilities and explains how malicious code can exploit them. In Section 4, the proof of concept implementation is discussed that was developed as a test bed for the vulnerabilities. Section 5 reflects on the security problems of Palm OS, proposes some suggestions and gives a short overview of the improvements in the future version of Palm OS. Finally, Section 6 concludes the paper.

2   Palm OS

Currently, the Palm OS operating system comes in two flavors: Garnet [9] and Cobalt [10]. Palm OS Garnet (version 5) is the version that is found on new Palm OS powered devices today. In the future, Palm OS Garnet will become the version for less powerful devices such as cell phones, while Palm OS Cobalt (version 6) will target PDAs. This paper focuses on Palm OS Garnet.

Palm OS is a single tasking operating system for ARM-based processors running on speeds from 100MHz to 400MHz. Palm OS based devices do not have nonvolatile memory. Memory is used for execution as well as storage and is partitioned in two logical regions: the *dynamic memory* is used for dynamic allocations and maintaining the execution state of programs and the *storage memory* stores data that has to be preserved. Data as well as applications are kept in structures called *records* and records are grouped in *databases*. Because data is stored in RAM, a device has to maintain a minimal voltage over the memory at all times. Resetting the device will only erase the dynamic memory, but it is possible to erase all memory by doing a *hard reset*.

Palm OS supports multiple wireless communication technologies including IrDA, Bluetooth, WiFi and GSM allowing users to 'beam' data or applications from one device to another. Palm OS implements a TCP/IP stack for networking wirelessly or by modem and newer Palm OS devices support mobile phone technology to make voice calls or send text messages.

Synchronization with the desktop is realized by *Hotsync*. This is an application that consists of a device component and a desktop component that lets the user synchronize his/her calendar and contacts between the applications on the device and those on the desktop. Hotsync is also used to install new software and to take backups.

A number of security features is supported in Palm OS. It is possible to *lock* the device, which will disable it until the user authenticates him/herself with a password.[1] Locking can be activated manually or automatically, e.g. when the

---

[1] Since a PDA is supposed to be a single user device, a username is not required.

device is turned off. Furthermore, some protection mechanisms for databases are provided. For example, database records can be made 'secret', meaning that the user must enter his/her password to be able to read or write the information in the record. Palm OS also has a cryptographic library that contains implementations of a limited number of algorithms for encryption, secure hashing and signing.

3   Vulnerabilities

We have assembled and verified a set of new and known vulnerabilities for Palm OS Garnet. Approximately half of the vulnerabilities comes from the work of Kingpin and Mudge [1]. The discussion of the vulnerabilities is structured according to the vulnerable operating system aspects: database management, event mechanisms, application and process management, communications, built-in security mechanisms, desktop components and the GUI. For each vulnerability, the problem is first explained and then the possible exploitations by malicious code are discussed.

3.1   Database Management

Full access to data [1]. Palm OS has no access control mechanism for databases. Direct memory access into the storage heap is disallowed, but when the database API is used, every application has full access to all databases stored on the device. It is possible to read and write information into database records, append or remove database records or create and remove entire databases. Even records that have been marked as secret (see Section 2) or databases that have been marked read-only can be deleted without restrictions.

Since Palm OS devices can contain sensitive information such as business cards, important documents and passwords, the lack of access control towards data poses an important threat. Malicious code can execute numerous malicious actions such as erasing, sending or modifying important data, storing information in existing databases or erasing log entries.

Program Infection or Destruction [1]. The fact that every application has full write access to the code of other applications opens the platform for a wide range of virus infection techniques.

A malicious program that is running on the device can replicate itself by writing its own code into another application by means of the database API. Or it could also simply destroy other applications by writing data in their code. We have experimented with program infection by means of a simple proof-of-concept infection program that replaces the first occurrence of the RET instruction of every user-installed program with the machine code of an infinite loop. This causes the execution of these applications to block the system.

Preventing the Deletion of Databases. Databases can be protected by means of the DmDatabaseProtect operation. Internally, Palm OS keeps a per-database counter with the number of times the database has been protected. Calling the protection function increases this counter by one. A database with a positive protection counter cannot be deleted.

The protection mechanism is easily circumvented because the protection function can also decrease the counter until the database can be deleted again. Beyond this obvious threat, the database protection mechanism can also be abused by malicious programs to protect themselves against removal. A malicious program can protect its own database and detect[2] when someone tries to remove it. In response to the removal attempt, the program could reprotect itself. This way, the user is unable to delete the database, even with applications such as Filez [11] that give the user much more low-level control over databases and their attributes than the default database management functionality of Palm OS.

3.2   Event Mechanisms

Palm OS applications are event-based and the operating system provides a number of event sources and event handling mechanisms:

1. *Launch codes* are sent by the operating system when certain events take place that are of interest to all applications, for example the completion of a Hotsync synchronization.
2. There is a publish-subscribe mechanism called *Notifications* that allows applications to register themselves with a notification service for a certain event and receive notification when the event takes place. An example of a notification is the launching of a particular application.
3. Through the *Alarm Manager*, applications can set a number of alarms. At a given time the application will get a warning for the alarm and can execute code in response to it.

All these event mechanisms allow malicious code to trigger their malicious actions with a high precision [1]. When a malicious program is installed on the device, it will start receiving launch codes. Once it has received its first launch code, it can register itself for notifications and set alarms, and become active on numerous occasions.

Hiding of Noticeable Actions. It is possible that malicious activity cannot be completely hidden for the user. Therefore a malicious program could carefully wait for a moment at which the user is not using or watching his PDA for a while. To choose such a moment, the following notifications could be used: the sysNotifyIdleTimeEvent notification is sent whenever the device is inactive for a short period, the sysNotifySleepNotifyEvent notification is sent whenever the device is put into standby mode.

User Interface Tracking. By registering for the sysNotifyEventDequeuedEvent notification, the application gets a notification whenever a user interface event

---

[2] By means of a Notification, see Section 3.2.

(such as the tapping of a button) is handled. This way, malicious programs can track tapped buttons and the information he/she enters. The security consequences are twofold: first, it allows for a fine grained selection of triggers. For example, a self-propagating program can track when the user presses the 'beam' button to send information to another device and react by sending itself instead, hoping that the receiving user will accept the transfer. Second, malicious programs can intercept confidential information entered by the user.

3.3   Application and Process Management

Hiding from the Application List. The database of each application has a bit that, when set, will hide the application from the list of launchable applications. When doing so, the application will still be listed in the dialogs for copying, moving and deleting applications.[3] Malicious applications could set their hidden bit for trivial hiding purposes.

Hiding Entirely From the User Interface. Every database has a type and an identification number, called a *creator id*. Databases that contain application code have the type appl. When the type of an executing applications' database is changed into a non-executable type (for example the data type or a custom type), it will no longer be seen as an executable but it will still receive launch codes and notifications as long as the device is not reset. Doing so will hide the program from the launch screen. Moreover, when the creator id of the executing application is also changed to another applications' creator id, the application will be regarded as a database of the other application and will also be hidden from the copy, move and delete dialogs. The executing code can only be deleted by removing the application whose creator id was taken. When the creator id of a built-in application is taken, the executing code cannot be deleted at all because the delete dialog only allows the removal of user-installed applications.

Thus, a malicious program can hide itself completely from the user interface and render itself unremovable while it can remain executing in the background. Third party database managers such as Filez will still allow the removal of the database.

Application Replacement. Besides a type and a creator id, every application on Palm OS has a name and a version number. Two vulnerabilities in the handling of these attributes exist that can be exploited to replace existing applications:

1. Installing an application that has the same creator id but a higher version number than a built-in application will replace the built-in application by the new one[1].
2. When an application is installed with the same name as an application installed by the user, the old application will be physically removed from the device and is completely overwritten by the new application.

---

[3] A user can visually notice installed applications either in the launch screen or in the copy, move and delete dialogs.

Consequently, malicious code can replace all applications that are installed on the device. The replacement of an application poses an obvious threat of making existing applications unusable, but these vulnerabilities can also be exploited to exhibit Trojan horse behavior. The functionality and appearance of existing applications can be mimicked for secretly executing malicious actions.

Occupying the Processor. Since Palm OS is a single tasking operating system without any process management capabilities, a malicious program can perform a denial of service attack by simply executing and not releasing the processor. An infinite loop is enough to block the entire system and force the user to reset.

3.4   Communications

Backdoor for Beamed Data [1]. The Exchange Manager is a library that allows data to be sent to another device using a high level transport-independent API. Data sent by the exchange manager typically travels over wireless protocols such as IrDA, Bluetooth or GSM protocols. An application can be registered to handle the reception of data of a certain type, for example contacts, meetings or applications. When data of the application type is received, by default a dialog will be shown asking the user for confirmation.

Every application can register itself to receive all beamed applications and can override the confirmation dialog, always accepting the received code. This way, a malicious application can open a backdoor that allows other self-replicating malicious programs to transfer themselves silently onto the system.

Detection of Devices in the Proximity. Low-level communication libraries such as the IrDA or Bluetooth library pose less of an infection threat than the Exchange Manager mainly because no servers are running for these protocols. They can however be used by malicious code to detect other devices that are in the proximity. For example, the IrDA library can be used to poll for other devices periodically and trigger a propagation with the Exchange Manager when a potential victim has been detected.

Detection of Communication Facilities. Self-propagating malicious code uses communication channels and network connections to copy itself onto other devices. PDAs typically only have short-lived connections, for example when data is sent over IrDA or Bluetooth. Sometimes the communication hardware is not always present. A number of notifications exist that are useful propagation triggers: the `sysExternalConnectorAttachEvent` is sent whenever an external device such as a WiFi adapter or a Hotsync cradle is attached and the `sysNotifyLibIFMediaEvent` is sent whenever a network interface is activated.

3.5   Built-in Security Mechanisms

Brute Force Password Guessing. Since entering a long password on a PDA can be an annoyance to the user, passwords are often chosen to be very short. The authentication mechanism of Palm OS is implemented by simply comparing the MD5 hash of the user-provided password and the original password stored in a (freely accessible) system database. Since passwords on a PDA are often significantly shorter than normal passwords, the MD5 hash of the password is vulnerable for a brute force attack.

Experiments on a device with a 144MHz processor have shown that all alphanumerical passwords of length 3 can be found within 15 seconds.

Password Removal. As mentioned earlier, a record can be protected by setting its secret bit. This requires the user to enter his/her password upon viewing or changing the information in the record. When a user has forgotten the password, he/she can remove the password. This deletes all records that have their secret bit on. However, there is an API call (`PwdRemove`) that removes the password without any further consequences.

This API call effectively undermines almost all security mechanisms of Palm OS. By removing the password, a malicious program can open the device and the information carried by it to persons that can physically approach the device.

3.6   Desktop Components

Surviving a Hard Reset. Every kind of malicious code has to reside in RAM, so when the user does a hard reset it would be erased. By setting the 'backup bit' of a database, it will be copied to the desktop upon synchronization. Malicious code can transfer its own database to the PC in order to survive a hard reset. After a hard reset, the next synchronization will restore all backed up databases.

Infection via Hotsync [1]. The Hotsync component on the desktop is the gateway to the PDA for all applications. By placing a copy of an application in a certain directory on the desktop and calling a function on a Hotsync library, the Hotsync installation program will install the file on the device.

Cross-platform malicious code that carries a Palm OS payload can exploit this weakness for infecting the device.

3.7   GUI

Hiding Dialogs. Two API calls exist for turning off the screen and for stopping its redrawing. Malicious code can abuse these calls for hiding noticeable actions from the user.

A possible technique is to first detect when the user wants to put the device into standby mode and then turning off the screen, but leaving the device on. The user cannot make a visual distinction between its device in this state or in standby mode. When the screen is turned off, a malicious program can operate without being detected by the user.

When malicious code wants to perform certain actions such as beaming itself to another device, some dialogs appear on the screen. A technique to hide these dialogs is to freeze the screen just before the dialog appears and release it when the dialog is gone, given that this latter moment can be determined.

4   Proof of Concept Implementation

To verify and experiment with these threats in practice, we have created a generic proof of concept implementation of one specific kind of malicious code: a worm. We have chosen a worm because it is a good vehicle for testing the full spectrum of discovered vulnerabilities and techniques. Malicious code typically combines a number of exploits. Therefore, the main purpose is not only to allow easy experimentation with isolated vulnerabilities but also with combinations thereof. The implementation is written in C and can flexibly combine exploits at compile-time. It consists of the skeleton of a worm and is structured along three phases: the *activation* phase hides and protects the worm and activates the other two phases, the *propagation* phase actively propagates the worm to other systems and the *execution* phase contains the payload. Table 1 shows the phase(s) to which each of the discussed exploits belongs.

Table 1. Vulnerabilities and the phase(s) to which they belong: Activation, Propagation or Execution

	A	P	E		A	P	E
Full access to data			•	Backdoor for beamed data	•		
Program infection or destruction		•	•	Detection of devices in the proximity	•		
Preventing the deletion of databases	•			Detection of communication facilities	•		
Hiding of noticeable actions	•			Brute force password retrieval			•
User interface tracking	•			Password removal			•
Hiding from the application list	•		•	Surviving a hard reset	•		
Hiding entirely from user interface	•			Infection via hotsync		•	
Application replacement			•	Hiding dialogs	•		
Occupying the processor			•				

We have found that it is very easy to use combinations of these exploits to create a proof of concept worm that is quasi invisible *and* virtually impossible to delete. We have used our implementation to create a self-propagating security utility with a benign payload. This utility uses a number of exploits discussed above to hide and protect itself. In the mean time, its benign payload tries to determine the user's password, warning him/her when it is not strong enough. As can be seen in Table 1, currently the vulnerabilities for the activation and execution phases are the main threats to Palm OS. The simplicity and relatively small size (less than 2000 lines of code) of our proof of concept implementation confirms that Palm OS is an easy target for malicious code.

5   Discussion

We have seen that Palm OS is vulnerable for numerous malicious code threats. The reason for this lies within Palm OS's security model: it is a secure operating system under the assumption that all applications can be fully trusted.

This assumption is reflected in two ways. First of all, the responsibility for enforcing various security rules is pushed up towards the application layer. A trusted benign application will behave well and will implement the enforcement logic, but an application with malicious intentions is completely free to ignore this enforcement request. Examples of security rules to be enforced by the applications are the read-only bit for a database and the secret bit for a record. Secondly, as illustrated extensively in Section 3, simple use of Palm OS's API can seriously harm the system and can be a large threat. Trusted applications will not misuse the API, but malicious applications are only limited by the creativity of their writers in the malicious actions they can perform. The fact that in the Palm OS world, new applications are frequently installed only worsens the untrusted code problem.

To tackle these problems, a number of changes to Palm OS could be implemented. First of all, memory protection should be introduced. Without it, no other security mechanism could be implemented securely. Furthermore, all existing security enforcement (e.g. for read-only databases and secret records) should be pulled down to the operating system. A number of new security mechanisms could also be added to Palm OS. The introduction of a code authentication mechanism would eliminate a great deal of the discussed malicious code threats. Unauthenticated code could be disallowed or be executed with limited permissions. In addition, an access control mechanism could be implemented that can limit access at least to databases but preferably also to API calls.

As can be seen in Table 1, most of the discovered vulnerabilities either belong to the activation phase or to the execution phase. Propagation phase techniques that actively propagate code to other devices are currently much less of a threat to Palm OS than they are to classical desktop operating systems. This can be explained by the fact that, except for the built-in exchange manager, Palm OS devices do not run server programs. Furthermore, Palm OS devices normally only have short-lived connections. Finally, Palm OS devices are less prone to buffer overflow attacks than most desktop operating systems because the address of the central application stack can not be determined easily. Actively propagating forms of malcode are most likely to propagate on the desktop platform and install their payload through Hotsync.

Palm OS Cobalt [10] introduces a number of interesting security-related changes. Most importantly, code can be signed to guarantee its integrity. Furthermore, memory protection is implemented, so no more direct memory writes can be made. Another novelty is the introduction of secure databases. These contain encrypted information and are only accessible through a configurable authorization manager that controls which operations may be executed on the database. Finally, programs that do not respond can be terminated by the user. Beside these positive evolutions, not all issues are solved. For example, the enforcement of database attributes (e.g. the read-only bit) is still not done by the operating system and secure databases are sent over the wire in plaintext when performing a synchronization. Unfortunately, code authentication is also not mandatory. Cobalt is a step in the good direction, but is certainly not perfect.

6   Conclusion

We have studied the vulnerabilities of Palm OS and have given potential malicious code threats that result from them. These threats and vulnerabilities were tested and verified in a proof of concept implementation. It was found that the platform is extremely vulnerable to malicious code. The reason is that Palm OS fully trusts all code. Although Palm OS devices are more and more equipped with wireless technologies, currently the main threat comes from passively propagating forms of malicious code. Suggested improvements are memory protection, system-level security enforcement, access control and code authentication.

Further study has to show the impact of Cobalt on the security of the platform in general and to the problem of malicious code in particular. Furthermore, a comparison will be made of this problem and the solutions on other operating systems for both PDAs and desktops.

References

1. Kingpin, Mudge: Security analysis of the palm operating system and its weaknesses against malicious code threats. In: Proceedings of the 10th USENIX Security Symposium, USENIX (2001) 135–152
2. Murmann, T., Rossnagel, H.: How secure are current mobile operating systems? In: Proceedings of the Eighth IFIP TC-6 TC-11 Conference on Communications and Multimedia Security, IFIP (2004) 47–58
3. Ghosh, A.K., Swaminatha, T.M.: Software security and privacy risks in mobile e-commerce. Communications of the ACM **44** (2001) 51–57
4. Pfitzmann, A., Pfitzmann, B., Schunter, M., Waidner, M.: Trustworthy user devices. In: Multilateral Security in Communications, Addison-Wesley (1999) 137–156
5. Symantec Security Response: The WinCE.Duts.A virus for Windows CE. http://securityresponse.symantec.com/avcenter/venc/data/wince.duts.a.html (2004)
6. Symantec Security Response: The SymbOS.Cabir worm for Symbian. http://securityresponse.symantec.com/avcenter/venc/data/epoc.cabir.html (2004)
7. Symantec Security Response: The Palm.Phage.Dropper virus for Palm OS. http://securityresponse.symantec.com/avcenter/venc/data/palm.phage.dropper.html (2000)
8. Vanhoof, J., Goovaerts, T.: Studie van de wormproblematiek op het Palm OS platform (Dutch). Master's thesis, Katholieke Universiteit Leuven (2004)
9. PalmSource: Palm OS Garnet. http://www.palmsource.com/palmos/garnet.html (2004)
10. PalmSource: Palm OS Cobalt 6.1. http://www.palmsource.com/palmos/cobalt.html (2004)
11. Software, N.: Filez 6.7. http://www.nosleeep.net (2005)

Implementation of Credit-Control Authorization with Embedded Mobile IPv6 Authentication

HyunGon Kim and ByeongKyun Oh

Dept. of Information Security, Mokpo National University,
Muan-Gun, Jeonnam, 534-729, Korea
{hyungon, obk}@mokpo.ac.kr

Abstract. In next generation wireless networks, an application must be capable of rating service information in real-time and prior to initiation of the service it is necessary to check whether the end user's account provides coverage for the requested service. However, to provide prepaid services effectively, credit-control should have minimal latency. In an endeavor to support real-time credit-control for Mobile IPv6 (MIPv6), we design an architecture model of credit-control authorization. The proposed integrated model combines a typical credit-control authorization procedure into the MIPv6 authentication procedure. We implement it on a single server for minimal latency. Thus, the server can perform credit-control authorization and MIPv6 authentication simultaneously. Implementation details are described as software blocks and units. In order to verify the feasibility of the proposed model, latency of credit-control authorization is measured according to various Extensible Authentication Protocol (EAP) authentication mechanisms. The performance results indicate that the proposed approach has considerably low latency compared with the existing separated models, in which credit-control authorization is separated from the MIPv6 authentication.

Keywords: Mobile node, prepaid, authorization, Mobile IPv6.

1 Introduction

The prepaid model has proved to be very successful in applications such as GSM networks, where network operators offering prepaid services have experienced substantial growth of their customer base and revenues. Prepaid services are now cropping up in many other wireless and wire line based networks as well. In next generation wireless networks, additional functionality is required beyond that specified in the Diameter base protocol[1]. For example, the 3GPP Charging and Billing requirements state that an application must be able to rate service information in real-time[2]. In addition, it is necessary to check whether the end user's account provides coverage for the requested service, prior to initiation of that service. When an account is exhausted or expired, the user must be denied the capacity to compile additional chargeable services. A mechanism that informs the user of the charges to be levied for a requested service is also needed.

J. Dittmann, S. Katzenbeisser, and A. Uhl (Eds.): CMS 2005, LNCS 3677, pp. 250–260, 2005.
© IFIP International Federation for Information Processing 2005

In addition, there are services such as gaming and advertising that may credit as well as debit from a user account.

For general purposes, the Diameter Credit-Control Application[3] was proposed to support prepaid services. It can be used to implement real-time credit-control for a variety of end user services such as network access, Session Initiation Protocol (SIP) services, messaging services, download services, etc. However, in the event that long latency is induced by authentication in the home network e.g. MIPv6 authentication[4], a practical approach should be considered to ensure real-time processing. Considering this, we design and implement an architecture model that is capable of MIPv6 service specific fast authorization for prepaid services.

2   Architecture of Credit-Control Authorization with Embedded MIPv6 Authentication

Fig. 1 illustrates the architecture of a credit-control authorization model with embedded MIPv6 authentication. It consists of a service element with embedded Diameter credit-control client, a Diameter credit-control server, a business support system, and MIPv6 authentication servers. i.e., a foreign authentication, authorization, and accounting server (AAAF) in the Mobile Node(MN)'s foreign network and a home AAA server (AAAH) in the MN's home network[6].

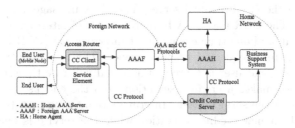

Fig. 1. Architecture of Credit-Control authorization with embedded MIPv6 authentication

The Diameter Credit-Control Application[3] defines the framework for credit control; it can provide generic credit-control authorization. In order to support real-time credit-control with an embedded MIPv6 authentication mechanism[5], a new type of server is needed, i.e., Diameter credit-control server. This server is the entity responsible for credit authorization for prepaid subscribers. It also acts as a prepaid server, performing real-time rating and credit control. It is located in the home domain and is accessed by service elements or Diameter AAA servers in real-time for the purpose of price determination and credit-control before a service event is delivered to the end user. It may also interact with business support systems. The service element can be an Access Router (AR), which is defined in MIPv6 basic service[4] or an AAA server in the foreign domain.

A Diameter credit-control client is an entity that interacts with a credit-control server. It monitors the usage of the granted quota according to instructions returned by the credit-control server. A business support system is usually deployed, and it includes at least the billing functionality. The credit-control protocol is the Diameter base protocol with the Diameter Credit-Control application. The AAA protocol with embedded credit-control protocols is used between the credit-control client and AAA server. However, the credit-control protocol is only used between the credit-control server and the credit-control client and between the credit-control server and AAA server. In this paper, to launch the credit control authorization model on a MIPv6 authentication infrastructure, it is assumed that credit-control client functionality is performed by AR in the MN's visited domain. It is also assumed that the AAAH server performs both basic AAAH server functionality and credit-control server functionality. The latter means that two server functionalities are implemented on a single host even if it is explicitly defined as an external interface.

3   Embedded Credit-Control Authorization Procedure

The Diameter Credit-Control Application[3] defines two Diameter messages, Credit-Control-Request (CCR) and Credit-Control-Answer (CCA). The CCR message requests credit-control authorization for a given service. When an end user requests a service, the request is issued by the credit-control client and is forwarded to the credit-control server. The CCA message acknowledges the CCR message. The CCR and CCA have four types of interrogation, initial, intermediate, final, and one-time events. First-interrogation (CCR-Initial) is used to first interrogate a requested prepaid service. The credit-control server will check whether the end user is a prepaid user and will rate the service event in real-time. It also makes a credit-reservation from the end user's account that covers the cost of the service event. Intermediate-interrogation (CCR-Update) is used to make a new credit reservation while the service is ongoing. Final-interrogation (CCR-Termination) is used to close credit-control authorization. One-time event (CCR-Event) is used when there is no need to maintain any state in the credit-control server, for example, requiring the price of the service.

Fig. 2 illustrates the initial credit-control authorization procedure with an embedded MIPv6 authentication procedure for Initial-interrogation (CCR-Init). It proceeds as follows:

(1) A user logs onto the network. An MN may make a data link connection using a data link protocol such as IEEE 802.11.
(2) Upon receipt of a Network Access Identifier (NAI) from the network, the AR with a credit-control client populates the Diameter ARR (Authorization-Authentication Registration Request) message with the Credit-Control AVPs (Attribute-Value Pair) set to CREDIT-AUTHORIZATION. MIPv6 specific AVPs are included. The ARR message requests MIPv6 authentication and credit-control authorization from the MIPv6 authentication

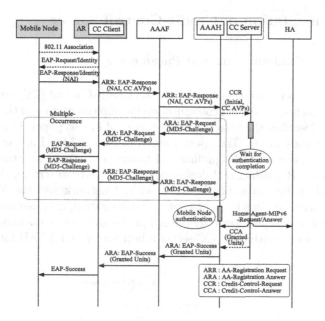

Fig. 2. Initial credit-control authorization with embedded MIPv6 authentication

server and credit-control server, respectively, in the home network. Then, the AAAF forwards the request to the AAAH.

(3) The AAAH may perform MIPv6 specific authentication and authorization as usual. It determines whether the user is a prepaid user and identifies from the Credit-Control AVPs. It then sends a Diameter CCR with CC-Request-Type set to INITIAL-REQUEST to the internal credit-control server to perform credit authorization and to establish a credit-control session (the AAAH may forward MIPv6 specific AVPs as received from the AR as input for the rating process).

(4) The credit-control server waits for authentication completion of the MN by the AAAH.

(5) After challenges and responses are processed between the MN and AAAH, the AAAH performs authentication of the MN. If it is successful, the AAAH sends a HOR (Home-Agent-MIPv6-Request) message to the Home Agent (HA) to perform binding update of the MN. It may receive a HOA (Home-Agent-MIPv6-Answer) from the HA.

(6) The reserved quota thus, Granted Units may be sent to the AAAH by the credit-control server. It may be included in the Diameter ARA (Authorization-Authentication Registration Answer) message. The AAAH sends it to the credit-control client through the AAAF.

(7) Upon receipt of a successful ARA, the AR starts the credit-control service and starts monitoring the granted units. The AR grants access to the end user.

4   Implementation of Credit-Control Server

4.1   System Configuration and Parameters

This chapter presents implementation of the Credit-Control (CC) server in detail. Fig. 3 presents the system configuration for implementation of the CC server and Table 1 describes the system parameters used in this paper. Certificate parameters are used in the Transport Layer Security (TLS). Each entity has a public IPv6 address and IP signaling and traffic are routed by a standard IPv6 routing scheme. Regarding real deployment for the MIPv6 service, the network is segmented by two subnets, the MN's visited network and the MN's home network. In order to launch credit-control authorization, it is assumed that CC client functionality is performed by the AR in the MN's visited networks and the CC server performs both basic CC server functionality and AAAH functionality.

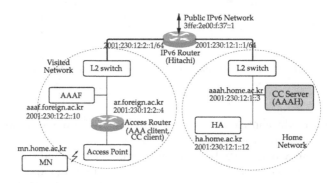

Fig. 3. System configuration for implementation

Table 1. System parameters

	System parameters
Platform	CC Server; SUN V880
	MN/AR/HA/AAAF; ZION Linux Pentium-III
Operatin System	Solaris 8/Red Hat 9(Kernel v2.4.20)
Link Capacity	100Mbps(100 Base-T)
Routing	IPv6 routing and Diameter message routing
Certificate Parameters	Certificate size; 493bytes
	ClientHello/ServerHello size; 60/66bytes
	ClientKeyExchange message size; 64bytes
	Finished message size; 12bytes
	CertificateVerify message size; 64bytes

4.2   Software Architecture and Functional Blocks

This section describes the implemented software architecture, blocks, and units in the CC server. Fig. 4 illustrates the implemented software architecture of the CC server. There are five software blocks, Low-layer Transport Block (LTB), Diameter Base Engine Block (DBEB), MIPv6 Security Application Block (MSAB), Credit-Control Block (CCB), EAP Block (EAPB), and Operation and Management Block (OMB). Each block acts as a process, and the UNIX System V IPC queue is utilized to communicate between blocks, i.e., processes. The DBEB performs the Diameter Base Protocol followed by [1], the MSAB performs the Diameter Mobile IPv6 Security Application followed by [5], the CCB performs the Diameter Credit-Control Application followed by [3], and the EAPB performs EAP Authentication Protocol followed by [7]. The OMB performs CC server operation and management functionality.

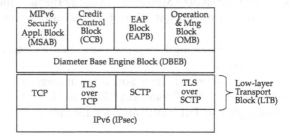

Fig. 4. Software architecture of the CC server

LTB (Low-layer Transport Block). Based on the IPv6 routing scheme, the LTB performs low-layer transport functionality followed by [8]. It has capable of processing multiple transport layer protocols such as TLS, Stream Control Transmission Protocol (SCTP)[9], TLS over SCTP, and TCP. Thus, the DBEB in the upper layer may choose a proper transport protocol corresponding to the peer's transport capability.

DBEB (Diameter Base Engine Block). The DBEB provides the following facilities: Delivery of AVPs, capabilities negotiation, error notification, extensibility through addition of new commands and AVPs, and basic services necessary for applications such as handling of user sessions or accounting. It consists of eight software units and three libraries, which provide the following functionalities respectively:

- Main Controller: performs initialization for power-up/reset and sending/ receiving primitives from/to internal units.
- PCMU (Peer Connection Managing Unit): performs low-layer peer connection management based on LTB functionality, such as connection establishment, monitoring, and release.

- RSU (Routing Service Unit): performs Diameter message routing service. A request is sent toward its final destination using a combination of Destination-Realm and Destination-Host AVPs. If the request cannot be processed locally, it is forwarded to other Diameter agents such as proxies, redirects, or relays.
- OMB_MU (OMB_Managing Unit): performs local operation and management functionality and cooperates with external OMB.
- AMU (Accounting Managing Unit): performs real-time accounting management by handling accounting messages. It collects accounting records for roaming subscribers according to an accounting state machine. Accounting records include session time, input octets, output octets, input packets, output packets, etc.
- PAMU (Path Authorization Managing Unit): checks that its peers are authorized to act in their roles, before initiating a connection.
- CEMU (Capabilities Exchange Managing Unit): performs capabilities negotiation in order to determine what Diameter applications are supported by each peer.
- USMU (User Session Managing Unit): manages user sessions according to a user session state machine.
- Three common libraries: provide transport layer management, CODEC, and DB interface by using a TML (Transport Managing Library), CDL (Coding & Decoding Library), and DIL (DB Interface Library).

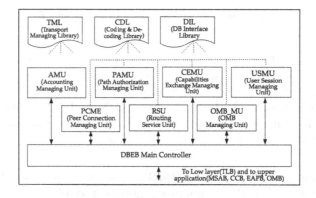

Fig. 5. DBEB software block in the CC server

CCB (Credit Control Block). As described above, the CC server provides credit-control authorization with embedded MIPv6 authentication. The MSAB performs MIPv6 authentication and, afterwards, the CCB performs authorization for a MN. To do this, MSAB and CCB are tightly coupled to exchange authentication results and credit-control authorization results. After successful MIPv6 authentication of the MN, the result is informed to the CCB to authorize the MN. The CCB consists of five software units, which provide the following functionalities respectively:

- Main Controller/Interface Handler: performs initialization for power up/ reset and sending/receiving primitives from/to internal units.
- Credit Handler: performs credit authorization and debits end user credit or refunds credit.
- CC Session Handler: manages credit-control sessions according to a Diameter credit-control session state machine.
- Diameter Message Handler: decodes messages such as CCR and CCA according to Diameter message format, and also encodes messages to be used by credit-control peer.
- Error Handler: handles errors and exceptions.

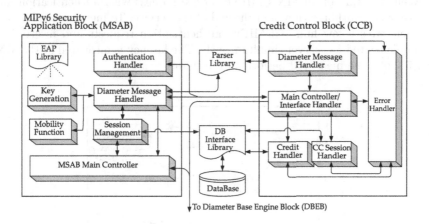

Fig. 6. CCB and MSAB software blocks in the CC server

MSAB (MIPv6 Security Application Block). The MSAB consists of six software units and one library, which provide the following functionalities respectively:

- Main Controller: performs initialization and sending/receiving primitives from/to internal units.
- Mobility Function: performs HA assignment and home address assignment of MN.
- Key Generation: performs key generation to be used for IPSec SA.
- Authentication Handler: performs authentication of MN and interacts with CCB for credit-control authorization.
- Diameter Message Handler: handles Diameter messages such as ARR, ARA, HOR, and HOA and message encoding and decoding.
- Session Management: manages MIPv6 authentication sessions according to a Diameter MIPv6 user session state machine.
- EAP Library: provides five EAP authentication mechanisms, EAP-MD5, EAP-TLS, EAP-TTLS, EAP-SRP, and PEAP[10].

EAPB (EAP Block) and OMB (Operation and Management Block).
The EAPB provides a standard mechanism for support of various EAP authentication mechanisms. It carries EAP packets between the Network Access Server (NAS), working as an EAP Authenticator, and a back-end authentication server, i.e., a CC server with AAAH. The OMB performs operation and management of the CC server itself. It interacts with other software blocks in the CC server.

5   Performance Results

Latency measurement is performed in order to evaluate the proposed credit-control authorization approach with embedded MIPv6 authentication according to several EAP authentication mechanisms. The latency is the amount of time between the start of an MN's MIPv6 service request with authentication and credit-control authorization, and the end of the service. To measure the latency, MN generates a few hundred MIPv6 authentication requests and inserts into the implemented CC server simultaneously. The latency is measured at the MN. Fig. 7 shows the measured performance results.

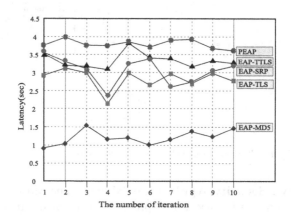

Fig. 7. Latency of CC authorization with MIPv6 authentication

Table 2 shows the average latency and CC server' processing time. It should be noted that the measured server's processing time depends on system processing capability such as CPU processing time, I/O operation capability, memory resources, and so on. In the case of EAP-MD5, the average latency is about 1.2 sec for one credit-control authorization with one MIPv6 authentication. The results indicate that EAP-TLS, EAP-TTLS, EAP-SRP, and PEAP require about 2.82 sec, 3.3 sec, 3.06 sec, and 3.8 sec latency, respectively.

Under the same conditions, we measure the latency of MIPv6 authentication alone for comparison with the latency of the proposed credit-control authorization scheme with MIPv6 authentication. The latter requires only 2% additional

Table 2. Average latency of CC authorization and CC server's processing time

EAP Authentication	Average Latency & Processing Time
EAP-MD5	1.2sec (CC server's processing time: 399msec)
EAP-TLS	2.82sec (CC server's processing time: 839msec)
EAP-TTLS	3.3sec (CC server's processing time: 1,105msec)
EAP-SRP	3.06sec (CC server's processing time: 1,018msec)
PEAP	3.8sec (CC server's processing time: 1,128msec)

latency relative to the former. In the case of EAP-MD5, the latter requires 1.224 sec additional latency. Thus, considerably lower latency is realized relative to that of the existing, separated models, wherein the credit-control authorization server is separated from the MIPv6 authentication server. In addition, the separated model may have additional latency such as the server's processing time, transport layer latency, data link latency, physical latency, and so on. Since a CC server must have a Diameter agent's transport capability[3,8] such as TCP, TLS, and SCTP, the transport layer may also require a hundred msec order delay.

6 Conclusions

This paper has presented an architecture model of credit-control authorization for MIPv6 services, which have recently drawn remarkable attention in IETF. From a real deployment point of view, we have attempted to realize a practical approach to credit-control authorization. The proposed integrated model combines a credit-control authorization procedure into the MIPv6 authentication procedure. In order to verify the feasibility of the proposed approach, we implemented it and measured the latency of credit-control authorization with MIPv6 authentication and compared the results with those yielded by existing schemes. From the performance results, we found that the proposed integrated model has considerably low credit-control authorization latency compared with the separated models, which separate credit-control authorization from MIPv6 authentication. Thus, the proposed integrated model is more effective than the separated models in terms of real-time processing.

References

1. Pat R. Calhoun, J. Loughney, E. Guttman, G. Zorn, J. Arkko: Diameter Base Protocol. RFC 3588 (2003)
2. 3rd Generation Partnership Project; Technical Specification Group Services and System Aspects, Service aspects; Charging and Billing(release 5). 3GPP TS 22.115(v.5.2.1) (2002)
3. Harri Hakala, Leena Mattila, Juha-Pekka Koskinen, Marco Stura, John Loughney: Diameter Credit-Control Application. draft-ietf-aaa-diameter-cc-06.txt (2004)
4. D. Johnson, C. Perkins, J. Arkko: Mobility Support in IPv6. RFC 3775 (2004)

5. Stefano M. Faccin, Franck Le, Basavaraj Patil, Charles E. Perkins: Diameter Mobile IPv6 Application. draft-le-aaa-diameter-mobileipv6-03.txt (2004)
6. Stefano M. Faccin, Frank Le, et al.: Mobile IPv6 Authentication, Authorization, and Accounting Requirements. draft-le-aaa-mipv6-requirements-03.txt (August 2004)
7. P. Eronen, Ed., T. Hiller, G. Zorn: Diameter Extensible Authentication Protocol (EAP) Application. draft-ietf-aaa-eap-10.txt (2004)
8. PB. Aboba, J. Wood: Authentication, Authorization and Accounting (AAA) Transport Profile. RFC 3539 (2003)
9. Stewart, R., Xie, Q., Morneault, K., Sharp, C., Schwarzbauer, H., Taylor, T., Rytina, I., Kalla, M., Zhang, L. and V. Paxson: Stream Control Transmission Protocol. RFC 2960 (2000)
10. B. Aboba, L. Blunk, J. Vollbrecht, J. Carlson, H. Levkowetz, Ed.: Extensible Authentication Protocol (EAP). RFC 3748 (2004)

Biometrics: Different Approaches for Using Gaussian Mixture Models in Handwriting

Sascha Schimke[1], Athanasios Valsamakis[2], Claus Vielhauer[1], and Yannis Stylianou[2]

[1] Otto-von-Guericke University of Magdeburg,
[2] University of Crete

Abstract. In this work in progress paper we discuss an established as well as a new approache to the use of Gaussian Mixture Models (GMMs) for handwriting biometrics. The technique of GMMs is well explored for the domain of speech processing and we evaluate ways to use them for handwriting biometrics, too.

1 Introduction

At present, certain biometric traits are very popular in the public discussion. Mainly these are fingerprint, face or iris recognition for the purpose of verification or identification. In our work we focus on the active trait of on-line handwriting biometrics and in particular signature identification. Most people are familiar with handwritten signature because of regularly usage for example to affirm contracts or sign forms.

In the following, we elaoarte on new approaches derived from speaker recognition and theoretically outline their adaptivity towards signature authentication.

2 Gaussian Mixture Models (GMMs)

Gaussian mixture models have been successfully used for speaker recognition tasks [2]. Here we suggest to use GMMs for signature recognition applications. The main idea is to represent the biometric features as the probability density function of one signee, with a mixture of Gaussians.

A Gaussin mixture density function is primarily a weighted sum of M constituent functions, and in notational form

$$p(\mathbf{x}|\lambda) = \sum_{i=1}^{M} a_i f_i(\mathbf{x}) \tag{1}$$

where $\mathbf{x}$ is a D-dimensional random vector, $f_i(\mathbf{x})$, $i = 1, 2 \cdots M$ are the constituent Gaussian density functions, and a_i are the mixture weights. Each constituent Gaussian density is a D-variate normal density function. For the GMM

J. Dittmann, S. Katzenbeisser, and A. Uhl (Eds.): CMS 2005, LNCS 3677, pp. 261–263, 2005.

function $p(\mathbf{x}|\lambda)$ to be a legitimate probability density function the constraint $\sum_{i=1}^{M} a_i = 1$ must be satisfied.

Each signee has its own density function, that is $p(\underline{x}|\lambda_s)$ where $\lambda_1, \lambda_2 \cdots \lambda_S$ are the different signees. The parameters of signee s's density are denoted as $\{a_i, m_i, \Sigma_i\}$, $i = 1, 2 \cdots M$. For identification, a maximum likelihood classifier is used. For a number of signees S represented by $\lambda_1, \lambda_2 \cdots \lambda_S$ our goal is to find the signee with maximum posterior probability for the feature vectors $X = \{x_1, x_2 \cdots x_T\}$ extracted by the signature to be tested. The probability of being signee λ_s given the feature vectors of the testing signature is given by the Bayes' formula

$$Pr(\lambda_s|X) = \frac{p(X|\lambda_s)Pr(\lambda_s)}{p(X)} \tag{2}$$

We can assume without loss of generality equal prior probabilities $Pr(\lambda_s)$ for all speakers. The denominator can be ignored as being a constant for all speakers. Finally the formula for the selection of one signee as the correct signee is

$$\hat{s} = \arg \max_{s=1,2\cdots S} p(X|\lambda_s) \tag{3}$$

and assuming independence among the feature vectors, we get

$$\hat{s} = \arg \max_{s=1,2\cdots S} \sum_{i=1}^{T} \log p(x_t|\lambda_s) \tag{4}$$

in which $p(x_t|\lambda_s)$ is given by Eq. (1).

3   On-line Handwriting Features for GMM

In this section we describe two different types of features, which can be extracted from signature data and which could be the basis for a GMM.

3.1   Spatial and Pen Movement Data and Features

The first kind of handwriting features are sample points of the pen movement while signing. These are in our case 5-tuples $(x_t, y_t, p_t, \theta_t, v_t)$, where x_t, y_t and p_t are the pen tip position coordinates and the pressure, respectively; θ_t is the direction of the stroke tangent in the point (x_t, y_t) and v_t is the velocity; t is the timeindex. This approach was firstly presented in [1].

3.2   Spectral Features for Signature Recognition

Another kind of feature data, which can be extracted from handwriting signals are features from the frequency domain. This is motivated from the domain of speech processing where often cepstral coefficients of speech segments are used.

The signature can be characterized as a random process This is true because no two signatures of the same person are exactly alike. The same is true for the signals x_t, y_t, p_t, θ_t and v_t. Having a repeated signal (i.e. periodic) in the time domain, in the frequency domain we have harmonics related to the period of the signal. What we need is the envelope of these harmonics, this characterizes the signature, namely the signee.

The procedure firstly is to take the peaks of the harmonics in the frequency domain. Secondly, in order to take the envelope, we compute the discrete cosine transform of the peaks. So, for each signal $(x_t, y_t, p_t, \dots)$ we produce one feature vector.

Acknowledgements

This work has been supported by the EU Network of Excellence SIMILAR (Proposal Reference Number: FP6507609). The contents of this publication are the sole responsibility of the authors and can in no way be taken to reflect the views of the EU.

References

1. Richiardi, J., Drygajlo, A.: 'Gaussian Mixture Models for On-line Signature Verification', in *Proceedings of WBMA'03*, 115–122, 2003.
2. Reynolds, D. A.: *A Gaussian Mixture Modeling Approach to Text-Independent Speaker*, PhD Thesis, Georgia Institute of Technology, August 1992.

INVUS: INtelligent VUlnerability Scanner

Turker Akyuz and Ibrahim Sogukpinar

Dept. of Computer Engineering,
Gebze Institute of Technology 41400 Gebze / Kocaeli,
{takyuz, ispinar}@bilmuh.gyte.edu.tr

Abstract. This paper presents a new vulnerability scanning model named as INVUS, which contains aspects of both network and host-based vulnerability scanners. INVUS model has client/server architecture and provides an option to repair the found vulnerabilities by working with the firewall.

1 Introduction

Vulnerability scanning tools are the proactive security tools that scan computer systems in order to find exploitable points before an attacker does [1]. Most of the current vulnerability scanning tools fall into one of the two categories: host-based and network-based. While network–based scanners view the system from attacker perspective and they do not install any agent software on the target host, host-based scanners view the system from perspective of a local user and scan for password problems, inappropriate access permissions or software configuration errors [2, 3]. The main idea of the INVUS model has been improved via combining the advantages of both network and host based vulnerability scanning tools.

2 INVUS Design and Implementation

Proposed model has client/server structure which means it consists of one server and one or more clients. A general view of the proposed model is shown in Figure 1. The model is implemented on Linux operating system by using C++ language.

INVUS core which is located on the target host is responsible to manage the vulnerability scanning process. Before starting the scanning process, the user establishes a connection between the client and the server and then selects the vulnerability types to be tested by using the interface. While selected network-based vulnerability types are sent to the INVUS Server VS Engine, host-based vulnerability types are sent to the INVUS Client VS Engine as scanning parameters.

INVUS Server VS Engine focuses on network-based scanning process. This process includes operating system detection, port scanning, service detection, vulnerability searching and vulnerability proving. Services running on open ports and detailed information about the software used for these services are obtained as the result of port scanning and service detection processes. Then scanning engine starts to find known vulnerabilities related to this software. On the other hand, INVUS Client VS Engine performs host-based vulnerability scanning process. By using the results

J. Dittmann, S. Katzenbeisser, and A. Uhl (Eds.): CMS 2005, LNCS 3677, pp. 264–265, 2005.

obtained from scanning engines, INVUS Core creates a report. The information related to the found vulnerabilities is obtained from the vulnerability database. Also, the user is given choice to close the ports which are thought as unnecessary. This process is implemented by the help of the firewall.

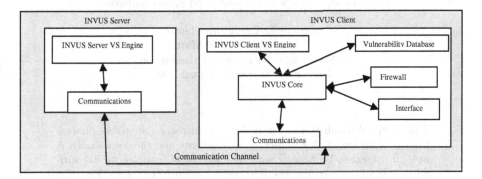

Fig. 1. INVUS model overview

3   Experimental Results and Conclusion

Proposed model has been implemented to conduct experiments. The number of host-based and network-based vulnerability types that are available to be scanned by the INVUS is increasing continuously. At that moment, INVUS can scan for 32 host-based vulnerability types; and 71 network-based vulnerability types. Some experiments were performed in order to illustrate the performance and usefulness of the INVUS model. INVUS was installed on eight different hosts running different Linux operating systems and versions. While three of these hosts were servers running services like web, ftp or mail services, the other five hosts were workstations. Results of the tests obtained from these hosts show that INVUS can detect all of the existing vulnerabilities that belong to the available vulnerability types.

In this work, a new model for vulnerability scanners is proposed. This model can scan a system for both network and host based vulnerabilities and as a result prepares comprehensive reports. By using these reports, administrators can patch vulnerabilities found. Also, the model can work with the firewall installed on the target host so vulnerable points can be repaired easily.

References

1. Venter, H. S., Eloff, J. H. P. Assessment of Vulnerability Scanners. *Network Security,* February 2003, Volume 2003, Issue 2, pp. 11-16.
2. Humphries,J.W, Carver,C.A, Pooch,U.W. Secure Mobile Agents for Network Vulnerability Scanning. *IEEE Workshop on Information Assurance and Security,* June 2000 pp 19-25.
3. Sharma, A., Martin, J.R., Anand, N., Cukier, M., Sanders, W.H. Ferret: A Host Vulnerability Checking Tool. *Proceedings of the 10th IEEE Pacific Rim International Symposium on Dependable Computing,* March 2004 pp. 389-394.

Personal Rights Management– Enabling Privacy Rights in Digital Online Content

Mina Deng[1,*], Lothar Fritsch[2], and Klaus Kursawe[1]

[1] Katholieke Universiteit Leuven,
[2] Univeristy of Frankfurt
{MDeng, KKursawe}@esat.kuleuven.be
Lothar.Fritsch@m-lehrstuhl.de

Abstract. With ubiquitous use of digital cameras, e.g. in mobile phones, privacy is no longer threatened by governments and companies only. A new threat exists by people, who take photos of unaware people with no risk and little cost anywhere in public and private spaces. Fast distribution via online communities and web pages expose an individual's private life to the public. Social and legal measures are taken to deal with this, but they are hardly enforcable. We propose a supportive infrastructure aiming for the distribution channel such that if the picture gets publicly available, the exposed individual has a chance to detect it and take action.

Protection of personal privacy has become a major issue. Most of the current work assumes an asymmetric model; the violator is an institution, while the victim is a person. Recently, a new privacy thread has emerged. An increasing number of people are equiped with miniature cameras, taking photos anywhere and anytime, thus endangering privacy when they publish the photos. Countermeasures, like penalties or a ban on cameraphones have proven insufficient, as a growing number of websites promoting such photos (e.g. the Mobile Asses website [1]) shows. As it is infeasible to enforce a broad ban on cameraphones or artificially inhibit their usage by technical measures (e.g., simulated shutter noise), we propose a novel way to complement such measures: we attack the distribution channel. If a picture of a person is taken and published, the victim has a good chance of being the first to find this picture, enabling her to request the pictures removal or invoke legal action in time.

Three major players are in our setting: the photographer (Bob), the individual (Alice), and the search engine. Bob is the photographer using a cameraphone. We assume that Bob should not to be prevented from taking the pictures and have his identity protected as long as he does not infringe the rights of anybody. Alice is being photographed by Bob. The interest of Alice is that she has some control over pictures taken of her, so we assume this picture should not be distributed without her consent. We grant her this option: If a picture of her is

---

* Mina Deng is funded by research grants of the Katholieke Universiteit Leuven, Belgium.

J. Dittmann, S. Katzenbeisser, and A. Uhl (Eds.): CMS 2005, LNCS 3677, pp. 266–268, 2005.

taken and published, she can find out early. Alice uses a receiver, which registers the identities of pictures taken in her vicinity. The receiver is her own mobile phone or a piece of hardware. It can also be integrated in the infrastructure provided by external parties, for instance, the owner of a discotheque or the GSM operators. Finally, the search engine searches the Internet for picture identities and makes them publicly available with a matching scheme.

The scenario: In the first step, Bob chooses to take a picture of unaware Alice. The camera generates and broadcasts a unique picture identifyer embedded into the picture (either by watermarking or perceptual hashing). On the other side, Alice's receiver picks up the picture identification information and stores it for later use. When Bob publishes Alice' picture, the search engines can find it and index it by the embedded ID. Alice sends requests to the search engine with all picture identities that her receiver picked up, and thus locates the picture taken by Bob. Hardware implementation: Our protocol must not require any significant changes to the devices' hardware. Three communication standards can be used to establish the link between camera phone and the receiver: Infrared, Bluetooth, and the GSM network. Infrared has a low bandwith and is easy to block, but can be directed; bluetooth is reasonably realiable and fast, but can be received by devices not in the camera range and poses a potential security risk. GSM is the most natural channel for a cellphone to communicate on, but requires support of the provider and will cover a high number of receivers. We recommend to use a combination: an infrared flash could trigger the receiver to listen to a bluetooth signal We are not protecting against a higly sophisticated attacker, but against users with both limited criminal energy and technical skills to prevent privacy violation from becoming a mass phenomena. In this, the contemporary DRM technologies for mobile devices can be applied to protect a user's personal privacy.

Software implementation: Embedding the information is done with digital watermarking [2,3]. In the our system, we identify the secretly photographed image rather than authenticating its integrity. A high level of robustness against malicious attacks is required, though the amount of data we need to embedd is relatively small (40 bits). We expect low resolution photos to allow for sufficient robustness in this setting. Perceptual hash functions can be used to identify the picture [4]. Their advantage is that the data is neither altered nor degraded. Occasional collisions do not pose a problem, as they make the user find irrelevant pictures; as long as this does not cause too much effort, is is acceptable. The final part of our protocol is a search engine that locates the pictures on the Internet. The special feature is the extraction of the identification information from the pictures to use it as an index. Similar technlogies are already in place, for example Digimarc's MarcSpider. Though technologies exist to fool such engines, one can expect a reasonable success rate in a practical setting.

References

1. ... *Mobile Asses.com - The real reason mobile phones have cameras!* . 2005.
2. R. J. Anderson F.A.P. Petitcolas and M. G. Kuhn. Information hiding-a survey. volume 87, pages 1062–1078, 1999.

3. S. Katzenbeisser and F.A.P. Petitcolas. *Information hiding techniques for steganography and digital watermarking.* Artech House, INC., 2000.
4. M. Kivanç Mihçak and R. Venkatesan. New iterative geometric methods for robust perceptual image hashing. In *ACM CCS-8 Workshop on Security and Privacy in Digital Rights Management*, pages 13–21, London, UK, 2002. Springer-Verlag.

Flexible Traitor Tracing for Anonymous Attacks

Hongxia Jin and Jeffery Lotspiech

IBM Almaden Research Center,
San Jose, CA, 95120
{jin, lotspiech}@us.ibm.com

Abstract. Copyrighted materials are divided into multiple segments
and each segment has multiple variations that are differently watermarked and encrypted. The combination of watermark and encryption
enables one to identify the actual users (traitors) who have engaged in
the piracy. In this paper, we shall present a traitor tracing scheme that
can efficiently and flexibly defend against anonymous attacks.

1 Introduction

This paper is concerned with content protection in a one-to-many type of
distribution system, for example, a pay-per-view TV system or for prere-
corded/recordable media. The security threat is a Napster-style "anonymous"
attack which comes in two forms. An attacker redigitizes the analogue output
from a device and redistributes the unprotected content (content attack). Or the
attacker extracts the decryption keys from the device and sells them on demand
(title key attack).

For both types of anonymous attack the only way to trace the users (traitors)
who engaged in the piracy is to use different versions for different users. The content is divided into multiple segments and each segment has multiple variations.
Each variation is differently watermarked and encrypted with a different key.
The keys are assigned such that any given device has access to only one variation for each segment. After recovering enough unauthorized copies of different
content, the scheme can determine the traitors.

Our scheme systematically allocates the variations based on an error-
correcting code. Furthermore, we concatenate codes [1]. In our construction,
variations in each segment are assigned following an inner code, which are then
encoded using an outer code. We call the nested code the *super code*. This super
code avoids the bandwidth problem by having a small number of variations at
any single point. For example, suppose both inner and outer codes are Reed-
Solomon codes. For the inner code, we can choose 16 variations at each of the 15
segments and hamming distance being 14. This effectively creates 256 versions
per movie. For the outer code, we can use 256 versions per movie throughout the
255 movie sequence and have a Hamming distance 252. This example can accommodate more than 4 billion users. and the extra bandwidth needed is about
10% of the bandwidth needed for a normal 2 hour movie. These parameters fit
very well in a practical setting.

J. Dittmann, S. Katzenbeisser, and A. Uhl (Eds.): CMS 2005, LNCS 3677, pp. 269–270, 2005.

2   A Flexible Scheme

Each device is assigned 255 keys, namely "sequence keys", from a key matrix with 255 columns and 256 rows, exactly one key from each column. Each key correponds to one movie in the sequence. It can be used to decrypt one of the 256 tables, each containing the encrypted 15 variant keys for that movie. The scheme can be flexible during deployment because only the outer code needs to be fixed to assign the sequence keys when the devices are manufactured. The inner code and those variant encrypting keys, even the necessity of an inner code are movie-by-movie decisions that can be delayed to the movie distribution time.

We improve our scheme by extending the number of rows in the key matrix for the sequence key assignment. For example, each sequence key comes with 1024 versions in the world even though there are only 256 versions per movie created from the inner code. Then there would be 1024 variant encrypting key tables. To keep this number at 256, we can use an array to index every 4 sequence keys into the same key k_i which is randomly chosen to encrypt the table i. Each k_i is encrypted with 4 sequence keys. The only overhead is the array of 1024 entries, which is negligible compared to the storage of a high-definition movie.

With this extension, we improve the flexibility of the inner code. It now can accommodate an inner code that creates more than 256 versions. The extension also achieves better traceability for key tracing. Intuitively with every recovered movie with q variations, we can trace down to $1/q$ of the population, assuming there is only a single user involved in the attack. A larger q means faster tracing.

Another important benefit of the extension is that the length of the movie sequence is in effect increased, without increasing the number of keys in each device. After 255 movies in our example, the scheme starts reusing columns. The attackers, noticing this, should use the same variation in a new movie that they previously used in an older movie at the same point in the sequence (column). This tactic would give tracing agency no new information from the new movie. But with our extension, the grouping of four sequence keys to each variation can be reshuffled in a new sequence of movies. The tactic at least reveals which of the possible four sequence keys the attackers have had in the first sequence.

Yet another important benefit of the extension is the improvement of the scheme's overall resistance to attacks. Every time the attacker redistributes keys, fewer keys remained in the system are useful for the future. When the number of exposed keys is big enough, the system is broken. Suppose the movies are randomly being attacked, a simple combinatorial analysis tells us that it takes $q \log q$ movies to expose all the q versions of keys in each column in the key matrix with high probability. Apparently, the extended scheme with a larger q can survive longer. As future work, we are continually interested in overcoming the practical barriers to bring the work to real practice.

Reference

1. H. Jin, J.Lotspiech and S.Nusser, "Traitor tracing for prerecorded and recordable media", ACM DRM workshop, Oct. 2004.

Efficient Key Distribution for Closed Meetings in the Internet

Fuwen Liu and Hartmut Koenig

Brandenburg University of Technology Cottbus,
Department of Computer Science,
PF 10 33 44, 03013 Cottbus, Germany
{lfw, koenig}@informatik.tu-cottbus.de

Abstract. Many emerging group oriented and collaborative applications such as audio/video conferences use the peer-to-peer paradigm. Confidentiality is an often demanded feature for such applications, e.g. in business meetings, to provide group privacy. To assure confidentiality in a meeting the partners have to agree upon a common secret key for encrypting their communication. This requires efficient distributed group key exchange protocols. We present the principle of the key distribution protocol TKD which achieves a lower key refreshment delay compared to existing key exchange protocols.

1 Motivation

In order to assure confidentiality in a peer-to-peer (P2P) meeting the partners have to agree upon a common secret key for encrypting their communication. It is intuitive that a decentralized key management protocol in which the members themselves manage the group key renewal should be deployed in P2P systems. In particular, real-time settings strongly require efficient decentralized key exchange protocols.

In this contribution we sketch the principle of a novel distributed key distribution protocol, called TKD (*token based key distribution*), which has been designed for small dynamic peer groups to support a secure and efficient group key renewal. Unlike other protocols it also provides a mutual authentication of the partners when entering the group. We focus on closed dynamic peer groups of less than 100 participants here. The entrance is by invitation. Many every-day life meetings such as business talks have usually a considerably smaller number of participants.

Decentralized group key management protocols can be divided into two groups: group key agreement and group key distribution protocols [1]. Among the group key agreement protocols, TGDH has proven to be the most efficient one [1], whereas the protocol of Rodeh et al. provides the best performance of existing key distribution protocols [2]. Both protocols, however, are not efficient enough for small group settings. TGDH intensively utilizes asymmetrical cryptographic computations. The Rodeh protocol requires two communication rounds. TKD is a group distribution protocol which has been proven more efficient than the both mentioned ones. It has been integrated in our P2P conference system BRAVIS [3]. TKD requires like other decentralized key management protocols an underlying group communication protocol with virtual synchrony.

J. Dittmann, S. Katzenbeisser, and A. Uhl (Eds.): CMS 2005, LNCS 3677, pp. 271–272, 2005.
© IFIP International Federation for Information Processing 2005

2 Principle of TKD

TKD is a token based protocol. The group members form a logical ring. The rotating token determines the group member responsible for generating a new group key and for distributing it to the members. The group key is renewed whenever the group composition changes (join, leave, and failure of peers). The token holder is further the group member who authenticates the joining partners using the IKEv2 protocol [4].

The group key renewal is based on the Diffie-Hellman (DH) key exchange principle [5]. When the token holder has generated a new group key it establishes a temporary secure channel to each member to deliver the new key. For this, each group member stores a shared DH secret with each other member. To set up the channels it uses the shared DH secrets and a newly generated nonce which is only valid for this group key renewal cycle. The Figure 1 shows the principle.

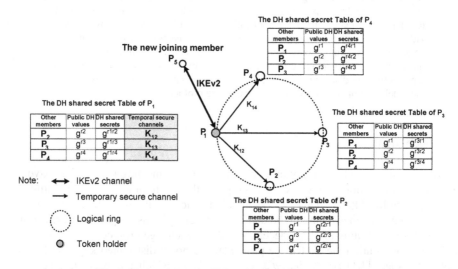

Fig. 1. Key exchange in TKD with temporal secure channels

The efficiency gain of TKD results from the main use of symmetric cryptographic operations and only one communication round for the group key renewal. Thus TKD considerably reduces the group key refreshment delay compared to TGDH and the Rodeh protocol.

References

1. Y. Kim, A. Perrig, and G. Tsudik: Tree-based Group Key Agreement. ACM Transactions on Information Systems Security (TISSEC) 7 (2004) 1, pp.60-96.
2. O. Rodeh, K. P. Birman, D. Dolev: Optimized Group Rekey for Group Communication Systems. Network and Distributed System Security Symposium 2000(NDSS'00), pp. 39-48.
3. The BRAVIS video conference system. http://www.bravis.tu-cottbus.de.
4. C. Kaufman: Internet Key Exchange (IKEv2) Protocol, draft-ietf-ipsec-ikev2-17.txt, September, 2004.
5. E. Rescorla: Diffie-Hellman Key Agreement Method. RFC 2631, June 1999.

Blind Statistical Steganalysis of Additive Steganography Using Wavelet Higher Order Statistics

Taras Holotyak[1], Jessica Fridrich[1], and Sviatoslav Voloshynovskiy[2]

[1] Department of Electrical and Computer Engineering, State University of New York at Binghamton, Binghamton, NY, 13902-6000, USA
{holotyak, fridrich}@binghamton.edu
[2] Department of Computer Science, University of Geneva, 24 rue Général Dufour, 1211 Geneva 4, Switzerland
svolos@cui.unige.ch

Development of digital communications systems significantly extended possibility to perform covert communications (steganography). This recalls an emerging demand in highly efficient counter-measures, i.e. steganalysis methods. Modern steganography is presented by a broad spectrum of various data-hiding techniques. Therefore development of corresponding steganalysis methods is rather a complex problem and challenging task. Moreover, in many practical steganalysis tasks second Kerckhoff's principle is not applicable because of absence of information about the used steganography method. This motivates to use blind steganalysis, which can be applied to the certain techniques where one can specify at least statistics of the hidden data. This paper focuses on the class of supervised steganalysis techniques developed for the additive steganography, which can be described as $y = f(x, s, K) = x + g(s, K)$, where stego image y is obtained from the cover image x by adding a low-amplitude cover image independent (± 1 embedding also known as LSB matching) or cover image dependent (LSB embedding) stego signals that may be also depended on secret stego key K and the secret data s. The function $g(.)$ represents the embedding rule.

The proposed method provides the stochastic interpretation of the blind steganalysis and consists of two main stages, i.e., data preprocessing and feature extraction. The data preprocessing targets at stego signal estimation that is performed in the wavelet domain from the mixture of cover image (presented by non-stationary Gaussian model) and stego signal (presented by stationary Gaussian model). Feature extraction is realized using model-based (polynomial) approximation of stego image pdf. In this case polynomial coefficients, which simultaneously are high order statistics, have created the feature set. Because the features are calculated from the estimated stego signal, they are more sensitive to steganographic modifications while suppressing the influence of the cover image.

The proposed method is tested on various classes of images that are known to pose problems for steganalysis – never compressed raw images from digital cameras. We test the methodology on the ± 1 embedding paradigm and LSB embedding. On raw grayscale digital camera images for ± 1 embedding, we obtained reliable detection results for message lengths above 0.5 bits per pixel (Fig. 1). For images coming from a homogenous source, such as raw grayscale images obtained using a single camera, relatively reliable detection is even possible at the embedding rate of 0.25 bits per pixel (for ± 1 embedding).

J. Dittmann, S. Katzenbeisser, and A. Uhl (Eds.): CMS 2005, LNCS 3677, pp. 273 – 274, 2005.

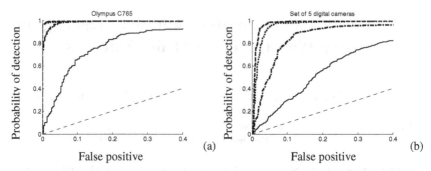

Fig. 1. ROCs for ±1 embedding for a single camera (Olympus C765) (a) and set of 5 digital cameras (Canon G2, Canon S40, Kodak DC290, Olympus C765, and Nikon D100) (b) with different embedding capacity: solid = 0.25 bits per pixel (bpp), dash-dotted = 0.5 bpp, dotted = 0.75 bbp, dashed = 1 bpp

The detection performance in decompressed JPEGs embedded with both cover image dependent and independent methods was nearly perfect even for embedding rates of 0.15 bits per pixel (Fig. 2).

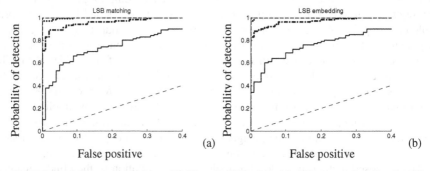

Fig. 2. ROCs for LSB matching (a) and LSB embedding (b) with different embedding capacity: solid = 0.05 bits per pixel (bpp), dash-dotted = 0.1 bpp, dotted = 0.15 bbp, dashed = 0.25 bpp in decompressed JPEG images

Acknowledgment

The work on this paper was supported by Air Force Research Laboratory, Air Force Material Command, USAF, under a research grant number F30602-02-2-0093 and FA8750-04-1-0112 (T. Holotyak and J. Fridrich) and Swiss National Foundation Professorship grant No PP002-68653/1 (S. Voloshynovskiy). The U.S. Government is authorized to reproduce and distribute reprints for Governmental purposes notwithstanding any copyright notation there on. The views and conclusions contained herein are those of the authors and should not be interpreted as necessarily representing the official policies, either expressed or implied, of Air Force Research Laboratory, or the U.S. Government. Authors would like to thank to Miroslav Goljan for many useful discussions.

Applying LR Cube Analysis to JSteg Detection

Kwangsoo Lee, Changho Jung, Sangjin Lee, HyungJun Kim, and Jongin Lim

Center for Information Security Technologies, Korea University, Korea
kslee@cist.korea.ac.kr

Abstract. JSteg is a steganographic method for JPEG images that can be viewed as LSB steganography. Recently, we proposed a new principle to detect the use of LSB steganography in digitized vector signals and showed how to apply it to gray-scale images. In this paper, we discuss how to apply it to JPEG images and show some experimental results for the JSteg-like algorithm.

Introduction: JSteg-like algorithm [1] is a steganographic method for JPEG images. It works by replacing the LSBs (least significant bits) of quantized DCT (discrete cosine transform) coefficients excepting the values of '0' and '1' with message bits. Thus, the JSteg-like algorithm can be viewed as the LSB steganography with an exception for usable DCT coefficients. Recently, we proposed the LR cube analysis to detect the use of LSB steganography in RGB color images [2]. It used RGB vectors as basic units and took advantage of the local correlation of these vectors. In [3], we described its general framework to use n-dimensional vectors as basic units for the applications to various types of digital signals and showed how to apply it to gray-scale images. So far, we have been working on the task whether the LR cube analysis can be applied to detect the JSteg-like algorithm for JPEG images; the answer is yes. This paper shows the method of how to apply the LR cube analysis for detecting the usage of JSteg-like algorithm.

Method Description and Experimental Results: Fig. 1 and Fig. 2 show the two basic ideas of the LR cube analysis. Fig. 1 represents the two types of comparable sets in Z^3 under the LSB embedding, where the δ is a positive odd integer and the two-sided arrows represent the possible changes of the vectors by LSB embedding. Given a vector signal, the sets can be classified into their complexities as shown in Fig. 2, where the complexity of a set means the number of different vectors contained in the set. We observed that the left and right δ-cubes are similarly distributed on their complexities before the LSB embedding, but the left (or right) δ-cubes' complexities tend to decrease (or increase) after the LSB embedding, respectively. The LR cube analysis measures a dissimilarity between their complexities by a well-known hypothesis test: the χ^2-test.

For the application of the LR cube analysis to JPEG format, we have investigated various kinds of vector samplings from the DCT coefficients. As a result, we developed the $(x, y; i, j)$ sampling; x and y indicate the numbers of joint blocks in x and y directions, and also, i and j indicate the numbers of joint

J. Dittmann, S. Katzenbeisser, and A. Uhl (Eds.): CMS 2005, LNCS 3677, pp. 275–276, 2005.
© IFIP International Federation for Information Processing 2005

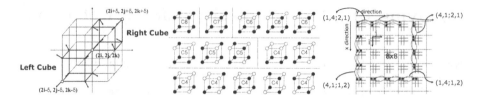

Fig. 1. LR cube model   **Fig. 2.** Cube complexities   **Fig. 3.** Vector sampling

coefficients in i and j directions of each jointed JPEG block, respectively. The vectors drawn by the $(x, y; i, j)$ sampling have the dimension $n = xyij$. Fig. 3 illustrates some of the efficient vector sampling.

The proposed method has been tested on the 518 uncompressed JPEG images of CBIR image database of Washington University [4] with their compressed images of 75%, and 50% qualities in order to take into consideration the quantization effect on the DCT coefficients. We embedded random messages into Y component data of the images by JSteg-like algorithm, where the message lengths are 5% and 10% of the capacity of each image.

We drew the 8-dimensional vectors from the Y component data by the (1,4; 1,2) and (1,4;2,1) samplings, and set the δ equal to 3. The below table shows the detecting performances of our method for each image set, when the decision thresholds of p-values were set to have the false positives about 0% and 5%. The most interesting result is that our method highly detected the low-rate embedding by the JSteg-like algorithm, even if it did not show any false detections.

Image quality	Decision threshold	Embedding rate			Decision threshold	Embedding rate		
		0%	5%	10%		0%	5%	10%
100%	0.99	0.000	0.602	0.940	0.58	0.464	0.830	0.995
75%	0.91	0.000	0.450	0.987	0.40	0.046	0.857	0.998
50%	0.89	0.000	0.419	0.960	0.47	0.043	0.757	0.990

Acknowledgements: This research was supported by the Ministry of Information and Communication (MIC), Korea, under the Information Technology Research Center (ITRC) support program supervised by the Institute of Information Technology Assessment (IITA).

References

1. D. Upham, http://www.funet.fi/pub/crypt/stegangraphy/jpeg-jsteg-v4.diff.gz.
2. K. Lee, C. Jung, S. Lee, and J. Lim, "Color Cube Anlysis for Detection of LSB Steganography in RGB Color Images", ICCSA 2005, LNCS vol. 3481, Springer-Verlag, Berlin Heidelberg, 2005, pp. 537–546.
3. K. Lee, C. Jung, S. Lee, and J. Lim: "New Steganalysis Methodology: LR Cube Analysis for the Detection of LSB Steganography", accepted to the *7th Information Hiding Workshop*, Barcelona, Spain, June 6-8, 2005.
4. http://www.cs.washington.edu/research/imagedatabase/groundtruth.

Digital Signatures Based on Invertible Watermarks for Video Authentication

Enrico Hauer[1], Jana Dittmann[2], and Martin Steinebach[1]

[1] Fraunhofer Institute IPSI, Dolivostr. 15, 64293 Darmstadt, Germany
Enrico.hauer@ipsi.fraunhofer.de
[2] Otto-von-Guericke-Unversity, Multimedia and Security Lab (AMSL),
Universitätsplatz 2, 39016 Magdeburg, Germany
Jana.dittmann@iti.cs.uni-magdeburg.de

1 Security Demands and Solution

For verification and authentication of the video material and recovery of the original video several security mechanisms are required. The security techniques to realize this solution are introduced in [1]:

1. The verification of the integrity is verified by hash functions.
2. Authenticity is verified by digital signatures using asymmetric cryptography and hash functions. The introduced scheme from [1] uses RSA signatures. The private key of the digital signature mechanism is used to sign the data and the corresponding public key is used for verification of the encrypted data. If the data can be verified the corresponding private key was used for the digital signature generation and the data seems to be authentic as well integer.
3. Furthermore the original content can be reproduced by inverting of the watermark with the well know techniques of Fridrich et al. [2]. Additional secret key cryptography (symmetric crypt function) protects the reproduction. The invertibility is necessary, because we use a digital watermark to embed the authentication message and signature into the media itself. Digital watermark, in this application fragile watermark, changes the data and the original data cannot be reconstructing. To invert the data, the watermark must be removed and the original data reconstructed. The watermark embeds the information into a non visual or acoustical channel of the data after the original data of the channel were compressed and encrypted. The compression realizes the new space for the watermark consisting of the encrypted selected data and security information.

2 Invertible Watermark for Video Material

In this paper we demonstrate the watermark information for one picture P of the video because the frame index as a part of the information is changed from picture to picture. The picture index controls the order of the frames.

The picture data are split into selected data $P_{selected}$ and remaining data $P_{remaining}$. The selected data are compressed and encrypted symmetrically with the secret

J. Dittmann, S. Katzenbeisser, and A. Uhl (Eds.): CMS 2005, LNCS 3677, pp. 277 – 279, 2005.

key $K_{sec\,ret}$. A following encryption establishes the dependency of the encrypted data from with the remaining data $P_{remaining}$. The selected data can only be recovered with no changes at the remaining data. After the decryption of the selected data the integrity of selected data are verified with a message authentication code HMAC with secret key $K_{sec\,ret}$. The public authentication of the picture data is realized with a RSA signature, because the signature can be check by the public key K_{public}.

The complete watermark information can be summarized to the following form:

$$W = E_{AES}\left(E_{AES}\left(C_{P_{selected}}, K_{sec\,ret}\right)K_{H}\left(P_{remaining}\right)\right)$$

$$+Index(P)$$

$$+MAC_{HMAC}((P_{selected} + Index(P)), K_{sec\,ret})$$

$$+S_{RSA}(H(P_{remaining} + Index(P))$$

$$+E_{AES}(E_{AES}(C_{P_{selected}}, K_{sec\,ret}), K(_{H(P_{remaining})})$$

$$+MAC_{HMAC}((P_{selected} + Index(P)), K_{sec\,ret})), K_{private}) \qquad (1)$$

Figure 1 demonstrates the embedding procedure. The LSB bits of the blue chrominance values at the DCT block position (5, 5) are the selected data and compressed by RLE to produce the free space to embed the watermark.

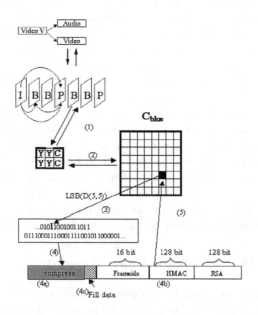

Fig. 1. Watermark embedding procedure

References

1. J. Dittmann., M. Steinebach, L. Ferri. Watermarking protocols for authentication and ownership protection based on timestamps and holograms. In: Proceedings of SPIE Vol. 4675, Security and Watermarking of Multimedia Contents IV, pp.240 - 251, San-Jose, January, ISBN 0-8194-4415-4, 2002
2. J. Fridrich, M. Golian, R.Du: Lossless Data Embedding – New Paradigm in Digital Watermarking, Special Issue on Emerging Applications of Multimedia Data Hiding, Vol. 2002, No.2, February 2002, pp. 185–196

A Theoretical Framework for Data-Hiding
in Digital and Printed Text Documents

R. Villán, S. Voloshynovskiy, F. Deguillaume, Y. Rytsar,
O. Koval, E. Topak, E. Rivera, and T. Pun

Computer Vision and Multimedia Laboratory - University of Geneva,
24, rue du Général-Dufour - 1211 Geneva 4, Switzerland
svolos@cui.unige.ch

In this work, we consider the text data-hiding problem as a particular instance of the well-known Gel'fand-Pinsker problem [1]. The text, where some message $m \in \mathcal{M}$ is to be hidden, is represented by $\mathbf{x}$ and called cover text. Each component x_i, $i = 1, 2, \ldots, N$, of $\mathbf{x}$ represents one character from this text. Here, we define a character as an element from a given language alphabet (e.g. the latin alphabet $\{A, B, \ldots, Z\}$). To be more precise, we conceive each character x_i as a data structure consisting of multiple component fields (features): *name*, *shape*, *position*, *orientation*, *size*, *color*, etc.

Assuming the knowledge of the conditional probability distribution $p(u|x)$, $|\mathcal{M}||\mathcal{J}|$ codewords $\mathbf{u}$ are generated independently at random and located into $|\mathcal{M}|$ bins, each of them with $|\mathcal{J}|$ codewords. Once generated, the codebook is revealed to both the encoder and the decoder. Given m to be communicated, the encoder produces the watermark $\mathbf{w}$ by finding first a jointly strongly typical pair $(\mathbf{x}, \mathbf{u}(m, j))$, where $\mathbf{u}(m, j)$ is the j-th codeword inside the bin corresponding to m, and then, by using a deterministic mapping $\mathbf{w} = \varphi^N(\mathbf{x}, \mathbf{u})$. The influence of the channel $p(v|w, x)$ is divided in two stages. In the first stage, $\mathbf{w}$ and $\mathbf{x}$ are combined via a deterministic mapping $\psi^N(\mathbf{w}, \mathbf{x})$ to give the stego text $\mathbf{y}$. In the second stage, $\mathbf{y}$ may suffer from some intentional or unintentional distortions. We denote by $\mathbf{v}$ the resulting distorted version of $\mathbf{y}$. Finally, $\mathbf{v}$ is fed to the decoder, which tries to obtain an estimate $\hat{m}$ of message m by using the jointly strongly typical decoding rule.

As a particular example of the Gel'fand-Pinsker scheme, let us consider the Scalar Costa Scheme (SCS) [2] where the stego text Y is obtained as $Y = W + X = \alpha' Q_m(X) + (1 - \alpha')X$, where $Q_m(\cdot)$ is a scalar quantizer corresponding to m and α' is a compensation parameter. For a practical implementation based on the SCS, we only need to select a character feature (e.g. color), and use it as the cover character X. We show in Fig. 1 the resulting SCS codebook and an illustration of how to use it for text data-hiding.

Based on the above framework, we propose two new methods for text data-hiding: *color quantization* and *halftone quantization*. The exploited character features are, respectively, *color* and *halftone pattern* (see Fig. 2). The main idea of these methods is to quantize the character feature in such a manner that the human visual system is not able to distinguish between the original and quantized characters, but it is still possible to do it by a specialized reader, e.g. a high dynamic range and/or high resolution scanner in the case of printed

J. Dittmann, S. Katzenbeisser, and A. Uhl (Eds.): CMS 2005, LNCS 3677, pp. 280–281, 2005.

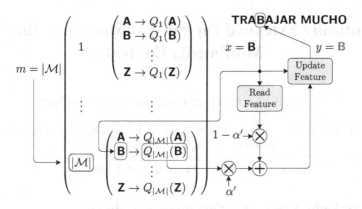

Fig. 1. SCS text data-hiding

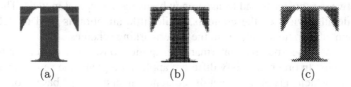

Fig. 2. Halftone quantization: (a) original character; (b) marked character for $m = 0$, screen angle $= 0°$; (c) marked character for $m = 1$, screen angle $= 45°$

documents. In particular, we show that the color quantization method works both for digital and printed documents, has high information embedding rate, is perceptually invisible, and is fully automatable.

Acknowledgment

This work was partially supported by the SNSF professorship grant no. PP002-68653/1, the IM2 project, and the European Commission through the programs IST-2002-507932 ECRYPT and FP6-507609 SIMILAR. The information in this document reflects only the author's views, is provided as is and no guarantee or warranty is given that the information is fit for any particular purpose. The user thereof uses the information at its sole risk and liability.

References

1. Gel'fand, S., Pinsker, M.: Coding for channel with random parameters. Problems of Control and Information Theory **9** (1980) 19–31
2. Eggers, J., Su, J., Girod, B.: A blind watermarking scheme based on structured codebooks. In: Secure Images and Image Authentication, IEE Colloquium, London, UK (2000) 4/1–4/6

Semantically Extended Digital Watermarking Model for Multimedia Content

Huajian Liu, Lucilla Croce Ferri, and Martin Steinebach

Fraunhofer IPSI - Integrated Publication and Information Systems Institute,
Dolivostr. 15, 64293 Darmstadt, Germany
{liu, ferri, steinebach}@ipsi.fraunhofer.de
http://www.ipsi.fraunhofer.de/merit/

1 Semantically Extended Watermarking Model

Most current watermarking algorithms utilize syntactic features to achieve a good tradeoff between robustness and transparency by using perceptual models. They focus only on a detailed view of the contents, while little attention is paid to define and apply the semantic content features in the watermarking schemes.

However, in some specific watermarking applications, such current approaches show their limits. In order to satisfy different application goals, the semantic structure of the data, which gives an overall content understanding based on specific application goals, has to be taken into account as a fundamental part in the design of the watermark scheme. The concept of "region of interest" (ROI) has been integrated into specific watermarking algorithms, where the semantic meaning of a ROI depends strongly on the type and goals of the targeted application.

In this paper we propose an extended watermarking model based on semantic content understanding and illustrate its advantages. In the proposed model, the semantic and syntactic features in content understanding correspond respectively to different layers of the watermarking system, the application layer and the algorithm layer. On the first layer, the application decides the important levels of different regions of the content. Combined with content understanding, a content classification process is applied according to the retrieved underlying semantic features, in which the content is segmented into regions of more or less interest. Based on the importance levels, watermarks are embedded into different regions respectively, which are controlled by a visual model obtained from the syntactic features. The watermark messages could also be related to the different regions according to the specific application field. In the watermark detection process, the regions of various interests are obtained again by the content understanding and targeted application goals. The watermarks can then be retrieved from every watermarked region.

2 Advantages of the Semantically Extended Watermarking Model

First, the proposed semantically extended watermarking model can help in solving some open technical issues in the digital watermarking field. One of them is the resynchronization of watermark information during the detection process after geometric transformations. By applying a semantic content retrieval, the watermark

J. Dittmann, S. Katzenbeisser, and A. Uhl (Eds.): CMS 2005, LNCS 3677, pp. 282–283, 2005.

detection algorithm can refer to the detected ROI positions, dramatically reducing the searching range and time and even directly finding the synchronization points. Another example can be an alternative solution to the problem of the permanent loss of data fidelity, caused by the most watermarking algorithms. For some special applications, extremely high fidelity requirements are specified. By applying image content understanding, different regions of an image can be identified with various importance levels, depending on the different application goals. The watermark can be embedded into the less important parts, avoiding affecting the fidelity of the most important parts, while the latter can still be protected by properly designing the watermarking scheme.

Furthermore, besides solving some technical issues, the "classical" functionality of digital watermarking can be extended by applying content understanding. For robust watermarking, such as copyright protection, the semantic watermarking model can enable the protection of specific objects with selective robustness to attacks, making object-based protection possible. For content integrity watermarking, semantic authentication can be achieved instead of only pixel-wise verification. Multiple security levels can be defined based on ROI specifications according to the different application goals.

As an application example, in our semantic watermarking scheme for human face images authentication [1], we consider human faces as objects of most interest and provide semantic protection with multiple levels of security in different regions. The application goal determines that the integrity of the face regions must be particularly ensured, including the position and quantity. A content understanding tool, the face detection algorithm [2], is applied to segment face regions from the background automatically. An authentication loop, embedded into the face regions, is defined to link all the faces together, while the background watermarks contain the total number of faces in the scene. In the watermark detection process, with the help of the located faces, the watermark synchronization can be achieved by an efficient local search even after slight background cropping. The highest security level is given to face regions and any adding, moving, changing and deleting faces are not allowed and will render the image unauthenticated. Background security level is lower compared to the face security. Content changing manipulations, caused by the common post processing, are allowed in the background, such as visual annotation and slight background cropping. Such semantic watermarking and multiple security levels partially enable to trace manipulations and to identify some kinds of attacks, which can help to infer the attacker's motives.

References

1. H. Liu, H. Sahbi, L. C. Ferri, M. Steinebach: Advanced Authentication of Face Images. In Proceeding of WIAMIS 2005, Montreux, Switzerland, April, 2005
2. H. Sahbi, D. Geman, N. Boujemaa: Face Detection Using Coarse-to-fine Support Vector Classifiers. In Proc. of the IEEE Inter. Conf. on Image Processing, 2002, pp. 925–928

An Architecture for Secure Policy Enforcement in E-Government Services Deployment

Nikolaos Oikonomidis, Sergiu Tcaciuc, and Christoph Ruland

Institute for Data Communication Systems, University of Siegen
{nikolaos.oikonomidis, sergiu.tcaciuc,
christoph.ruland}@uni-siegen.de

1 Introduction

Citizens interact at regular intervals with municipalities or municipal organizations. Public administrations offer a variety of services like requests/processing of certificates and (local) tax payment. An effective and efficient service provision brings benefits to both municipalities and the involved citizens/customers of a particular service. Due to the fact that exchanged data in forms and documents may contain private or/and sensitive data, it is imperative to introduce security mechanisms that guarantee to citizens a trustworthy means of communication via a network that may be insecure, such as the Internet. Further, cross-border services involve different municipalities and other public authorities in the processes. The described work is derived from research for "eMayor", a project funded by the EU committee. eMayor addresses the specific audience of Small and Medium sized Governmental Organizations (SMGOs) across Europe. The project looks especially at transactions that are performed on a European level. This paper focuses on an architecture for secure policy enforcement within eGovernment platforms, such as the eMayor platform.

2 Secure Policy Enforcement

The approach chosen for modeling the overall architecture of eMayor relies on the Reference Model of Open Distributed Processing (RM-ODP) [1]. At first, the identified requirements together with the legal frameworks formed the Enterprise Viewpoint. This viewpoint resulted into a specification of a community of the platform users and the respective business objects that derive from the community specification. The identified scenarios have been converted into processes. The Information Viewpoint has presented and analyzed various information objects that exist in the eMayor context and the relations between them. Additionally, since Information Objects pass from various states through their life-cycle, their respective state transitions have been specified as well. The interaction between system components on the functional level and their respective interfaces have been described in the Computational Viewpoint. Engineering and Technology Viewpoints have been placed in the implementation phase.

The system design resulted into the specification of an architecture as a set of modules, each one comprising certain functionalities. *User Interface* handles the interaction of the user with the eMayor platform, required for the actual processing of the

J. Dittmann, S. Katzenbeisser, and A. Uhl (Eds.): CMS 2005, LNCS 3677, pp. 284–285, 2005.
© IFIP International Federation for Information Processing 2005

service. *Service Handling* represents the core of the system and has dependencies to all other modules. *Format Transformation* is responsible for transforming legal documents from a country-bound local format to a universal format for use within the eMayor environment and vice versa. *Content Routing* provides the routing functionality for forwarding requests and legal documents from one municipality to another. *Municipal Systems Adaptation* is the linking point to the existing (legacy) systems of the municipalities. *Persistent Storage* handles data storage to databases. *Output Notification and Printing* provide support for notification and printing services. Finally, *Policy Enforcement* encapsulates the enforcement of a series of functionalities which are defined in municipal policies. Such functionalities include, e.g., auditing, access control, digital signature verification and other security mechanisms. Within the Information Viewpoint, a policy information object has been specified. Such a policy object represents the constraints, conditions, and rules that have to be respected and enforced by the platform. *Security Services Policy* implements the security services that are required. *Access Control Policy* regulates access control to the requested municipal services. *Audit Policy* controls how actions are recorded in the system for auditing purposes. *Policy Subject* represents the entity which will invoke one or more *Policy Action* objects. A *Policy Action* may take effect on a *Policy Object*. The result of a *Policy Action* or even one ore more *Policy Objects* are related to the *Policy Target*. One or more *Policy Pre Condition*, *Policy Condition* and *Policy Post Condition* objects control the invocation of one or more *Policy Action* objects depending on the policy type. A subject of research is modeling of policies that control the secure execution of the municipal services. In other terms, a *Service Execution Policy* will define the steps that have to be taken during the system's operation regarding the required security services and the pre-/post conditions that should be fulfilled.

Policy Enforcement is implemented in the policy enforcement module, which resides in the eMayor platform of each municipality. Components of the policy enforcement module comprise different sets of functionalities in order to enforce the appropriate policies. *Policy Enforcement Management* is the component that exposes the module's functionality as a set of "enforcer" interfaces. *Policy Evaluation* component contains all elements which are responsible for taking a decision if a request or functionality complies to the appropriate policy, whereas *Policy Retrieval* component queries the respective policy repositories and retrieves the appropriate policy. The model of the components and their communication within the policy enforcement package derives from the XACML specification [2]. The current research objective is to provide an extension to XACML for enforcement of other types of policies apart from access control policies.

References

1. Information technology, Open Distributed Processing - Reference Model: Architecture, ISO, 1996
2. Core Specification, eXtensible Access Control Markup Language (XACML) Version 2.0, OASIS, 2005

Some Critical Aspects of the PKIX TSP

Cristian Marinescu and Nicolae Tapus

University "Politehnica" Bucharest, Romania
cristian.marinescu@omicron.at, ntapus@cs.pub.ro

Abstract. Authentication, non-repudiation, and digital signatures, require the ability to determine if a data token existed at a certain moment in time when the creator's credentials were valid. Time-stamps are tokens which contain a verifiable cryptographic link between a time value and a data representation. The paper presents some critical aspects of the X.509 Public Key Infrastructure Time Stamp Protocol, trying to suggest some possible improvements to the protocol.

Keywords: PKI, security, time-stamp, TSA, PKIX TSP.

1 The PKIX Time Stamp Protocol

In an effort to solve some of the current security problems, many security solutions and services require the ability to establish the existence of data at a certain moment in time. Time-stamps (TSs) are a digital solution to this problem, providing the proof that the signed data existed prior to the indicated time. The Time Stamping Authority (TSA) is the trusted third party (TTP) that generates the digital TS and guarantees that the time parameter is correct. TSs can indicate weather or not an electronic signature was generated before the private key expired or was compromised, non-repudiation and authenticity beeing guaranteed if this is the case [6]. The moment when the document was time-stamped is also an important part of the requirement to present undeniable information about who, what and *when* e-documents were issued, in order to be used in a court of law [5].

RFC3161 specifies a simple time-stamp scheme based on digital signatures and a typical client-server architecture. The PKIX TSP specifies the format of the packets, along with some possible transport protocols and some verifications to be done by the server and by the client. The communication mechanism consists of a one-step transaction: the TSP client sends a request to the TSA; the server has to check, upon receiving a packet, that it contains a valid TS request, and to send a valid TS token back [1]. The requester has the responsibility to verify that the received TS token is what it has requested. The verifier does not have to be the same as the requester, any third party may check the TS. In case of a dispute, the claimer has to provide the TS, to prove that the data existed at the specified moment. It should also be noted that this does not prove sole possession or origination of the data, other mechanisms should be used in conjunction with a TSA to accomplish this task.

J. Dittmann, S. Katzenbeisser, and A. Uhl (Eds.): CMS 2005, LNCS 3677, pp. 286–288, 2005.
© IFIP International Federation for Information Processing 2005

2   Some Critical Aspects of the PKIX TSP

Like many PKI standards, the PKIX TSP does not consider real-life conditions, such as incompatibility problems, software bugs, or the interconnection of software modules. This rather *optimistic* approach can cause security problems, even though a certain abstraction is quite unavoidable in a standardization process. The resulting protocol has been designed to be a part of the PKI, and therefore should not be regarded as a stand-alone solution [3].

RFC3161 suggests several transport protocols that can be used: e-mail, FTP, HTTP, and raw sockets. Unfortunately, the standard specifies more options for the raw sockets solution and disregards the basic rule of network protocols to completely ignore the underlying transport layer. The raw socket polling support is unlikely to simplify any implementation, and just adds unnecessary complexity to the protocol. Under these circumstances, interfacing an HTTP solution to a raw socket implementation is difficult to achieve because the protocol behaves different depending on the transport layer. Since interoperability is in our opinion an important issue, we argue that the next version of the standard should dispense with the polling operations.

The standard contains some questionable *features*, like the *ordering* field or the *policy* information, which can cause problems if implemented like the standard suggests. The main benefit of the *policy* field, like defined by RFC3161, should be the possibility to provide more information about the conditions under which a TS may be used, the availability of a log, etc. Unfortunately, it is neither specified what policies must be provided, nor what the TSA should do under these policies. Another unsolved problem is the procedure to be used for advertising and parsing the supported policies. In order to be able to request a certain policy, the client has to find out the available policies, but at the moment, this has to be solved outside the standard . We suggest to define a frame inside the standard, so that the client could optionally start by parsing first the available policies and other parameters of the TSA.

Another issue is generated by the usage of the *ordering* field in the TS token. If the field is set to true, all TSs generated by the same TSA can be ordered based on the time parameter. Otherwise, ordering the TSs is just possible if the difference of the time parameters is greater than the sum of the accuracies. This is rather a mistake, ordering TSs generated by the same TSA should always be possible, any other approach is not acceptable. Establishing a timeline is an important feature of TS schemes in general. We strongly suggest to avoid the usage of the *ordering* field, any practical implementation should serialize the TS generation process, in order to guarantee the timeline.

The several security considerations specified by RFC3161, are rather thin and insufficient. In case that the key expires or gets compromised, the certificate has to be revoked with a specified reason, but auditing, notarizing or even applying a new signature to all existing TSs is difficult to achieve and a tremendous task to accomplish [4], even if assuming that all the generated TSs have been stored locally (which is normally not required). This still does not solve the problem in case that the private key of the TSA gets compromised, because in most cases it is difficult to find out the exact moment when this happened. In our opinion, a much more simple approach, borrowed from the linking schemes, would be to embed information from the previous generated token in the TS; another solution, borrowed from the distributed schemes, would be to time-stamp the same message digest at two or more different TSAs. A protocol improvement should include this possibility, since this would not just increase the security of the scheme, but also solve one of the biggest PKI problems [2].

In an effort to prevent the *man-in-the-middle* attack, RFC3161 makes an *interesting* recommendation: to consider any response as suspect if it takes too much time between request and reply. We argue that this approach is futile, since the time necessary to process a request is not an indisputable argument for an attack; it can be just the sign of a simple network congestion. The question that also rises is how to define *an acceptable period of time*, since this parameter would be different depending on the transport protocol [4]?

The TS is done on a message digest, having no constraints on the data format, but this apparent simplicity hides another problem when time-stamping CMS digital signatures. As defined, the TS token is placed inside a client's CMS digital signature as an unsigned/unauthenticated attribute within the signer info, with a special OID. Since two different CMS data structures are needed (the one to be signed and the one to place the TS inside), the implementation can be rather complex. RFC3126 tried to solve this problem by extending CMS to include TSs, but we believe that it would have been better if the TSA would have time-stamped not just a hash but also the signature of the requester, if desired [4].

The virtual world of the PKIX TSP does not consider security threats, and interoperability issues. Unfortunately, it is impossible for practical implementations to avoid all the problems presented, if an RFC3161 compliant version is the goal. This is in our opinion the main reason why a second version should improve and correct at least some of these mistakes. Failing to solve them will have negative effects on the acceptance of RFC3161 as the *de facto* time-stamp standard of the Internet.

References

1. Adams, C., et al: RFC3161 Internet X.509 Public Key Infrastructure Time-Stamp Protocol (TSP), ftp://ftp.rfc-editor.org/in-notes/rfc3161.txt (2001)
2. Adams, C. and Lloyd S.: Understanding PKI, Addison-Wesley, NY, USA (2002)
3. Housley, R. and Polk, T.: Planning for PKI - Best Practices Guide for Deploying Public Key Infrastructure, John Wiley & Sons, NY, USA (2001)
4. Marinescu, C., et al: A Case Study of the PKI Time Stamp Protocol Based On A Practical Implementation, in: Proceedings of the CSCS15, Bucharest, (2005)
5. Merill, C.R.: Time is of the Essence, CIO Magazine, http://www.cio.com/archive/031500_fine.html (2000)
6. Pinto, F. and Freitas, V.: Digital Time-stamping to Support Non Repudiation in Electronic Communications, in: Proceedings of the SECURICOM'96, CNIT, Paris, (1996) 397-406

Motivations for a Theoretical Approach to WYSIWYS

Antonio Lioy, Gianluca Ramunno, Marco Domenico Aime, and Massimiliano Pala

Politecnico di Torino, Dip. di Automatica e Informatica,
Corso Duca degli Abruzzi 24, Torino Italy
{lioy, ramunno, m.aime, massimiliano.pala}@polito.it

The statement "What You See Is What You Sign" (WYSIWYS) expresses a functional requirement for digital signatures of electronic documents, in particular when considering legally binding signatures. However this statement is intrinsically wrong. In fact a signer never really sees what he digitally signs, namely the bits of the electronic document, but he sees only one of the possible representations of these bits. This is due to the theory and the technology underlying the actual implementations of the digital signatures. Moreover, while the acronym refers only to the presentation on the signer side, in legal settings the presentation on the recipient side must be also taken into account as well as the relation between the twos.

The current status of research in this field can be summarized as follows. Many different definitions of WYSIWYS can be found and sometime this requirement is described only through some of its supposed effects. Therefore a clear and unambiguous definition of WYSIWYS is still missing. Conversely many security threats related to the document presentation have been described. In addition some theoretical and practical solutions have been proposed to design applications capable to properly present the electronic documents. Anyway many proposals take into account only a subset of the problems to be solved while others guarantee a correct presentation at the price of compromising their usability. We think this is the current situation first because the *exact* requirements for the document presentation on both the signer and the verifier side have not been clearly identified. Then because of the lack of a theoretical and comprehensive model to deal with these requirements. In this short paper we intend to show one of the possible directions the research in this field could move towards.

Fig. 1.1(a) shows a simplified and high level model of a Signature Creation System (SCS). The document bit string is displayed by the Document Presenter (DP), a set of software components and of a hardware device; it is then digitally signed by means of software components and of the Signature Creation Device (SCD), often a hardware device. First, there is the need to guarantee that the input to both the SCD and the DP is exactly the same bit string, that of the document being signed. This can be achieved by designing a proper architecture for the SCS (e.g. CEN-CWA14170). Similar considerations hold on the verifier side about the input to the DP and the Signature Verification Device (SVD) in a Signature Verification System (SVS), see Fig. 1.1(b).

Now, what relation does exist between the bit string to be signed or verified and what the human being reads, namely between the DP input (I_S or I_V) and its output (O_S or O_V)? *What do the signer and the verifier see?* What is really displayed by the DP? We can say that it depends on how the sequence of bits is "interpreted" by the DP. It takes input the document bit string and transforms it into physical quantities that appear as symbols and images meaningful for the human being. Therefore both the signer and verifier always see the result of transformations applied to the document bit

J. Dittmann, S. Katzenbeisser, and A. Uhl (Eds.): CMS 2005, LNCS 3677, pp. 289–290, 2005.
© IFIP International Federation for Information Processing 2005

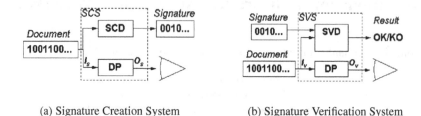

(a) Signature Creation System   (b) Signature Verification System

Fig. 1. Simplified models of a SCS and a SVS

string: the signer sees the DP output (O_S) of the SCS while the verifier sees the DP output (O_V) of the SVS.

Given that, we think that the WYSIWYS functional requirement should be defined as follows: *"the presentations O_S on the signer side and O_V on the verifier side must be semantically equivalent at each verification done by any verifier at anytime after the signature creation and by using any computer system, application or configuration".*

The legal rules for legally valid digital signatures can impose stricter constraints on the document presentation and these constraints may differ from country to country. Anyway we think that, from the functional perspective, the above constraint is the minimum to be met. In our opinion, in fact, there is no need for the two physical presentations to be identical. Moreover this is a goal really difficult to achieve because of the variety of systems and platforms deployed and of their possibly different configurations. An example of different physical presentations with the same semantic is given by the use of the fax machine. An order placed by fax is not to be invalidated simply because on the recipient side the quality is lower than on the sender side, if it is possible to verify that the received document is semantically complete and unambiguous. Thus imposing the same physical presentation would be an oversized constraint. Instead, the use of a less featured DP on the recipient side should be possible.

Let F_S be the sequence of transformations done by the DP over the document bits on the signer side, then $O_S = F_S(I_S)$. Let F_V be the sequence of transformations done by the DP on the verifier side, then $O_V = F_V(I_V)$. Let *doc* be the document bit string sent as input to the DP both on the signer and the verifier side and $\overset{sem}{\equiv}$ the semantical equivalence operator. Then the WYSIWYS requirement can be expressed as $F_S(doc) \overset{sem}{\equiv} F_V(doc)$ and this has to be true any time (after the signing time) the F_V transformations are performed and whatever hardware-software platform and configuration is used.

To define the real technical requirements and constraints to be applied to the SCS and SCV architecture in order to satisfy the WYSIWYS requirement as defined above, we need to model the sequences of transformations F_S and F_V. This could be done by defining an abstract model based on the actual hardware-software architectures, by formalizing F_S and F_V in terms of mathematical functions and by studying the properties they must have to satisfy $F_S(doc) \overset{sem}{\equiv} F_V(doc)$ independently from the time when and the platform where the F_V transformations are performed.

Such a theoretical and comprehensive model could be used as a reference to evaluate the trustworthiness of existing applications as well as to design new usable WYSIWYS architectures.

Secure XMaiL or How to Get Rid of Legacy Code in Secure E-Mail Applications

Lars Ewers[1], Wolfgang Kubbilun[2], Lijun Liao[3], and Jörg Schwenk[3]

[1] Alsenstr. 23, 44789 Bochum, Germany
lars.ewers@web.de
[2] MediaSec Technologies GmbH, Berliner Platz 6-8, 45127 Essen, Germany
wkubbilun@mediasec.de
[3] Hörst Görtz Institute for IT Security, Ruhr-University Bochum
{lijun.liao, joerg.schwenk}@rub.de

Abstract. E-mail is one of the oldest applications on the internet. Clients have to adhere to message formats that have been defined in RFC 822 [13] back in 1982, and at the same time be able to transport all types of content. Additionally, there are severe restrictions for the use of both encryption and digital signatures due to the adherence to RFC822. In this paper we propose a new approach based on our XMaiL project: Using the XMaiL parser, we transform header and body of the mail into an XML object. This transformation preserves both the MIME and the PKCS#7 structure of the mail. We describe the security enhancements that are possible using XMaiL such as selective encryption and signature of parts of the e-mail, or signature of critical fields in the header of the mail.

1 Introduction

E-mail and the WWW are the two most important applications on the Internet, but e-mail is much older: RFC 822 [13] dates from August 13th, 1982, and the ASCII-based text format described therein is the basis for all mails sent on the internet today.

E-mail is one of the most dangerous internet applications: it is used to send computer viruses, spyware, malware, SPAM and Phishing mails to users [14]. This is partly due to the fact that mail clients must be able to understand many different data formats specific to e-mail.

Legacy Code. To include more than just text in mails, the "Multipurpose Internet Mail Extension" (MIME, RFC 2045 – 2049, [13]) defined a platform independent way to include arbitrary data in RFC 822 based mails. The different multipart message formats can be used to give mails a tree based structure. Although the basic MIME data types are also used in the http protocol, the structuring of data with multipart types and boundary ASCII sequences is only used in e-mail.

In 1998 MIME was extended to Secure MIME (S/MIME, RFC 2311, 2312, 2630, 2632, 2633 [13]) by introducing new, binary MIME types based on PKCS#7 [12], X.509 [15] and ASN.1 [2]. The interpretation of these binary data types can not be delegated to helper applications, but has to be done by the mail application itself. This

J. Dittmann, S. Katzenbeisser, and A. Uhl (Eds.): CMS 2005, LNCS 3677, pp. 291 – 300, 2005.
© IFIP International Federation for Information Processing 2005

is not a trivial task: After a good start with S/MIME implementations in at least three popular e-mail clients (Netscape Messenger, Microsoft Outlook and Outlook Express), the abandonment of the Messenger 4.x product line by Netscape was a serious drawback. It took the Mozilla project years to come up with a new S/MIME implementation.

OpenPGP (RFC 1847, 3156 [13]) is a valid alternative to S/MIME, but it does not add new security features, and it also increases code complexity because of its binary format.

With the rapid development of the WWW, many of its standards were included in e-mail: HTML [7] coded mails have become fairly standard, and they may include hyperlinks and thus force the mail client to understand HTTP. It is to be expected that XHTML and the whole XML [16] standards family will follow soon.

Due to this steadily increasing number of data formats that have to be supported by mail clients, the development and support of mail clients becomes more and more difficult. Additionally, companies who have to store their mails for a long time due to legal reasons will need special databases to store this large amount of data in a structured way, and will also have to archive the client software needed to display it.

Security. S/MIME and OpenPGP have a common weakness when used to secure e-mails: They can only sign and encrypt the Body part of an e-mail, most parts of the Header remain insecure. The only exception is the address of the sender, included in the "FROM:" line: Each e-mail application should check if this address is identical to the one included in the PGP public key, or in the Subject or SubjectAltName fields of the X.509 certificate. Thus this field is only secure when the e-mail client has been implemented correctly.

All other fields of the Header remain insecure, even such important ones as "TO:" and "DATE:". Sending signed SPAM mails is thus possible by simply exchanging the "TO:"-line with an automated script, and is computationally easy since the signature has to be generated only once. Replay attacks are also possible.

As an example, consider a signed mail from a bank to one customer telling him that his account is nearly empty. Replaying this mail, and changing the "TO:" field, will generate a lot of confusion. If in addition the customer is asked to follow a link and enter his password, then combining this attack with a DNS attack on the bank's domain name, can be a serious threat.

Digital Signatures in S/MIME. Digitally signed content always comes as a pair in S/MIME and CMS. There are two options for signing content: clear signed (S/MIME data type multipart/signed) and opaque signed (CMS/PKCS#7 data type SignedData).

In theory these data structures can be nested, but in practice the mail clients restrict an e-mail to one such pair. (This holds for signature generation and verification.) As a result, header fields can never be signed, because the header must not contain S/MIME or CMS constructs.

Organisation of the paper. Section 2 gives a rough overview of e-mail security, including some research on XML. In Section 3, the basic ideas behind the XMaiL approach are presented. Section 4 goes into detail by discussing security enhancements of the XMaiL data format. Smooth transition scenarios from RFC 822 to XMaiL are discussed in Section 5. Our XMaiL parser described in Section 6 plays an important role here. Section 7 shows how normal mail and webmail can be displayed with XSLT, and future research is described in Section 8.

2 Related Work

The deployment of secure e-mail is limited because both S/MIME and OpenPGP are distributed applications, i.e. the user has to understand the security issues connected to encryption and digital signatures. There is a snapshot of the importance of secure e-mail in today's e-commerce in [6].In addition, encrypted e-mails can no longer be scanned for SPAM, viruses or other malware. Therefore there is a trend to centralize the encryption and signature of e-mails, ranging from automated client applications [5] to secure mail gateways (e.g. [4]). The XMaiL data format allows to combine both distributed and centralized security features, e.g. the content of the mail is signed by the user, but the authenticity of the sender's address and the encryption are guaranteed by the mail gateway.

Secure e-mails are considered to be one component in the fight against SPAM [11]. S/MIME or OpenPGP are used to authenticate the identity of the sender. Additionally, the authors mention that it would be desirable to secure header fields like the "RECEIVED:" lines. We move in this direction by signing security related header fields.

In [10] it has been proposed that in order to fight SPAM, the domain of the sender should be signed. With our approach this is easily possible, since we can split a "name@domain" mail address into a <name> and a <domain> tag, and only select the <domain> element to be digitally signed by the mail gateway.

Since XML is a very general data description language and since the two most important cryptographic primitives encryption and digital signature are available as XML co-standards [17, 18] it is a simple statement that all data formats contained in a secure e-mail can be replaced by XML structures. This idea has been published as the „eXtensible Mail Transport Protocol (XMTP)" [19] in 2000. However, this approach did not take into account the internal structure of e-mails and is thus not applicable to the ideas presented in this paper.

There is an ongoing debate about the advantages of binary and text based data formats [20]. However, the XML and ASN.1 standardization bodies are approaching each other, by defining XML based coding for ASN.1 (XER, see [2]), and by studying the advantages of a binary XML format [21].

3 XMaiL Data Format

Our approach is to model this structure as closely as possible using XML Schema. The final goal is to be able to transform an e-mail to XML, and to be able to transform this XML data back to the original e-mail. Advantages of this approach are the following:

- After transformation, e-mails can be stored in a structured form in any XML database. No special technology is needed to search this database.
- A complex workflow can be applied to the XMaiL inside a company, but it can be transformed to a valid MIME mail when sent over the internet.
- Important header fields can be secured by copying them as invisible Tags into the XML body of the message and signing them, or by first transforming them into an

XMaiL, selecting them for signature with XPath, and then transforming them back to a normal mail.

- A complex workflow can be secured by including multiple signatures.
- Knowledge of mail transport protocols (SMTP, POP3, IMAP), RFC 822 and XML is sufficient to build secure e-mail applications.
- XMaiLs can be easily displayed through a webmail interface.

Table 1. A small example from RFC 822 and its translation to XMaiL.

```
          From: John Doe <jdoe@machine.example>
          To: Mary Smith <mary@example.net>
               Subject: Saying Hello
          Date: Fri, 21 Nov 1997 09:55:06

This is a message just to say hello. So, "Hello".
```
```
               <?xml version="1.0" ... ?>
          <XMaiL xmlns="http://www.xmlemail.org">
                       <Header>
                        <From>
     <Mailbox>John Doe &lt;jdoe@machine.example&gt;</Mailbox>
                        </From>
<To><Address>Mary Smith &lt;mary@example.net&gt;</Address></To>
               <Subject>Saying Hello</Subject>
          <Date>Fri, 21 Nov 1997 09:55:06</Date>
               <Mime-Version>1.0</Mime-Version>
                       </Header>
                        <Body>
                        <Text>
                        <Plain>
     This is a message just to say hello. So, "Hello".
                       </Plain>
                       </Text>
                       </Body>
                      </XMaiL>
```

The XMaiL format informally described in Table 1 is defined with an XML Schema (available at xmlemail.org). This Schema is modelled after RFC 2822, MIME and S/MIME. In the XMaiL Parser, Java classes are automatically generated from this Schema, and the mail is parsed with JavaMail. The content of these Java classes is then stored in XMaiL format.

4 Improving the Security of E-Mails

Today's e-mail clients support HTML, which is often the default format for sending mails. Following the development of the World Wide Web, there is a clear migration path to XHTML and XML/XSLT. In these future mail clients, we can also expect support for XML Signature and XML Encryption, or at least it could be added with modest cost.

In XMaiL, the two XML security standards replace both S/MIME and OpenPGP, and for the first time we have a fully text based security standard. Table 2 compares the structure of a multipart/signed S/MIME message with an equivalent signed

Table 2. Equivalent of a clear signed S/MIME message in XMaiL, with two additional signed header fields (marked by underscores). Since the CMS type application/pkcs7-signature is a binary data type, only its structure is give with grey background.

RFC 2822, MIME & S/MIME	XMaiL
	```<?xml version="1.0" ...>```
	```<XMaiL xmlns="http://...">```
	```<Header>```
...	...
From:	```<From ID="Fromtobesigned"/>```
To:	```<To ID="Totobesigned"/>```
Subject:	```<Subject/>```
Date:	```<Date/>```
...	...
MIME-Version: 1.0	```<MIME-Version>1.0</Mime-version>```
	```</Header>```
Content-Type:	```<Body>```
multipart/signed;	```<MultipartSigned```
protocol="application/x-pkcs7-	```protocol="application/x-pkcs7-```
signature";	```signature"```
micalg=SHA-1;	```>```
boundary="-----12345------"	
-----12345------	```<MIMEMail ID="Mailtobesigned">```
Here is the real MIME mail	```Here is the real MIME mail```
(optionally with attachments)	```(optionally with attachments)```
-----12345------	```</MIMEMail>```
Content-Type:	```<Signature Id="MyFirstSignature"```
application/pkcs7-signature;	```xmlns="http://www.w3.org/2000/```
name="smime.p7s";	```09/xmldsig#">```
Content-Transfer-Encoding:	```<SignedInfo>```
Base64	```<CanonicalizationMethod```
	```Algorithm="..."/>```
PKCS7:	```<SignatureMethod```
Content-Type:	```Algorithm="..."/>```
pkcs7-signedData	```<Reference URI="#Mailtobesigned"```
Version: 1	```Type="...">```
	```<DigestMethod```
	```Algorithm="..."/>```
	```<DigestValue>```
	```345x3rvEPOOvKtMup4Nbe8nk=...```
	```</DigestValue>```
	```</Reference>```
Digest-Algorithms:	```<Reference URI="#Fromtobesigned"```
Digest-Algorithm:	```Type="http://www.w3.org/2000/09/```
Algorithm:	```xmldsig#XMaiL">```
sha1	```<DigestMethod```
(2B:0E:03:02:1A)	```Algorithm="http://www.w3.org/```
Parameter:	```2000/09/xmldsig#sha1"/>```
Content:	```<DigestValue>```
PKCS7:	```hhdudkas1sdi743rundiu23=...```
Content-Type:	```</DigestValue>```
pkcs7-data	```</Reference>```
	```<Reference URI="#Totobesigned"```
	```Type="http://www.w3.org/2000/```
	```xmldsig#XMaiL">```
	```<DigestMethod```
	```Algorithm="http://www.w3.org/```
	```2000/09/xmldsig#sha1"/>```

Table 2. *Continued*

```
                                    <DigestValue>
                                      7dshdiw74hdh3h39j939=...
                                    </DigestValue>
                                    </Reference>
                                  </SignedInfo>
                                  <SignatureValue>
                                    MC0CFFrVLtRlk34FG6H9OGg5=...
                                  </SignatureValue>
                                  <KeyInfo>
                                    <X509Data> <!--ID public key-->
                                      <X509IssuerSerial>
                                        <X509SerialNumber>
                                          549
                                        </X509SerialNumber>
                                      </X509IssuerSerial>
                                    </X509Data>
    Certificates:                   <X509Data> <!-- cert chain -->
      Certificate:                    <!--Client cert-->
        Root-Zertifikat               <X509Certificate>
      Certificate:                      MIICXTCCA..
        CA-Zertifikat                 </X509Certificate>
      Certificate:                    <!-- Intermediate cert -->
        Client-Zertifikat(549)        <X509Certificate>
    SignerInfos:                        MIICPzCCA...
      SignerInfo:                     </X509Certificate>
        Serial-Number: 549            <!-- Root cert -->
        ...                           <X509Certificate>
      Signature:                        MIICSTCCA...
        0F:9B:46:5B:44:...            </X509Certificate>
    -----12345------                </X509Data>
                                    </KeyInfo>
                                  </Signature>
                                </MultipartSigned>
                              </Body>
                            </XMaiL>
```

XMaiL message. (This should not be confused with the XMaiL output by our Parser prototype when applied to a S/MIME message; the result is much more complicated, because we have to adhere to the CMS syntax. See xmlemail.org for example results of our parser.)

Table 2 also shows the additional possibilities of secure XMaiL compared to S/MIME and OpenPGP. The hash value which is signed not only covers the mail body, but also two important fields in the mail header, the "TO:" and the "FROM:" field. In our example there is still only one signature, but in principle there can be different signatures by different signers, e.g. a signature by the sender of the mail covering the mail body, and another signature from the company mail gateway covering the "FROM:" header field and thus certifying that the e-mail is indeed valid for the company.

The verification and visualization of signatures must no longer be implemented by the mail client, but can use standard XML technology: standard libraries (e.g. [1]) to decrypt or verify signatures, and XSLT stylesheets which display the successfully verified parts of an e-mail in a different colour.

The only part of Table 2 which is not XML are the different X.509 certificates, which are only included in base64 coded form. This is an approach also followed in

WS-Security (binary X.509 security tokens), but one can also think of a Certification Authority which issues the same certificate both in X.509 and XML format.

5 XMaiL and SMTP

If we transform the RFC 822 header of an e-mail to XMaiL as in Table 2, the current SMTP infrastructure will no longer be able to transport it. There are two ways to cope with this problem:

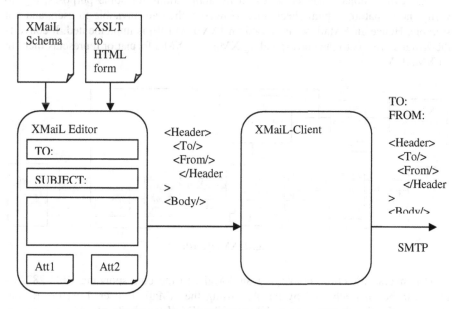

Fig. 1. Generating an RFC 822 header from an XMaiL

The first possibility is to transform the RFC 822 header only to XMaiL to compute the signature, and then transform it back for SMTP transport. This approach works if the signed RFC 822 header fields are not modified during transport. To verify the signature, the header can be transformed to XMaiL again. If some unsigned header fields have changed (e.g. the "RECEIVED:" fields), this does not affect the signature.

The second possibility is to generate the RFC 822 header from the XMaiL header part for SMTP transport. Figure 1 shows this possibility. When such an e-mail is received, the signed parts of the <Header> element are displayed rather than the corresponding fields in the RFC 822 header.

6 XMaiL Parser Prototype

The XMaiL API structure is illustrated in Figure 2. It begins with the XMaiL schemas: XMaiL_Schema.xsd and smime.xsd. The former defines the basic data formats of an XMaiL, and includes the latter schema which is to be extended with the

PKCS#7 [12] data formats. Using the XML binding compiler (*xjc*) of Sun [9], Java objects can be generated from the schemas.

We first consider the process to convert an RFC 2822 e-mail to the corresponding XMaiL. The core component is the XMaiL Parser. It takes RFC 2822 e-mails as input. To convert an RFC 2822 email without cryptographic components, the JavaMail API [8] converts it to JavaMail objects. The XMaiL API then picks up information from the JavaMail objects and generates the XMaiL objects. The current JavaMail API is not able to handle the PKCS#7 data formats. Hence to handle S/MIME e-mails the Bouncy Castle Crypto API [3] is additionally applied.

The XMaiL objects can be accessed by applications for some purposes, e.g. to verify the signatures, spam check, etc.. However, they are invisible to users and not storable. Hence an XMaiL writer based on JAXB API [9] is implemented. It converts the XMaiL objects to the corresponding XMaiL in XML format or represents them in an XMaiL Viewer.

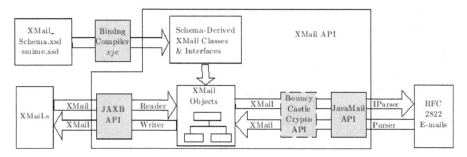

Fig. 2. XMaiL API

The inverse direction, converting an XMaiL to the corresponding RFC 2822 e-mail, can be also achieved by the API using the XMaiL IParser. First the Reader generates XMaiL objects from an XMaiL. The XMaiL can be from a file, or from an Editor, as in Figure 1. The XMaiL IParser either provides an interface for the normal email-client, e.g. Firefox, Outlook Express, to access the XMaiL, or converts the XMaiL to the RFC 2822 e-mail.

7   Displaying XMaiLs with XSLT

The XMaiL format closes the gap between "normal" mail and webmail: The e-mail is displayed in the same way in the mail client and in the browser, only the retrieval method is different. It will also be possible to display the validity of the signature in a web browser, provided this browser is capable of verifying XML signatures.

Figure 3 shows a MIME message transformed to XMaiL and displayed with the Mozilla Browser using an "Outlook Express" XSLT transformation.

With the application of the XMaiL IParser as plug-ins (described in Section 6), the XMaiLs can also be displayed with normal e-mail clients, e.g. Firefox and Outlook Express.

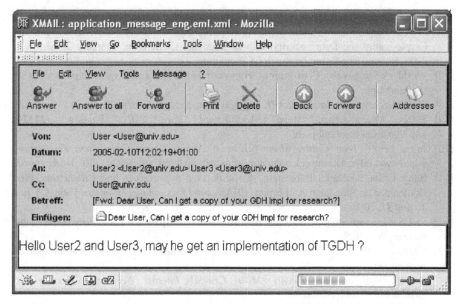

Fig. 3. The example mail transformed to XMaiL format and displayed using XSLT. The text part needs some more work.

8 Future Work

The main goal of the XMaiL project is to give a proof-of-concept implementation that demonstrates a possible migration path from RFC 822 to XML based mail formats. The first step in this path is the XMaiL gateway which transform all kinds of mails (including the binary formats of S/MIME and OpenPGP) to XML and back. The interaction between Parser and iParser still needs some tuning, and OpenPGP has to be included.

The next step will be the implementation of an XMaiL editor with SMTP support, and an XMaiL viewer with POP3. Both tools will add and remove RFC 822 header lines, and will use Apache XML security routines. We will investigate if with XForms and XSLT a standard browser can be used, and how different signature levels can be displayed.

References

[1] Apache XML Security. http://xml.apache.org/security/.
[2] ASN.1 Information Site. http://asn1.elibel.tm.fr.
[3] The Legion of the Bouncy Castle, Bouncy Castle Crypto APIs. http://www.bouncycastle.org/
[4] IronMail Gateway. http://www.ciphertrust.com
[5] Lars Eilebrecht, *Ciphire Mail: Email Encryption and Authentication.* Financial Cryptography and Data SecurityNinth International Conference, February 28-March 3, 2005, Roseau, The Commonwealth Of Dominica.

[6] Simson L. Garfinkel, Jeffrey I. Schiller, Erik Nordlander, David Margrave, and Robert C. Miller, *Views, Reactions and Impact of Digitally-Signed Mail in e-Commerce*. Financial Cryptography and Data SecurityNinth International Conference, February 28-March 3, 2005, Roseau, The Commonwealth Of Dominica.

[7] World Wide Web Consortium, *Hypertext Markup Language*. http://www.w3c.org/MarkUp/

[8] SUN Microsystems, *JavaMail API*. http://java.sun.com/products/javamail/

[9] SUN Microsystems, *Java Architecture for XML Binding (JAXB)*. http://java.sun.com/xml/jaxb/

[10] Jason Levitt, *Tech Guide: Many Strategies Against Spam Can't Stem Frustration*. http://www.informationweek.com/story/showArticle.jhtml?articleID=13101046&pgno=3

[11] Barry Leiba, Nathaniel Borenstein, *A Multifaceted Approach to Spam Reduction*. First Conference on Email and Anti-Spam (CEAS) *2004* Proceedings *Mountain View, CA July 30 and 31, 2004*

[12] PKCS #7: Cryptographic Message Syntax Standard. http://www.rsasecurity.com/rsalabs/node.asp?id=2129

[13] Internet Engineering Task Force, *Request for Comments No. vwxy*. www.ietf.org/rfc/rfcvwxy.txt .

[14] SANS Institute, *The Twenty Most Critical Internet Security Vulnerabilities*. http://www.sans.org/top20

[15] http://www.itu.int/rec/recommendation.asp?type=folders&lang=e&parent=T-REC-X.509

[16] World Wide Web Consortium, *eXtended Markup Language*. http://www.w3.org/XML/

[17] XML Signature WG, http://www.w3.org/Signature/

[18] XML Encryption WG, http://www.w3.org/Encryption/2001/

[19] Mediaone, *eXtensible Mail Transport Protocol*. http://xml.coverpages.org/xmtp20000508. html

[20] Darren P Mundy, David Chadwick and Andrew Smith, *Comparing the Performance of Abstract Syntax Notation One (ASN.1) vs eXtensible Markup Language (XML)*. TERENA Networking Conference, 19-22 May 2003, Zagreb, Croatia.

[21] XML Binary Characterization Working Group, http://www.w3.org/XML/Binary/

Integrating XML Linked Time-Stamps in OASIS Digital Signature Services

Ana Isabel González-Tablas[1] and Karel Wouters[2]

[1] Carlos III University (Madrid),
Computer Science Department - SeTI
aigonzal@inf.uc3m.es
[2] Katholieke Universiteit Leuven,
Department Electrical Engineering - ESAT, Cosic
karel.wouters@esat.kuleuven.be

Abstract. The technique of electronic time-stamping allows a client to get an electronic proof of the existence of a document at a specific point in time. A simple way to achieve this is to produce a digital signature over the pair (document,time). Linked time-stamps have an advantage over these simple time-stamps because they construct a verifiable link between time-stamps. In this paper, we discuss how to include linked time-stamps in the OASIS Digital Signature Services standard. We highlight the problem points when introducing a sub-profile of this standard, and we describe some additional structures that are needed to accommodate a broad range of linked time-stamping schemes.

Keywords: Linked time-stamping, Digital Signature Services, XML security.

1 Introduction

In recent years, time-stamping implementations have become popular in several countries. Studies, performed by the European Committee for Standardization [10], clearly identified the need for time-stamps when using electronic signatures. This has been followed by a range of standardization efforts [1,3]. With the rise of XML as a language to structure communications, XML formats for security protocols were proposed too. In 2002, the OASIS Digital Signature Services Technical Committee (DSS TC) was formed[8]. Its purpose is to develop techniques to support the processing of digital signatures, including the development of a profile for time-stamping, with a focus on XML formats. At the moment of this writing, the time-stamping profile includes support for so-called independent time-stamp tokens. In this paper, we investigate the possibility of including linked time-stamp tokens in the DSS standard, driven by the believe that this kind of time-stamp is more desirable in certain settings, despite its complexity. In the next two sections we give an overview of existing time-stamping schemes and the OASIS DSS standard. This is followed by a description of the structures for linked time-stamp requests and verifications, and its processing.

J. Dittmann, S. Katzenbeisser, and A. Uhl (Eds.): CMS 2005, LNCS 3677, pp. 301–310, 2005.

2   Time-Stamping Schemes

Digital time-stamping is a set of techniques that enables us to determine if a certain digital document has been created before a given time. A trusted third party – a Time-Stamping Authority (TSA) – implements this by creating time-stamps, the digital assertions that a given document was presented to the TSA at a given time. A common practise is to time-stamp documents that represent new inventions and discoveries (log files, financial audit reports). This helps to establish first-to-invent claims or document authenticity [13]. Time-stamping can also play a role in Public Key Infrastructures (PKI). In this context, time-stamps are used to extend the lifetime of digital signatures: a time-stamp on a digital signature can prove that the signature was generated before the certificate on the signature key-pair was revoked. We distinguish two classes of time-stamping schemes, which are described below.

2.1   Schemes Producing Independent Time-Stamps

Simple schemes generate time-stamps that are independent of other time-stamps. A classical example is the digital signature of a TSA on a pair (`time`,`document`), which is standardised in RFC3161 [3] and in ISO/IEC FDIS 18014-2 [2]. A limitation of these schemes is that they assume a high level of trust in the TSA, and possible fraudulent behaviour of the TSA remains undetected. The time-stamping profile [9] of DSS is aimed at this kind of time-stamp.

2.2   Schemes Producing Linked Time-Stamps

Linking schemes limit the required trust in the TSA by including data from other time-stamps into the computation of the issued time-stamp, such that they depend on each other. Linking happens in three phases:

Aggregation: in the first step, all documents received by the TSA within a small time interval – the aggregation round – are considered as being submitted simultaneously. The output of the aggregation round is a binary string that securely depends on all the documents submitted in that round.

Linking: the output of the aggregation round is linked to previously computed aggregation round values. The resulting value cannot be computed without the existence of previous aggregation round values. This establishes a one-way order between aggregation round values, such that so-called *relative temporal authentication* is obtained: time-stamps of different aggregation rounds can be compared.

Publication: from time to time (e.g., each week), the TSA publishes the most recent time-stamp in a widely witnessed medium, such as a newspaper. By doing this, the TSA commits itself to all of the previously issued time-stamps. The published values are used for verifying time-stamps and they enable other parties to check if the TSA is behaving properly.

Examples of linking schemes can be found in Bayer *et al.* [4], and Buldas *et al.* [6]. In these cases, the linking can be visualised by a graph and optimised in time-stamp size. In Benaloh *et al.* [5] and Merkle [12], some aggregation schemes are proposed.

3   OASIS Digital Signature Services Standard

In October 2002, the Digital Signature Services Technical Committee (DSS TC) was formed within OASIS. The purpose of this TC is to develop techniques (a standard) to support the processing of digital signatures. The core document specifies a simple client/server protocol on which the actual services are built. These services are specified by profiles. The core protocols support the creation and verification of signatures and time-stamps. The core document is aimed at XML Digital Signatures [7] and CMS Signatures [11]. The standard accommodates RFC3161 time-stamps [3] and a DSS XML time-stamp format [9]. XML elements, taken from the W3C XML Digital Signature standard are prefixed by 'ds:' while elements from the OASIS DSS standard are not prefixed. The new elements, proposed in this paper, are prefixed by 'tsp:'.

The DSS core protocol is composed of two operational types: one for signature generation and one for signature verification. A typical use of the protocols is submitting a document or its digest value to a DSS server through a <SignRequest> element. The DSS server will return a signature on the submitted values, in a <SignResponse> element. Later on, the signature can be submitted to the DSS server for verification, by sending a <VerifyRequest> element. The essence of the response is a valid/invalid indication, returned in a <VerifyResponse> element. The DSS core standard also specifies an XML structure for independent time-stamp tokens. The DSS <TimeStamp> children are <ds:Signature> and <RFC3161TimeStampToken>. The element <RFC3161TimeStampToken> allows for the inclusion of a base64-encoded RFC3161 time-stamp. In the <ds:Signature> case, a <TstInfo> element is placed in <ds:Object> and covered by the signature. This <TstInfo> element is a XML translation of the RFC3161 TSTInfo structure.

The *XML Timestamping Profile* of OASIS DSS [9] restricts the services of the DSS core to a time-stamping protocol. The main restriction is that only hash values (no documents) can be sent to the TSA. Furthermore, for the <SignRequest/OptionalInputs>, two values for <SignatureType> are proposed to identify the time-stamping schemes mentioned above. Finally, the TSA can include only a <SigningTime> optional output in the <VerifyResponse>.

The current DSS standard does not specify a structure to integrate linked time-stamps. The authors have knowledge of at least two large commercial TSAs that have deployed a linked time-stamp service. Furthermore, these time-stamping schemes have some advantages over simple schemes. Therefore, we think that linked time-stamps should not be ignored in the OASIS DSS standard. Moreover, as far as we know, there exists no other XML standard that allows for an easy integration of this class of time-stamping schemes. We should note that the X9.95 proposal by ANSI is based on an XML translation of ASN.1 structures; our approach differs by the fact that we start from a standard, based on XML Digital Signatures. In this paper, we present a possible path to include linked time-stamps in the DSS standard through a subprofile of the OASIS DSS XML time-stamping profile in [9]. Our subprofile defines a new XML *linked* time-stamp token, as a sibling of the <ds:Signature> and <RFC3161TimeStampToken>.

4   Integrating XML Linked Time-Stamps in the XML Time-Stamping Profile of OASIS DSS

4.1   Issuing Protocol

In this section, we describe the XML elements that are exchanged when a client wants to get a certain document time-stamped by the TSA. The main contribution is the definition of a linked time-stamp format, which allows to model most linked time-stamps. This definition is based on previous work in [15], in which an example XML fragment can be found.

Element <SignRequest>

– Element <SignRequest/OptionalInputs/SignatureType> The content of the optional input <SignatureType> should identify the requested linking scheme. An example for identifying an existing linking scheme could be ee:cyber:timestamp.
– Element <SignRequest/InputDocuments/DocumentHash> As described in [8], the digest value contained in each <DocumentHash> is the result of applying a digest method, specified in the same element, to one or more documents. If a client wants to time-stamp the same content with several digest algorithms, several <InputDocuments> elements can be included, each containing a <DocumentHash> element with a different digest algorithm. This is useful if one of the hash functions gets compromised as shown in [14].

Element <SignResponse> The server must return a <Timestamp> signature object as defined in [9]. The new <tsp:LinkedTimestamp> element will be a child of the <SignResponse/SignatureObject/Timestamp> element. Its structure is presented in Figure 1 and we describe its key aspects below.

– Element <InputDocuments>. This element should be copied from the <SignRequest> element. In the DSS TST profile [9], these values are copied into the signature, so the resulting time-stamp contains them by default. As in our profile, it is optional to sign these values directly, we need to copy them somewhere else to reconstruct the input of the aggregation (or linking) operation.
– Element <TstInfo>. This element is optional and can contain values as discussed in the DSS core.
– Element <ds:Signature>. In our profile, the signature is optional and can only contain <ds:Reference> elements pointing to the <InputDocuments>, <tsp:BindingInfo> and/or <TstInfo> children of its <tsp:LinkedTimestamp> parent. This signature can be discarded from the time-stamp, once the linking round finishes. After that stage, the evidence value of the time-stamp lies in the binding information, rather than in the signature.
– Element <tsp:BindingInfo>. This element should contain the binding information of the linked time-stamp. This element is used as follows:

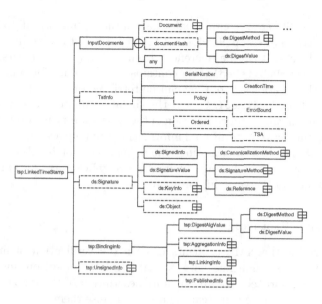

Fig. 1. tsp:LinkedTimestamp element

- The <tsp:DigestAlgValue> element contains the digest value that is passed on to the linking scheme. This value is obtained as follows: First, we build a node set using an XPath expression which selects the **descendant-or-self** elements and attributes of the <DigestMethod> and the <DigestValue> in the <DocumentHash> elements that have been copied into <tsp:LinkedTimestamp/dss:InputDocuments> element. Optionally, we can also attach <TstInfo> to the node set. Next, we take the **excl-CN14** transform of this node set which should result in an octet string. This octet string is hashed using the specified digest method in <tsp:DigestAlgValue>.

- The <tsp:AggregationInfo> element, if present, specifies the aggregation algorithm and the necessary data to compute the output of the aggregation round using the <tsp:DigestAlgValue> element.

- The <tsp:LinkingInfo> element contains the algorithm and data to compute the value of the linking round, given the output of the aggregation round.

    * <tsp:Head> contains linking information from time-stamps issued before this one.

    * <tsp:Tail> contains information from time-stamps after this one. It is computed by the TSA at the end of the linking round. In most cases, this element will not be present in the <SignResponse> element, as the necessary information is not available at the time of generating the time-stamp. This information will be added in the verifying protocol. How this affects the signature, is discussed in the next section.

* <ds:Object> contains information that is 'unnatural' to include directly into <tsp:Head> or <tsp:Tail>, but is used in some linking schemes. It can be referenced from within these elements.
- The <tsp:PublishedInfo> contains round values for linking rounds, plus the location where they can be retrieved or verified.
- Element <tsp:UnsignedInfo>. If the signature on an existing time-stamp should remain valid after completion of the time-stamp with values generated after this time-stamp, additional information can be placed here. As it is not covered by the signature, adding things here will not break the signature. This element will not be present in the <SignResponse> element, but it will be added in the verifying protocol.

4.2 Verifying Protocol

Here, we describe the XML elements used in the verification of linked time-stamps. The biggest challenge here is enabling its comparison and extension within the DSS approach. We give a short description of these operations, and describe how the DSS elements can be used to realise them.

- **Verify a time-stamp TS1 against another time-stamp TS2.**
  Upon this request, the verifier should get a response from the server indicating one of the following cases: (a) TS1 was issued before TS2 ('earlier'), (b) TS1 was issued after TS2 ('later'), (c) an error. The server can determine the response using the times in the signed information, or using the linking information between the two time-stamps directly. Our protocol also allows the verification of a timestamp TS1 alone, not against another one.
- **Update a time-stamp TS1 to a published value PV or to an arbitrary second time-stamp TS2.**
  Updating a time-stamp means that the linking information in that time-stamp is updated such that the link between the time-stamp and a certain other value can be computed with the information held in the time-stamp. Updating TS1 to a PV means one of the following cases: (a) the completion of the time-stamp within its same round, or (b) the extension to the last published value. Depending on the time when the update is requested, a completion (a) or an extension (b) should be returned. For most linking schemes, the extension to the PV should include the completion of an (incomplete) time-stamp.
  If a completion is done, the signed <tsp:BindingInfo> is replaced by a new <tsp:BindingInfo>. If an extension is done, the new linking information can be placed in <tsp:UnsignedInfo> or in <tsp:BindingInfo>. In the last case, a new <ds:Signature> has to be computed to replace the one present in the time-stamp, if the signature is still needed.
  Extending the time-stamp TS1 to other time-stamp TS2 means that the server should include in the response enough information (chain of digest values and optionally published values) to allow the client to verify the temporal relationship between TS1 and TS2. In most cases this means building

the hash chain that passes through both time-stamps TS1 and TS2. As in the case of updating to a PV, this new information can be signed or not. It is assumed in the protocol that TS1 has been issued earlier than TS2. If it is not this case, the server should return a response indicating that the client can change their order and make a new request for the extension.

Next, we describe the elements that allow the functionality above.

Element <VerifyRequest> Important modified children of this element are:

- Element <OptionalInputs>. Contrary to [9], in this protocol the following optional inputs are allowed.
  - Element <tsp:RelativeTimestamp> can contain a <Timestamp> child, a second time-stamp TS2. Alternatively, its URI attribute can refer to TS2 (using, for example, the serial number). This is an optional element, but is mandatory if the optional input <tsp:CompareLinkedTimestamp> is present in the verify request. The time-stamp TS1 in the <SignatureObject> element will be updated or compared to TS2.
  - Element <tsp:CompareLinkedTimestamp> is an empty element which indicates that time-stamp TS1 must be compared to the time-stamp TS2 contained in the <tsp:RelativeTimestamp> optional input, that must be present in this case.
  - Element <UpdateLinkedTimestamp> indicates that the client wants to update his time-stamp TS1. This optional element has an URI attribute that can contain one of the following items: a local reference to the ID attribute of the <tsp:RelativeTimestamp> optional input, a reference to a published value, or an empty reference. If in the last case, TS1 should be updated to the most recent published value.
- Element <SignatureObject>. The client sends a <Timestamp> element containing the time-stamp TS1.
- Element <InputDocuments>. The client must only send <DocumentHash> elements; <Document> elements are not allowed.

Element <VerifyResponse> This element contains the TSA's response. It holds a status code and optionally and updated time-stamp.

- Element <Result>. Our profile defines additional <ResultMinor> children of <Result>, all of them prefixed with urn:oasis:names:tc:dss:1.0: resultminor:. If the verification is successful, the server returns:
  - ValidLinkedTimestamp_Earlier: TS1 has been found earlier than TS2.
  - ValidLinkedTimestamp_Later: TS1 has been found later than TS2.
  - LinkedTimestamp_Updated: TS1 was updated.
  Otherwise, if verification has failed, the following <ResultMinor> codes may be returned:
  - IncorrectTimestamp: The time-stamp fails to verify, indicating that the time-stamp was modified, or that the time-stamp has been computed incorrectly.

- **IncomparableTimestamps**: TS1 cannot be compared to TS2. A possible reason might be that they are in the same aggregation round.
- **IncorrectOrder**: Updating TS1 to a certain value V failed because V existed prior to TS1. We only allow forward extensions in our protocol.
- **NoPublishedValue**: There is no new published value yet.

– Element <OptionalOutputs>. Our profile defines <tsp:UpdatedLinked-Timestamp>, as an optional child of <OptionalOutputs>. This element shall contain the original linked time-stamp TS1 with some additional information added to it (completion or extension information). Optionally, the added information can be signed, depending on where the information is added, as explained above.

4.3   Processing of XML Linked Time-Stamp Tokens

Signing Protocol Upon receiving a <SignRequest> a DSS server will form a <SignatureObject/Timestamp/tsp:LinkedTimeStamp> as follows: First, it copies <SignRequest/InputDocuments> into a <tsp:LinkedTimeStamp> element. Then, optionally, the server computes a <TstInfo> element and enters it as the second child of <tsp:LinkedTimeStamp>. Next, the server computes the <tsp:BindingInfo> as it is described in section 4.1 and a <ds:Signature> element according to [7], which are entered as the third and fourth child of <tsp:LinkedTimeStamp>. The server may include <ds:Signature/Signed-Info/Reference> elements pointing to <InputDocuments>, <TstInfo> (optional) and <tsp:BindingInfo> elements. Then, an appropriate <Result> element is generated, depending on if the previous steps were successful. Finally, the <Result> and the <SignatureObject> elements are entered into a <SignResponse>, and returned to the requester.

Verifying Protocol Upon receiving a <VerifyRequest>, a DSS server will perform the following steps. If this fails, the appropriate error will be returned in the <Result> element.

– **Verification.**
  There must exist a <SignatureObject/Timestamp/tsp:Linked TimeStamp> element (TS1) present as a child of the <VerifyRequest>. First, the server gets the <TstInfo> element if present, and verifies that the <Policy> contained in it is acceptable according to the relying party's policy. Then, the server gets the <tsp:BindingInfo> element and verifies that the <tsp:BindingInfo/tsp:DigestAlgValue> element value has been computed taking as inputs the children of <InputDocuments> and, optionally, the <TstInfo> element. After that, the server must verify the <tsp:AggregationInfo> (if present) and <tsp:LinkingInfo> elements as specified by the <tsp:BindingInfo> algorithm. This includes retrieving the trust anchors (published reference values) needed to check the time-stamp and comparing them to the reference values stored in <tsp:Head>, <tsp:Tail> and <tsp:PublishedInfo>. If the element

<ds:Signature> is present, the server performs the standard checks on the signature keys as specified in the OASIS DSS standard. After checking that the <ds:Reference> elements point to <InputDocuments>, <TstInfo> and <tsp:BindingInfo> elements, the server must verify all digests and the signature according to [7].

– **Comparison.**
 If there exists a <tsp:CompareLinkedTimeStamp> optional input, the server should verify that there is also a <tsp:RelativeTimestamp> optional input. In this case, the server must retrieve the <tsp:LinkedTimestamp> element TS2 from the element <tsp:RelativeTimestamp> and verify it as described above (*Verification* step). Then, the server builds the chain of digests between the two time-stamps according to the binding algorithm and the time-stamping policy. This step will determine the temporal relation between the time-stamps.

– **Update.**
 If there exists a <tsp:UpdateLinkedTimeStamp> optional input which contains an URI attribute pointing to <tsp:RelativeTimestamp> optional input, and it has not been verified during the *Comparison* step, the server must verify it. If the URI attribute points to a published value PV or another time-stamp TS3, the server should verify that it is a correct identifier, and retrieve and verify PV or TS3. Then, the server should build the chain of digests that passes through the time-stamp TS1 and the requested extension point (TS3, PV or most recent PV). If the linked time-stamp can be extended to that extension point, the extension information is placed in <tsp:BindingInfo> or in <tsp:UnsignedInfo>, depending on the binding algorithm and the time-stamping policy.

5   Implementation

To implement the scheme, we can start from a standard DSS implementation, with adjustments to handle linked time-stamp requests. The implementation will have a first presentation tier which receives the request, verifies the syntax and determines to which service module it has to be dispatched.

The service modules in the second tier will determine the nature of the request (time-stamp generation/verification), and will pass the request to a suitable plug-in component in a third tier. If the server supports several linking schemes, the element <SignRequest/OptionalInputs/SignatureType> indicates the specific linked time-stamp scheme asked by the client and this should help the server to allocate the requests; otherwise the server should know which one should be applied. In the case of <VerificationRequest>s, there is no specific indication of the applied linked time-stamp in the main body, but the <LinkedTimeStamp> element should carry enough information to allow the server to identify which kind of linked time-stamp contains, and therefore, which linked time-stamp module it may be assigned to.

6 Conclusions

In this paper, we sketched a path to include linked time-stamp tokens in the OASIS DSS standard [8] by making a sub-profile of the existing time-stamping profile [9] for this standard. We discussed several points at which our subprofile collides with the original profile, and we think that some changes to the standard could help the integration of linked time-stamps. We hope to have an impact in the DSS standardization body to which we will present a fully elaborated version of this paper.

References

1. ISO/IEC 18014-1. Information technology – Security techniques – Time-stamping services – Part 1: Framework, 2002.
2. ISO/IEC 18014-2. Information technology – Security techniques – Time-stamping services – Part 2: Mechanisms producing independent tokens, 2003.
3. C. Adams, P. Cain, D. Pinkas, and R. Zuccherato. Internet X.509 Public Key Infrastructure Time-Stamp Protocol (TSP). www.ietf.org/html.charters/pkix-charter.html, April 2002.
4. Dave Bayer, Stuart Haber, and W. Scott Stornetta. Improving the Efficiency and Reliability of Digital Time-Stamping. In *Sequences II: Methods in Communication, Security and Computer Science*, pages 329–334. Springer-Verlag, 1993.
5. J. Benaloh and M. de Mare. One-way Accumulators: A Decentralized Alternative to Digital Signatures. In T. Helleseth, editor, *Advances in Cryptology - Proceedings of EuroCrypt '93*, volume 765 of *Lecture Notes in Computer Science*, pages 274–285, Lofthus, Norway, May 1993. Springer-Verlag.
6. Ahto Buldas, Helger Lipmaa, and Berry Schoenmakers. Optimally Efficient Accountable Time-Stamping. In *Public Key Cryptography - PKC'2000*, number 1751 in Lecture Notes in Computer Science, pages 293–305. Springer-Verlag, 2000.
7. D. Eastlake, J. Reagle, and D. Solo. XML-Signature Syntax and Processing. www.w3.org/Signature, February 2002.
8. T. Perrin et *al.* OASIS Digital Signature Services TC. Digital Signature Service (DSS) Core Protocols, Elements and Bindings, Working Draft 26. www.oasis-open.org, June 2004.
9. T. Perrin et *al.* OASIS Digital Signature Services TC. XML Timestamping DSS Profile, Working Draft 06. www.oasis-open.org, June 2004.
10. European Committee for Standardization CEN. CWA 14171: Procedures for Electronic Signature Verification. www.cen.eu.org, 2001.
11. R. Housley. Cryptographic Message Syntax. http://www.ietf.org/html. charters/smime-charter.html, April 2002.
12. Ralph C. Merkle. Protocols for public key cryptosystems. In *Proceedings of the IEEE Symposium on Security and Privacy*, pages 122–134, 1980.
13. Surety. Surety AbsoluteProof Solution Suite . www.surety.com.
14. Xiaoyun Wang, Dengguo Feng, Xuejia Lai, and Hongbo Yu. Collisions for Hash Functions MD4, MD5, HAVAL-128 and RIPEMD. Rump session of CRYPTO 2004, available at http://eprint.iacr.org/2004/199.pdf, August 2004.
15. Karel Wouters, Bart Preneel, Ana Isabel González-Tablas, and Arturo Ribagorda. Towards an XML Format for Time-Stamps. In *ACM Workshop on XML Security 2002*. ACM, ACM, November 2002.

Trustworthy Verification and Visualisation of Multiple XML-Signatures

Wolfgang Kubbilun[1], Sebastian Gajek[2], Michael Psarros[2], and Jörg Schwenk[2]

[1] MediaSec Technologies GmbH, Berliner Platz 6-8, 45127 Essen, Germany
wkubbilun@mediasec.de
[2] Horst Görtz Institute for IT Security, Ruhr-University Bochum, Germany
{sebastian.gajek, michael.psarros, joerg.schwenk}@nds.rub.de

Abstract. The digital signature is one of the most important cryptographic primitives. It provides data integrity, message authentication and non-repudiation, which are required attributes in security critical services, such as electronic commerce, voting or health care. Whereas previous data formats for digital signatures concentrated on signing the entire document, the XML signature standard is feasible to secure complex workflows on a document with multiple signatures.

In a proof of concept implementation we demonstrate that verifying and trustworthily displaying of signed documents is realizable in standard Web browsers. The focus of our work are multisigned XML documents that introduce new requirements particularly in the field of presentation.

Keywords: Visualisation, WYSIWYS, XML, XML Signature, XPath, XSL Transformation, Web Browser.

1 Introduction

Electronic data exchange over TCP/IP networks made an overwhelming development in the past years and resulted in an increased need for security critical services. A major building block to secure documents are digital signatures. They have enormous practical relevance in fundamental services, such as electronic commerce, digital voting or health care. Signing and verifying of electronic documents is very crucial as it preserves the document's integrity and authenticity. For this reason, cryptographic algorithms (e.g., RSA, DSA, ECC-DSA) have been studied and are believed to be secure [1]. However, in practice this (single) assumption is insufficient to provide a sophisticated level of security. For instance, in legal proceedings one must also prove that the signed document has been presented correctly, i.e., one must show that the document and its content are clearly assigned to the signer (see e.g. [2]). As the typical user can only verify what she sees[1] the content of a digitally signed document must be visualised as well as information about the signer and the verification process (including the certificate chain).

---

[1] This is referred to as the *What You See is What you Sign (WYSIWYS) paradigm* (see section 2).

J. Dittmann, S. Katzenbeisser, and A. Uhl (Eds.): CMS 2005, LNCS 3677, pp. 311–320, 2005.

An additional aggravation is that in today's workflows several internal and external business instances process an electronic document. Generally, documents pass a hierarchical network of responsibilities (e.g., employees, supervisors) with different roles and access rights. To enhance the workflow (see section 4.1 for a further discussion) new constraints on digital documents have to be made: it is necessary to sign a document manifoldly. Multiple signing means to sign both the entire and certain parts of the document in unspecific order by multiple parties. Due to these requisitions of digital signing several new assumptions of the WYSISWS paradigm have to be made. Solving this paradigm in an user-convenient manner would dramatically enhance the use of digitally signed documents and broaden possible fields of application.

Our goal is to demonstrate the benefits of XML Signatures [3] and argue and elaborate that this technology is particularly suitable to design digital processes which require multisigned documents. More precisely, we employ XML and XSLT technologies [4] to fit the above named assumptions of the WYSWYS paradigm and mirror the results in a view, which can be presented, e.g., by standard web browsers. Finally, we show in a proof of concept that the Apache implementation [5] of the XML signature specification can be used for this approach.

The remainder sections are structured as follows: in section 2 we briefly introduce the presentation problem and discuss related works in section 3. In section 4 we propose an approach to solve the presentation problem based on XML technologies. In section 5 we prove the feasibility of our idea and provide a proof of concept implementation. Finally, we summarize our work and discuss future work in section 6.

2   The Presentation Problem

As mentioned in the introduction, cryptographically proven secure signature algorithms are not sufficient for providing an over-all security in practice; the presentation of the signed document is also decisive. A general problem results from the fact that electronic, respectively, electronically signed documents are processed by machines and displayed in an user-compatible manner, i.e., machines interpret data to the user's convenience and adequately present it [6]. However, this presentation can be incomplete, incorrect or ambiguous, which yields to a mis-interpretation of significant information including a distorted view of the document's integrity and authenticity. This is called the presentation problem [7,8,9,6]. For a trustworthily presentation of digital signatures, further assumptions[2] have to be fulfilled, which we briefly summarise:

The presentation must be *definite*. In particular, the presentation of signed data must be unambiguous. A verifying person must always be aware of what has been signed. In practice, she is restricted by several factors. Depending on, for example, the displaying device or layout she might be interfered to see the

---

[2] We concentrate on basic problems, as a complete discussing would go beyond the paper's scope.

proper document. A frequently mentioned example is the use of white font on white background, which hides the actual content. Moreover, active content is (in this context) crucial. On the one hand it provides a level of dynamics, which is required today for a more user-friendly presentation. On the other hand this level of dynamics might inherent the capability to disguise the actual content's presentation [10].

In addition, the presentation must be *transparently*. This issue is particularly essential in legal disputes proving non-repudiation: surveyors must trace that the document led to this presentation. In cases of a dispute, the presentation must be reproducible. This is only feasible, if the document format is known, i.e., if each byte and its function is disclosed. For this reason, a definite separation of content and presentation enables a more convenient solution to a higher level of transparency.

Perhaps the most important aspect, specifically when considering an entire system, is that the document must be displayed *securely*. So far, we considered the semantic and syntactic requirements of a document format. We did neither consider the application nor the system, which are threatened by certain attacks (e.g., Trojan horses [7]). An electronic document can only be trustworthily displayed when the intrinsic system is not compromised and sound. In other words, the system and its application are trusted. This is an ultimate prerequisite, or else a digital signature is not tamper-proof. Note that the argumentation is invertible: a trusted system, respectively, an application on its own is insufficient to present an electronic document trustworthily. In addition a suitable document format is needed, which enables the document's content to be displayed unambiguously (as discussed before).

In the case of multiple signatures, these requirements become more complex. As a trusted system is not part of this paper, we presuppose an uncompromised and sound system for the present work and concentrate on definitiveness and transparency.

3   Previous Works

In the past, several commercial and open document formats/standards have been proposed (see e.g. [11,12,13,14]) which are able to present electronically signed documents.

A basic approach is to transform the content into an image (see e.g. [15]). The user sees a static effigy of the document. The benefit of this approach is that a static document does not contain any active content, i.e., it circumvents the possibility of altering the content. This approach is from todays point of view impracticable as static documents are hardly editable, hardly processible and unqualified for multi-party business models. Another basic approach is encoded text as used in common signature standards (e.g. S/MIME [12], CMS [13]). However, the encoded text based standards have shortcomings. They define how to embed the signature—even multiple signatures (cf. [14])—into the document format. In contrast to XML, they do not define how to present the content;

the presentation depends on its application and, hence, is interpreted product-specifically.

The most tangential work was proposed by Scheibelhofer [8]. First of all, he deployed the benefits of XML technologies in the context of signing and verifying electronic documents. He developed an Internet terminal [16] aiming at signing, validating and trustworthily displaying electronic documents. Mainly, his approach is construed for single-signed documents. Our idea goes beyond. Although we use similar techniques, we also take into account the usage of multiple XML signatures. Furthermore, we do not provide an architecture for a signing terminal, instead we demonstrate that validating and visualising XML-signed documents is feasible in standard Web browsers.

4   Verification and Visualisation of Signed XML Documents

4.1   The Need for Multiple Signatures

Many business processes require multiple signatures. Usually the responsible persons do not sign at the same time and the same place. For example, the business process of creating an invoice by a fictive software company might require four different signatures: the confirmation of a person that certain goods have been packaged and shipped, the responsible sales person signing for special agreements that have been made with the customer, another signature by a controlling instance (the company's invoice department) and, finally, the signature of the general manager. Nevertheless, the different process participants are not willing—and partly not able—to sign the document in its completeness due to their restricted areas of responsibility. In this sense the person responsible for packaging for example will not be willing to sign special sales conditions. Therefore, if such a workflow is mapped to the digital world, the according responsibilities have to be mapped too; otherwise the new solution will not have the needed acceptance by all participants.

XML signatures provide two features which make them especially attractive for application scenarios that require complex signing processes: the use of XPath [17] expressions and the support for multiple signatures. The XML signature standard [3], published in february 2002 by the World Wide Web consortium as a W3C recommendation, defines an XML based format for digitally signed data. The data to be signed is referenced through Uniform Resource Identifiers (*URIs*) and may be XML as well as arbitrary digital content. The use of URIs enables the signing of external data sources like file or network resources. The XML signature is calculated over a list of XML references of which every reference contains the URI, the used hash algorithm and the hash value.

Additionally, the XML standard lists five different transformations—including XPath—which can be applied to the XML reference to be signed.[3] The

---

[3] Note that not all of these transformations are defined to be required. The implementation of XPath for example is *recommended* but not required by [3].

XML reference is first transformed before the according hash value is calculated. Hence, the transform or list of transforms respectively, act as a pre-processing step within the XML signature creation process. This fact has a great impact on the visualisation of the XML signature: the data secured by the signature might differ from the referenced source. This aspect is also addressed explicitly by [3] (see [3] chapters 8.1.2 and 8.1.3).

The primary purpose of XPath is to identify particular parts of an XML document (or more precisely: subsets of the XML document's node set). Furthermore, XPath also provides some basic operations for the manipulation of strings, numbers and booleans. As a conclusion, XPath expressions are sufficient to identify definite parts of a document that have to be signed.

An XML document may contain more than one signature. In particular, if it comprises some signatures securing parts of the document by the use of XPath, another signature covering the entire document's content may additionally be inserted. Every signature is represented by a <Signature> tag, which hosts any relevant data, such as key material, references and their according digests. Therefore each XML signature can be validated independently from the other ones.

The named properties of the XML signature are powerful features and, if properly used, enable an appropriate design of business processes in the digital domain. Nevertheless, they also result in new requirements regarding the validation and visualisation process of a signed XML document[4]: if the content of a PKCS#7 container comprising multiple signatures is manipulated all signatures will become invalid. In contrast to that a signed XML document may contain both valid and invalid signatures. The use of URIs and transformations in the XML references can additionally complicate the presentation problem, especially regarding the aspects of definitiveness and transparency. In the following we present an approach to overcome these problems. One important design goal thereby is the use of standard Web browsers for the verification and visualisation of the signed XML documents.

4.2   Visualisation Based on XSL Transformations

We propose to utilize the XSLT technology in order to present the signatures of an XML document to a human viewer. XSL transformations defined by [4] operate on an XML source tree and generate a result tree (possibly but not necessarily in XML format). The transformation is achieved by patterns defined by the XSLT, which are applied to the input. A popular application of XSLT is the transformation of XML input into HTML or XHTML output. We also make use of XSLT to generate a compact view of the XML signatures' signed data that can be displayed by a standard HTML browser. Moreover, we use XSLT to mark the signed data parts of the XML signatures for the visualisation, which will be explained below.

We describe our approach in a more detail before we discuss its advantages. Fig. 1 depicts the workflow representing our main idea: First the signed XML

---

[4] In the following a *signed XML document* means an XML document containing signatures according to the XML signature standard [3].

input document is validated against the XML schema defined by [3]. This step assures the syntactic correctness of the input. After that each XML signature of the input document is evaluated. The results comprising the signature's status and information about the signer are delivered to the XSLT facility[5]. Then the XPath expressions of the signatures, which define their signed data (in our application environment[6]) are extracted from the according `<Reference>` tags and passed to the XSLT component as well.

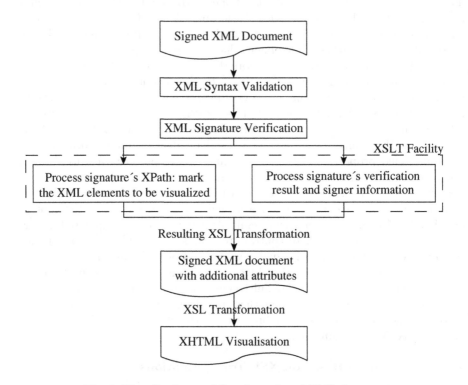

Fig. 1. Visualisation workflow for a signed XML document

The XSLT facility takes the original signed XML document as a basis for the resulting view of the document. It processes the XPath expressions of each signature to determine its signed data to be visualised. During this step every XML tag that belongs to the signed data part is provided with an additional attribute called `signatureID`. The value of this attribute is set to an unique id (e.g., the name of the signer), so that we are later able to distinguish the signed data parts of different signatures in the resulting XML document. After

---

[5] The XSLT facility is the component of our system, which is able to process XSL transformations.

[6] Note that in the given context we have documents in mind, which only use XPath as transformation—as already indicated in Section 4.1. Nevertheless, the outlined approach can be extended to cover additional transformations defined by [3].

processing all signatures this version of the signed XML document is stored as an intermediary result.

The intermediary result represents a machine readable version of the visualisation that we display to the human viewer. The values of the `signatureID` attributes act as a kind of highlighting in XML format. In the next step this highlighting must be transferred to a human readable view. Again we use an XSL transformation to produce an XHTML version of the original signed XML document. The highlighting given by the `signatureID` attributes is visualised and connected to the signer's identity. An example of such a visible highlighting is a box that is drawn around the signed data. Based on the status of the signature that the XSLT facility gets as input the highlighted parts of the XML document can be displayed in an adequate manner, such as a green box in case of a valid signature and a red box otherwise.

Our approach fits the requirement to present the validity of each XML signature contained in the input file individually to the human viewer. Moreover, the signed data of a given signature is visualised within its textual context. Thereby, the model of authorisation that comes along with a multisigned document is mirrored by our view. Another advantage is that any standard Web browser can display the XHTML result. This aspect leads to the idea to construct a Web based service, which offers verification services for signed and multisigned XML documents, i.e., to offer a centralised XML verification. Such a service may be offered either by a PKI operating entity in a local or by a trusted third party (e.g., a trust center) in a global application environment.

The use of the XSLT technology to prepare the visualisation for the human viewer facilitates particularly the support of different display devices. Based on the machine readable version of the visualisation different XSL transformations can be supplied to present the visualisation results also on devices with limited display capabilities (e.g., mobile phones). The format of the presentation results is thereby not restricted to XML or XHTML.

5   Proof of Concept Implementation

We use the Apache Java implementation [5] of the XML signature standard and the Apache XSLT processor Xalan [18] for our proof of concept realization. First we implement a Java module that takes a signed XML document as input, parses it, finds all contained XML signatures and finally does the validation of the signatures. This module makes intensive use of the named Apache library to do the verification.

After that the module extracts the XPath expressions that have been used during the creation of the XML signatures. In order to do so it loops through all references of a signature's `<SignedInfo>` element and identifies transformations of type XPATH. To export the xpath transformations out of the XML document the Java module creates an output file in form of an XSL transformation. The XPath expressions of the signed XML document are then written to the XSL output file. Thereby, the according XSL patterns are constructed to attach an unique signer id to each elements belonging to the signed data part of the signature. In detail we write a `<template>` element to the output file whereas we set the `match` attribute to the exported XPath while the content of the element is set to the signer id. To simplify the implementation we use the id attribute of the signature's `<SignedInfo>` tag even if this attribute is declared to be optional by the XML signature standard [3]. Furthermore, we output the XPath expressions of a given signature only if the validation process of this signature evaluates to be valid. In other words, we only highlight the valid signatures of an input document.

After the processing of the Java module has been finished the resulting XSL transformation is passed to the Xalan library (building the XSLT facility in our implementation). The transformation is then triggered by the Java module. The resulting XML document represents the machine readable version of the visualisation which we mentioned in Section 4.2. Regarding the representation for the human viewer we decided to develop an XSL transformation that transfers the content data of the XML document into an XHTML version. The signed data part of each signature is thereby surrounded by a box. Additionally, the text content of a border is displayed in dark colours if the according signer id is clicked whereas all other text of the document is faded out. Nevertheless, this is just a matter of design. Other forms of the visualisation are imaginable – dependant on the capabilities of the targeted display device – provided that the assignment of the signed parts to the signer is obvious.

As a sample business process requiring multiple signatures we created a fictive invoice document in XML format (see Fig. 2). We attached three different XML signatures to the document:

- the signer (with the id *Technician*) confirms that the invoiced software packages have actually been delivered,
- the signer *Salesperson* electronically signs the agreed prices as well as the invoice recipient's contact details and
- the signature *InvoiceDepartment* finally covers the entire document and confirms that the invoice document has correctly passed the prescribed workflow. In addition it guarantees the integrity of the document as a whole.

We applied our proof of concept implementation to the fictive invoice document and generated the according XHTML document. This document mirrors the different roles and the assigned authorisations of the signers: the technician, for instance, is not able to confirm the correctness of the pricing information, so she does not sign for it. It is therefore essential that the visualisation of her signature unambiguously presents to the viewer exactly those parts of the document that she actually signed. Our prototype implementation fits this requirement.

Fig. 2 shows the result when the signer id of the sales responsible is clicked: the numbers, prices and the invoice recipient are displayed in darker colours meaning that the sales responsible signed exactly these data. The delivery date of the invoiced products, for example, which is faded out and surrounded by another box is not part of her signature. We tested the output document with the

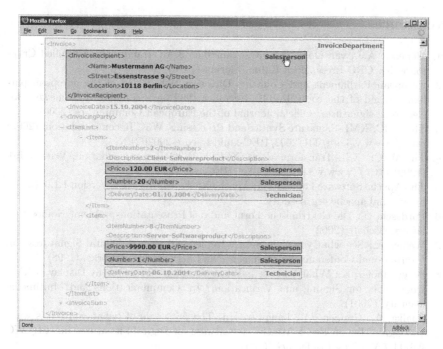

Fig. 2. Visualisation of signed XML invoice document

Mozilla Firefox (version 1.0) and with the Microsoft Internet Explorer (version 6) browsers.

6   Conclusion and Future Work

Our investigations of the XML signature standard and especially the implementation that we described in section 5 demonstrate the suitability of the XML signature for multisigned XML documents. XML signatures allow the design of digital workflows considering the different roles and according authorisations of the signers. The XSL transformations turned out to be an appropriate technology to realize a browser based visualisation system for signed XML documents. Moreover the Apache Software Foundation provides an usable implementation of the XML signature standard with [5], as our visualisation prototype shows.

Future research includes the investigation of more application examples that need multiple signatures and to define adequate visualization styles for them. Another area is to clearly define enhancements for current browsers (e.g., inclusion of XML signature verification) such that the display of signed documents on the WWW will be possible by simply providing a signed XML document and a (signed) XSLT transform.

The authors want to acknowledge the contribution of Lars Ewers regarding the proof of concept implementation of our approach.

References

1. Menezes, A.J., van Oorschot, P.C., Vanstone, S.A.: Handbook of Applied Cryptography. CRC Press, Boca Raton, Florida (1996)
2. European Parliament and Council: Directive 1999/93/ec of the european parliament and of the council of 13 december 1999 on a community framework for electronic signatures. Official Journal of the European Communities (2000)
3. The W3C: XML-Signature Syntax and Processing, W3C Recommendation. (2002) http://www.w3.org/TR/2002/REC-xmldsig-core-20020212/.
4. The W3C: XSL Transformations (XSLT), W3C Recommendation, Version 1.0. (1999) http://www.w3.org/TR/1999/REC-xslt-19991116.
5. The Apache Software Foundation: Apache XML Security API, Version 1.1.0. (2004) http://xml.apache.org/security.
6. Pordesch, U.: Die elektronische Form und das Präsentationsproblem. Nomos Verlagsgesellschaft (2002)
7. Weber, A.: See what you sign: Secure Implementations of Digital Signatures. In: International Conference on Intelligence and Services in Networks. (1998)
8. Scheibelhofer, K.: What You See Is What You Sign - Trustworthy Display of XML Documents for Signing and Verification. In: Communications and Multimedia Security. (2001)
9. Spalka, A., Cremers, A., Langweg, H.: The fairy tale of 'what you see is what you sign' - Trojan Horse Attacks on Software for Digital Signature. In: IFIP WG 9.6/11.7 Working Conference. (2001)
10. Kain, K., Smith, S., Asokan, R.: Digital Signatures and Electronic Documents: A Cautionary Tale. In: Communications and Multimedia Security. (2002)
11. Callas, J., Donnerhacke, L., Finney, H., Thayer, R.: OpenPGP Message Format. Network Working Group. (1998) Request for Comment 2440.
12. Hoffman, P.: Enhanced Security Services for S/MIME. Network Working Group. (1999) Request for Comment 2634.
13. Housley, R.: Cryptographic Message Syntax. Network Working Group. (1999) Request for Comments 2630.
14. Kaliski, B.: PKCS #7: Cryptographic Message Syntax Version 1.5. Network Working Group. (1998) Request for Comment 2315.
15. Utimaco AG: WYSIWYS - What you see is what you sign. (2003) http://www.utimaco.com/eng/content_pdf/wysiwys.pdf.
16. Scheibelhofer, K.: Signing XML Documents and the Concept of "What You See Is What You Sign". Institute for Applied Information Processing and Communications, Graz University of Technology. (2001)
17. The W3C: XML Path Language (XPath), W3C Recommendation, Version 1.0. (1999) http://www.w3.org/TR/1999/REC-xpath-19991116.
18. The Apache Software Foundation: Apache Xalan-Java, Version 2.6.0. (2004) http://xml.apache.org/xalan-j/.

Experience XML Security
The XML-Security Plug-In for Eclipse

Dominik Schadow

Pasingerstrasse 28, 82152 Planegg, Germany
info@xml-sicherheit.de,
http://www.xml-sicherheit.de

Abstract. The XML-Security Plug-In is a freely available plug-in for
the Eclipse platform and provides versatile XML security features in an
educational software like environment. Users can experiment with XML
security and inform themselves about the corresponding W3C recommendations. The aim of the plug-in is to raise interest in XML security functions and especially encourage users to sign and encrypt their
personal data and messages. This is a common aim with CrypTool, an
educational software for modern cryptography. This article will explain
the basic features of the XML-Security Plug-In and give a perspective
on the cooperation with the more general CrypTool.

1 Introduction

Security features for the Extensible Markup Language (XML) are basically defined by two recommendations of the World Wide Web Consortium (W3C):
XML-Signature Syntax and Processing[1] and XML Encryption Syntax and
Processing[2]. These two recommendations are available for almost three years
now and used in lots of commercial and non-commerical products and services:
Apache XML Security[1] and IBM XML Security Suite[2] are surely the most well-
known. But as standard cryptography, XML security lacks of end user acceptance.

One reason for that is, besides the relatively short availability of only three
years, certainly the absence of easy to use educational software in the XML
(security) area with the main focus on practical execution. Normal users are
not interested in reading extensive W3C recommendations and gaining all their
knowledge from theoretical studies. Furthermore a deep and broad knowledge
of XML security can only be achieved by a combination of practical experience
and theory, not only by studying the corresponding recommendations.

The *XML-Security Plug-In* tries to bridge this lack of user acceptance. Therefore the main focus lies clearly on easy practical execution of the W3C recommendations on digital signatures and encryption for end users. The plug-in is the
result of the authors diploma thesis 2004 at the University of Applied Sciences

---

[1] See http://xml.apache.org/security
[2] See http://www.alphaworks.ibm.com/tech/xmlsecuritysuite

J. Dittmann, S. Katzenbeisser, and A. Uhl (Eds.): CMS 2005, LNCS 3677, pp. 321–329, 2005.

Furtwangen. Since then the plug-in has been continuously enhanced with new features and possibilities.[3]

The plug-in requires an Eclipse[3] platform and extends it with versatile XML security features like digital signatures and encryption. As mentioned before, the main objective is to provide users an easy-to-use tool with rich functionality to experiment with XML security. Users can sign and encrypt their own existing XML documents; there is no limitation on sample files. The educational part - the theory behind XML security with its various recommendations and extensive information on how to use the plug-in - is located in the included online help.

In order to provide an easy and useful access to XML security, the XML-Security Plug-In consists of these five components

1. Canonicalization (with or without comments)
2. Digital Signatures
3. Verification
4. Encryption
5. Decryption

The XML-Security Plug-In addresses users with knowledge in XML and basic knowledge in modern cryptography, especially in the different signature and encryption algorithms (like AES or RSA). Experience in XML security is not necessary.

Users with no or little knowledge in modern cryptography can use the excellent educational software *CrypTool*[4] as a starter or reference tool. CrypTool brings out a good introduction for cryptographic knowledge as well as an extensive reference tool for cryptography and supports beginners in learning cryptographic basics needed for the XML-Security Plug-In.

2   Standard Cryptography

2.1   CrypTool

As in the XML-Security Plug-In, practical experience plays the important role in the software CrypTool. The application lets the user apply and analyse complex cryptographic mechanisms and reveals the inner working of digital signatures and hybrid encryption with interactive data flow diagrams. An extensive online help with information about digital signatures, hash functions and much more is available.[4]

CrypTool comes as a stand-alone application for Windows and addresses both cryptography beginners and advanced users. It is completely available in English and German. The used programming language is C/C++, therefore a Win32 environment is required.

---

[3] See http://www.eclipse.org
[4] See http://www.cryptool.com

The aim of CrypTool is to teach cryptographic methods and standards with a modern and interesting tool and to sensitize employees and end users in IT-security as well as to enable a deeper knowledge and awareness for cryptography. The methods available include both classical methods like Caesar encryption algorithm and modern cryptosystems like AES and DES algorithms. Asymmetric algorithms like RSA and DSA, based on both the factorization problem and on elliptic curves, are also available.

The development of CrypTool startet in 1996 and is basically done by the Deutsche Bank with the support of the universities of Darmstadt, Siegen and Karlsruhe. In this nine years history the software gained several awards like the European Information Security Award 2004[5] and some other German awards. The current version is 1.3.05, the next release is 1.3.10 and will be available soon.

2.2   Cooperation of CrypTool and XML-Security Plug-In

As described before, CrypTool and XML-Security Plug-In have an identical focus on end users in different areas of cryptography. CrypTool addresses beginners as well as advanced users, whereas the XML-Security Plug-In focuses on advanced users.

Cooperation between the CrypTool and the XML-Security Plug-In is useful (and indeed considered in practice) because they share the same aim. Plus the XML-Security Plug-In provides a focus on XML which is missing in the more general CrypTool to date. Moreover plans for a redesign and redevelopment of CrypTool have been in mind of the CrypTool authors for a while now. The opinion poll[6] on the CrypTool home page came to a clear decision for the programming language Java: 213 votes totally, 126 people voted for Java.[7] 56 users voted for the combination Java and Standard Widget Toolkit (SWT) of Eclipse, 70 for the combination of Java and Swing. One reason for this decision may be the much longer availability of Java Swing, whereas SWT is relatively new and not so much known outside the Eclipse community yet.

Based on this voting, the new *JCrypTool* will, as the *J* indicates, be completely developed in Java and will be available as an Eclipse Rich Client Platform (RCP) for multiple platforms. Due to the advantages of SWT and Eclipse, better performance and integration, SWT is the prefered technology.

As CrypTool itself, JCrypTool will be available in German and English. For the first time extensive XML security features - signatures, verification, encryption and decryption as well as the theoretical information - will be available in this educational software.

More information or a release plan are not yet available, the development process is still in an early stage. All information will be published on the Cryp-Tool and on the XML-Security Plug-in home page.

---

[5] See http://2004.rsaconference.com/europe/awards.aspx
[6] Poll available on CrypTool home page, results made available by CrypTool officers.
[7] As at June 2005.

3   XML-Security Plug-In

3.1   Plug-In Structure

The XML-Security Plug-In is a free of charge available plug-in for Eclipse version 3.0 and above. Besides Eclipse only an up to date Java Runtime Environment (JRE) or J2SE Development Kit (JDK) version 5.0 or newer is required. The XML-Security Plug-In can be used at no costs (freeware) in private, education and teachings as well as non-commercial and commercial environments. Redistribution is admitted and welcome, however commercial redistribution requires the explicit allowance of the developer.

To support the users in learning XML security, the design of the plug-in is as open as possible. This means that all the necessary data for a digital signature or encryption has to be entered or selected by the user. Depending on the wizard, different amounts of information are required before the XML document can be secured. By intention, the plug-in wizards provide many different functional choices. Therefore the user must perform quite a lot of explicit selection steps before a wizard can finish successfully.

In order to provide an easy access to its features, the XML-Security Plug-In extends the Eclipse workbench in different views. The most important extension point is available in standard Eclipse editors, as shown in the following figure. Moreover functions of the plug-in can be called via navigator or package explorer view.

Fig. 1. Context menu in an Eclipse editor

Every extension point consists of the same menu and contains the same structure. Nevertheless there are some differences between these extension points. The most important one is that a text selection can only be signed with a call from the context menu of an editor. The possibility of signing or encrypting a text selection shows a special feature of XML security: to secure only one or more elements, element content or parts of a document (document fragment).

It is possible to combine the wizards of the plug-in. A signed document can be encrypted subsequently and vice versa. Both ways are possible deliberately, even though it is more common and suggestive to sign first and encrypt afterwards. By comparing both possibilities, first sign - then encrypt and first encrypt - then sign, the user can easily compare these two sequences and discover the pros and cons for each one by own experience.

The signed and/ or encrypted XML document can be used outside of the plug-in and shared with other users. It is also possible to verify foreign XML signatures which were not created with the XML-Security Plug-In. Each signature which contains a valid KeyInfo element can be verified. The decryption of XML documents encrypted with other tools should be possible too, but depends on the used algorithms.

3.2   Apache XML Security API

The XML security application programming interface (API) shipped with the plug-in is the already mentioned Apache XML Security API version 1.2.1. This API is available as open source and comprises an extensive implementation of the W3C recommendations. Digital signatures are completely and stably implemented, every part of the W3C recommendation can be used. Encryption functionality grows with every release and catches up to digital signatures. Not every part of the encryption recommendation is completely and stably implemented yet. The range and the quality of the whole API are surely a result of the continuous enhancement by the large Apache community.

One point of criticism is the incomplete documentation and the basic code samples. Corresponding to the todo list this will be changed in future versions.[8]

There are special terms of license[9] for the Apache XML-Security API contained in the plug-in. These terms of license are only valid for the Apache XML-Security API (*xmlsec.jar*).

3.3   Basic Security Profile

Both the Digital Signature Wizard and the Encryption Wizard support the Basic Security Profile version 1.0 working group draft (BSP)[5] by the Web Services-Interoperability Organization (WS-I)[10]. The WS-I is an open industry organization, the BSP therefore consists of a set of non-proprietary web services specifications. The main objective of both the profile and the organization is higher service interoperability across platforms, operating systems and programming languages.

Using this profile in the plug-in activates different restrictions in the respective wizard. Due to the fact that the BSP does not allow enveloping signatures and discourages enveloped signatures, the Digital Signature Wizard preselects

---

[8] See Todo List on the Apache XML Security home page.
[9] See http://www.apache.org/licenses/LICENSE-2.0
[10] See http://www.ws-i.org

detached signatures for example. Other restraints affect the available algorithms; here the profile encourages the usage of RSA algorithms.[11]

3.4 Canonicalization

Canonicalization provides a comprehensible way to XML security. The user can select between the two types of exclusive XML canonicalization; one removes comments, the other one maintains them.[6] The intention of these commands is to point out to the user what happens to an XML document during the canonicalization process and to make the differences between a canonicalized and a non-canonicalized XML document visible.

A canonicalized (normalized) XML document has some significant differences to a standard XML document: among other things the canonicalized XML document is encoded in UTF-8, empty elements are converted to start-end tag pairs and whitespace outside of the document element and within start and end tags is normalized.[7]

3.5 Digital Signatures

Digital signatures are the most complex part of the plug-in. A wizard supports the user in the creation process and lets him enter step by step the necessary information to create a digital signature. With its versatile possibilities the wizard encourages users to combine different settings of digital signatures. Short annotations in this and every other wizard inform the user about the current wizard page and the required settings.

The first choice on the first wizard page refers to the data to be signed. Possible selections are *document, selection* and *XPath*. *Document* signs the complete XML document, *selection* an existing and well-formed text selection in the openend editor and *XPath* a document fragment specified by the entered or selected XPath expression.

The XML digital signature recommendation offers different kinds of signatures. All in common is that the signature object itself appears in XML syntax, but the data to secure can consist of XML or arbitrary data. Everything that can be referenced through a Uniform Resource Identifier (URI) can be signed. Because of that the user can choose between the standard W3C signature types *enveloping, enveloped* and *detached* in the wizard.

In an enveloping signature, the signed data appears inside the signature element. Signed data surrounding the XML signature is called enveloped signature. A separated signature (in the same document as the data or outside) is called a detached signature.[8]

The complete first page of the digital signature wizard is shown in the next figure. Every wizard has the same standard layout, with short help information at the top, content in the middle and navigation buttons at the bottom.

---

[11] See section 8 of the Basic Security Profile working draft.

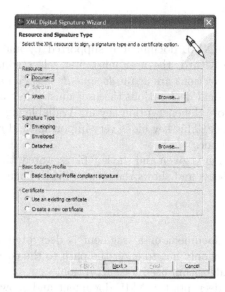

Fig. 2. First page of the digital signature wizard

On the following wizard page the user has either to enter the necessary information for an existing Java KeyStore or to create a new one with the help of the wizard. A newly created certificate is stored in the current project directory and can be reused in future signing processes inside and outside of the plug-in.

The third and last page finally allows the user to select the algorithms to use for the signature. Necessary information are the algorithms for canonicalization and transformation as well as a message digest and a signature algorithm.

After all the information is given, the wizard signs the selected document (-fragment) and shows the secured XML document to the user.

3.6 Verification

Verification lets the user quickly verify any signed XML document that contains a valid KeyInfo element. Corresponding to the XML digital signature recommendation, the KeyInfo element is an optional element that enables the recipient to obtain the key needed to validate the signature.[12] In the plug-in the KeyInfo element is required for verification and contains the users' certificate.

The result of the verification, a valid or invalid signature, is directly shown to the user. The fast verification result makes it easy to manipulate parts of an XML document and to see, which manipulation breaks a signature and which does not. This way the user can experience the special feature of XML signatures where only document fragments are signed and the rest of the XML document remains in an insecure state.

---

[12] See section 4.4 of the XML-Signature Syntax and Processing recommendation

3.7   Encryption

The encryption of an XML document is supported by another wizard. As in the digital signature wizard, the user must first select which data should be encrypted. Possible selections are again *document, selection* and *XPath*.

Besides some optional declarations the user must select an encryption algorithm and a file to store the encryption key in. Available algorithms are AES or Triple-DES for example. This key file is very important and required to decrypt the XML document later.

After all information is given and the key file is stored, the wizard takes care of the encryption process and shows the secured XML document to the user.

3.8   Decryption

An encrypted XML document or a fragment is decrypted with the help of a small wizard. The user only has to enter the path to the correct key file and to select the transport algorithm used for encryption.

The wizard then decrypts the XML document and shows the result to the user. Decryption will fail if a wrong key file is used.

3.9   Online Help

The online help contains the educational and theoretical parts of the XML-Security Plug-In and consists of two main sections. First it includes extensive information about the two W3C recommendations on digital signatures and encryption as well as related specifications or recommendations like canonicalization and the Basic Security Profile. The second section of the online help contains extensive support and hints for the first steps with the plug-in, its usage and possibilities.

The online help is easily accessible in the Eclipse workbench all the time and is completely in German. In the new Eclipse platform version 3.1 the online help will be available in a special view as *Dynamic Help* too. This way help information can always be visible in the same perspective and not only in a separate window.

4   Conclusions

The XML-Security Plug-In provides an easy and practical access to XML security and the W3C recommendations for end users without much previous knowledge or experience. Users can get in touch with cryptography for XML in an interesting and practical way and learn all aspects of XML security by experimentation. In addition to the practical experience the theoretical background is available in the online help.

CrypTool is a recommendable starting and lookup tool for classic and modern cryptography and contains all the basics needed to understand XML security and to work reasonable with the XML-Security Plug-In. Both tools can easily be used together and extend each other in various ways.

The intention of the plug-in is to interest and sensitize more users for the need of cryptography and to show them, how easily XML documents can be secured with the W3C recommendations. To support this aim, the usage of the XML-Security Plug-In is totally free of charge and continuously enhanced with new possibilities and features.

The latest version of the XML-Security Plug-In, tutorials, documentation, user discussion group and much more are available on the plug-in home page www.xml-sicherheit.de. Critical user feedback and suggestions are always welcome and appreciated.

References

1. Eastlake III, D., Reagle, J., Solo, D.: XML-Signature Syntax and Processing. RFC 3275, March 2002. http://www.ietf.org/rfc/rfc3275, and W3C Recommendation, 12 February 2002. http://www.w3.org/TR/xmldsig-core/
2. Eastlake III, D., Reagle, J.: XML Encryption Syntax and Processing. W3C Recommendation, 10 December 2002. http://www.w3.org/TR/xmlenc-core/
3. Schadow, D.: Ein praktisches XML Signatur- und Verschluesselungstool. Datenschutz und Datensicherheit, 4 (2005) 193–196
4. Deutsche Bank: CrypTool. eLearning Program for Cryptology, 29 March 2005. http://www.cryptool.com
5. Barbir, A., Gudgin, M., McIntosh, M., Morrison, K.: Basic Security Profile - Version 1.0 (WGD), Work-ing Group Draft, 12 May 2004, http://www.ws-i.org/Profiles/BasicSecurityProfile-1.0.html
6. Boyer, J.: Canonical XML. W3C Recommendation, 15 March 2001. http://www.w3.org/TR/xml-c14n
7. Boyer, J., Eastlake III, D., Reagle, J.: Exclusive XML Canonicalization. W3C Recommendation, 18 July 2002. http://www.w3.org/TR/xml-exc-c14n
8. Eastlake III, D., Niles, K.: Secure XML - The New Syntax for Signatures and Encryption. Boston: Addison-Wesley (2003)

How to Make a Federation Manageable

Christian Geuer-Pollmann

European Microsoft Innovation Center,
Ritterstrasse 23, 52072 Aachen, Germany
chgeuer@microsoft.com
http://www.microsoft.com/emic/

Abstract. Nowadays, the setup of seamless, cross-organizational working environments is a challenging task, mainly because of security-related problems. The available options for cross-domain collaboration are often dysfunctional, expensive and not in line with the organization's business needs. Despite the proliferation of claims-based mechanisms like SAML, WS-Trust or WS-Federation, additional guidance is necessary how to effectively apply these technologies. The architectural pattern and ideas presented in this talk are an attempt to solve a common class of problems in collaboration space.

The opinions expressed in this keynote presentation are my personal ones, and do not represent or endorse my employer's point of view in any way. This presentation is highly influenced by the current thinking and work inside the EMIC security group. In particular I would like to thank Laurent Bussard, Joris Claessens, Stéphanie Deleamont and Mark Gilbert

1 How It Is Today – Surviving in Security Management Hell

1.1 A Problem Statement

In this keynote talk, I would like to tell a story about the security management nightmares information workers encounter when they have cross-partner collaborations with people in other organizations. During our daily work, we often come into situations where we have to share data or services with our partners. A typical example (from our own site) is proposal preparation: multiple partners want to collaboratively share documents and other files, so that these data objects are accessible to a small set of people, and these files are continually changed by many people. Working with multiple companies is a common situation for many people: sales forces during contract negotiation, companies that expose services to government bodies, or consultants working for a customer.

The problem is that the set of collaborating people is an ad-hoc formed group that consists of people from different organizations. These organizations understandably shield their internal networks against the outside world. This is normally done by firewalls which limit external communication channels to well-understood protocols like HTTP and e-mail. The underlying assumption of this compartmentalization process is that the majority of interactions happen inside the organization's network, so that it's fine to constrain outbound and inbound resource access. The administrators have to balance the organization's security needs with the employee's user experience and comfort level.

J. Dittmann, S. Katzenbeisser, and A. Uhl (Eds.): CMS 2005, LNCS 3677, pp. 330 – 338, 2005.

While this compartmentalization helps administrators to assess their network's attack surface, it is a serious obstacle for the people who want to collaborate. In situations where only few cross-partner interactions happen, sending documents forth and back via e-mail is a minor annoyance for users. In other scenarios, e-mail exchanges just don't work or do not scale well. For instance, in situations where more sophisticated interactions are necessary, such as access to specific services, shielding of the internal network is dysfunctional, because users are forced to choose non-favorable (non-manageable or insecure) options. We've seen many options people normally turn to and I will quickly outline the two that are the most successful (but still fairly dysfunctional).

1.2 Dysfunctional Option #1: Do-It Yourself Service Hosting – Wrestling with the IT Department

Imagine a scenario where the collaborating people need a service for shared file storage. Bob offers that his company could host this service in the company's DMZ. The DMZ is the 'demilitarized zone', a network perimeter outside of the company's internal core network. The DMZ has less restrictive permissive security policies than the internal network. One advantage of this approach is that the service is operated inside a controlled area by Bob's own company, so that the service security is controlled by one of the partners. The other advantage is that the IT department is aware of the fact that people from other organizations have access to resources inside the company.

Unfortunately, there are also three downsides with this approach: First of all, somebody (Bob) has to persuade the IT department that there is a business justification to deploy this specific service inside the company's DMZ. This is usually a hassle that few people in big organizations would like to go through. The ones that do are rarely successful in a time scale under three months of lobbying, which is not very appropriate for short term engagements.

The second problem is user management: somebody (usually Bob) has to ask all the collaboration partners about which of their employees have to get access to the service. For each of these people, a guest account has to be created. During the life cycle of the project, this set of users will change, thus requiring Bob to make sure that the company's IT department gets notified of the changes.

The last problem is that the IT department also has to make sure that the access control lists for the service are in line with the business needs, so that Bob has to specifically instruct the administrators about access rights.

As a conclusion, this option respects corporate (security) policy, but has a high price tag with respect to management overhead and setup time.

1.3 Dysfunctional Option #2: Service Outsourcing – Bypassing Your Company's Security Controls

Another option for the user is to host the service at a 3rd party site, e.g. at an application service provider. One potential advantage is that the costs of setting up the service may be slightly lower, because the company's IT department does not have to provide the infrastructure. Nevertheless, the costs for user management are the same, as accounts for people from different organizations have to be set up and maintained. One big advantage of this approach is that the potentially vulnerable services do not have to be hosted inside the company's network, thus reducing the threats to the network itself. The direct drawback is, that potentially critical and sensitive data that the partners want to share, is hosted outside their own trusted networks. In addition, this solution has very bad audit characteristics: neither the company's IT department nor the executives of the company may be aware of the fact that the company's business relies on outsource services, and if something goes wrong, it can be very hard to figure out what happened.

The next section describes our fundamental beliefs how collaborations work. Section 3 on *"How it should be"* outlines our thoughts how collaboration (and the necessary authentication and authorizations) should work ideally. The mechanisms that will help solving these problems are federations and 'claims-based security', described in section 4. Section 5 *"How to apply these tools"* provides an architectural overview how we believe federations and the claims-based security model can be utilized to solve our problem. Section 6 *"What it brought us"* assesses and outlines the benefits for the different stake holders. The document concludes with a brief outlook.

2   Our Beliefs Regarding Collaboration

Before going into the details of the scenario, I would like to outline the beliefs we have and the assumptions we make, in order to know how a 'potential' solution could be:

2.1   Trust Across Organizations Depends on People Who Trust Each Other

When it comes to cross-organizational collaboration, the decision to work together is often done by people who know each other personally. The fact that two or more companies collaborate in general may not directly help people during their daily work. The actions that are performed in a particular collaboration should be traceable back to these people. This means that actions in the collaboration are justified because two humans trusted each other and intended to collaborate. When for instance two people exchange information, this exchange should be tied to an existing collaboration. The collaboration itself is tied to the people in the organizations who rooted the trust and bootstrapped the project.

2.2   Whoever Makes a Decision Should Have the Tool to Enforce That Decision

Much frustration arises from the fact that people like administrators have to make or enforce decisions that are beyond their duties. Business people who start a new project should control who of their colleagues works on 'their' project. This means that the business people should be responsible for assigning people and resources to their project and for defining the roles of these people and resources. In return, administrators should be freed from implementing these specific user and role assignments for the business people, while having the confidence that the network remains protected.

2.3 Collaborations Must Be Visible and Manageable Inside the Company

Another source of frustration is missing information, which people would need to get their job done. Ongoing collaborations (and their specific details) should be visible to various people in the company. For instance, the CEO should have a tool at hand to easily find out whether somebody inside her company collaborates with a specific partner. Administrators should be able to determine whether other partner organizations have access to a specific resource inside their network. Administrators should also have the chance to associate inbound messages to certain collaborations. That would enable administrators to temporarily block message exchanges with a certain partner, if they learn that this partner has a network security problem.

3 How It Should Be – A Fairy Tale

Now that I've described our beliefs, let me walk you through a quick scenario that describes how collaborations could work, and how technology can be used to help, instead of having to wrestle with it.

3.1 Bootstrapping Trust

Alice and Bob have known each other for a long time and have worked together on past projects. Based on their past experience, they trust each other personally and plan to work together on a collaborative project. Alice works for the company 'Contoso Ltd', whereas Bob works for 'Fabrikam, Inc'. We also assume that both have a mid-level managerial position inside their companies' hierarchy, so that they are permitted to start collaborations on their own, on behalf of their respective companies. Alice and Bob agree to start a specific collaboration.

The first thing Alice and Bob have to do is to give this new collaboration between Contoso and Fabrikam a name, like 'Project X'. The name is necessary to distinguish between parallel projects that exist in the same partner organizations. It is necessary that these different projects can be distinguished from each other.

Alice and Bob have to exchange their 'corporate business cards'. A corporate business card is similar to the root certificate of a corporate certification authority, enriched with additional information like the network address of the company's 'security token service' (STS). An STS (described in the section 4) is a service that can issue and validate security tokens for a given trust domain. By exchanging the corporate business cards, the two companies' IT systems can validate each others security tokens, thus creating a federation.

3.2 Enacting a 'Constrained' Federation

After agreeing to start the project, assigning it a name and exchanging business cards, Alice and Bob instruct their corporate IT systems that the project now has to be started. Basically, Alice tells Contoso's IT system:

> "I ('Alice@Contoso') have started a project with Fabrikam.
> My peer contact there is Bob@Fabrikam. The project is
> called 'Project X'. Here is Fabrikam's business card, so now

you can validate tokens they issue. The project should be enacted now, and it should expire in three months from now. If somebody has questions about that collaboration, just ask me, because I (Alice) am the project's business owner from our side."

Bob does the same inside his own network. After this step, the *constrained* federation is enacted, i.e. both companies know about the project and can validate each other's security tokens. 'Constrained' means that the federation must only be used in the scope of the specific project, i.e. it must not be used for other purposes.

Unfortunately, nobody can (yet) do anything inside the project, because neither people, nor resources are associated with it. Both Alice and Bob have to decide what people from their own organization are assigned to the project. 'Being assigned' to the project means that these people are authorized to request specific (branded) security tokens that can only be used inside that particular project. This also applies to resources: Messages with project-bound security tokens must only be forwarded to services that are associated to the project.

4 Federations and the Claims-Based Security Model – Our Knight in Shining Armor

4.1 What's in a Federation

Nowadays, federated identity management is a solution for the user management problems in the above scenarios. Multiple technology proposals, ranging from SAML, Shibboleth and the Liberty Alliance to WS-Trust and WS-Federation, attempt to provide solutions for federating trust domains. Regardless of what specific technology is used, the main question is: *"What does it practically help, now that we've set up an identity federation with our partners?"* The easy answer is that a federation helps entities inside one organization to authenticate subjects from another organization. Simply speaking, when a service receives a security token, it can be validated whether the token was issued by a partner organization. This is very similar to signed e-mail in which a recipient can be sure that the mail originated in a particular organization. So using federation technologies, one can implement the first step to a cross-organizational single sign-on.

The unanswered (and tough) question is how a recipient (like a service) can validate whether the subject is *authorized* to perform certain actions, like invoking the service. The fact that an incoming e-mail comes from one of the collaboration partners does not mean that the sender of the e-mail is part of the specific collaboration project and is authorized by the business owner inside the partner organization. Without asking "Does your colleague Greg work on our project", it is impossible to validate whether an incoming request is authorized or not.

4.2 Claims-Based Security

In a 'claims-based' system, security decisions are performed based on 'claims' that are supplied by a requestor. In this context, a claim is "an assertion of the truth of something, typically one which is disputed or in doubt" [3]. SAML and WS-Trust/WS-Federation are claims-based systems. A claim could be an X.509 certificate, which asserts that the subject that holds the corresponding private key is 'known' to the CA under the given distinguished name. Other classes of claims could be a username, a SAML assertion or a capability (from a capability-based security system). In our example, a claim is a statement by one of the partners that a certain user or service is associated with the project. Such a claim can only be validated by parties which are part of the constrained federation.

Claims are statements by a claim provider about a particular subject. To ensure that these claims really originate from the claim provider, claims can be protected using data origin authentication mechanisms like digital signatures or message authentication codes. Multiple claims can be combined, in order to build a higher-order claim. These higher-order claims are called 'security tokens', i.e. a security token contains one or more claims. By their very nature, security tokens can have an arbitrary amount of complexity. Comparing this with an X.509 certificate, the X.509 certificate is very simple because of its well-defined semantics (ignoring that X.509v3 extensions and OIDs make it harder).

A client that aims to invoke a service may not be in possession of the appropriate security token that is necessary to invoke a particular service. Imagine a client that possesses a username/password pair or a Kerberos ticket that are only valid within the corporate network. With these security tokens alone, it is impossible to invoke a service in another trust boundary, because these security tokens are not understood or will not be accepted by the target service.

This dilemma is solved by token transformers, so-called 'security token services' (STS). An STS is a service that can take an existing security token (like username/password) and transform it into another token that will be valid inside another trust boundary. This transformation can be either issuing a new token or validating an existing token. To get a token issued, the client asks the STS: "Please, I have this token here that you can recognize, please give me a token that I can use over there." During token validation, the recipient of a security token asks the STS: "I received this token here and I do not understand the claims inside the token. Could you please bring it into a form that I can understand?"

The concept of security token services, together with a very simple language to request and validate security tokens is specified in the WS-Trust specification [1]. The WS-Federation specification [2] is a guideline based on WS-Trust, which describes how to combine different STSs in order to implement identity, account, attribute and authorization federation, as well as delegation across different trust realms. For further reference, the 'Laws of Identity' [3] provide an excellent background how identity systems in general (and the claims used therein specifically) should be constructed in order to be acceptable for the different stakeholders.

5 How to Apply the Tools – A Simplified Architectural Overview

The following illustration provides a simplified overview on the solution architecture: Both Alice and Bob setup the constrained federation inside their respective organizations.

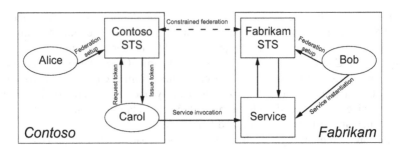

The constrained federation is established by Alice and Bob inserting the entry about the project into their companies' security token services. After this entry, each STS knows *that* the project exists and what the security token of the partner's STS is. In addition to that, Alice instructs Contoso's STS that Carol is part of the project. This means that the Contoso STS will issue project-bound security tokens to Carol if requested by her. On the peer side at Fabrikam, Bob dynamically creates a service and 'adds' that service to the project by inserting that association into the Fabrikam STS.

Besides just associating Carol to the project, Alice also needs a way to attribute Carol's STS entry with roles statements or similar claims. So Alice needs to be able to express that Carol is an 'editor' or 'reviewer' inside the 'Project X' collaboration. With that additional claims embedded into the cross-organizational security token, the Fabrikam STS can decide not only whether the invoked service belongs to the 'Project X', but also whether the specific operation is permitted to users with the role. This decision can be taken by the Fabrikam STS because the security token contains role claims, and because Bob inserted the "'Project X'-Editors can write on services associated to Project X, reviewers can only read" into the STS. This information can be only provided by Bob, because Bob is the business owner of the service and the collaboration, and should be able to answer (and maintain) such information.

One important aspect to note down is that 'regular' users (which are not system administrators) will be able to insert security-critical information into the company's overall security system. This implies that 'regular users' will be able to 'open the door' to the company's internal network to people which do not belong to the company. This implies a serious threat to the network: It must be ensured that only services which are associated to the project will accept incoming messages from external parties. In order to ensure this, the company's network must have strong enforcement components that permit message delivery only to services that belong to the project. An additional mechanism to reduce the threat potential is to have dynamic service instantiation and strong process isolation, so that services are only associated to a single project. As a first step, conservative deployments could instantiate the exposed services inside the company's DMZ or another compartmentalized area.

6   What It Brought Us – Problems Solved?

To conservative security people, this scenario should be frightening: regular users (who usually have no security education) will be able to expose resources inside the company to external people. So what does this apparently risky idea bring? There are multiple stakeholders impacted:

6.1 IT and Network Administrators

- The first advantage for administrators is that they can concentrate on systems administration work, without being disturbed with user management and change requests to specific access control lists.
- Administrators have the complete overview of what resources are exposed to other companies inside the corporate STS. The corporate STS has a complete view on what constrained federations exist. For each of these federations, the central corporate STS provides information which services are associated with the federation. In addition, the STS provides the information who the other companies are that have access to these services. All this information is necessary to perform audits over the IT systems and to determine the potential attack surface and threats that the corporate network is exposed to.
- Each incoming message must have a valid security token attached. Messages without valid security tokens can be blocked easily. In case of suspicious messages, the attached security token enables administrators to find the business owner both inside their own company, as well as in the partner companies. Therefore, malicious messages that have been sent by people inside partner companies can, in corroboration with the partner company, be linked to an individual inside that partner company.
- Administrators can also decide that all interactions (both inbound and outbound) with a particular partner can be blocked as long as necessary. For instance, collaborations can be 'put on hold' if certain partners have security problems with their IT infrastructures. The corporate STS is the single point of control to enforce such policies.
- As a last point, administrators have the confidence that proprietary data, that is shared across partners, is not stored outside the federation, e.g. on 3rd-party IT systems like an application service provider. This assures that this data is protected either by their own or by the partner's network.

6.2 Top Executives

- Top-level managers like e.g. a CEO can extract valuable business information from the central STS, e.g. "Who inside my own organization works together with this partner company?"
- If necessary, top-level managers can use the central STS in order to enforce business decisions, e.g. "We terminate (or suspend) all collaborative business with this specific partner."
- Another interesting option is to prevent the setup of certain collaborations: "For the time being, no new collaborations with these specific partner organizations can be established without further vice president approval".

6.3 Mid-level Managers

The mid-level managers are people like Alice and Bob. These people are the core of the collaborations.

- With the approach presented in this paper, these people have an effective tool to establish new collaborations, which gives them full control over the business-related details of the collaboration.
- This tool provides a minimum-effort mechanism to directly associate employees and resources to collaborations.
- It ensures that their business relationships are automagically visible to the top-level management. This gives them confidence that each collaboration they establish will be in line with the company's overall partner strategy.
- As a last point, the STS is *the* central tool to maintain their relationships with other partners. For instance, it is easy to determine "What collaborations and projects do me and my team own?"

7 Conclusions

This paper presented our view on how security management for distributed systems could be enhanced, in particular for situations where cross-organizational collaboration is a business necessity. The driving force during the development of this architecture was to focus on the business needs of the different stakeholders. We believe that the developed security architecture correctly reflects how human trust relationships in cross-partner collaborations work. The next steps will be to validate that such a system is manageable at a broad scale. This validation is expected to happen in the scope of collaborative research projects, like the European FP6 project TrustCoM.

One common aspect for aspect for software companies is that the employees have to use new software themselves before rolling the products out to clients. For ourselves, the main challenge will be to apply this new model to our own collaborative working environment.

References

1. Martin Gudgin, Anthony Nadalin: *WS-Trust*, (February 2005) http://msdn.microsoft.com/ws/2005/02/ws-trust/
2. Chris Kaler, Anthony Nadalin: *WS-Federation*, (July 2003)http://msdn.microsoft.com/ws/2003/07/ws-federation/
3. Kim Cameron: *The Laws of Identity*, (May 2005),http://www.identityblog.com/stories/2005/05/13/TheLawsOfIdentity.doc

XML Signatures in an Enterprise Service Bus Environment

Eckehard Hermann and Dieter Kessler

Research & Development XML Integration,
Uhlandstraße 12
64297 Darmstadt, Germany
{Eckehard.Hermann, Dieter.Kessler}@softwareag.com

Abstract. The goal of service oriented architectures (SOA) is to allow a message based and loosely coupled interaction between different web services. This approach allows the orchestration of web services in distributed, heterogeneous applications where the different services can be implemented in different programming languages, run on different machines and be based on different protocols. The adoption of web services to integrate systems within an organization and with partners is strongly dependent on the security standards that accompany service oriented architectures (SOA). The XML (Extensible Markup Language) Signature standard plays a key role here. For protecting such a distributed application, XML Signatures are used on several levels and for different challenges, for example to guarantee the integrity and authenticity of the exchanged messages and their authentication information, as well as the audit trails and to provide non-repudiation. The paper describes the role of XML Signatures for protecting Enterprise Service Bus (ESB) based SOA applications.

1 Introduction

1.1 Background - Enterprise Service Bus

The phrase "Enterprise Service Bus" describes an architectural pattern in which applications are created by composing software components together in such a way that complete business processes are reflected. In an ESB, the software components are packaged as high-level "services", which are platform-neutral and which can be described in terms of the documents which they take as input and the documents which they produce as output. These input and output documents are formatted as XML. An ESB-based application therefore involves XML documents, being routed from one software component to the next, where each one performs a particular processing step on the document. ESBs differ architecturally from earlier "hub and spoke" integration patterns. The central role within the "hub and spoke" architecture is played by a broker, which connects all services. In contrast, an ESB is a message oriented middleware (MOM) that allows all services to communicate directly with each other. Another difference is that an ESB is independent of the transfer protocol: the SOAP binding defines how the messages are bound to the different protocols such as TCP/IP or HTTP.

J. Dittmann, S. Katzenbeisser, and A. Uhl (Eds.): CMS 2005, LNCS 3677, pp. 339–347, 2005.

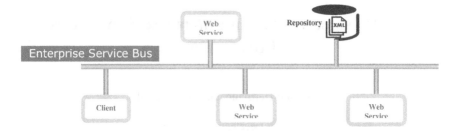

Fig. 1. Orchestration of internal and external services with an ESB

It can be argued that ESB architectures have been in existence for many years, but the addition of XML technologies has made ESBs much easier to implement. These XML technologies include:

- SOAP (Simple Object Access Protocol, since SOAP 2.0 it is no longer an abbreviation): For enveloping XML documents which are exchanged among services in an ESB, and for routing
- WSDL (Web Services Description Language): For describing the different services, orchestrated by the ESB
- XML Schema: For describing XML documents used by an ESB
- XSLT (Extensible Stylesheet Language Transformation): For converting an XML document from one format to another
- XML Signature: For securing the service oriented architecture on different levels

1.2 XML Signature

The data to be signed with an XML Signature is referenced via a URI with the help of Reference elements which are part of a SignedInfo element of an XML signature. The data to be signed can be transformed, using the Transforms element, prior to forming the hash value for the canonical form of the referenced data. This hash value which is subsequently computed for the referenced and transformed data is entered in the SignedInfo part of the XML signatures as the DigestValue element. When the DigestValue has been generated for all references, the canonical form is created from the SignedInfo element of the Signature element and a second hash value is computed for the result. This hash value is encrypted using the signer's private key. It constitutes the actual digital signature and is attached to the XML signatures as the SignatureValue. All referenced documents are thereby endowed with one digital signature [1].

1.3 Secure the Service Oriented Architecture

Like other applications, a service oriented architecture is protected by addressing the following requirements and finding an adequate answer to the related questions:

- **Authentication** - Who is attempting to gain access?
- **Authorisation** - Which resources is this client allowed to access?

```
<Signature ID?>
  <SignedInfo>
    <CanonicalizationMethod/>
    <SignatureMethod/>
    (<Reference URI? >
      (<Transforms>)?
      <DigestMethod>
      <DigestValue>
    </Reference>)+
  </SignedInfo>
  <SignatureValue>
  (<KeyInfo>)?
  (<Object ID?>)*
</Signature>
```

Fig. 2. XML Digital Signature Syntax [2]

- **Integrity** - Has the data or system been tampered with?
- **Confidentiality** - Can the data be read while in transit or storage?
- **Non-repudiation** - Can a sender deny having sent a message?
- **Auditing** - Is there a record of client access to data?
- **Availability** - Is this system vulnerable to a denial-of-service attack?

For securing a SOA, XML Signature is a key concept to address the authentication, integrity and non-repudiation topics directly, and authorization and auditing indirectly. In the following the role of XML Signature in the different areas is discussed.

2 Importance of XML Signature

2.1 Motivation

As mentioned above, Enterprise Service Bus based applications orchestrate different web services into one distributed application. Each request is processed as one business transaction. To be able to analyse and reproduce the different steps in case of an attack, (during a business transaction) a legally relevant audit trail is important. It can also be used as input information for intrusion detection systems to prevent future attacks after the same schema. To give an audit trail legal relevance, it is necessary to know when and by whom the trails were created and if it was possible to manipulate the audit trail. A whole new dimension is added by the cascading nature of applications, which is given in case of an ESB based SOA. Each web service participating in a business transaction, as well as the ESB itself, writes its own audit trail, each of which must be protected.

Normally web services are not directly used by a human user. At the very least, there is a client application between the web service and the user, in more complex scenarios like an ESB based application, there are a web service client, the ESB and probably several cascading web services. In the worst case, each of these services needs to authenticate and authorize the user. To allow the services to check the authentication result and to authorize the requesting user, but on the other hand free the user from having to logon multiple times (which would require a distributed administration of authorization rules), a single sign on mechanism and centralized point of administering access rights is necessary.

In a distributed environment where messages travel from the sender to the receiver via several hosts and services, it is important for the receiver to be able to prove that the message arrived unchanged, by whom it was sent, and perhaps at what exact time it was sent or arrived.

Digital signatures and especially XML Signature can be a solution for these issues, as discussed in the following.

2.2   Identity Federation in a Distributed Web Services Environment

One of the most critical topics of a distributed heterogeneous application, especially if legacy systems are involved, is the authentication and authorization of the requesting client. Independent applications and components that are wrapped by a web service and which are orchestrated to one distributed web service application normally have their own authentication and authorization behavior, running in their own independent domain.

2.2.1   The Identity Provider

The orchestration of these components via web services also includes the orchestration of the authentication and probably the centralisation of the access right administration, to allow the definition of overall security policies. The problem of different domains where user Bob in domain A is not equal to user Bob in Domain B can be solved by the introduction of a trusted third party, the Identity Provider, which plays the role of a central point of authentication and user management. All the different participating web services have to trust the Identity Provider and its user and role mapping decisions. The Identity Provider has to know that the identity of a client e.g. "Joe" authenticated as "Bob" in domain A is the "Steve" in domain B.

The authentication has to be done by the Identity Provider. After a successful authentication, the Identity Provider provides the identity of the authenticated user in the different domain. This identity information can now be placed as part of the message, sent to the distributed web service application, which allows the participating web services to find out the user's identity and authorize the user depending on his local a ccess rights. To exchange messages between web services, the SOAP protocol, defined in XML is used. A SOAP message consists of a header and content section. The SOAP header contains meta information, necessary for routing and processing the data provided in the content section of the SOAP message. The distinction between the content and meta data sections of a SOAP message makes it possible to place the identity information as part of the SOAP Header, which is defined by the Web Service Security standard [7].

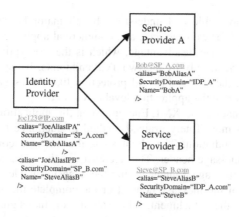

Fig. 3. Identity provider and multiple service providers as identity federation [4]

2.2.2 Identity Federation

The complete concept of this single sign-on approach is based on the trust relationship between the different web services and the Identity Provider and the integrity and authenticity of the identity information, placed in the messages. To guarantee integrity and authenticity, the identity data is digitally signed by the Identity Provider. Because the protocol that is used to exchange the message and the message themselves are in XML, the signature created by the Identity Provider is also an XML Signature. To validate the integrity and authenticity of the identity information, the web services have to validate the XML Signature signing the identity information and created by the Identity Provider. Beside the identity information, the XML Signature is also placed in the message as part of the SOAP header. [7]

2.3 Message Integrity and Non-repudiation

In an open architecture like the SOA, it is vital to protect the messages that are being transmitted from client to server and further from the server to other services within or even outside a closed network. Because of the human-readable format of XML messages, attackers are very much attracted. When orders are being passed over the internet, the issuer, the order object and sometimes the bank details are transmitted. If this happened over an unprotected line, attackers would have a very easy job in forging and spoofing messages either from the client or from the service.

It is therefore very important to have a tool to guarantee that the message was not modified in transit and that each party can be sure that no other fraudulent party is participating. One of the first countermeasures is the usage of SSL [10].

- SSL allows the client to determine that the service is the real service that he is supposed to communicate with. The SSL server (i.e. the service provider) sends his certificate, which is checked by the client (application).
- SSL guarantees message integrity. All traffic between the two TCP endpoints is protected from forgery.
- SSL encrypts all traffic, so that the (even plain text XML) messages cannot be read by unauthorized parties.

SSL is widely available and understood by all major browsers. Also, SSL can easily be configured for web services, and commercial applications usually support it as well. But SSL has one disadvantage, which is that encryption and other security functions are performed only by the two TCP endpoints. If the message needs to be secured further on, then an end-to-end protection like the usage of XML Signature and XML Encryption in the application level is required.

Using XML Signature and XML Encryption on the application level takes up more coding but gives a more finely grained method to guarantee the message integrity, privacy and non-repudiation. The client signs the message content and places the signature into the message header. The references of the XML Signature point to the signed data in the message content. Using the Transforms element, it is possible to protect only parts of the message context or the complete message and in case of a multipart message the attachment. The validity of the signature guarantees the receiving service the integrity and authenticity of the message.

2.4 Signed Audit Trails

One of the most critical issues in terms of the legal requirements is a method that enables the provider of a service to prove that certain activities have taken place and data have been processed in a particular way by the providing service. The best instrument for this task is the signed audit trail.

Audit trails are basically the protocol about what happened at a specific service. Now, when we look at the SOA architecture, we will quickly see that one action triggered by a client can lead to multiple (sub-) actions carried out by other web services. In order to backtrack the end user's transaction accurately, this requires the collaboration of all participating services to add meaningful and important information to this trail. Audit trails are providing the following capabilities:

- They guarantee non-repudiation. I.e., if dealing with a customer order, the manufacturer can prove that a certain order was placed by a certain principal.
- They also give the client a tool by which he can review (double-check) his orders.
- Audit trails should provide enough qualitative information to re-build the business transaction, in case of problems like attacks, disk crashes, breakdowns and outages of the service did happen.

Certain features are required for different levels of trust that an audit trail can provide:

- Identification and authentication of the client. Can the client be identified uniquely and could he authenticate himself in a trustworthy way? This must be logged in case of a non-repudiation requirement.
- The usage of single sign-on. The identity of the caller should be the same for all subsequent web service requests within this transaction. Optionally, each service may log the time and principal identification in case of any doubt.
- If the authenticated client is been given a certain role, this needs to be logged as well. All participating services must state clearly for which account the action was carried out.

- One of the most critical issues is the quality of the signing certificate. Normally, a batch signature with an advanced signature is sufficient. Sometimes there may be the need for a qualified signature.
- In order to trust all related parties, and that all the applications work reliably to a certain degree, is a certification required? This will certainly improve the trustworthiness of the whole application. Still, this is a very costly process and needs to be evaluated thoughtfully.

Because of the complexity of an enterprise service bus, the creation of audit trails is similarly complex. A central utility is a good start to implement signed audit trails.

Within the suggested environment, a native XML server with the cryptographic capability to handle electronic signatures is the ideal solution. In addition to the bus type communication of the application data, each service itself has a direct line to the logging process (i.e. an XML server). Given that the XML server supports transactions, each (sub-) service carries forward the data required to complete an audit log for the whole service request.

The above suggestion will also work in a widely distributed environment. This is due to the fact that the XML server itself can be configured to act like a protected service.

3 The Software AG ESB Approach

The Software AGs Enterprise Service Bus, the Enterprise Service Integrator (ESI), is also confronted with the security issues discussed above.

3.1 Identity Federation

For Software AG, single sign on is a very important topic. One of the most common use cases of the ESI is the web service integration of legacy applications running in a mainframe environment. By default, mainframe applications run in a closed environment with a closed and limited set of users. If such applications are integrated into a distributed web application, accessible via the Inter- or Intranet, a strong security policy has to be defined. Authentication, authorization and user handling are very sensitive topics for such applications. For most of the use cases it is important to authorize the primary user, who initiated the business transaction. Because of the multi-tier architecture of distributed web services applications, authenticating the requesting user is done by the web service client and not in the backend system. In such a case, the mainframe application has to trust the authentication and user's identity information provided by the authenticating entity, as well as the integrity of the transmitted data. A strong trust relationship is given by digitally signing the authentication assertions and the identity data.

The ESI handles signed authentication and authorization assertions and supports a role based access control approach. This requirement is provided by the support of SAML (Secure Assertion Markup Language) [9] based Web Service Security. The security assertions are digitally signed by the Identity Provider and the signature is validated by the ESI and the mainframe application before the requesting user is authorized to execute the request.

3.2 Message Integrity and Non-repudiation

The ESI demonstrates the design of a middleware that allows companies to implement message integrity with or without the knowledge of the underlying web services. The usage of XML Signatures (i.e. the validation process of incoming messages as well as the automatic signature generation of outgoing responses) can be carried out without the service noticing this additional feature. In case the signature and data integrity keeps its important role beyond the mere transport and time of conversation, the web service can make active use of the signature features of the ESI.

Furthermore it should be pointed out that in most cases of message authentication a digital signature does not provide enough information. Typically a timestamp needs to be added to the signature. The digitally signed document (or a hash thereof) together with date and time information guarantees for both sender and addressee that a certain message or document was only sent once (not replayed) and, if used with a signed response, to prove to the sender that his original document was not modified in transit plus that it was accepted at a certain time. This "receipt" provides the legal binding to business transactions being originated by the web service request.

3.3 Signed Audit Trails

Most of the various web services within a distributed web service application that participate in processing a request as well as the ESI itself write their own audit trails. To guarantee integrity of the audit trails, the ESI follows two different approaches.

1. At the end of a business transaction all audit trails, written during this business transaction, are referenced and digitally signed with one detached XML Signature.

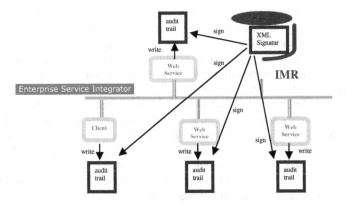

Fig. 4. ESI based application with several audit trail documents

2. A higher degree of security is obtained by writing the audit trail directly into the Integrated Metadata Repository (IMR), which is part of the Enterprise Service Integrator. The locking and security concept of the IMR guarantees protection against parallel manipulation of the audit trails until the transaction is committed. Before the transaction is committed, the audit trail is digitally signed with an XML Signature, containing a timestamp as well.

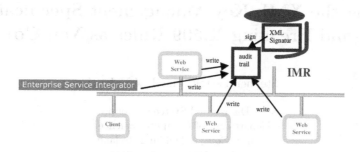

Fig. 5. ESI based application with one central audit trail document

4   Conclusion

In protecting distributed web services applications, XML signatures play a very important role. In case of business transactions single sign on, message integrity and non-repudiation are important security requirements that can be addressed. Other problems can only be solved by using XML Signatures, such as signing the audit trails of several components located at different places and involved in one business transaction with one signature. An additional dimension is introduced in case the signed audit trails have to be archived over a long time. In such cases, XML Signature can also be used to guarantee integrity and non-repudiation for a long time, including the possibility of renewal of the XML Signatures by resigning periodically. An approach is given by the Long-term Archive and Notary Services (LTANS) Internet-Draft [8]. Long-term archiving is one of the next important steps to take, and in which XML Signatures will play a key role.

References

[1] René Kollmorgen, Dieter Kessler, Eckehard Hermann, Frank Jung: Digital signatures in XML, http://asia.cnet.com/builder/architect/system/0,39009336,39100045,00.htm
[2] XML Signature Syntax and Processing, http://www.w3.org/TR/xmldsig-core/
[3] Eugene Kuznetsov: XML Web services security best practices, http://www.builderau. com.au/manage/work/0,39024674,39130825,00.htm
[4] Liberty ID_FF Architecture Overview, Version: 1.2-errata-v1.0, https://www. projectliberty. org/ specs/draft-liberty-idff-arch-overview-1.2-errata-v1.0.pdf
[5] Software AG ESI Security and SOA Security white papers, http://www.softwareag.com
[6] SOAP Version 1.2 Part 0, http://www.w3.org/TR/2003/REC-soap12-part0-20030624/
[7] OASIS Web Service Security: SOAP Message Security, http://docs.oasis-open.org/ wss/2004/01/oasis-200401-wss-soap-message-security-1.0.pdf
[8] Long-term Archive And Notary Services (LTANS) Internet-Draft, http://ietfreport.isoc.org/ids/draft-ietf-ltans-ers-02.txt
[9] SAML v2.0, OASIS, http://www.oasis-open.org/specs/index.php#samlv2.0
[10] IETF Working Group on Transport Layer Security, http://www1.treese.org/ietf-tls/

Using the XML Key Management Specification (and Breaking X.509 Rules as You Go)

Stephen Farrell[1] and José Kahan[2]

[1] Distributed Systems Group,
Department of Computer Science,
Trinity College, Dublin 2, Ireland
stephen.farrell@cs.tcd.ie
https://www.cs.tcd.ie/Stephen.Farrell/
[2] W3C / ERCIM,
INRIA Rhône-Alpes,
ZIRST, 655 av. de l'Europe, Montbonnot,
FR-38334 ST ISMIER CEDEX, France
jose.kahan@w3.org
http://www.w3.org/People/Jose/

Abstract. Implementing X.509 based public-key infrastructure requires following a complex set of rules to establish if a public key certificate is valid. The XML Key Management Specification has been developed as one way in which the implementation burden can be reduced by moving some of this complexity from clients and onto a server. In this paper we give a brief overview of the XML key management specification standard, and describe how, in addition to the above, this system also provides us with the means to sensibly break many of the rules specified for X.509 based public key infrastructure.

1 Introduction

In this paper we will describe how the XML Key Management Specification (XKMS) [1,2] can be used as a kind of intranet "front-end" to an X.509 based Public Key Infrastructure (PKI). Such PKIs mainly try to follow the rules specified in most detail in RFC 3280 [3].

Once we have seen how an XKMS responder can be used in such a situation we will then examine a number of ways in which the responder can offer better service to clients, by breaking the rules of X.509!

2 The XML Key Management Specification

The XML Key Management Specification (XKMS) [1] is a W3C Recommendation designed to ease the costs of PKI deployment without sacrificing its benefits. It is suitable for use in conjunction with the XML-Signature [4] and XML-Encryption [5] W3C Recommendations as well as in other application contexts,

J. Dittmann, S. Katzenbeisser, and A. Uhl (Eds.): CMS 2005, LNCS 3677, pp. 348–357, 2005.

such as email. As stated, XKMS is a W3C Recommendation, the pinnacle of the W3C standards process: it has been reviewed by W3C Members and other interested parties and there exists enough implementation and interoperability proof to validate its concepts. The XKMS W3C Recommendation was published on 28 June 2005 though the original W3C Note on XKMS dates from 2001.

We will now give a brief overview of XKMS - a companion paper [6] describes XKMS in more detail and also reports on interoperability status. XKMS consists of two different parts: the XML Key Information Service Specification (X-KISS) and the XML Key Registration Service Specification (X-KRSS). X-KISS defines a protocol to support the delegation by an application to a service of the detailed processing of key information associated with an XML-Signature, XML-Encryption, or other usage of the XML-Signature <ds:KeyInfo> element. X-KRSS defines a protocol for the registration of a public key by a key pair holder, with the intent that the key subsequently be usable in conjunction with X-KISS or a PKI. XKMS is designed to be protocol independent and it proposes bindings [2] over SOAP/1.2 as well as plain HTTP.

2.1 X-KISS

Reducing the complexity of applications using XML-Signature is one of the key objectives of the protocol design. X-KISS clients are relieved of the complexity of the underlying PKI used to establish trust relationships. These relationships may be based upon a different specification, such as X.509/PKIX, or PGP[7].

In addition, sometimes the information provided by a signer can be insufficient for performing cryptographic verification or to be able to decide whether to trust a signature. Alternatively, the information provided by the signer may be in a format that is not supported by the client. In these cases communication with an X-KISS service can be useful as a way to get that "missing" information.

Examples where the key information could be insufficient for the client include:

- The key may be specified by a name only.
- The key may be encoded in an X.509 certificate that the client cannot parse.
- In the case of an encryption operation, the client may not know the public key of the recipient (e.g., just having a name).

X-KISS works via two different services: Locate and Validate.

Locate resolves a <ds:Keyinfo> element but does not require the service to make an assertion concerning the validity of the data in the <ds:Keyinfo> element. Validate does all that Locate does, but in addition, the client obtains an assertion (at that time, according to that responder) specifying the status of the binding between the public key and other data, for example a name or a set of extended attributes. Furthermore the service represents that each of the other data elements returned are bound to the same public key.

2.2 X-KRSS

X-KRSS handles the registration and subsequent management of public key information. An X-KRSS service may bind information such as a name, an identifier or other attributes, to a public key, on reception of a client request. The key may be generated by the client or by the service on request. The Registration protocol may also be used for subsequent management operations including recovery of the private key and reissue or revocation of the key binding. The protocol provides ways of authenticating the requester and the possession of a private key. Additionally it provides a means of communicating the private key to the client in the case that the private key is generated by the registration service.

The operations constituting X-KRSS are:

- `Register`: Information is bound to a public key through a key binding. Generation of the key pair may be performed by either the client or the Registration service.
- `Reissue`: A previously registered key binding is updated. It is similar to the initial registration of a key and the principal reason a client would make a Reissue request is to cause the registration service to generate new credentials in the underlying PKI, e.g., X.509 Certificates.
- `Revoke`: A previously registered key binding may be revoked. A revocation request need only contain sufficient information to identify the key binding to be revoked and the authority for the revocation request.
- `Recover`: The private key associated with a key binding is recovered. The private key must have been previously escrowed with the recovery service, for example by means of the X-KRSS registration of a server generated key.

2.3 Using XKMS as a PKI Front-End

PKIs aim to allow every user and every application to verify the identity of everyone with which they communicate and to ensure that the counter-party identity is appropriate for the transaction and also that the identity/key binding is still valid (not revoked). Unfortunately, the infrastructure needed to support this places such burdensome demands on application developers that it can be difficult to develop a secure application that achieves all of these goals simultaneously.

In order to verify a given signed document, a party must locate the corresponding public-key certificate, verify its validity, and parse it to extract the corresponding public-key. Traditionally with PKI, these operations are carried out by a (PKI) client application. This requires complex configuration settings, e.g., rules/configuration for mapping application identities to X.500 names. Moreover, as different PKIs can have different conventions, this can complicate the integration of PKI with applications.

In XKMS, these trust decisions are delegated to a common server, so that they can be centralized and applied consistently across platforms. The only configuration information that an XKMS client needs is the URL of the server and the public key the server will be using to sign its replies. Different trust models can be supported by using different server URLs.

Figure 1 gives an example of one way in which XKMS can validate requests between a client and an application server (we assume that both the client and application server have previously used X-KRSS to register their public keys in the XKMS service). The workflow is as follows:

1. The client uses the `Validate` request to get a public key for the server.
2. The client sends a signed request to the application server; the request includes a copy of the client's public-key certificate and is encrypted with the server's public key.
3. The application server decrypts the request, and forwards the client's public key certificate to the XKMS service using a `Validate` request, asking to validate it and to extract the public-key contained within.
4. The application server processes the client request.

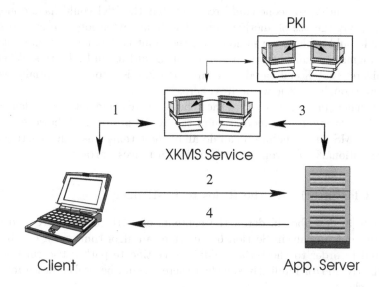

Fig. 1. Validating a request using XKMS

Note that in the preceding example, the XKMS service does not sign or verify the signature of the client's request. These operations have to be done locally. Also note that the PKI that is behind the XKMS responder is completely transparent to the client - it could be based on X.509 or something else. Likewise, this transparency allows for the exchange of one PKI with another one with minimal change for the client and application server code. Finally, the client and the application server could contact different XKMS services; in this case, one XKMS server could act as client to get the required information from the other server.

In addition to acting as a relatively straightforward "front-end" for the usual X.509 based PKI, XKMS is also intended to be usable in other contexts, in particular where PGP [7] based data formats are used instead of X.509 based ones or where a PKI is built from scratch based on "native" XML formats like the `<ds:KeyInfo>` structure defined in XML-Signature [4].

3   Breaking X.509 Rules Using XKMS

in this paper we are interested in considering how an XKMS responder, placed in front of an X.509 PKI can usefully break the rules of that PKI in order to provide better service to the responder's clients. We first consider the types of rule which can be broken, and then give a number of examples where breaking each type of rule is of benefit.

Many of the rule-breaks, or "cheats", we outline below might be considered to be features of a PKI. For example, if an XKMS responder uses a different name for an entity, someone could respond that the PKI could have done the same thing via the use of another SubjectAltName extension. However, even if some PKI could achieve the same effect, the point is that for a given deployed PKI, changing the name of the entity is cheating, at least in PKI terms. Whether this indicates that X.509 based PKIs are too rigid, is a topic potentially worth discussing though not one we address here.

Note that many, but not all, of the "cheats" here could also be implemented by a *non-conformant* implementation of the SCVP protocol [8], however a conforming XKMS implementation can do all of these things, as well as acting as a more "traditional" PKI front-end when circumstances warrant.

3.1   A Classification of the Rules-to-Be-Broken

RFC 3280 [3] describes in detail the contents of certificates and related data structures and (mainly in Section 6) describes an algorithm which can be implemented in order to check the validity of certificate paths. The rules which are explicitly and/or implicitly specified therein could be broken down into the following classes:

- **Certificate content.** Rules as to how to interpret the content of a certificate.
- **Certificate status checking.** Rules stating whether or not a previously issued certificate remains valid.
- **Valid path constraints.** Rules which valid certificate paths follow (many of these are derived from the validation algorithm).

For each of these classes we will give examples of how breaking related rules can be useful. Note that the classes themselves are not really significant, but they do help to organize our presentation and also help us to find additional ways in which we can break X.509 rules!

3.2 Certificate Content Related Rules

We begin by breaking the most basic rules of X.509 based PKI. We will go into more detail on the first rule-break, for later ones we leave the details of the XKMS messaging required as an exercise for the reader.

Changing the Name of the Certificate Holder. In many cases organizations will have gone to much trouble to ensure that the certificate holder (subject and/or subjectAlternateName) fields contain unique values, for example, via the inclusion of employee numbers or other serial numbers. Non-human entities (like applications) may have similarly constructed names for consistency. This makes these names cumbersome and unsuitable for many applications, for numerous reasons, not least the fact perhaps the applications didn't actually exist when the PKI naming debate was raging within the enterprise. An XKMS responder can therefore usefully maintain its own translation of names, perhaps via a set of tables and/or some algorithm. In this way, an entity known to the PKI as `"L=Internet;O=Example Org; CN=Joseph User+SN=123456798"` might sensible be mapped to `"joe"`. In terms of XKMS processes, the steps that occur could be as follows:

1. Application received XML-Signature produced by Joe, with Joe's X.509 certificate in a `<ds:KeyInfo>`.
2. Application does a Validate containing that `<ds:KeyInfo>`, but without ever looking "inside".
3. Responder does PKI things to validate the certificate and then maps from the subject field (above) and the name of the application (or other context) to `"joe"`.
4. Responder returns a binding containing the appropriate ds:keyValue and a `<ds:KeyName>` containing simply the string `"joe"`.
5. Application correctly accepts that XML-Signature is from Joe and does further XML processing on the relevant documents.

In a variation on the above, the responder could simply *invent a pseudonym* for the certificate holder each time it sees a new XKMS-client/application pair (or following many other algorithms). This would make the application less likely to cause privacy problems since application state would contain the pseudonym and not a real identity. It would also make it harder to correlate the same user's actions over multiple applications.

Another related "cheat" would be where the responder uses some *name resolution* service (like DNS), and maps from the requested name to one present in a certificate (or vice-versa). This could be useful to handle load-balancing and other cases where the names currently in X.509 certificates don't match those that the application requires. Of course, this means putting some "trust" in whatever resolver is used by the XKMS responder, but that may well be as secure, and cheaper than, frequently getting new X.509 certificates.

Hidden Key Escrow. In response to a query from an application which is about to do an encryption operation (e.g. an S/MIME enabled mail user agent), an XKMS responder could produce a response which contains a public key for which the corresponding private key is known to some other application (e.g. an outbound SMTP server). In the example, the mail client will (unknown to it!) encrypt for the SMTP server, which can decrypt, presumably then apply some useful policy checks, and subsequently re- encrypt for the intended recipient. Say that now the SMTP server uses the XKMS responder to find the intended recipient's key. Either via configuration, or even some visible and/or hidden values in the KeyBinding returned (e.g. a proprietary X.509 extension), to the mail client, the XKMS responder can know how to respond.

Ignoring Expiration. X.509 certificates expire, unfortunately. For many applications, there is no real need to update certificates other than to handle the fact that certificates expire. XKMS can rescue us here by simply checking the notBefore and notAfter values in a certificate and running the RFC 3280 validation algorithm for some time in that interval, that is, the responder can ignore the certificate's validity period entirely. In this way, Joe can go on using the same certificate indefinitely possibly saving money for the organization (if certificate renewal is a chargeable service). For any application which has its own concept of account revocation or expiry this mode of operation is entirely sufficient (i.e. the notAfter field of the X.509 certificate adds no value in such cases).

Creating An Entirely New Certificate. In response to a locate or validate request a responder could do the standard PKI operations to validate some certificate for the public key in question, but then create a new certificate, issued by the responder (or at least signed using a key under the responder's control) which will be more likely to satisfy the application requirements. Basically, this allows the responder to include any of the above "cheats" in an X.509 certificate, which is useful if the ultimate X.509 relying party will trust the responder-issued certificate. This is slightly different from normal PKI models, in that the responder may for example change the subject field to better match the application requirements.

This "cheat" also allows the responder to *handle potential cryptographic weaknesses*, for example related to hash-function robustness. If the responder has a local repository of certificates, then it can perhaps be confident that those certificates retain their integrity even if the hash functions used therein are currently considered weak. The newly created certificate can then use better hash functions or else countermeasures like long, random serial numbers in order to create a certificate which will be acceptable to the X.509 relying-party.

If the responder is creating new certificates for some application where the certificate is only used for a short period, then the responder could *re-use serial numbers* in order to make it simpler to handle revocation of such certificates. For example, if the XKMS client application uses the certificate for a CMS [9] based confidentiality service, but throws away the certificate shortly after use, then the responder could use a small set of serial numbers for all certificates. The net effect is that CRLs never get long enough to cause problems, while relying party applications can do standard revocation checks. This "cheat" shows that even the most fundamental "rule" of X.509 (that an issuer MUST NOT re-use serial numbers) can usefully be broken!

Covert Channel. Where a responder creates new certificates there are many X.509 fields which can be used as a kind of covert channel between the XKMS responder and intermediaries who see the certificate or perhaps the private key holder (if the certificate is carried end-to-end in an encrypting application). Such a covert channel could be used to carry (or link to) authorization information or any other application data. The fields that could be used in this way without affecting the use of the public key contained in the certificate include the serial number, unique identifiers, issuer, subject, algorithm identifiers (both inner and outer), and many of the standard extensions. The version number could also potentially be used, though probably at the expense of suffering decoding errors in intermediaries. Note that if CMS is used for encryption then the serial number covert channel gets through to the private key holder even if the certificate does not. Although a similar trick can be done using short-lived X.509 certificates, this "cheat" differs in two respects: the certificates are likely to be even more short lived since an XKMS client will more frequently contact its responder, hence the covert channel has higher bandwidth. Secondly, the XKMS protocol inherently supports us in doing this, whereas in an X.509 context a modified LDAP server might be the best way to implement this.

3.3   Certificate Status Related Rules

Handing revocation of certificates has always been a really problematic area for X.509 based PKIs. In this section we will examine ways in which we can help by breaking the rules of X.509.

Entirely Ignoring Revocation. The most obvious way to solve the revocation problem is to get rid of it. This is straightforward enough - the responder simply runs the validation algorithm but skips the certificate status checking stages entirely. It may be useful to for the responder to keep its own, application-specific blacklist as well as a global blacklist and to use that as the basis on which it decides the Status of KeyBindings.

Ignoring Business Motivated Revocations. If an enterprise pays a service provider to operate a PKI on their behalf then that service provider might create a CA for that purpose. When the customer no longer wants to use that service, the service provider might revoke that CA's certificate, thus potentially invalidating all of the end entity certificates issued by that CA. An XKMS responder is in a useful position to ignore this revocation in order to provide business continuity where the customer is switching from one service provider to another, or to an in-house PKI. More generally, one could perhaps argue that leveraging the flexibility of XKMS makes many business transitions easier, when compared with X.509 compliant solutions.

Ignoring Authority Revocation. Access to the required CRLs or OCSP responders for end entity certificates may be possible in many circumstances. However, for some PKIs it will be hard to find the relevant CRLs or OCSP responders in order to ensure that no CA on the path has been revoked. An XKMS responder could usefully maintain its own list of revoked CAs and therefore not have to attempt to access these ARLs or equivalent.

Ignoring Revocation Timing. An XKMS responder could be configured so as to ignore revocation timing information (e.g. the next update field etc.) and could simply periodically access certificate status information, presumably from a fairly reliable source. This amounts to having the XKMS responder (administrator) choose the level of acceptable risk, in terms of potential missed revocations. In many circumstances the XKMS responder will be in a much better position than the X.509 certificate issuer to properly evaluate this risk - thus leading to a more easily deployed system.

3.4   Path Validation Related Rules

X.509 based PKIs define a range of certificate extensions which are aimed at controlling which paths are valid and which are not. There are many cases where we may want to disagree with the constraints that CA's would like to impose and XKMS allows this to be done easily.

Ignoring All Certificate Policy Checks. Certificate policies, even if initially sensible, may well not last as long as certificates, for example introducing new applications into a bridge-CA structure may make many issued certificates useless. An XKMS responder could therefore effectively "strip" out all certificate policy handling, and in particular all policy mapping.

Ignoring Basic Constraints. A responder could totally ignore the basic constraints extension (or its path length constraint) and treat an end entity as a CA. This could be useful to integrate with some quasi-standard or less frequently seen PKIs such as those used in some grid computing environments [10].

4   Conclusions

We have given a brief outline of XKMS and one of its main use cases: use as a locally trusted intranet server. However, by showing ways in which XKMS can usefully be used to break restrictive X.509 rules, we have also demonstrated that XKMS can be used as more than just a front-end for X.509 based (or other) PKIs.

It should also be clear that we could have given many more examples - in fact one could possibly construct an interesting "cheat" for almost all certificate and CRL fields, and for almost all MUST or SHOULD statements in RFC 3280 [3]. However, we are, of course, not recommending that XKMS implementers implement these "cheats" - they each only make sense in specific contexts. We do expect that over time, some of them (or others) will be found to be useful enough to warrant inclusion in XKMS implementations - perhaps at some stage some might even find their way back into the X.509 related standards!

Finally, the fact that there are so many potentially useful ways in which the X.509 PKI rules can be broken, given the opportunity offered by XKMS, may indicate that those rules are somewhat too onerous, at least when an on-line trusted server is available as is the case with XKMS (and, whenever it is finally completed, with SCVP).

References

1. P. Hallam-Baker and S. H. Mysore (eds.): XML Key Management Specification (XKMS 2.0). Recommendation, W3C (2005) http://www.w3.org/TR/2005/REC-xkms2-20050628/.
2. P. Hallam-Baker and S. H. Mysore (eds.): XML Key Management Specification (XKMS 2.0) Bindings. Recommendation, W3C (2005) http://www.w3.org/TR/2005/REC-xkms2-bindings-20050628/.
3. R. Housley, W. Polk, W. Ford, D. Solo: Internet X.509 Public Key Infrastructure Certificate and Certificate Revocation List (CRL) Profile. RFC, IETF (2002) http://www.ietf.org/rfc/rfc3280.txt.
4. D. Eastlake et al (eds.): XML-Signature Syntax and Processing. Recommendation, W3C (2002) http://www.w3.org/TR/2002/REC-xmldsig-core-20020212/.
5. D. Eastlake and J. Reagle (eds.): XML Encryption Syntax and Processing. Recommendation, W3C (2002) http://www.w3.org/ TR/2002/REC-xmlenc-core-20021210/.
6. G. Alvaro, S. Farrell, T. Lindberg, R. Lockhart, Y. Zhang: XKMS Working Group Interoperability Status Report. In: to appear in Proceedings of EuroPKI 2005, Univerrsity of Kent, Canterbury, England. (2005) http://www.europki.org/.
7. P. Zimmermann: Pretty Good Privacy (PGP), PGP User's Guide. Technical report, MIT (1994)
8. T. Freeman, R. Housley, A. Malpani, D. Cooper, T. Polk: Simple Certificate Validation Protocol (SCVP). Internet Draft, IETF (2005) http://www.ietf. org/internet-drafts/draft-ietf-pkix-scvp-18.txt.
9. R. Housley: Cryptographic Message Syntax. RFC, IETF (2004) http://www.ietf.org/rfc/rfc3852.txt.
10. S. Tuecke, V. Welch, D. Engert, L. Pearlman, M. Thompson: Internet X.509 Public Key Infrastructure (PKI) Proxy Certificate Profile. RFC, IETF (2004) http://www.ietf.org/rfc/rfc3820.txt.

Author Index

Lecture Notes in Computer Science

For information about Vols. 1–3587

please contact your bookseller or Springer